Computer-Related Risks

Peter G. Neumann

SRI INTERNATIONAL

ACM Press

New York, New York

▲▼ ADDISON-WESLEY
PUBLISHING COMPANY

Reading, Massachusetts • Menlo Park,
California • New York • Don Mills, Ontario
Wokingham, England • Amsterdam
Bonn • Sydney • Singapore • Tokyo
Madrid • San Juan • Milan • Paris

Sponsoring Editors: Peter S. Gordon/Helen M. Goldstein
Senior Production Supervisor: Helen M. Wythe
Copyeditor: Lyn Dupré
Production: Superscript Editorial Production Services (Marsha Finley)
Composition: Windfall Software (Paul C. Anagnostopoulos/Caroline McCarley, using ZzTEX)
Text Design: Jennie Bush, Designworks
Cover Design: Eileen R. Hoff
Manufacturing Coordinator: Evelyn M. Beaton
Nhora Cortes-Comerer, Executive Editor, ACM Press Books

Many of the designations used by manufacturers and sellers to distinguish their products are claimed as trademarks. Where those designations appear in this book, and Addison-Wesley was aware of a trademark claim, the designations have been printed in initial caps or all caps.

Material drawn from *Inside Risks* articles by Bob Charette, Robert Dorsett, Donald Norman, Ronni Rosenberg, and Marc Rotenberg is noted explicitly in the text. Other columns contributed by the author to *Inside Risks* are also included. Items from the *ACM Software Engineering Notes* are cited throughout. In addition, several previously published papers have been adapted for inclusion here, with appropriate permissions. Section 3.1 is based on an article by Neumann and Parker [115]. Other articles by the author adapted here are: Section 5.8, drawn from [112]; Section 7.3, drawn from [109]; Section 7.6, drawn from [111]; part of Section 8.2, drawn from [108].

The views in the book reflect the personal opinions of the author, the named contributors, and other quoted individuals, and in no way represent the views of the Association for Computing Machinery, SRI International, Addison-Wesley Publishing Company, or any other organization.

Library of Congress Cataloging-in-Publication Data

Neumann, Peter, 1932–
    Computer-related risks / Peter G. Neumann.
      p. cm.
    Includes bibliographical references and index.
    ISBN 0-201-55805-X
    1. Electronic digital computers—Reliability. 2. Risk management.
  I. Title.
QA76.5.N424   1995
363.1—dc20

             94-25875
             CIP

1 2 3 4 5 6 7 8 9 10-CRS-9897969594

TO MY DAUGHTER, Hellie,
who loves high-tech things
—except when they don't work

IN MEMORY OF Chris, John, Elsa, and J.B.,
who provided great inspiration.

Preface

THIS BOOK IS BASED on a remarkable collection of mishaps and oddities relating to computer technology. It considers what has gone wrong in the past, what is likely to go wrong in the future, and what can be done to minimize the occurrence of further problems. It may provide meat and potatoes to some readers and tasty desserts to others—and yet may seem almost indigestible to some would-be readers. However, it should be intellectually and technologically thought-provoking to all.

Many of the events described here have been discussed in the on-line computer newsgroup, the *Forum on Risks to the Public in the Use of Computers and Related Systems* (referred to here simply as *RISKS*), which I have moderated since its inception in 1985, under the auspices of the Association for Computing Machinery (ACM). Most of these events have been summarized in the quarterly publication of the ACM Special Interest Group on Software Engineering (SIGSOFT), *Software Engineering Notes (SEN)*, which I edited from its beginnings in 1976 through 1993 and to which I continue to contribute the "RISKS" section. Because those sources represent a fascinating archive that is not widely available, I have distilled the more important material and have added further discussion and analysis.

Most of the events selected for inclusion relate to roles that computers and communication systems play in our lives. Some events exhibit problems with technology and its application; some events illustrate a wide range of human behavior, such as malice, inadvertent actions, incompetence, ignorance, carelessness, or lack of experience; some events are attributable to causes over which we have little control, such as natural disasters. Some of the events are old; others are recent, although some of the newer ones seem strangely reminiscent of earlier ones. Because such events continue to happen and because they affect us in so many different ways, it is essential that we draw realistic conclusions from this collection — particularly if the book is to help us avoid future disasters. Indeed, the later chapters focus on the technology itself and discuss what can be done to overcome or control the risks.

As we go to press, further events continue to occur, such as another roller-coaster crash, the Dante II robotic exploration of the Mt. Spurr volcano crater, and another squirrel whose a-gnawing habit of chewing powerlines brought down the entire Nasdaq stock market. Stay tuned to the *Risks Forum* for late-breaking developments.

I hope that the events described and the conclusions drawn are such that much of the material will be accessible to readers with widely differing backgrounds. I have attempted to find a middle ground for a diverse set of readers, so that the book can be interesting and informative for students and professionals in the computer field, practitioners and technologists in other fields, and people with only a general interest in technology. The book is particularly relevant to students of software engineering, system engineering, and computer science, for whom it could be used as a companion source. It is also valuable for anyone studying reliability, fault tolerance, safety, or security; some introductory material is included for people who have not been exposed to those topics. In addition, the book is appropriate for people who develop or use computer-based applications. Less technically oriented readers may skip some of the details and instead read the book primarily for its anecdotal material. Other readers may wish to pursue the technological aspects more thoroughly, chasing down relevant cited references — for historical, academic, or professional reasons. The book is relatively self-contained, but includes many references and notes for the reader who wishes to pursue the details further. Some readers may indeed wish to browse, whereas others may find the book to be the tip of an enormous iceberg that demands closer investigation.

In my presentations of the cases, I have attempted to be specific about the causes and actual circumstances wherever specifics were both available and helpful. Inevitably, the exact causes of some of the cases still remain unknown to me. I also have opted to cite actual names, although I realize that certain organizations may be embarrassed by having some of their old dirty laundry hung out yet again. The alternative would have been to make those cases anonymous—which would have defeated one of the main purposes of the book, namely, to increase reader awareness of the pervasiveness and real-life nature of the problems addressed here.

The Organization of the Book

Chapter 1 presents an introduction to the topic of computer-related risks. Chapters 2 through 6 consider examples from the wealth of cases, from several perspectives. Chapters 7 and 8 reflect on that experience and consider what must be done to avoid such risks in the future. Chapter 9 provides conclusions. The individual chapters are summarized as follows:

- Chapter 1, "The Nature of Risks," characterizes the various sources of risks and the types of effects that those risks entail. It also anticipates what might be done to prevent those causes from having serious effects.

- Chapter 2, "Reliability and Safety Problems," examines the causes and effects in various cases in which reliability problems have been experienced, over a wide range of application areas.

- Chapter 3, "Security Vulnerabilities," considers what the most prevalent types of security vulnerabilities are and how they arise.

- Chapter 4, "Causes and Effects," makes a case for considering reliability problems and security problems within a common framework, by pointing out significant conceptual similarities as well as by exploring the risks of not having such a common framework.

- Chapter 5, "Security and Integrity Problems," reviews many cases in which different types of security violations have been experienced, over a variety of application areas.

- Chapter 6, "Threats to Privacy and Well-Being," discusses threats to privacy, to individual rights, and to personal well-being.

- Chapter 7, "A System-Oriented Perspective," considers the subject matter of the book from a global system perspective. It considers techniques for increasing reliability, fault tolerance, safety, and security, including the use of good software engineering practice.

- Chapter 8, "A Human-Oriented Perspective," considers the pervasive roles of people in achieving low-risk systems.

- Chapter 9, "Implications and Conclusions," considers the foregoing chapters in retrospect. It draws various conclusions and addresses responsibility, predictability, weak links, validity of assumptions, risks in risk assessment, and risks inherent in the technology.

Challenges for the reader are suggested at the end of each chapter. They include both thought-provoking questions of general interest and exercises that may be of concern primarily to the more technically minded reader. They are intended to offer some opportunities to reflect on the issues raised in the book. At the urging of my EditriX, some specific numbers are given (such as number of cases you are asked to examine, or the number of examples you might generate); however, these numbers should be considered as parameters that can be altered to suit the occasion. Students and professors using this book for a course are invited to invent their own challenges.

Appendix A provides useful background material. Section A.1 gives a table relating *Software Engineering Notes (SEN)* volume and issue numbers to dates, which are omitted in the text for simplicity. Section A.2 gives information on how to access relevant online sources, including *RISKS*, *PRIVACY*, and *VIRUS-L* newsgroups. Section A.3 suggests some selected further readings. The back of the book includes a glossary of acronyms and terms, the notes referred to throughout the text, an extensive bibliography that is still only a beginning, and the index.

How to Read the Book

Many different organizations could have been used for the book. I chose to present the experiential material according to threats that relate to specific attributes (notably reliability, safety, security, privacy, and well-being in Chapters 2 through 6) and, within those attributes, by types of applications. Chapters 7 and 8 provide broader perspectives from a system viewpoint and from a human viewpoint, respectively. That order reinforces the principal conclusions of the book and exhibits the diversity, perversity, and universality of the problems encountered.

Alternatively, the book could have been organized according to the causes of problems—for example, the diverse sources of risks summarized in Section 1.2; it could have been organized according to the effects that have been experienced or that can be expected to occur in the future—such as those summarized in Section 1.3; it could have been organized according to the types of defensive measures necessary to combat the problems inherent in those causes and effects—such as the diverse types of defensive measures summarized in Section 1.4. Evidently, no one order is best suited to all readers. However, I have tried to help each reader to find his or her own path through the book and have provided different viewpoints and cross-references.

The book may be read from cover to cover, which is intended to be a natural order of presentation. However, a linear order may not be suitable for everyone. A reader with selective interests may wish to read the introductory material of Chapter 1, to choose among those sections of greatest interest in Chapters 2 through 6, and then to read the final three chapters. A reader not particularly interested in the technological details of how the risks might be avoided or reduced can skip Chapter 7.

Certain cases recur in different contexts and are interesting precisely because they illustrate multiple concepts. For example, a particular case might appear in the context of its application (such as communications or space), its types of problems (distributed systems, human interfaces), its requirements (reliability, security), and its implications with respect to software engineering. Certain key details are repeated in a few essential cases so that the reader is not compelled to search for the original mention.

Acknowledgments

I am deeply indebted to the numerous people who contributed source material to the *Risks Forum* and helped to make this book possible. My interactions with them and with the newsgroup's countless readers have made the *RISKS* experience most enjoyable for me. Many contributors are identified in the text. Others are noted in the referenced items from the ACM *Software Engineering Notes.*

I thank Adele Goldberg, who in 1985 as ACM President named me to be the Chairman of the ACM Committee on Computers and Public Policy and gave me the charter to establish what became the *Risks Forum* [50]. Peter Denning, Jim Horning, Nancy Leveson, David Parnas, and Jerry Saltzer are the "old reliables" of the *RISKS* community; they contributed regularly from the very beginning. I am delighted to be able to include the "CACM Inside Risks" guest columns written by Bob Charette (Section 7.10), Robert Dorsett

(Section 2.4.1), Don Norman (Section 6.6), Ronni Rosenberg (Section 8.4), Marc Rotenberg (Section 6.1), and Barbara Simons (Section 9.7). I thank Jack Garman and Eric Rosen for the incisive articles they contributed to *Software Engineering Notes*, discussing the first shuttle launch problem [47] and the 1980 ARPAnet collapse [139], respectively. I also thank Matt Jaffe for his extemporaneous discussion on the Aegis system in response to my lecture at the Fifth International Workshop on Software Specification and Design in 1989. (My summary of his talk appears in [58].)

I would like to express my appreciation to John Markoff of *The New York Times*. Our interactions began long before the Wily Hackers [162, 163] and the Internet Worm [35, 57, 138, 150, 159]. John has been a media leader in the effort to increase public awareness with respect to many of the concepts discussed in *RISKS*.

I am grateful to many people for having helped me in the quest to explore the risks involved in the design and implementation of computer systems — especially my 1960s colleagues from the Multics effort, F.J. Corbató (Corby), Bob Daley, Jerry Saltzer, and the late E.L. (Ted) Glaser at MIT; and Vic Vyssotsky, Doug McIlroy, Bob Morris, Ken Thompson, Ed David, and the late Joe Ossanna at Bell Laboratories. My interactions over the years with Tony Oettinger, Dave Huffman, and Edsger W. Dijkstra have provided great intellectual stimulation. Mae Churchill encouraged me to explore the issues in electronic voting. Henry Petroski enriched my perspective on the nature of the problems discussed here. Two of Jerry Mander's books were particularly reinforcing [87, 88].

Special thanks go to Don Nielson and Mark Moriconi for their support at SRI International (formerly Stanford Research Institute). The on-line *Risks Forum* has been primarily a *pro bono* effort on my part, but SRI has contributed valuable resources — including the Internet archive facility. I also thank Jack Goldberg, who invited me to join SRI's Computer Science Laboratory (CSL) in 1971 and encouraged my pursuits of reliability and security issues in a socially conscious context. Among others in CSL, Teresa Lunt and John Rushby have been particularly thoughtful colleagues. Liz Luntzel—without whom, et cetera—provided cheerful assistance. Donn Parker and Bruce Baker provided opportunities for inputs and outputs through their International Information Integrity Institute (I-4) and as part of SRI's Business and Policy Group.

Maestro Herbert Blomstedt has greatly enriched my life through his music and teaching over the past 10 years. My Tai Chi teachers

Martin and Emily Lee [77] contributed subliminally to the writing of this book, which in a Taoist way seems to have written itself.

I thank Lyn Dupré, my high-tech EditriX, for her X-acting X-pertise (despite her predilection for the "staffed space program" and "fisherpersons" — which I carefully eschewed, in Sections 2.2.1 and 2.6, respectively); the high-TeX Marsha Finley (who claims she did only the dog work in burying the bones of my LaTeX style, but whose bark and bite were both terrific); Paul Anagnostopoulos, who transmogrified my LaTeX into ZzTeX; Peter Gordon of Addison-Wesley for his patient goading; and Helen Wythe, who oversaw the production of the book for Addison-Wesley. I am indebted to the anonymous reviewers, who made many useful suggestions — although some of their diverse recommendations were mutually incompatible, further illustrating the difficulties in trying to satisfy a heterogeneous audience within a single book.

I am pleased to acknowledge two marvelous examples of non-proprietary software: Richard Stallman's Gnu Emacs and Les Lamport's LaTeX, both of which were used extensively in the preparation of the text.

I would be happy to hear from readers who have corrections, additions, new sagas, or other contributions that might enhance the accuracy and completeness of this book in any future revisions.

I thank you all for being part of my extended family, the *RISKS* community.

Contents

 CHAPTER 1

The Nature of Risks

We essay a difficult task; but
there is no merit save in
difficult tasks.

OVID

COMPUTER SYSTEMS ENABLE US to do tasks that we could not even dream of doing otherwise—for example, carrying out extremely complex operations, or searching rapidly through mammoth amounts of information. They can also fail to live up to our expectations in many different ways, sometimes with devastating consequences.

This book analyzes a large collection of problems experienced to date, and provides insights that may be helpful in avoiding such consequences in the future. Hindsight can be valuable when it leads to new foresight. I hope that this book will serve that purpose, helping us to attain a safer, sounder, and more secure future in our interactions with and dependence on computers and related technologies.

1.1 Background on Risks

This book refers to vulnerabilities, threats, and risks in computers and related systems. Strict definitions always tend to cause arguments about subtle nuances, and tend to break down in specific cases. Because the primary emphasis in this book is on the big picture, we seek definitions that are intuitively motivated.

- A **vulnerability** is a weakness that may lead to undesirable consequences.

1

- A **threat** is the danger that a vulnerability can actually lead to undesirable consequences—for example, that it can be exploited intentionally or triggered accidentally.

- A **risk** is a potential problem, with causes and effects; to some authors, it is the harm that can result if a threat is actualized; to others, it is a measure of the extent of that harm, such as the product of the likelihood and the extent of the consequences. However, explicit measures of risk are themselves risky (as noted in Section 7.10) and not a major concern here. What is important is that avoiding risks is an exceedingly difficult task that poses a pervasive problem.

1.1.1   Terminology

The following intuitively based English language terms are applied to computer and communication systems throughout this book, and are introduced here. These definitions are generally consistent with common technical usage. (Each term tends to have a conceptual meaning as well as a relative qualitative meaning.) Further definitions are given as they are needed.

- **Reliability** implies that a system performs functionally as is expected, and does so consistently over time. Reliability is also a measure of how well a system lives up to its expectations over time, under specified environmental conditions. Hardware reliability relates to how well the hardware resists malfunctions. Software reliability relates to how well the system satisfies certain functional requirements. Reliability in its various forms is the main concern of Chapter 2.

- **Security** implies freedom from danger, or, more specifically, freedom from undesirable events such as malicious and accidental misuse. Security is also a measure of how well a system resists penetrations by outsiders and misuse by insiders. Security in its many manifestations is the main topic of Chapters 3 and 5.

- **Integrity** implies that certain desirable conditions are maintained over time. For example, system integrity relates to the extent to which hardware and software have not been altered inappropriately. Data integrity relates to data items being as they should be. Personnel integrity relates to individuals behaving in an appropriate manner. Integrity encompasses avoidance of both accidental and intentional corruption.

These three terms appear to overlap significantly, and indeed that is the case no matter how carefully definitions are chosen. These concepts *are* inherently interrelated; uses of technology must necessarily consider them together. Furthermore, there is never an absolute sense in which a system is secure or reliable.

1.1.2   **Perspective**

Increasingly, we depend on computer systems to behave acceptably in applications with extremely **critical requirements,** by which we mean that the failure of systems to meet their requirements may result in serious consequences. Examples of critical requirements include protection of human lives and resources on which we depend for our well-being and the attainment, with high assurance, of adequate system reliability, data confidentiality, and timely responsiveness, particularly under high-risk situations. A challenge of many computer-system designs is that the entire application environment (rather than just the computer systems) must satisfy simultaneously a variety of critical requirements, and must continue to do so throughout its operation, maintenance, and long-term evolution. The satisfaction of a single requirement is difficult enough, but the simultaneous and continued satisfaction of diverse and possibly conflicting requirements is typically much more difficult.

The collection of diverse failures presented here is representative of computer-related problems that have arisen in the past. Understanding the reasons for these cases can help us at least to reduce the chances of the same mistakes recurring in the future. However, we see that similar problems continue to arise. Furthermore, major gaps still exist between theory and practice, and between research and development.

We take a broad, system-oriented view of computer-related technologies that includes computer systems, communication systems, control systems, and robots, for example. We examine the role of computers themselves from a broad perspective. Hardware, software, and people are all sources of difficulties. Human safety and personal well-being are of special concern.

We explore various inherent limitations both of the technology and of the people who interact with it. Certain limitations can be overcome—albeit only with significant effort. We must strive to promote the development and systematic use of techniques that can help us to identify the intrinsic limitations, and to reduce those that are not intrinsic—for example, through better systems and better operational practices. We also must remain keenly aware of the limitations.

There are many pitfalls in designing a system to meet critical requirements. Software-engineering techniques provide directions, but no guarantees. Experience shows that even the most carefully designed systems may have significant flaws. Both testing and formal verification have serious deficiencies, such as the intrinsic incompleteness of the former and the considerable care and effort necessary in carrying out the latter. All in all, there are no easy answers.

Unfortunately, even if an ideal system were designed such that its specifications were shown to be consistent with its critical requirements, and then the design were implemented correctly such that the code could be shown to be consistent with the specifications, the system would still not be totally trustworthy. Desired behavior could be undermined by the failure of the underlying assumptions (whether implicit or explicit), even temporarily. Such assumptions are far-reaching, yet often are not even stated—for example, that the requirements are complete and correct, that there are no lurking design flaws, that no harmful malicious code has been inserted, that there are no malicious users (insiders or outsiders), that neither the data nor the system has been altered improperly, and that the hardware behaves predictably enough that the expected worst-case fault coverage is adequate. In addition, human misuse or other unanticipated problems can subvert even the most carefully designed systems.

Thus, there is good news and there is bad news. The *good news* is that computer system technology is advancing. Given well-defined and reasonably modest requirements, talented and diligent people, enlightened and altruistic management, adequate financial and physical resources, and suitably reliable hardware, systems can be built that are likely to satisfy certain stringent requirements *most of the time*. There have been significant advances—particularly in the research community—in techniques for building such computer systems. The *bad news* is that guaranteed system behavior is impossible to achieve—with or without people in the operational loop. There can always be circumstances beyond anyone's control, such as floods, lightning strikes, and cosmic radiation, to name a few. Besides, people are fallible. Thus, there are always inherent risks in relying on computer systems operating under critical requirements—especially those that are complex and are necessary for controlling real-time environments, such as in fly-by-wire aircraft that are aerodynamically unstable and cannot be flown without active computer control. Even the most exhausting (but still not exhaustive) testing leaves doubts. Furthermore, the development community tends to be slow in adopting those emerging research and development concepts that are practical, and in discarding many other ideas that are not practical. Even more important, it is inherent in a development effort and in system operation that all potential disasters cannot be foreseen—yet it is often the unforeseen circumstances that are the most disastrous, typically because of a combination of circumstances involving both people and computers. A fundamental conclusion is that, even if we are extremely cautious and lucky, we must still anticipate the occurrences of serious catastrophes in using computer systems in critical applications. This concept is also explored by Charles Perrow, who illustrates why accidents must be considered to be *normal*, rather than *exceptional*, events [126].

Because most of the examples cited here illustrate what has gone wrong in the past, the casual reader may wonder if anything has ever gone right. I have always sought to identify true success stories. However, there are few cases in which system developments met their requirements, on budget, and on time; even among those, there have been many developmental and operational problems.

The technological aspects of this book consider how we can improve the state of the art and enhance the level of human awareness, to avoid in the future the problems that have plagued us in the past. It is important to consider the collection of examples as representing lessons from which we must learn. We must never assume infallibility of either the technology or the people developing and applying that technology. Indeed, in certain situations, the risks may simply be too great for us to rely on either computers or people, and it would be better not to entrust the application to automation in the first place. For other applications, suitable care in system development and operation may be sufficient to keep the risks within acceptable limits. But all such conclusions depend on an accurate assessment of the risks and their consequences, an assessment that is typically lacking.

1.2 Sources of Risks

Some of the many stages of system development and system use during which risks may arise are listed in Sections 1.2.1 and 1.2.2, along with a few examples of what might go wrong. Indeed, every one of these categories is illustrated throughout the book with problems that have actually occurred. Techniques for overcoming these problems are considered in Chapter 7.

1.2.1   Sources of Problems Arising in System Development

Problems may occur during each stage of system development (often involving people as an underlying cause), including the following:

- *System conceptualization:* For example, inappropriate application of the technology when the risks were actually too great, or avoidance of automation when use of the technology would have been beneficial
- *Requirements definition:* Erroneous, incomplete, or inconsistent requirements
- *System design:* Fundamental misconceptions or flaws in the design or specification of either the hardware or the software
- *Hardware and software implementation:* Errors in chip fabrication or wiring, program bugs, accidentally or intentionally installed malicious code capable of causing unanticipated effects (for example, Trojan horses such as time bombs and logic bombs, or viruses in the floppy-disk shrinkwrap—see Section 3.1)
- *Support systems:* Poor programming languages, faulty compilers and debuggers, misleading development tools, editing mistakes
- *Analysis of system concepts and design:* Analyses based on false assumptions about the physical world, the operating environment, or human behavior; erroneous models, erroneous simulations
- *Analysis of the implementation—for example, via testing or code verification:* Incomplete testing, erroneous verification, mistakes in debugging
- *Evolution:* Sloppy redevelopment or maintenance, misconceived system upgrades, introduction of new flaws in attempts to fix old flaws, incremental escalation applied to inordinate complexity (the straw that breaks the camel's back)
- *Decommission:* Premature removal of a primary or backup facility before its replacement is fully operational; hidden dependence on an old version that is no longer available but whose existence is necessary (for example, for compatibility); inability to decommission a system before its operation becomes unmanageable (the albatross effect)

1.2.2   Sources of Problems in System Operation and Use

Problems may also arise during system operation and use (typically involving people or external factors), including the following:

- *Natural environmental factors:* Lightning, earthquakes, floods, extreme temperatures (as in the *Challenger* loss), electromagnetic and other interference including cosmic radiation and sunspot activity, and myriad other natural occurrences

- *Animals:* Sharks, squirrels, monkeys, and birds are included as causative factors in the cases presented here, and—indirectly—a cow; a pig appears in Section 5.3, trapped in an electronic-mail spoof
- *Infrastructural factors:* Loss of electrical power or air conditioning
- *Hardware malfunction:* Equipment malfunctions, due to causes such as physical aging, transient behavior, or general-sense environmental causes, such as those noted in the preceding three items
- *Software misbehavior:* Unexpected behavior resulting from undetected problems in the system-development process, or from subsequent system changes, or from faulty maintenance after installation (see Section 1.2.1)
- *Communication media failures:* Transmission outages, natural interference, jamming
- *Human limitations in system use:* System operators, administrators, staff, users, or unsuspecting bystanders may cause problems throughout, for example,
    - *Installation:* Improper configuration, faulty initialization, incompatible versions, erroneous parameter settings, linkage errors
    - *Misuse of the overall environment or of the computer systems:* Such problems include *unintentional misuse* such as entry of improper inputs, lack of timely human response, misinterpretation of outputs, improper response to warning messages, execution of the wrong function; they also include *intentional misuse,* such as penetrations by supposedly unauthorized users, misuse by authorized users, malicious insertion of Trojan horses, fraud, and so on. (See Section 3.1.)

1.3 Adverse Effects

There are many areas in which computers affect our lives, and in which risks must be anticipated or accommodated. Several of these areas are listed here, along with just a few types of potential risks associated with the causes listed in Sections 1.2.1 and 1.2.2. All of these areas are represented in the following text.

- *Computers and communications:* Loss or corruption of communication media, nondelivery or corruption of data, insertion of bogus or spoofed electronic-mail messages or commands, loss of privacy through wire taps and computer taps—Section 2.1 and Chapter 5

- *Computers that are used in space applications:* Lost lives, mission failures, launch delays, failed experiments, large financial setbacks — Section 2.2

- *Computers that are used for defense and warfare:* Misidentification of friend or foe, failure to attack, failure to defend, accidental attacks, accidental self-destruction, "friendly fire" — Section 2.3

- *Computers that are used in transportation:* Deaths, delays, fires, sudden acceleration, inability to brake or control a vehicle, inability to escape from an automatically controlled vehicle after power interruption — Section 2.4 for civil aviation, Section 2.5 for railroads, and Section 2.6 for shipping

- *Computers used in controlling safety-critical applications:* Deaths, injuries, delays, inconvenience — Section 2.7 for control systems, Section 2.8 for robots

- *Computers and related systems used in health care and in otherwise safeguarding health and safety:* Deaths, injuries, psychological disabilities, misdiagnosis, mistreatment, incorrect billing — Sections 2.9.1 and 2.9.2; loss of privacy of personal information — Chapter 6

- *Computers and related systems whose use causes health problems:* Physical harm (carpal-tunnel syndrome and other repetitive-strain injuries, radiation effects), computer-related stress, mental anguish — Section 2.9.2

- *Computers used in electrical power:* Deaths, injuries, power outages, long-term health hazards including radiation effects in nuclear-power systems — Section 2.10

- *Computers that manage money:* Fraud, violations of privacy; losses and disruptions of market facilities such as shutdown of stock exchanges and banks, both accidental and intentional — Sections 5.6 and 5.7

- *Computers that control elections:* Accidentally wrong results and election frauds involving computer or external manipulation — Section 5.8

- *Computers that control jails and prisons:* Technology-aided escape attempts and successes, mistakes that accidentally release inmates, failures in computer-controlled locks — Section 5.9

- *Computers used in law enforcement:* False arrests and false imprisonments, failure to apprehend suspects — Section 6.5

- *Computers that enforce system and data integrity:* Insertion of Trojan horses, viruses, denials of service, spoofing attacks, subversions — Chapter 5

- *Computers that protect data privacy:* Invasions of privacy, such as undesired data accessibility or tracking of individuals — Chapter 6

- *Computers in general:* Accidentally false results, delays, and losses of data — for example, Sections 2.11, 5.2, 5.5, and 7.2; victimization by intentional system misuses such as the malicious insertion of Trojan horses and bogus messages — Sections 5.1, 5.3, and 5.4

- *Computers that otherwise adversely affect people's lives:* Personal aggravation including being falsely declared dead, being billed incorrectly, and other nuisances — Section 6.4; adverse effects of mistaken identities — Section 6.5

1.4   Defensive Measures

Given these potential sources of risks and their consequent adverse effects, appropriate countermeasures are essential. Chapter 7 includes discussion of techniques for increasing reliability, safety, security, and other system properties, and protecting privacy. That chapter also addresses techniques for improving the system-development process, including system engineering and software engineering.

The reader who is technically inclined will find useful discussions throughout, and many pointers to further references — in various sections and in the summaries at the end of each chapter. Reliability and safety techniques are considered in Section 7.7. Security techniques are considered in Sections 3.8 and 6.3, and in several of the sections of Chapter 7 (particularly Section 7.9). Assurance of desired system properties in turn relies heavily on software engineering and system-development approaches considered in Sections 7.6 and 7.8. The reader who is primarily interested in the illustrative material may wish to skip over those sections.

1.5   Guide to Summary Tables

Chapters 5 and 6, and most sections of Chapter 2, conclude with tables that summarize the cases discussed therein. For each case or group of cases, the apparent causative factors are indicated. For each of the summary tables, the abbreviations and symbols used for the column headings and for the table entries are as defined in Table 1.1. In particular, the column headings in each of the summary tables relate to the most prevalent sources of problems itemized in Section 1.2. The summary-table entries exhibit the relevance of each causative factor. In particular, a ○ indicates a negative causative factor that contributed to the problem, and a ● indicates the primary causative factor. When multiple cases are

TABLE 1.1 Summary of table abbreviations

Column heading	Problem sources and examples
Req def	Requirements definition, omissions, mistakes
Sys des	System design, flaws
HW impl	Hardware implementation, wiring, chip flaws
SW impl	Software implementation, program bugs, compiler bugs
Sys use	System use and operation, inadvertent mistakes
Misuse	Willful system misuse (particularly in Chapters 5 and 6)
HW malf	Hardware, communication, or other equipment malfunction
Envir	Environmental problems, natural causes, acts of God
Analysis	Analysis of concepts, design, implementation, etc.
Evol, maint	Evolution, maintenance, faulty upgrades, decommission

Table entry	Meaning
○	Deleterious cause contributing to the problem
●	Primary deleterious cause
(○)	Deleterious cause among some of the grouped cases
?	Possible but unconfirmed cause
★	Restorative factor helping to overcome the problem

aggregated into a single row of a summary table, a ○ in parentheses indicates that some of those cases exhibit the column attribute. Occasionally when multiple events involving different factors contributed to a particular case, those events are identified by parenthesized numbers in the text, and those numbers are also referred to in the summary tables (for example, as in Table 2.2). In a few cases, positive factors helped to ameliorate a particular problem—for example, through detection and manual recovery; in those instances, the presence of a positive or restorative factor is denoted by a ★ in the column corresponding to the relevant factor (as in Table 2.2).

1.6 **Summary of the Chapter**

This introductory chapter provides a brief overview of the types of harmful causes and adverse effects that can arise in connection with the use of computers. It introduces the enormous variety of problems that we confront throughout this book.

Preliminary Challenges for the Reader

C1.1   Examine the sources of risks given in Section 1.2. Identify those sources that have affected your life. Describe how they have done so.

C1.2   Examine the illustrative list of adverse consequences given in Section 1.3. Identify those consequences that have affected your life. Describe them.

C1.3   Describe an incident in which your work with computer systems has been adversely affected, and analyze why that happened and what could have been done to avoid or mitigate the effects.

C1.4   (Essay question) What are your expectations of computer-communication technologies? What effects do you think these technologies might have on civilization, both in the short term and in the long term? What kinds of risks do you think might be acceptable, and under what circumstances? Is the technology making life better or worse? Be specific in your answers. (This challenge is a preliminary one. Your views may well change after you read the rest of the book, at which time you may wish to reassess your answers to this question.)

CHAPTER 2

Reliability and Safety Problems

If anything can go wrong,
it will (and at the worst
possible moment).
A VARIANT OF MURPHY'S LAW

ONE OF THE MOST IMPORTANT CHALLENGES in the design of computer-related systems is to provide meaningful assurances that a given system will behave dependably, despite hardware malfunctions, operator mistakes, user mistakes, malicious misuse, and problems in the external environment—including lightning strikes and power outages that affect system performance, as well as circumstances outside the computer systems relating to processes being controlled or monitored, such as a nuclear meltdown.

With respect to reliability issues, a distinction is generally made among faults, errors, and failures in systems. Basically, a **fault** is a condition that could cause the system to fail. An **error** is a deviation from expected behavior. Some errors can be ignored or overcome. However, a **failure** is an error that is not acceptable. A **critical failure** is a failure that can have serious consequences, such as causing damage to individuals or otherwise undermining the critical requirements of the system.

The following 11 sections of this chapter present past events that illustrate the difficulties in attaining reliability and human safety. These events relate to communication systems and computers used in space programs, defense, aviation, public transit, control systems, and other applications. Many different causes and effects are represented. Each application area is considered in summary at the end of the section relating to that area.

It is in principle convenient to decouple reliability issues from security issues. This chapter considers reliability problems, whereas security is examined in Chapters 3 and 5. In practice, it is essential that both reliability and security be considered within a common framework, because of factors noted in Chapter 4. Such an overall system perspective is provided in Chapter 7. In that chapter, a discussion of how to increase reliability is given in Section 7.7.

2.1 Communication Systems

Communications are required for many purposes, including for linking people, telephones, facsimile machines, and computer systems with one another. Desirable requirements for adequate communications include reliable access and reliable transmission, communication security, privacy, and availability of the desired service.

2.1.1 Communications Reliability Problems

This section considers primarily cases in which the reliability requirements failed to be met for communications involving people and computers. Several security-related communications problems are considered in Chapter 5.

The 1980 ARPAnet collapse. In the 1970s, the ARPAnet was a network linking primarily research computers, mostly within the United States, under the auspices of the Advanced Research Projects Agency (ARPA) of the Department of Defense (DoD). (It was the precursor of the Internet, which now links together many different computer networks worldwide.) On October 27, 1980, the ARPAnet experienced an unprecedented outage of approximately 4 hours, after years of almost flawless operation. This dramatic event is discussed in detail by Eric Rosen [139], and is summarized briefly here.

The collapse of the network resulted from an unforeseen interaction among three different problems: (1) a hardware failure resulted in bits being dropped in memory; (2) a redundant single-error-detecting code was used for transmission, but not for storage; and (3) the garbage-collection algorithm for removing old messages was not resistant to the simultaneous existence of one message with several different time stamps. This particular combination of circumstances had not arisen previously. In normal operation, each net node broadcasts a status message to each of its neighbors once per minute; 1 minute later, that message is then rebroadcast to the iterated neighbors, and so on. In the absence of bogus status messages, the garbage-collection algorithm is relatively sound. It keeps only the most recent of the status messages received from any given node, where **recency** is defined as the larger of two close-together 6-bit time stamps, modulo 64. Thus, for example, a node could delete any message that it had already received via a shorter path, or a message that it had originally sent that was routed back to it. For simplicity, 32 was considered a permissible difference, with the numerically larger time stamp being arbitrarily deemed the more recent in that case. In the situation that caused the collapse, the correct version of the time stamp was 44 [101100 in binary], whereas the bit-dropped versions had time stamps 40 [101000] and 8 [001000]. The garbage-collection algorithm noted that 44 was more recent than 40, which in turn was more recent than 8, which in turn was more recent than 44 (modulo 64). Thus, all three versions of that status message had to be kept.

From then on, the normal generation and forwarding of status messages from the particular node were such that *all of those messages* and their successors with newer time stamps had to be kept, thereby saturating the memory of each node. In effect, this was a naturally propagating, globally contaminating effect. Ironically, the status messages had the highest priority, and thus defeated all efforts to maintain the network nodes remotely. Every node had to be shut down manually. Only after each site administrator reported back that the local nodes were down could the network be reconstituted; otherwise, the contaminating propagation would have begun anew. This case is considered further in Section 4.1. Further explanation of the use of parity checks for detecting any arbitrary single bit in error is deferred until Section 7.7.

The 1986 ARPAnet outage. Reliability concerns dictated that logical redundancy should be used to ensure alternate paths between the New England ARPAnet sites and the rest of the ARPAnet. Thus, seven separate circuit links were established. Unfortunately, all of them were routed through the same fiber-optic cable, which was accidentally severed near White Plains, New York, on December 12, 1986 (*SEN 12,* 1, 17).[1]

The 1990 AT&T system runaway. In mid-December 1989, AT&T installed new software in 114 electronic switching systems (Number 4 ESS), intended to reduce the overhead required in signaling between switches by eliminating a signal indicating that a node was ready to resume receiving traffic; instead, the other nodes were expected to recognize implicitly the readiness of the previously failed node, based on its resumption of activity. Unfortunately, there was an undetected latent flaw in the recovery-recognition software in every one of those switches.

On January 15, 1990, one of the switches experienced abnormal behavior; it signaled that it could not accept further traffic, went through its recovery cycle, and then resumed sending traffic. A second switch accepted the message from the first switch and attempted to reset itself. However, a second message arrived from the first switch that could not be processed properly, because of the flaw in the software. The second switch shut itself down, recovered, and resumed sending traffic. That resulted in the same problem propagating to the neighboring switches, and then iteratively and repeatedly to all 114 switches. The hitherto undetected problem manifested itself in subsequent simulations whenever a second message arrived within too short a time. AT&T finally was able to diagnose the problem and to eliminate it by reducing the messaging load of the network, after a 9-hour nationwide blockade.[2] With the reduced load, the erratic behavior effectively went away by itself, although the software still had to be patched correctly to prevent a recurrence. Reportedly, approximately 5 million calls were blocked.

The ultimate cause of the problem was traced to a C program that contained a break statement within an if clause nested within a switch clause. This problem can be called a programming error, or a deficiency of the C language and its compiler, depending on your taste, in that the intervening if clause was in violation of expected programming practice. (We return to this case in Section 4.1.)

The Chicago area telephone cable. Midmorning on November 19, 1990, a contractor planting trees severed a high-capacity telephone line in suburban Chicago, cutting off long-distance service and most local service for 150,000 telephones. The personal and commercial disruptions were extensive. Teller machines at some banks were paralyzed. Flights at O'Hare International Airport were delayed because the air-traffic control tower temporarily lost contact with the main Federal Aviation Administration air-traffic control centers for the Chicago area. By midafternoon, Illinois Bell Telephone Company had done some rerouting, although outages and service degradations continued for the rest of the day.[3]

The New York area telephone cable. An AT&T crew removing an old cable in Newark, New Jersey, accidentally severed a fiber-optic cable carrying more than 100,000 calls. Starting at 9:30 A.M. on January 4, 1991, and continuing for much of the day, the effects included shutdown of the New York Mercantile Exchange and several commodities exchanges; disruption of Federal Aviation Administration (FAA) air-traffic control communication in the New York metropolitan area, Washington, and Boston; lengthy flight delays; and blockage of 60 percent of the long-distance telephone calls into and out of New York City.[4]

Virginia cable cut. On June 14, 1991, two parallel cables were cut by a backhoe in Annandale, Virginia. The Associated Press (perhaps having learned from the previously noted seven-links-in-one-conduit separation of New England from the rest of the ARPAnet) had requested two separate cables for their primary and backup circuits. Both cables were cut at the same time, because they were adjacent!

Fiber-optic cable cut. A Sprint San Francisco Bay Area fiber-optic cable was cut on July 15, 1991, affecting long-distance service for 3.5 hours. Rerouting through AT&T caused congestion there as well.[5]

SS-7 faulty code patch. On June 27, 1991, various metropolitan areas had serious outages of telephone service. Washington, D.C. (6.7 million lines), Los Angeles, and Pittsburgh (1 million lines) were all affected for several hours. Those problems were eventually traced to a flaw in the Signaling System 7 protocol implementation, and were attributed to an untested patch that involved just a few lines of code. A subsequent report to the Federal Communications Commission (written by Bell Communications Research Corp.) identified a mistyped character in the April software release produced by DSC Communications Corp. ("6" instead of "D") as the cause, along with faulty data, failure of computer clocks, and other triggers. This problem caused the equipment and software to fail under an avalanche of computer-generated messages (*SEN, 17,* 1, 8-9).

Faulty clock maintenance. A San Francisco telephone outage was traced to improper maintenance when a faulty clock had to be repaired (*SEN, 16,* 3, 16-17).

Backup battery drained. A further telephone-switching system outage caused the three New York airports to shut down for 4 hours on September 17, 1991. AT&T's backup generator hookup failed while a Number 4 ESS switching system in Manhattan was running on internal power (in response to a voluntary New York City brownout); the system ran on standby batteries for 6 hours until the batteries depleted, unbeknownst to the personnel on hand. The two people responsible for handling emergencies were attending a class on power-room alarms. However, the alarms had been disconnected previously because of construction in the area that was continually triggering the alarms! The ensuing FAA report concluded that about 5 million telephone calls had been blocked, and 1174 flights had been canceled or delayed (*SEN 16*, 4; *17*, 1).

Air-traffic control problems. An FAA report to a House subcommittee listed 114 "major telecommunication outages" averaging 6.1 hours in the FAA network consisting of 14,000 leased lines across the country, during the 13-month period from August 1990 to August 1991. These outages led to flight delays and generated safety concerns. The duration of these outages ranged up to 16 hours, when a contractor cut a 1500-circuit cable at the San Diego airport in August 1991. That case and an earlier outage in Aurora, Illinois, are also noted in Section 2.4. The cited report included the following cases as well. (See *SEN 17*, 1.)

- On May 4, 1991, four of the FAA's 20 major air-traffic control centers shut down for 5 hours and 22 minutes. The cause: "Fiber cable was cut by a farmer burying a dead cow. Lost 27 circuits. Massive operational impact."
- The Kansas City, Missouri, air-traffic center lost communications for 4 hours and 16 minutes. The cause: "Beaver chewed fiber cable." (Sharks have also been known to chomp on undersea cables.) Causes of other outages cited included lightning strikes, misplaced backhoe buckets, blown fuses, and computer problems.
- In autumn 1991, two technicians in an AT&T long-distance station in suburban Boston put switching components on a table with other unmarked components, and then put the wrong parts back into the machine. That led to a 3-hour loss of long-distance service and to flight delays at Logan International Airport.
- The failure of a U.S. Weather Service telephone circuit resulted in the complete unavailability of routine weather-forecast information for a period of 12 hours on November 22, 1991 (*SEN 17*, 1).

Problems in air-traffic control systems are considered more generally in Section 2.4, including other cases that did not involve communications difficulties.

The incidence of such outages and partial blockages seems to

TABLE 2.1 Summary of communications problems

Case	Req def	Sys des	HW impl	SW impl	Sys use	HW malf	Envir	Anal-ysis	Evol, maint
				Source of the Problems					
1980 ARPAnet	o	o	o	o		●		o	
1986 ARPAnet	o	o	o			o	●		
1990 AT&T		o		o		?		o	●
Chicago, IL						o	●		
New York, NY						o	●		
Annandale, VA						o	●		
Bay Area, CA						o	●		o
SS-7 patch		o		o	o	o		o	●
Clock repair						o			●
NY power goof			o		o	o	o		●
ATC outages	(o)	(o)	(o)	(o)	(o)	(o)	(o)	(o)	(o)

be increasing, rather than decreasing, as more emphasis is placed on software and as communication links proliferate. Distributed computer-communication systems are intrinsically tricky, as illustrated by the 1980 ARPAnet collapse and the similar nationwide saturation of AT&T switching systems on January 15, 1990. The timing-synchronization glitch that delayed the first shuttle launch (Section 2.2.1) and other problems that follow also illustrate difficulties in distributed systems. A discussion of the underlying problems of distributed systems is given in Section 7.3.

2.1.2   **Summary of Communications Problems**

Section 2.1 considers a collection of cases related to communications failures. Table 2.1 provides a brief summary of the causes of these problems. The column heads relate to causative factors enumerated in Section 1.2, and are as defined in Table 1.1 in Section 1.5. Similarly, the table entries are as defined in Table 1.1.

The causes and effects in the cases in this section vary widely from one case to another. The 1980 ARPAnet outage was triggered by hardware failures, but required the presence of a software weakness and a hardware design shortcut that permitted total propagation of the contaminating effect. The 1986 ARPAnet separation was triggered by an environmental accident, but depended on a poor implementation decision. The 1990 AT&T blockage resulted from a programming mistake and a network design that permitted total propagation of the contaminating effect. A flurry of cable cuttings (Chicago, New York area, Virginia, and the San Francisco Bay Area) resulted from digging accidents, but the effects in each case were exacerbated by designs that made the systems particularly vulnerable. The SS-7 problems resulted from a faulty code patch and the absence of testing before that patch was installed. The New York City telephone outage resulted from poor network administration, and was complicated by the earlier removal of warning alarms.

In summary, the primary causes of the cited communications problems were largely environmental, or were the results of problems in maintenance and system evolution. Hardware malfunctions were involved in most cases, but generally as secondary causative factors. Software was involved in several cases. Many of the cases have multiple causative factors.

The diversity of causes and effects noted in these communications problems is typical of what is seen throughout each of the sections of this chapter relating to reliability, as well as in succeeding chapters relating to security and privacy. However, the specific factors differ from one type of application to another. As a consequence, the challenge of avoiding similar problems in the future is itself quite diversified. (See, for example, Chapter 7.)

2.2   Problems in Space

In this section, we consider difficulties that have occurred in space programs, involving shuttles, probes, rockets, and satellites, to illustrate the diversity among reliability and safety problems.

One of the most spectacular uses of computers is in the design, engineering, launch preparation, and real-time control of space vehicles and experiments. There have been magnificent advances in this area. However, in the firm belief that we must learn from the difficulties as well as the successes, this section documents some of the troubles that have occurred.

Section 2.2.1 considers problems that have arisen in the shuttle program, plus a few other related cases involving risks to human lives. Section 2.2.2 considers space exploration that does not involve people on board.

2.2.1   **Human Exploration in Space**

Despite the enormous care taken in development and operation, the space program has had its share of problems. In particular, the shuttle program has experienced many difficulties. The National Aeronautics and Space Administration (NASA) has recorded hundreds of anomalies involving computers and avionics in the shuttle program. A few of the more instructive cases are itemized here, including several in which the lives of the astronauts were at stake. Unfortunately, details are not always available regarding what caused the problem, which makes it difficult to discuss how that problem could have been avoided, and which may at times be frustrating to both author and reader.

The order of presentation in this section is more or less chronological. The nature of the causes is extremely diverse; indeed, the causes are different in each case. Thus, we begin by illustrating this diversity, and then in retrospect consider the nature of the contributing factors. In later sections of this chapter and in later chapters, the presentation tends to follow a more structured approach, categorizing problems by type. However, the same conclusion is generally evident. The diversity among the causes and effects of the encountered risks is usually considerable — although different from one application area to another.

The first shuttle launch (STS-1). One of the most often-cited computer-system problems occurred about 20 minutes before the scheduled launch of the first space shuttle, *Columbia*, on April 10, 1981. The problem was extensively described by Jack Garman ("The 'Bug' Heard 'Round the World" [47]), and is summarized here. The launch was put on hold for 2 days because the backup computer could not be initialized properly.

The on-board shuttle software runs on two pairs of primary computers, with one pair in control as long as the simultaneous computations on both agree with each other, with control passing to the other pair in the case of a mismatch. All four primary computers run identical programs. To prevent catastrophic failures in which both pairs fail to perform (for example, if the software were wrong), the shuttle has a fifth computer that is programmed with different code by different programmers from a different company, but using the same specifications and the same compiler (HAL/S). Cutover to the backup computer would have to be done manually by the astronauts. (Actually, the backup fifth computer has never been used in mission control.)

Let's simplify the complicated story related by Garman. The backup computer and the four primary computers were 1 time unit out of phase during the initialization, as a result of an extremely subtle 1-in-67 chance timing error. The backup system refused to initialize, even though the primary computers appeared to be operating perfectly throughout the 30-hour countdown. Data words brought in one cycle too soon on the primaries were rejected as noise by the backup. This system flaw occurred despite extraordinarily conservative design and implementation. (The interested reader should delve into [47] for the details.)

A software problem on shuttle (STS-6). The Johnson Space Center Mission Control Center had a pool of four IBM 370/168 systems for STS mission operations on the ground. During a mission, one system is on-line. One is on hot backup, and can come on-line in about 15 seconds. During critical periods such as launch, reentry, orbit changes, or payload deployment, a third is available on about 15 minutes notice. The third 370 can be supporting simulations or software development during a mission, because such programs can be interrupted easily. Prior to STS-6, the 370 software supported only one activity (mission, simulation, or software development) at a time. Later, the Mature Operations Configuration would support three activities at a time. These would be called the Dual and Triple Mission Software deliveries. STS-6 was the first mission after the Dual Mission Software had been installed. At liftoff, the memory allocated to that mission was saturated with the primary processing, and the module that allocated memory would not release the memory allocated to a second mission for Abort Trajectory calculation. Therefore, if the mission had been aborted, trajectories would not have been available. After the mission, a flaw in the software was diagnosed and corrected (*SEN 11*, 1).

Note that in a similar incident, Mercury astronauts had previously had to fly a manual reentry because of a program bug that prevented automatic control on reentry (*SEN 8*, 3).

Shuttle *Columbia* return delayed (STS-9). On December 8, 1983, the shuttle mission had some serious difficulties with the on-board computers. STS-9 lost the number 1 computer 4 hours before reentry was scheduled to begin. Number 2 took over for 5 minutes, and then conked out. Mission Control powered up number 3; they were able to restart number 2 but not number 1, so the reentry was delayed. Landing was finally achieved, although number 2 died again on touchdown. Subsequent analysis indicated that each processor failure was due to a single loose piece of solder bouncing around under 20 gravities. Astronaut John Young later testified that, had the backup flight system been activated, the mission would have been lost (*SEN 9*, 1, 4; *14*, 2).

Thermocouple problem on *Challenger* (STS-19). On July 29, 1985, 3 minutes into ascent, a failure in one of two thermocouples directed a computer-controlled shutdown of the center engine. Mission control decided to abort into orbit, 70 miles up—50 miles lower than planned. Had the shutdown occurred 30 seconds earlier, the mission would have had to abort over the Atlantic. NASA has reset some of the binary thermocouple limits via subsequent software changes. (See *SEN 14*, 2.)

***Discovery* launch delay (STS-20).** An untimely—and possibly experiment-aborting—delay of the intended August 25, 1985, launch of the space shuttle *Discovery* was caused when a malfunction in the backup computer was discovered just 25 minutes before the scheduled launch. The resulting 2-day delay caused serious complications in scheduling of the on-board experiments, although the mission was concluded successfully. A reporter wrote, "What was puzzling to engineers was that the computer had worked perfectly in tests before today. And in tests after the failure, it worked, though showing signs of trouble."[6] (Does that puzzle you?)

Arnold Aldrich, manager of the shuttle program at Johnson, was quoted as saying "We're about 99.5 percent sure it's a hardware failure." (The computers were state of the art as of 1972, and were due for upgrading in 1987.) A similar failure of the backup computer caused a 1-day delay in *Discovery*'s maiden launch in the summer of 1984 (*SEN 10*, 5).

Near-disaster on shuttle *Columbia* (STS-24). The space shuttle *Columbia* came within 31 seconds of being launched without enough fuel to reach its planned orbit on January 6, 1986, after weary Kennedy Space Center workers mistakenly drained 18,000 gallons of liquid oxygen from the craft, according to documents released by the White House panel that probed the shuttle program. Although NASA said at the time that computer problems were responsible for the scrubbed launch, U.S. Representative Bill Nelson from Florida flew on the mission, and said that he was informed of the fuel loss while aboard the spacecraft that day.

> According to the appendix [to the panel report], Columbia's brush with disaster . . . occurred when Lockheed Space Operations Co. workers "inadvertently" drained super-cold oxygen from the shuttle's external tank 5 minutes before the scheduled launch. The workers misread computer evidence of a failed valve and allowed a fuel line to remain open. The leak was detected when the cold oxygen caused a temperature gauge to drop below approved levels, but not until 31 seconds before the launch was the liftoff scrubbed.[7]

The *Challenger* disaster (STS-25). The destruction of the space shuttle *Challenger* on January 28, 1986, killed all seven people on board. The explosion was ultimately attributed to the poor design of the booster rockets, as well as to administrative shortcomings that permitted the launch under cold-weather conditions. However, there was apparently a decision along the way to economize on the sensors and on their computer interpretation by removing the sensors on the booster rockets. There is speculation that those sensors might have permitted earlier detection of the booster-rocket failure, and possible early separation of the shuttle in an effort to save the astronauts. Other shortcuts were also taken so that the team could adhere to an accelerating launch schedule. The loss of the *Challenger* seems to have resulted in part from some inadequate administrative concern for safety—despite recognition and knowledge of hundreds of problems in past flights. Problems with the O-rings—especially their inability to function properly in cold weather—and with the booster-rocket joints had been recognized for some time. The presidential commission found "a tangle of bureaucratic underbrush": "Astronauts told the commission in a public hearing . . . that poor organization of shuttle operations led to such chronic problems as crucial mission software arriving just before shuttle launches and the constant cannibalization of orbiters for spare parts." (See the *Chicago Tribune*, April 6, 1986.)

Shuttle *Atlantis* computer fixed in space (STS-30).[8] One of *Atlantis'* main computers failed on May 7, 1989. For the first time ever, the astronauts made repairs—in this case, by substituting a spare processor. It took them about 3.5 hours to gain access to the computer systems by removing a row of lockers on the shuttle middeck, and another 1.5 hours to check out the replacement computer. (The difficulty in making repairs was due to a long-standing NASA decision from the Apollo days that the computers should be physically inaccessible to the astronauts.) (See *SEN 14*, 5.)

Shuttle *Atlantis* backup computer on ground delays launch (STS-36). A scheduled launch of *Atlantis* was delayed for 3 days because of "bad software" in the backup tracking system. (See *SEN 15*, 2.)

Shuttle *Discovery* misprogramming (STS-41). According to flight director Milt Heflin, the shuttle *Discovery* was launched on October 6, 1990, with incorrect instructions on how to operate certain of its programs. The error was discovered by the shuttle crew about 1 hour into the mission, and was corrected quickly. NASA claims that automatic safeguards would have prevented any ill effects even if the crew had not noticed the error on a display. The error was made before the launch, and was discovered when the crew was switching the shuttle computers from launch to orbital operations. The switching procedure involves shutting down computers 3 and 5, while computers 1 and 2 carry on normal operations, and computer 4 monitors the shuttle's *vital signs*. However, the crew noticed that the instructions for computer 4 were in fact those intended for computer 2. Heflin stated that the problem is considered serious because the ground prelaunch procedures failed to catch it.[9]

Intelsat 6 launch failed. In early 1990, an attempt to launch the $150 million *Intelsat 6* communications satellite from a Titan III rocket failed because of a wiring error in the booster, due to inadequate human communications between the electricians and the programmers who failed to specify in which of the two satellite positions the rocket had been placed; the program had selected the wrong one (Steve Bellovin, *SEN 15*, 3). Live space rescue had to be attempted. (See the next item.)

Shuttle *Endeavour* computer miscomputes rendezvous with *Intelsat* (STS-49). In a rescue mission in May 1992, the *Endeavour* crew had difficulties in attempting to rendezvous with *Intelsat 6*. The difference between two values that were numerically extremely close (but not identical) was effectively rounded to zero; thus, the program was unable to observe that there were different values. NASA subsequently changed the specifications for future flights.[10]

Shuttle *Discovery* multiple launch delays (STS-56). On April 5, 1993, an attempt to launch *Discovery* was aborted 11 seconds before liftoff. (The engines had not yet been ignited.) (There had been an earlier 1-hour delay at 9 minutes before launch, due to high winds and a temperature-sensor problem.) Early indications had pointed to failure of a valve in the main propulsion system. Subsequent analysis indicated that the valve was operating properly, but that the computer system interpreted the sensor incorrectly—indicating that the valve had not closed. A quick fix was to bypass the sensor reading, which would have introduced a new set of risks had there subsequently been a valve problem.[11]

This *Discovery* mission experienced many delays and other problems. Because of the Rube Goldberg nature of the mission, each event is identified with a number referred to in Table 2.2 at the end of the section. (1) The initial attempted launch was aborted. (2) On July 17, 1993, the next attempted launch was postponed because ground restraints released prematurely. (3) On July 24, a steering-mechanism failure was detected at 19 seconds from blastoff. (4) On August 4, the rescheduled launch was postponed again to avoid potential interference from the expected heavy Perseid meteor shower on August 11 (in the aftermath of the reemergence of the comet Swift-Tuttle). (5) On August 12, the launch was aborted when the engines had to be shut down 3 seconds from blastoff, because of a suspected failure in the main-engine fuel-flow monitor. (An Associated Press report of August 13, 1993, estimated the expense of the scrubbed launches at over $2 million.) (6) The *Columbia* launch finally went off on September 12, 1993. *Columbia* was able to launch two satellites, although each had to be delayed by one orbit due to two unrelated communication problems. (7) An experimental communication satellite could not be released on schedule, because of interference from the payload radio system. (8) The release of an ultraviolet telescope had to be delayed by one orbit because communication interference had delayed receipt of the appropriate commands from ground control.

Shuttle *Columbia* aborted at -3 seconds (STS-55). On March 22, 1993, *Columbia*'s main engines were shut down 3 seconds before liftoff, because of a leaky valve. (The mission finally went off on April 26, 1993.)

Columbia launch grounded due to safety software (STS-58). The planned launch of *Columbia* on October 14, 1993, had to be scrubbed at the last minute because of a "glitch in the computer system designed to ensure safety on the ground during launches."[12] The launch went off successfully 4 days later.

Apollo: The moon was repulsive. The *Apollo 11* software reportedly had a program flaw that resulted in the moon's gravity appearing repulsive rather than attractive. This mistake was caught in simulation. (See *SEN 9*, 5, based on an oral report.)

Software mixup on the Soyuz spacecraft. According to *Aviation Week* (September 12, 1988, page 27), in the second failed reentry of the Soviet Soyuz-TM spacecraft on September 7, 1988, the engines were shut down in the last few seconds due to a computer problem: "Instead of using the descent program worked out for the Soviet-Afghan crew, the computer switched to a reentry program that had been stored in the Soyuz TM-5 computers in June for a Soviet-Bulgarian crew. Soviet officials said . . . that they did not understand why this computer mixup occurred." Karl Lehenbauer noted that the article stated that the crew was committed to a reentry because they had jettisoned the orbital module that contained equipment that would be needed to redock with the Mir space station. The article also noted that Geoffrey Perry, an analyst of Soviet space activities with the Kettering Group, said "the crew was not flying in the same Soyuz that they were launched in, but instead were in a spacecraft that had been docked with the Mir for about 90 days. Perry said that is about half the designed orbital life of the Soyuz." (See *SEN 13*, 4.)

2.2.2   Other Space-Program Problems

The problems itemized in Section 2.2.1 involved risks to human lives (except for the *Intelsat 6* launch, which is included because of the rescue mission). Some of these cases necessitated extra-vehicular human actions as well. Next, we examine problems relating to uninhabited space missions.

Atlas-Agena went beserk due to missing hyphen. On what was expected to be the first U.S. spacecraft to do a Venus flyby, an Atlas-Agena became unstable at about 90 miles up. The $18.5 million rocket was then blown up on command from the control center at Cape Kennedy. Subsequent analysis showed that the flight plan was missing a hyphen that was a symbol for a particular formula.[13]

Mariner I **lost.** *Mariner I* was intended to be the first space probe to visit another planet (Venus). Apparent failure of an Atlas booster during launch on July 22, 1962, caused the range officer to destroy the booster rather than to risk its crashing in a populated area.

However, in reality, the rocket was behaving correctly, and it was the ground-based computer system analyzing the launch that was in error — as the result of a software bug and a hardware failure. The software bug is noteworthy. The two radar systems differed in time by 43 milliseconds, for which the program supposedly compensated. The bug arose because the overbar had been left out in the handwritten guidance equations in the expression *R dot bar sub n.* Here *R* denotes the radius; the dot indicates the first derivative — that is, the velocity; the bar indicates smoothed rather than raw data; and *n* is the increment. When a hardware fault occurred, the computer processed the track data incorrectly, leading to the erroneous termination of the launch.[14]

There had been earlier erroneous reports that the problem was due to a comma that had been entered accidentally as a period in a DO statement (which really was a problem with the Mercury software, as noted in the next item). The confusion was further compounded by a report that the missing overbar might have been the interchange of a minus sign and a hyphen, but that was also false (*SEN 13*, 1). This case illustrates the difficulties we sometimes face in trying to get correct details about a computer failure.

DO I=1.10 bug in Mercury software. Project Mercury's FORTRAN code had a syntax error something like DO I=1.10 instead of DO I=1,10. The substitution of a comma for a period was discovered in an analysis of why the software did not seem sufficiently accurate, even though the program had been used successfully in previous suborbital missions; the error was corrected before the subsequent orbital and moon flights, for which it might have caused problems. This case was reported in *RISKS* by Fred Webb, whose officemate had found the flaw in searching for why the program's accuracy was poor (*SEN 15*, 1). (The erroneous 1.10 would cause the loop to be executed exactly once.)

Ohmage to an Aries launch. At White Sands Missile Range, New Mexico, a rocket carrying a scientific payload for NASA was destroyed 50 seconds after launch because its guidance system failed. The loss of the $1.5-million rocket was caused by the installation of an improper resistor in the guidance system.[15] (The flight was the twenty-seventh since the first Aries was launched in 1973, but was only the third to experience failure.)

***Gemini V* lands 100 miles off course.** *Gemini V* splashed down off-course by 100 miles because of a programmer's misguided short-cut. The intended calculation was to compute the earth reference point relative to the sun as a fixed point, using the elapsed time since launch. The programmer forgot that the earth does not come back to the same point relative to the sun 24 hours later, so that the error cumulatively increased each day.[16]

Titan, Orion, Delta, Atlas, and Ariane failures. The disaster of the space shuttle *Challenger* (January 28, 1986) led to increased efforts to launch satellites without risking human lives in shuttle missions. However, the *Challenger* loss was followed by losses of the Titan III (34-D) on April 18, 1986; the Nike Orion on April 25, 1986 (although it was not reported until May 9); and the Delta rocket on May 3, 1986. The Titan III loss was the second consecutive Titan III failure, this launch having been delayed because of an accident in the previous launch during the preceding August, traced to a first-stage turbo-pump. A subsequent Titan IV loss is noted in Section 7.5. A further Titan IV blew up 2 minutes after launch on August 2, 1993, destroying a secret payload thought to be a spy satellite.[17] The failure of the Nike Orion was its first, after 120 consecutive successes. The Delta failure followed 43 consecutive successful launches dating back to September 1977. In the Delta-178 failure, the rocket's main engine mysteriously shut itself down 71 seconds into the flight—with no evidence of why! (Left without guidance at 1400 mph, the rocket had to be destroyed, along with its weather satellite.) The flight appeared normal up to that time, including the jettisoning of the first set of solid rockets after 1 minute out. Bill Russell, the Delta manager, was quoted thus: "It's a very sharp shutdown, almost as though it were a commanded shutdown." The preliminary diagnosis seemed to implicate a short circuit in the engine-control circuit. The May 22, 1986, launch of the Atlas-Centaur was postponed pending the results of the Delta investigation, because both share common hardware. The French also had their troubles, when an Ariane went out of control and had to be destroyed, along with a $55 million satellite. (That was its fourth failure out of 18 launches; 3 of the 4 involved failure of the third stage.) Apparently, insurance premiums on satellite launches skyrocketed as a result. (See *SEN 11*, 3.) Atlas launches in 1991, August 1992, and March 1993 also experienced problems. The first one had to be destroyed shortly after liftoff, along with a Japanese broadcasting satellite. The second went out of control and had to be blown up, along with its cable TV satellite. The third left a

Navy communications satellite in a useless orbit, the failure of the $138 million mission being blamed on a loose screw. The losses in those 3 failed flights were estimated at more than $388 million. The first successful Atlas flight in a year occurred on July 19, 1993, with the launch of a nuclear-hardened military communications satellite.[18]

Voyager missions. *Voyager 1* lost mission data over a weekend because all 5 printers were not operational; 4 were configured improperly (for example, off-line) and one had a paper jam (*SEN 15*, 5).

Canaveral rocket destroyed. In August 1991, an off-course rocket had to be destroyed. A technician had apparently hit a wrong key while loading the guidance software, installing the ground-test version instead of the flight software. Subsequently, a bug was found before a subsequent launch that might have caused the rocket to err, even if the right guidance software had been in place (Steve Bellovin, *SEN 16*, 4).

Viking antenna problem. The *Viking* probe developed a misaligned antenna due to an improper code patch. (An orally provided report is noted in *SEN 9*, 5.)

Phobos 1 and 2. The Soviets lost their *Phobos 1* Mars probe after it tumbled in orbit and the solar cells lost power. The tumbling resulted from a single character omitted in a transmission from a ground controller to the probe. The change was necessitated because of a transfer from one command center to another. The omission caused the spacecraft's solar panels to point the wrong way, which prevented the batteries from staying charged, ultimately causing the spacecraft to run out of power. *Phobos 2* was lost on March 27, 1989, because a signal to restart the transmitter while the latter was in power-saver mode was never received.[19]

Mars Observer vanishes. The *Mars Observer* disappeared from radio contact on Saturday, August 21, 1993, just after it was ready to pressurize its helium tank (which in turn pressurizes the hydrazine-oxygen fuel system), preparatory to the rocket firings that were intended to slow down the spacecraft and to allow it to be captured by Martian gravity and settle into orbit around Mars. The subsequent request to switch on its antenna again received no response. Until that point, the mission had been relatively trouble free—except that the spacecraft's instructions had to be revised twice to overcome temporary problems. Speculation continued as to whether a line leak or a tank rupture might have occurred. Glenn Cunningham, project manager at the Jet Propulsion Laboratory, speculated on several other possible scenarios: the *Observer's* on-board clock could have stopped, the radio could have overheated, or the antenna could have gone askew. Lengthy analysis has concluded that the most likely explanation is that a change in flight plan was the inadvertent cause. The original plan was to pressurize the propellant tanks 5 days after launch; instead, the pressurization was attempted 11 months into the flight, in hopes of minimizing the likelihood of a leak. Apparently the valves were not designed to operate under the alternative plan, which problem now seems most likely to have been the cause of a fuel-line rupture resulting from a mixture of hydrazine and a small amount of leaking oxidizer.[20]

Landsat 6. *Landsat 6* was launched on October 5, 1993. It was variously but erroneously reported as (1) having gotten into an improper orbit, or (2) being in the correct orbit but unable to communicate. On November 8, 1993, the $228 million *Landsat 6* was declared officially *missing.* The object NASA had been tracking turned out to be a piece of space junk.[21]

These problems came on the heels of the continued launch delays on another *Discovery* mission, a weather satellite that died in orbit after an electronic malfunction, and the Navy communications satellite that was launched into an unusable orbit from Vandenburg in March 1993 ($138 million). Shuttle launches were seriously delayed.[22]

Galileo troubles en route to Jupiter. The $1.4 billion Galileo spacecraft en route to Jupiter experienced difficulties in August 1993. Its main antenna jammed, and its transmissions were severely limited to the use of the low-gain antenna.

Anik E-1, E-2 failures. Canadian Telesat's *Anik E-1* satellite stopped working for about 8 hours on January 21, 1994, with widespread effects on telephones and the Canadian Press news agency, particularly in the north of Canada. Minutes after *Anik E-1* was returned to service, *Anik E-2* (which is Canada's main broadcast satellite) ceased functioning altogether. Amid a variety of possible explanations (including magnetic storms, which later were absolved), the leading candidate involved electron fluxes related to solar coronal holes.

Xichaing launchpad explosion. On April 9, 1994, a huge explosion at China's Xichiang launch facility killed at least two people, injured at least 20 others, and destroyed the $75 million *Fengyun-2* weather satellite. The explosion also leveled a test laboratory. A leak in the on-board fuel system was reported as the probable cause.[23]

Lens cap blocks satellite test. A Star Wars satellite launched on March 24, 1989, was unable to observe the second-stage rocket firing because the lens cap had failed to be removed in time. By the time that the lens was uncovered, the satellite was pointing in the wrong direction (*SEN 14, 2*).

2.2.3   Summary of Space Problems

Table 2.2 provides a brief summary of the problems cited in Section 2.2. The abbreviations and symbols used for table entries and column headings are as in Table 1.1.

From the table, we observe that there is considerable diversity among the causes and effects, as in Table 2.1, and as suggested at the beginning of Section 2.2.1. However, the nature of the diversity of causes is quite different from that in Table 2.1. Here many of the problems involve software implementation or hardware malfunctions as the primary cause, although other types of causes are also included.

The diversity among software faults is evident. The STS-1 flaw was a subtle mistake in synchronization. The STS-49 problem resulted from a precision glitch. The original STS-56 launch postponement (noted in the table as subcase (1)) involved an error in sensor interpretation. The *Mariner I* bug was a lexical mistake in transforming handwritten equations to code for the ground system. The Mercury bug involved the substitution of a period for a comma. The Gemini bug resulted from an overzealous programmer trying to find a short-cut in equations of motion.

The diversity among hardware problems is also evident. The multiple STS-9 hardware failures were caused by a loose piece of solder. The STS-19 abort was due to a thermocouple failure. STS-30's problem involved a hard processor failure that led the astronauts to replace the computer, despite the redundant design. The original STS-55 launch was aborted because of a leaky valve. Two of the STS-56 delays (subcases 3 and 5) were attributable to equipment problems. The *Mariner I* hardware failure in the ground system was the triggering cause of the mission's abrupt end, although the

TABLE 2.2 Summary of space problems

Case	Req def	Sys des	HW impl	SW impl	Sys use	HW malf	Envir	Analysis	Evol, maint
				Source of the Problems					
STS-1 Columbia		○		●				○ ★	
STS-6 Challenger		○		●					○
STS-9 Columbia						○	●		
STS-19 Challenger						●			
STS-20 Discovery				?		?			
STS-24 Columbia					●		○		
STS-25 Challenger	○	○		○	○		●	○	
STS-30 Atlantis						●		★	★
STS-36 Atlantis				●					
STS-41 Discovery					●★	○		★	
STS-49 Endeavour				●					
STS-56 Discovery				1●		3,5●	2,4,7,8●		
STS-55 Columbia						●			
Apollo				●				★	
Soyuz				?		?	○		
Mercury (see STS-6)				●					
Atlas-Agena					●				○
Mariner I		○		●		●			
Mercury				●				★	
Aries			●						
Gemini V				●					
Titan III						●			
Delta-178						●			
Voyager 1					●	○			○
Viking				○					●
Phobos 1					●				○
Phobos 2					○	○			●
Observer		?	?	?	?	?	?		
Landsat 6			?	?	?	?	?		
Galileo				●					
Anik E-1,2							●		
Intelsat 6 (see STS-49)			●		○				○

software bug noted previously was the real culprit. The mysterious shutdown of the Delta-178 main engine adds still another possible cause.

Several cases of operational human mistakes are also represented. STS-24 involved a human misinterpretation of a valve condition. STS-41 uncovered incorrect operational protocols. The Atlas-Agena loss resulted from a mistake in the flight plan. Voyager gagged on output data because of an erroneous system configuration. The loss of *Phobos 1* was caused by a missing character in a reconfiguration command.

The environmental causes include the cold climate under which the *Challenger* was launched (STS-25), weightlessness mobilizing loose solder (STS-9), and communication interference that caused the delays in *Discovery*'s placing satellites in orbit (STS-56, subcases 7 and 8).

Redundancy is an important way of increasing reliability; it is considered in Section 7.7. In addition to the on-board four primary computers and the separately programmed emergency backup computer, the shuttles also have replicated sensors, effectors, controls, and power supplies. However, the STS-1 example shows that the problem of getting agreement among the distinct program components is not necessarily straightforward. In addition, the backup system is intended primarily for reentry in an emergency in which the primary computers are not functional; it has not been maintained to reflect many of the changes that have occurred in recent years, and has never been used. A subsystem's ability to perform correctly is always dubious if its use has never been required.

In one case (Apollo), analytical simulation uncovered a serious flaw before launch. In several cases, detected failures in a mission led to fixes that avoided serious consequences in future missions (STS-19, STS-49, and Mercury).

Maintenance in space is much more difficult than is maintenance in ground-based systems (as evidenced by the cases of STS-30 and *Phobos*), and consequently much greater care is given to preventive analysis in the space program. Such care seems to have paid off in many cases. However, it is also clear that many problems remain undetected before launch.

2.3 **Defense**

Some of the applications that stretch computer and communication technology to the limits involve military systems, including both defensive and offensive weapons. We might like to believe that more money and effort therefore would be devoted to solving problems of safety and lethality, system reliability, system security, and system assurance in defense-related systems than that expended in the private sector. However, the number of defense problems included in the *RISKS* archives suggests that there are still many lessons to be learned.

2.3.1 **Defense Problems**

In this section, we summarize a few of the most illustrative cases.

Patriot clock drift. During the Persian Gulf war, the Patriot system was initially touted as highly successful. In subsequent analyses, the estimates of its effectiveness were seriously downgraded, from about 95 percent to about 13 percent (or possibly less, according to MIT's Ted Postol; see *SEN 17,* 2). The system had been designed to work under a much less stringent environment than that in which it was actually used in the war. The clock drift over a 100-hour period (which resulted in a tracking error of 678 meters) was blamed for the Patriot missing the scud missile that hit an American military barracks in Dhahran, killing 29 and injuring 97. However, the blame can be distributed — for example, among the original requirements (14-hour missions), clock precision, lack of system adaptability, extenuating operational conditions, and inadequate risks analysis (*SEN, 16,* 3; *16,* 4). Other reports suggest that, even over the 14-hour duty cycle, the results were inadequate. A later report stated that the software used two different and unequal versions of the number 0.1 — in 24-bit and 48-bit representations (*SEN 18,* 1, 25). (To illustrate the discrepancy, the decimal number 0.1 has as an endlessly repeating binary representation 0.0001100110011 . . . . Thus, two different representations truncated at different lengths are *not* identical — even in their floating-point representations.) This case is the opposite of the shuttle *Endeavour* problem on STS-49 noted in Section 2.2.1, in which two apparently identical numbers were in fact representations of numbers that were unequal!

***Vincennes* Aegis system shoots down Iranian Airbus.** Iran Air Flight 655 was shot down by the USS *Vincennes'* missiles on July 3, 1988, killing all 290 people aboard. There was considerable confusion attributed to the Aegis user interface. (The system had been designed to track missiles rather than airplanes.) The crew was apparently somewhat spooked by a previous altercation with a boat, and was working under perceived stress. However, replay of the data showed clearly that the airplane was ascending — rather than descending, as believed by the Aegis operator. It also showed that the operator had not tracked the plane's identity correctly, but rather had locked onto an earlier identification of an Iranian F-14 fighter still on the runway. Matt Jaffe [58] reported that the altitude information was not displayed on the main screen, and that there was no indication of the rate of change of altitude (or even of whether the plane was going up, or going down, or remaining at the same altitude). Changes were recommended subsequently for the interface, but most of the problem was simplistically attributed to human error. (See *SEN 13*, 4; *14*, 1; *14*, 5; *14*, 6.) However, earlier Aegis system failures in attempting to hit targets previously had been attributed to software (*SEN 11*, 5).

"Friendly Fire" — U.S. F-15s take out U.S. Black Hawks. Despite elaborate precautions designed to prevent such occurrences, two U.S. Army UH-60 Black Hawk helicopters were shot down by two American F-15C fighter planes in the no-fly zone over northern Iraq on April 14, 1994, in broad daylight, in an area that had been devoid of Iraqi aircraft activity for many months. One Sidewinder heat-seeking missile and one Amraam radar-guided missile were fired. The fighters were operating under instructions from an AWACS plane, their airborne command post. The AWACS command was the first to detect the helicopters, and instructed the F-15s to check out the identities of the helicopters. The helicopters were carrying U.S., British, French, and Turkish officers from the United Nations office in Zakho, in northern Iraq, and were heading eastward for a meeting with Kurdish leaders in Salahaddin. Both towns are close to the Turkish border, well north of the 26th parallel that delimits the no-fly zone. All 26 people aboard were killed.

After stopping to pick up passengers, both helicopter pilots apparently failed to perform the routine operation of notifying their AWACS command plane that they were underway. Both helicopters apparently failed to respond to the automated "Identification:

Friend or Foe" (IFF) requests from the fighters. Both fighter pilots apparently did not try voice communications with the helicopters. A visual flyby apparently misidentified the clearly marked ("U.N.") planes as Iranian MI-24s. Furthermore, a briefing had been held the day before for appropriate personnel of the involved aircraft (F-15s, UH-60s, and AWACS).

The circumstances behind the shootdowns remained murky, although a combination of circumstances must have been present. One or both helicopter pilots might have neglected to turn on their IFF transponder; one or both frequencies could have been set incorrectly; one or both transponders might have failed; the fighter pilots might not have tried all three of the IFF modes available to them. Furthermore, the Black Hawks visually resembled Russian helicopters because they were carrying extra external fuel tanks that altered their profiles. But the AWACS plane personnel should have been aware of the entire operation because they were acting as coordinators. Perhaps someone panicked. An unidentified senior Pentagon offical was quoted as asking "What was the hurry to shoot them down?" Apparently both pilots neglected to set their IFF transponders properly. In addition, a preliminary Pentagon report indicates that the controllers who knew about the mission were not communicating with the controllers who were supervising the shootdown.[24]

"Friendly fire" (also called fratricide, amicicide, and misadventure) is not uncommon. An item by Rick Atkinson[25] noted that 24 percent of the Americans killed in action—35 out of 146—in the Persian Gulf war were killed by U.S. forces. Also, 15 percent of those wounded—72 out of 467—were similarly victimized by their colleagues. During the same war, British Warrior armored vehicles were mistaken for Iraqi T-55 tanks and were zapped by U.S. Maverick missiles, killing 9 men and wounding 11 others. Atkinson's article noted that this situation is not new, citing a Confederate sentry who shot his Civil War commander, Stonewall Jackson, in 1863; an allied bomber that bombed the 30th Infantry Division after the invasion of Normandy in July 1944; and a confused bomber pilot who killed 42 U.S. paratroopers and wounded 45 in the November 1967 battle of Hill 875 in Vietnam. The old adage was never more appropriate: With friends like these, who needs enemies?

Gripen crash. The first prototype of Sweden's fly-by-wire Gripen fighter plane crashed on landing at the end of its sixth flight because of a bug in the flight-control software. The plane is naturally unstable, and the software was unable to handle strong winds at low speeds, whereas the plane itself responded too slowly to the pilot's controls (*SEN 14*, 2; *14*, 5). A second Gripen crash on August 8, 1993, was officially blamed on a combination of the pilot and the technology (*SEN 18*, 4, 11), even though the pilot was properly trained and equipped. However, pilots were not informed that dangerous effects were known to be possible as a result of large and rapid stick movements (*SEN 19*, 1, 12-13).

F-111s bombing Libya jammed by their own jamming. One plane crashed and several others missed their targets in the 1986 raid on Libya because the signals intended to jam Libya's antiaircraft facilities were also jamming U.S. transmitters (*SEN 11*, 3; *15*, 3).

Bell V22 Ospreys. The fifth of the Bell-Boeing V22 Ospreys crashed due to the cross-wiring of two roll-rate sensors (gyros that are known as *vyros*). As a result, two faulty units were able to outvote the good one in a majority-voting implementation. Similar problems were later found in the first and third Ospreys, which had been flying in tests (*SEN 16*, 4; *17*, 1). Another case of the bad outvoting the good in flight software is reported by Brunelle and Eckhardt [18], and is discussed in Section 4.1.

Tornado fighters collide. In August 1988, two Royal Air Force Tornado fighter planes collided over Cumbria in the United Kingdom, killing the four crewmen. Apparently, both planes were flying with identical preprogrammed cassettes that controlled their on-board computers, resulting in both planes reaching the same point at the same instant. (This case was reported by Dorothy Graham, *SEN 15*, 3.)

Ark Royal. On April 21, 1992, a Royal Air Force pilot accidentally dropped a practice bomb on the flight deck of the Royal Navy's most modern aircraft carrier, the *Ark Royal*, missing its intended towed target by hundreds of yards. Several sailors were injured. The cause was attributed to a timing delay in the software intended to target an object at a parametrically specified offset from the tracked object, namely the carrier. [26]

Gazelle helicopter downed by friendly missile. On June 6, 1982, during the Falklands War, a British Gazelle helicopter was shot down by a Sea Dart missile that had been fired from a British destroyer, killing the crew of four (*SEN 12*, 1).

USS *Scorpion*. The USS *Scorpion* exploded in 1968, killing a crew of 99. Newly declassified evidence suggests that the submarine was probably the victim of one of its own conventional torpedoes, which, after having been activated accidentally, was ejected. Unfortunately, the torpedo became fully armed and sought its nearest target, as it had been designed to do.[27]

Missiles badly aimed. The U.S. guided-missile frigate *George Philip* fired a 3-inch shell in the general direction of a Mexican merchant ship, in the opposite direction from what had been intended during an exercise in the summer of 1983 (*SEN 8*, 5). A Russian cruise missile landed in Finland, reportedly 180 degrees off its expected target on December 28, 1984 (*SEN 10*, 2). The U.S. Army's DIVAD (Sgt. York) radar-controlled antiaircraft gun reportedly selected the rotating exhaust fan in a latrine as a potential target, although the target was indicated as a low-priority choice (*SEN 11*, 5).

Air defense. For historically minded readers, there are older reports that deserve mention. Daniel Ford's book *The Button*[28] notes satellite sensors being overloaded by a Siberian gas-field fire (p. 62), descending space junk being detected as incoming missiles (p. 85), and a host of false alarms in the World-Wide Military Command and Control System (WWMCCS) that triggered defensive responses during the period from June 3 to 6, 1980 (pp. 78–84) and that were eventually traced to a faulty integrated circuit in a communications multiplexor. The classical case of the BMEWS defense system in Thule, Greenland, mistaking the rising moon for incoming missiles on October 5, 1960, was cited frequently.[29] The North American Air Defense (NORAD) and the Strategic Air Command (SAC) had 50 false alerts during 1979 alone—including a simulated attack whose outputs accidentally triggered a live scramble/alert on November 9, 1979 (*SEN 5*, 3).

Early military aviation problems. The *RISKS* archives also contain a few old cases that have reached folklore status, but that are not well documented. They are included here for completeness. An F-18 reportedly crashed because of a missing exception condition if . . . then . . . without the else clause that was thought could not possibly arise (*SEN 6*, 2; *11*, 2). Another F-18 attempted to fire a missile that was still clamped to the plane, resulting in a loss of 20,000 feet in altitude (*SEN 8*, 5). In simulation, an F-16 program bug caused the virtual plane to flip over whenever it crossed the equator, as the result of a missing minus sign to indicate south latitude.[30] Also in its simulator, an F-16, flew upside down because the program deadlocked over whether to roll to the left or to the right (*SEN 9*, 5). (This type of problem has been investigated by Leslie Lamport in an unpublished paper entitled "Buridan's Ass" — in which a donkey is equidistant between two points and is unable to decide which way to go.)

2.3.2 Summary of Defense Problems

Table 2.3 provides a brief summary of the causative factors for the cited problems. (The abbreviations and symbols are given in Table 1.1.)

The causes vary widely. The first six cases in the table clearly involve multiple causative factors. Although operator error is a common conclusion in such cases, there are often circumstances that implicate other factors. Here we see problems with system requirements (Patriot), hardware (Osprey), software (lack of precision in the Patriot case, a missing exception condition in the F-18, and a missing sign in the F-16), and the user interface (Aegis). The Black Hawk shootdown appears to have been a combination of errors by many different people, plus an overreliance on equipment that may not have been turned on. The environment also played a role — particularly electromagnetic interference in the F-111 case.

TABLE 2.3 Summary of defense problems

Case	Req def	Sys des	HW impl	SW impl	Sys use	HW malf	Envir	Anal- ysis	Evol, maint
				Source of the Problems					
Patriot	○	○		●	●	○	○	○	○
Aegis	○		○	●	○		○	○	○
Black Hawks				●	?				
Gripen				○	○		○	○	
F-111		○			○		●		
Osprey			●	○			○		
Tornado					●				
Ark Royal				???					
Gazelle					●				
Scorpion		○			●		○		

2.4 **Civil Aviation**

This section considers the basic problems of reliable aviation, the risks involved, and cases in which reliability and safety requirements failed to be met. The causes include human errors and computer-system failures. The effects are serious in many of the cited cases.

2.4.1   **Risks in Automated Aviation**

The 1980s saw a tremendous increase of the use of digital electronics in newly developed airliners. The regulatory requirement for a flight engineer's position on larger airplanes had been eased, such that only two pilots were then required. The emerging power of advanced technology has resulted in highly automated cockpits and in significant changes to flight management and flight-control philosophies.

Flight management. The Flight Management System (FMS) combines the features of an inertial navigation system (INS) with those of a performance-management computer. It is most often used in conjunction with screen-based flight instrumentation, including an artificial horizon and a navigation display. The crew can enter a flight plan, review it in a plan mode on the navigation display, and choose an efficiency factor by which the flight is to be conducted. When coupled with the autopilot, the FMS can control virtually the entire flight, from takeoff to touchdown. The FMS is the core of all modern flight operations.

Systems. As many functions as possible have been automated, from the electrical system to toilet-flush actuators. System states are monitored by display screens rather than more than 650 electromechanical gauges and dials. Most systems' data items are still available via 10 to 15 synoptic pages, on a single systems display. It is not feasible for the pilots to monitor long-term changes in any onboard system; they must rely on an automatic alerting and monitoring system to do that job for them. Pilots retain limited control authority over on-board systems, if advised of a problem.

Flight control. In 1988, the Airbus A320 was certified; it was the first airliner to use a digital fly-by-wire flight-control system. Pilots

Section 2.4.1 originally appeared as a two-part *Inside Risks* column, *CACM 37*, 1 and 2, January and February 1994, written by **Robert Dorsett**—who is the author of a Boeing 727 systems simulator and *TRACON II* for the Macintosh.

control a conventional airliner's flight path by means of a control column. The control column is connected to a series of pulleys and cables, leading to hydraulic actuators, which move the flight surfaces. Fly-by-wire control eliminates the cables, and replaces them with electrical wiring; it offers weight savings, reduced complexity of hardware, the potential for the use of new interfaces, and even modifications of fundamental flight-control laws—resulting from having a computer filter most command inputs.

Communications. All new airliners offer an optional ARINC Communication and Reporting System (ACARS). This protocol allows the crew to exchange data packets, such as automatically generated squawks and position reports, with a maintenance or operations base on the ground. Therefore, when the plane lands, repair crews can be ready, minimizing turnaround time. ACARS potentially allows operations departments to manage fleet status more efficiently, in real time, worldwide, even via satellite.

Similar technology will permit real-time air-traffic control of airliners over remote locations, such as the Pacific Ocean or the North Atlantic, where such control is needed.

Difficulties. Each of the innovations noted introduces new, unique problems. The process of computerization has been approached awkwardly, driven largely by market and engineering forces, less by the actual need for the features offered by the systems. Reconciling needs, current capabilities, and the human-factors requirements of the crew is an ongoing process.

For example, when FMSs were introduced in the early 1980s, pilots were under pressure to use all available features, all the time. However, it became apparent that such a policy was not appropriate in congested terminal airspace; pilots tended to adopt a heads-down attitude, which reduced their ability to detect other traffic. They also tended to use the advanced automation in high-workload situations, long after it clearly became advisable either to hand-fly or to use the autopilot in simple heading- and altitude-select modes. By the late 1980s, airlines had started click-it-off training. Currently, many airlines discourage the use of FMSs beneath 10,000 feet.

Increased automation has brought the pilot's role closer to that of a manager, responsible for overseeing the normal operation of the systems. However, problems do occur, and the design of modern interfaces has tended to take pilots out of the control loop. Some research suggests that, in an emergency situation, pilots of conventional aircraft have an edge over pilots of a modern airplane with an equivalent mission profile, because older airplanes require pilots to participate in a feedback loop, thus improving awareness. As an example of modern philosophies, one manufacturer's pre-flight procedure simply requires that all lighted buttons be punched out. The systems are not touched again, except in abnormal situations. This design is very clever and elegant; the issue is whether such an approach is sufficient to keep pilots in the loop.

Displays. The design of *displays* is an ongoing issue. Faced with small display screens (a temporary technology limitation), manufacturers tend to use tape formats for airspeed and altitude monitoring, despite the cognitive problems. Similarly, many systems indications are now given in a digital format rather than in the old analog formats. This display format can result in the absence of trend cues, and, perhaps, can introduce an unfounded faith in the accuracy of the readout.

Control laws. Related to the interface problem is the use of *artificial control laws*. The use of unconventional devices, such as uncoupled sidesticks, dictates innovations in control to overcome the device's limitations; consequently, some flight-control qualities are not what experienced pilots expect. Moreover, protections can limit pilot authority in unusual situations. Because these control laws are highly proprietary—they are not standardized, and are not a simple consequence of the natural flying qualities of the airplane—there is potential for significant training problems as pilots transition between airplane types.

Communications. The improvement of *communications* means that ground personnel are more intimately connected with the flight. The role of an airliner captain has been similar to that of a boat captain, whose life is on the line and who is in the sole position to make critical safety judgments—by law. With more real-time interaction with company management or air-traffic control, there are more opportunities for a captain to be second-guessed, resulting in distributed responsibility and diminished captain's authority. Given the increasingly competitive, bottom-line atmosphere under which airlines must operate, increased interaction will help diminish personnel requirements, and may tend to impair the safety equation.

Complexity. The effect of *software complexity* on safety is an open issue. Early INSs had about 4 kilobytes of memory; modern FMSs are pushing 10 megabytes. This expansion represents a tremendous increase in complexity, combined with a decrease in pilot authority. Validating software to the high levels of reliability required poses all but intractable problems. Software has allowed manufacturers to experiment with novel control concepts, for which the experience of conventional aircraft control gathered over the previous 90 years provides no clear guidance. This situation has led to unique engineering challenges. For example, software encourages modal thinking, so that more and more features are context-sensitive.

A Fokker F.100 provided a demonstration of such modality problems in November 1991. While attempting to land at Chicago O'Hare, the crew was unable to apply braking. Both the air and ground switches on its landing gear were stuck in the air position. Since the computers controlling the braking system thought that the plane was in the air, not only was the crew unable to use reverse thrust, but, more controversially, they also were unable to use nosewheel steering or main gear braking—services that would have been available on most other airliners in a similar situation.

As another example, the flight-control laws in use on the Airbus A320 have four distinct permutations, depending on the status of the five flight-control computers. Three of these laws have to accommodate individual-component failure. On the other hand, in a conventional flight-control system, there is but one control law, for all phases of flight.

Regulation. The regulatory authorities are providing few direct standards for high-tech innovation. As opposed to conventional aircraft, where problems are generally well understood and the rules codified, much of the modern regulatory environment is guided by collaborative industry standards, which the regulators have generally approved as being sound. Typically a manufacturer can select one of several standards to which to adhere. On many issues, the position of the authorities is that they wish to *encourage* experimentation and innovation.

The state of the industry is more suggestive of the disarray of the 1920s than of what we might expect in the 1990s. There are many instances of these emerging problems; Boeing and Airbus use different display color-coding schemes, not to mention completely different lexicons to describe systems with similar purposes. Even among systems that perform similarly, there can be significant discrepancies in the details, which can place tremendous demands on the training capacity of both airlines *and* manufacturers. All of these factors affect the safety equation.

2.4.2 Illustrative Aviation Problems

There have been many strange occurrences involving commercial aviation, including problems with the aircraft, in-flight computer hardware and software, pilots, air-traffic control, communications, and other operational factors. Several of the more illuminating cases are summarized here. A few cases that are not directly computer related are included to illustrate the diversity of causes on which airline safety and reliability must depend. (Robert Dorsett has contributed details that were not in the referenced accounts.)

Lauda Air 767. A Lauda Air 767-300ER broke up over Thailand, apparently the result of a thrust reverser deploying in mid-air, killing 223. Of course, this event is supposed to be impossible in flight.[31] Numerous other planes were suspected of flying with the same defect. The FAA ordered changes.

757 and 767 autopilots. Federal safety investigators have indicated that autopilots on 757 and 767 aircraft have engaged and disengaged on their own, causing the jets to change direction for no apparent reason, including 28 instances since 1985 among United Airlines aircraft. These problems have occurred despite the autopilots being triple-modular redundant systems.[32]

Northwest Airlines Flight 255. A Northwest Airlines DC-9-82 crashed over Detroit on August 17, 1987, killing 156. The flaps and the thrust computer indicator had not been set properly before takeoff. A computer-based warning system might have provided an alarm, but it was not powered up—apparently due to the failure of a $13 circuit breaker. Adding to those factors, there was bad weather, confusion over which runway to use, and failure to switch radio frequencies. The official report blamed "pilot error." Subsequently, there were reports that pilots in other aircraft had disabled the warning system because of frequent false alarms.[33]

British Midland 737 crash. A British Midland Boeing 737-400 crashed at Kegworth in the United Kingdom, killing 47 and injuring 74 seriously. The right engine had been erroneously shut off in response to smoke and excessive vibration that was in reality due to a fan-blade failure in the left engine. The screen-based "glass cockpit" and the procedures for crew training were questioned. Cross-wiring, which was suspected — but not definitively confirmed — was subsequently detected in the warning systems of 30 similar aircraft.[34]

Aeromexico crash. An Aeromexico flight to Los Angeles International Airport collided with a private plane, killing 82 people on August 31, 1986 — 64 on the jet, 3 on the Piper PA-28, and at least 15 on the ground. This crash occurred in a government-restricted area in which the private plane was not authorized to fly. Apparently, the Piper was never noticed on radar (although there is evidence that it had appeared on the radar screen), because the air-traffic controller had been distracted by *another* private plane (a Grumman-Yankee) that had been in the same restricted area (*SEN 11*, 5). However, there were also reports that the Aeromexico pilot had not explicitly declared an emergency.

Collisions with private planes. The absence of technology can also be a problem, as in the case of a Metroliner that collided with a private plane that had no altitude transponder, on January 15, 1987, killing 10. Four days later, an Army turboprop collided with a private plane near Independence, Missouri. Both planes had altitude transponders, but controllers did not see the altitudes on their screens (*SEN 12*, 2).

Air France Airbus A320 crash. A fly-by-wire Airbus A320 crashed at the Habsheim airshow in the summer of 1988, killing 3 people and injuring 50. The final report indicates that the controls were functioning correctly, and blamed the pilots. However, there were earlier claims that the safety controls had been turned off for a low overflight. Dispute has continued to rage about the investigation. One pilot was convicted of libel by the French government for criticizing the computer systems (for criticizing "public works"), although he staunchly defends his innocence [6]. There were allegations that the flight-recorder data had been altered. (The flight recorder showed that the aircraft hit trees when the plane was at an altitude of 32 feet.) Regarding other A320 flights, there have been reports of altimeter glitches, sudden throttling and power changes, and steering problems during taxiing. Furthermore, pilots have complained that the A320 engines are generally slow to respond when commanded to full power.[35]

Indian Airlines Airbus A320 crash. An Indian Airlines Airbus A320 crashed 1000 feet short of the runway at Bangalore, killing 97 of the 146 passengers. Some similarities with the Habsheim crash were reported. Later reports said that the pilot was one of the airline's most experienced and had received "excellent" ratings in his Airbus training. Airbus Industrie apparently sought to discredit the Indian Airlines' pilots, whereas the airlines expressed serious apprehensions about the aircraft. The investigation finally blamed human error; the flight recorder indicated that the pilot had been training a new copilot (*SEN 15*, 2; *15*, 3; *15*, 5) and that an improper descent mode had been selected. The crew apparently ignored aural warnings.

French Air Inter Airbus A320 crash. A French Air Inter Airbus A320 crashed into Mont Sainte-Odile (at 2496 feet) on automatic landing approach to the Strasbourg airport on a flight from Lyon on January 20, 1992. There were 87 people killed and 9 survivors. A combination of human factors (the integration of the controller and the human–machine interface, and lack of pilot experience with the flightdeck equipment), technical factors (including altimeter failings), and somewhat marginal weather (subfreezing temperature and fog) was blamed. There was no warning alarm (*RISKS 13*, 05; *SEN 17*, 2; *18*, 1, 23; *19*, 2, 11).

Lufthansa Airbus A320 crash. A Lufthansa Airbus A320 overran the runway after landing at Warsaw Airport, killing a crew member and a passenger, and injuring 54 (70 people were aboard). There was a delay after the pilot attempted to actuate the spoilers and reverse thrust, apparently due to supposedly protective overrides in the safety system. Peter Ladkin suggested that this delay was most likely due to an improper requirements specification that prevented the pilot from taking the proper action. There was also a serious problem in the reporting of surface wind, which was given orally and which was updated only every 3 minutes. A strong tailwind existed, which had shifted by 120 degrees and doubled in speed since the previous report.[36] Lufthansa later concluded there had been a problem with the braking logic, the fix to which was to change the recommended landing configuration (*SEN 19*, 2, 11).

Ilyushin Il-114 crash. A prototype Ilyushin Il-114 regional turboprop crashed on July 5, 1993, when the digital engine-control system inadvertently commanded one propeller to feather just after takeoff. The pilots could not compensate for the resultant yaw.[37]

Korean Airlines Flight 007 off-course. Korean Airlines 007 was shot down on September 1, 1983, as it was leaving Soviet airspace, about 360 miles off course; all 269 people aboard were killed. The most plausible explanation was that the autopilot was not switched to inertial navigation when the plane passed over the checkpoint on its heading 246 outbound from Anchorage. This explanation now seems to have been confirmed, based on the blackbox flight recorder that the Russians recovered and disclosed, and analysis of the limitations of the inertial navigation system—which has now been improved.[38] There were reports that Arctic gales had knocked out key Soviet radars, and that Sakhalin air defense forces were trigger-happy following earlier U.S. Navy aircraft overflight incursions. There were also various contrary theories regarding intentional spying that took the plane over Sakhalin at the time of a planned Soviet missile test—which was scrubbed when the flight was detected.

Air New Zealand crash. On November 28, 1979, an Air New Zealand plane crashed into Mount Erebus in Antarctica, killing 257. A critical error in the on-line course data had been detected the day before, but had not been reported to the pilots of the excursion trip—which wound up many miles off course. Unfortunately, this was the first flight in that area under instrument controls (*SEN 6, 3; 6, 5*).

Autopilot malfunction breaks off two engines. A Boeing KC-135 had two engines break off during Desert Storm operations. An autopilot malfunction apparently put the plane into a roll that overstressed the airframe.[39]

Three engines failed on a DC-8. Responding to a discussion on the unlikeliness of two engines having failed (in connection with the British Midlands crash noted previously), a Transamerica Airlines pilot reported that three of the four engines of his DC-8/73 had failed simultaneously on a military flight to the Philippines. He was able to restart them during descent, but the fourth one failed after landing. The cause was attributed to the specific-gravity adjustments on the fuel controls having been set improperly for the fuel being used.[40]

Birds in flight. Birds colliding with an Ethiopian Airlines 737 were responsible for a crash that killed 31 people (*SEN 14, 2*).

Lightning strikes. A Boeing 707 at 5000 feet over Elkton, Maryland, was hit by lightning in 1963; a wing fuel tank exploded, killing all passengers (*SEN 15*, 1).

Traffic Collision Avoidance System (TCAS). TCAS is a system intended to prevent mid-air collisions. There have been various problems, including the appearance of ghost aircraft[41] and misdirected avoidance maneuvers. On February 3, 1994, two commercial planes came within 1 mile of each other over Portland, Oregon. Instead of moving apart, they apparently came closer to each other because of their reactions to the TCAS warning (*SEN 19*, 2, 12).

Communication outages that seriously affected air traffic. As noted in Section 2.1, telephone-system outages have resulted in air-traffic control system outages and major airport shutdowns—in Chicago, New York, San Diego, Kansas City (cable cuts), New York again (due to power problems), and Boston (due to a maintenance mistake that interchanged unmarked components). The FAA reported that, during a 12-month period in 1990 and 1991, there were 114 major telecommunications outages affecting air traffic, including 20 air-traffic control centers that were downed by a single fiber cable cut on May 4, 1991 (*SEN 17*, 1). There was an earlier problem in Aurora, Illinois, where a cable cut prevented radar data from reaching the air-traffic control (ATC) center, which resulted in several close calls (*SEN 10*, 5).

Other air-traffic control problems. We include here only a sampling of other items from the *RISKS* archives relating to air-traffic control problems. During the software-triggered AT&T long-distance telephone outage of January 15, 1990 (discussed in Section 2.1), air travel was essentially crippled (*SEN 17*, 1). The FAA has reported many other ATC center outages (for example, *SEN 5*, 3; *11*, 5) and near-misses—some that were reported officially and others that were not (*SEN 10*, 3). Causes included lightning strikes, blown fuses, and computer problems (*SEN 17*, 1). There have been numerous reports of ghost aircraft on controller screens (for example, *SEN 12*, 4; *16*, 3). In addition, a software bug brought down the Fremont, California, ATC Center for 2 hours on April 8, 1992; shortly afterward, on April 17, 1992, 12 of 50 of their radio frequencies stopped working, for unspecified reasons (*SEN 17*, 3). The installation of a new air-traffic control system in Canada was beset with frozen radar screens, jets appearing to fly backward, and blackouts of radar data (*SEN 17*, 4). There were earlier reports of flawed ATC radars, with planes mysteriously disappearing from the

display screens (*SEN 12*, 1). O'Hare Airport in Chicago reported a
near-miss of two American Airlines' planes due to controller errors resulting from the assignment of an incorrect plane designator
(*SEN 12*, 3). Two planes had a near-miss over Cleveland on August 24, 1991, due to a controller accidentally assigning the wrong
frequency that blocked contact with one of the planes (*SEN 16*,
4). Delta and Continental planes missed colliding by about 30 feet
on July 8, 1987; the Delta plane was 60 miles off course, reportedly because of a miskeyed navigation heading (similar to the KAL
007?), but also because previously recommended safety measures
had been ignored (*SEN 12*, 4). There were also various reports of
near-misses on the ground — for example, 497 in 1986 alone.[42] In
light of all these troubles, it is wonderful that air travel works as
well as it does. On the other hand, most of us have experienced the
long delays caused by the necessity of using manual or semiauto-
matic backup systems. The concept of fail-safe operation is clearly
important here.

Air-traffic control impersonations. Two other cases are worth reporting,
because they involved bypasses of the air-traffic control systems.
A radio operator with a "bizarre sense of humor" masqueraded as
an air-traffic controller using an approach channel for the Miami
International Airport; he transmitted bogus instructions to pilots
on at least two occasions, one triggering a premature descent (*SEN
12*, 1). Similar events occurred in Virginia, in 1994, when a phony
controller referred to as the "Roanoake Phantom" instructed pilots
to abort landings and to change altitudes and direction.

2.4.3   **Summary of Aviation Problems**

Table 2.4 provides a brief summary of the causes of the cited
problems. (The abbreviations and symbols are given in Table 1.1.)

The table suggests that the pilots and their interactions with
their environment are the predominant targets of blame attributed
in the civil aviation problems included here. Hardware and software problems are also involved or suspected in several cases. In
the A320 cases, for example, blame has been officially placed on
the pilots; however, serious questions remain about the influence
of software and interface problems. Unfortunately, there are cases
in which examination of the flight recorders and subsequent investigations cannot resolve the residual ambiguities completely.

Any system whose design requires almost perfect performance
on the part of its human operators and air-traffic controllers is

TABLE 2.4 Summary of aviation problems

Case	Req def	Sys des	HW impl	SW impl	Sys use	HW malf	Envir	Analysis	Evol, maint
					**Source of the Problems**				
Lauda		•							
NW 255	o	o			•	o	o	o	o
Brit.Midland			o		•		o	o	o
Aeromexico					•		o		
Air France			?	?	•		o		
Indian Air			?	?	•		o		
Air Inter			o	?	•		•		
Lufthansa	o	o	?	?	o		o		
Ilyushin		o	?	?			o		
KAL 007		o			•		o		
Air NZ					•		o		
KC-135						•	o		
DC-8					•	o	o		
ATC outages	(o)	(o)	(o)	(o)	(o)	(o)	(o)	(o)	(o)
ATC attacks	(o)				misuse		(o)		

clearly risky. The cases collected here suggest that there are still too many weak links, even in redundant systems, and that people are often the weakest link—even when they have had ample training and experience. Much greater effort is needed to make the systems more robust and less susceptible to failure, irrespective of the sources of difficulties (the systems, the people, or the environments). Air-traffic-control outages, birds, and lightning are not unusual events, and must be anticipated. Under normal conditions, however, flying commercial airlines is significantly safer per passenger mile than is driving on the highways and back roads.

2.5 Trains

Sic transit gloria mundi[43]

2.5.1   Transit Problems

Public transportation is a valuable cog in the mobility of a modern civilization, ideally reducing traffic congestion, pollution levels, and stress levels. A few cases illustrating the difficulties of maintaining reliable rail-transportation systems are noted in this section. Problems at sea are noted in Section 2.6. (Air travel is discussed in Section 2.4.)

Southern Pacific Cajon crash. A Southern Pacific potash unit train lost its brakes on May 11, 1989, while descending the Cajon Pass near San Bernardino in California. The train reached 90 miles per hour before jumping the track. Three people were killed, and eight were injured; 11 homes were destroyed. Apparently, the tonnage had been calculated incorrectly at 6150 instead of 8950, which resulted in an incorrect estimation of the effort required to brake. However, faulty dynamic brakes were later detected on the four lead engines and on one of the two pushers.[44]

Train wreck in Canada despite computer controls. In Canada, on February 8, 1986, an eastbound freight train had a head-on collision with a westbound transcontinental passenger train carrying about 120 people. Approximately 26 people were killed. Despite fail-safe computer safety controls (which worked correctly), the freight train had just left a parallel-track section and was 75 yards into the single-track section. Human operations were blamed.[45]

42 die in Japanese train crash under manual standby operation. In Japan, on May 14, 1991, a head-on collision of two trains killed 42 people and injured 415, 1.5 miles from a siding on which the trains were supposed to have passed each other. Hand signals were being used because of a malfunction in the automatic signaling system.[46]

Chinese train accident; failing safety systems not blamed. On November 15, 1991, in China, the express train *Freedom* rammed into the side of another express train that was switching to a siding in preparation for being passed; 30 people were killed, and more than 100 were injured. The subsequent investigation showed that *Freedom*'s driver was 1 minute early, and had mistakenly sped up in response to a signal to slow down. *Freedom*'s automatic warning system and automatic brakes were both known to be faulty before the accident, and yet were not blamed. Sloppy administrative practice was seemingly ignored by the report of the investigation.[47]

Head-on train collision in Berlin. At 2:23 P.M. on April 9, 1993 (Good Friday), an Intercity train leaving Berlin collided head-on with a train approaching Berlin just outside the city limits, near Wannsee. During the workweek, only one track was being used, while the other track was under construction to electrify this section of the tracks.

Consequently, the trains were going only 30 kilometers per hour. However, on this day—a holiday—both tracks were supposedly in use. Unfortunately, the *Fahrdienstleiter* (the supervisor in charge of setting the switches and overseeing the signals) set the switch improperly—to one-way traffic (workday) instead of two-way traffic (holiday). The computer reacted properly by setting the outbound signal to *halt*. The supervisor believed that this event was a defect in the system, and overrode the signal by setting the temporary extra signal (which is for use precisely when the track is under construction) to *proceed* without telephoning anyone to investigate the supposed signal error. The supervisor overlooked the fact that a nonregularly scheduled train was approaching the switch, and believed that the track was free. Both engineers in the other train and a passenger were killed, and over 20 people were injured.[48]

London train crashes into dead end. One man was killed and 348 were injured when a packed rush-hour train ran into the end-of-track buffer at 5 miles per hour, at the Cannon Street Station in London on January 8, 1991. Blame was placed on brake failure and on the fact that the train equipment was 30 to 40 years old (*SEN 16*, 2).

Automatic London trains crash. Two Docklands Light Railway trains equipped for automatic control crashed on March 10, 1987, with one train hanging off the end of the track 30 feet above ground. The train that was crashed into had been running under manual control because of previous failures. There were no injuries. The blame was placed on "unauthorized tests" having been conducted prior to required modifications. (See *SEN 12*, 4; *16*, 3.)

British Rail Clapham train crash due to loose wire. One commuter train plowed into the back of another on December 12, 1988, at Clapham Junction in south London, killing 35 and injuring almost 100. An earlier installation error was blamed, leaving a wire from an old switch that came into contact with the new electromagnetic signaling system. The fail-safe design had been expected to result in a red light in case of a short. The worker originally responsible for leaving the loose wire testified that he had worked for 12 hours on that day with only a 5-minute break.[49]

British Rail trains disappear; signaling software problem. Computer software problems in the British Rail signaling center at Wimbledon (controlling the Clapham Junction area) left operators "working blind" after train movements were wiped off control screens on at least one occasion. The problem was attributed to two different faults. Discovery of this problem led to all trains in the area being halted.[50]

London Underground tragedy: Man trapped in door. On February 3, 1991, a passenger attempting to get on a Northern Line Underground train to stay with his friends opened the door of a departing train by using a mechanism ("butterfly clasp") normally used only in emergency circumstances. Use of the clasp triggers no alarms. The man's arm was caught in the door and he was killed when his body hit the tunnel wall and was swept under the train (Peter Mellor, reporting in *SEN 16*, 2).

Another London Underground problem: Fail-safe doors stay open. On March 12, 1990, the double doors on a London Underground train remained open while the train traveled between four consecutive stations. The supposedly "fail-safe" door-control system failed, and the driver was given no indication that the doors were open.[51]

London Underground wrong-way train in rush hour. A confused driver drove an empty London Underground train northbound on south-bound tracks on the Piccadilly Line out of Kings Cross during the evening rush hour on March 12, 1990. Seeing the oncoming train, the driver of a stationary train with 800 passengers managed to reach out and manually short the circuit, thereby averting the crash. New warning lights have now been added.[52]

London Underground train leaves station without its driver. On April 10, 1990, an Underground train driver broke the golden rule of never leaving the cab of a fully automated train; he was checking a door that had failed to close properly. The door finally shut, and the train automatically took off without him — although there was no one to open the doors at the next station. (He took the next train.) As it turned out, the driver had taped down the button that started the train, relying instead on the interlock that prevented the train from starting when the doors were open. Indeed, the risks of this short-cut were probably not evident to him.[53]

A very similar event was reported on December 2, 1993, when a driver improperly left his Picadilly Line train when the doors did not close. The train took off with 150 passengers, and went through the Caledonian Road station without stopping. The train finally stopped automatically at a red light, and was boarded by personnel following in the next train. (Martyn Thomas, *SEN 19*, 2, 2).

Autumn leaves British Rail with signal failure. British Rail installed a new Integrated Electronic Control Centre (ICC), with three independent safety systems, intended to overcome problems with the old electromechanical processes. Unfortunately, the ICC worked properly only when the tracks were clear of debris. This fault mode was discovered in November 1991, during the system's first autumn, when leaves formed an insulating paste that prevented the wheels from making contact with sensors, causing the trains to disappear from the computer system. The problem was created by external clutch brakes having been replaced with disc brakes, which make less contact with the tracks. The temporary fix was to have each train include one car with the old brakes.[54]

Removal of train's dead-man switch leads to new crash cause. Four standing train engines rolled downhill for about 25 miles, with top speed of 75 miles per hour, crashing into a parked train. The engineer had fallen from the train and lost consciousness. The intelligent-system electrical replacements for the old dead-man's switch failed, apparently because they were designed to work *only when there was an engineer on board.*[55]

British Rail Severn Tunnel crash under backup controls. Subsequent to earlier problems with the signals that caused control to revert to a backup system on December 7, 1991, a British Rail train went through the Severn Tunnel at a slow pace (20 miles per hour), after having received a proceed-with-caution signal. The train was struck by another train running behind it at higher speed. The question of what kind of a signal the second train had received was not answered.[56]

Bay Area Rapid Transit: Murphy rides the rails. On November 20, 1980, the San Francisco BART system had a terrible day. Six different trains experienced serious malfunctions within a few hours. These problems were, in order, (1) doors that would not close, (2) failure of automatic controls, (3) brake failure on a train that then got stuck in a switch *en route* to the yards, (4) another brake failure, (5) smoking brakes, and (6) overheated brakes. During the same period, the controlling computer crashed, grinding the entire network to a halt for almost $1/2$ hour, while waiting for cutover to the backup system. The morning rush hour on December 8, 1980, saw another set of problems. Both the main computer and the backup failed, and lights went out in the control center (apparently due to a faulty power supply) (*SEN 6*, 1). Early in BART's life, there were reports of doors automatically opening in the middle of the cross-bay tunnel, because the station-to-station distance on that leg was longer than had been programmed into the control system (noted by Bill Park, in *SEN 8*, 5).

BART power outage; breakers break in Bay-to-Breakers. On May 17, 1987, BART had a power failure in which 17 switches kicked open in the rush to get runners to the Bay-to-Breakers race. A train was stalled in a tunnel beneath 7th Street in Oakland, and 150 passengers had to walk for 20 minutes to get out. Engineers could not identify the cause and were unable to restore power in the computer-controlled system. Five hours later, the switches suddenly closed again, just as mysteriously as they had opened (*SEN 12*, 3). On July 7, 1987, BART finally announced that the cause had been identified — a faulty switch and a short circuit caused by the use of a battery charger.[57]

San Francisco Muni Metro ghost trains. The San Francisco Muni Metro under Market Street was plagued with gremlins for many years, including a ghost-train problem in which the signaling system insisted that there was a train outside the Embarcadero Station blocking a switch. Although there was no such train, operations had to be carried on manually — resulting in increasing delays until finally passengers were advised to stay above ground. This situation lasted for almost 2 hours during the morning rush hour on May 23, 1983, at which point the nonexistent train vanished as mysteriously as it had appeared in the first place. (The usual collection of mechanical problems also has been reported, including brakes catching fire, brakes locking, sundry coupling problems, and sticky switches. There is also one particular switch, the *frog* switch, that chronically causes troubles, and unfortunately it is a weakest-link single point of failure that prevents crossover at the end of the line.) (See *SEN 9*, 3.) On December 9, 1986, the ghost-train problem reappeared, again involving the Embarcadero station from 6 A.M. until 8:14 A.M. On the very same day, BART had another horrible series of problems; "doors, signals, switches, brakes, and even a speedometer broke."[58]

Muni Metro crash; operator disconnected safety controls. On April 6, 1993, a San Francisco Municipal Railway car was headed for the car barns when it crashed into the rear of another car that had stalled in the Twin Peaks Tunnel. Fifteen people were hospitalized. The investigation showed that the operator had disabled the safety controls, permitting him to run the car faster than the control limits dictated.[59]

Water seepage stops computer-controlled monorail. In August 1988, water seeped into the programmable-logic controller of Sydney's new automated monorail and halted the system. One breakdown trapped dozens of passengers in a sealed environment for over 2 hours.[60]

Roller-coaster accidents blamed on computers. At Worlds of Fun in Kansas City, Missouri, one train rear-ended another on the season's opening day, March 31, 1990, on the 1-year-old computer-controlled roller coaster, *Timber Wolf*; 28 people were injured. The fix was to run with only one train until new sensors and redundant controls could be installed.[61]

A remarkably similar accident occurred on July 18, 1993, at Pennsylvania's Dorney Park. An occupied train on the *Hercules* roller coaster ran into an empty train outside the loading platform, injuring 14 passengers. The trains operate with no brakes for the 1-minute, 50-second ride; once they leave the station, they are free-wheeling (except when being towed uphill). A faulty sensor was blamed, which was supposed to detect the train leaving the station, which in turn would enable the computer system to release the restraints on the empty train so that it could move into the loading area. The temporary fix was to run with only one train, until three new safety measures could be added: a backup sensor, where the first one failed; a control-panel modification that displays all trains on the track; and a manually deployable brake on each train. Strangely, the sensor that failed was the only one that did not have a backup.[62] Gary Wright observed that *Timber Wolf* and *Hercules* were both built in 1989 and designed by the same firm, Curtis D. Summers, Inc. The same construction company may have been used as well.

Section 5.5 notes another roller-coaster crash in which 42 people were killed, attributed to electromagnetic interference.

2.5.2   **Summary of Train Problems**

Table 2.5 provides a brief summary of the causes of the cited problems. (The abbreviations and symbols are given in Table 1.1.)

TABLE 2.5 Summary of railroad problems

Case	Req def	Sys des	HW impl	SW impl	Sys use	HW malf	Envir	Analysis	Evol, maint
SP Cajon					●	○	○	○	
Canada					●		○		
Japan					●	○	○		
China					●	○	○		○
Berlin					●		○		○
Cannon St.						●	○		○
Docklands					●	○	○		○
Clapham Jn.			●		○	○	○		○
Wimbledon				●			○		
Door closes	○	○	○		●		○		
Doors open		?	?			?	○		
Wrong way	○	○	○		●		○		
Train leaves	○	○	○		●		○		○
Track leaves		○	○				●		
No dead-man	○	●					○		○
Severn					●	○	○		
BART problems		○	○	○		●	○		
BART outage						●	○		
Muni ghosts		?	?	?		?	?		
Muni crash		○		○	●		○		○
Sydney						○	●		
Roller coasters		●	○	○		○	○		

Operational problems predominate, including several in handling single-track sections and sidings. Quite a few cases are attributed to operator mistakes. However, there are also system-design problems (as in the roller-coaster crashes) and equipment problems (brake failures in the Cajon Pass, Cannon Street, and BART cases). Software was a critical factor in the Wimbledon signaling center screen vanishings. As usual, there are also a few cases in which the cause is not clear, even after detailed analysis. For example, whoo (!) knows what caused the Muni Metro ghost trains? Gremlins?

2.6 **Ships**

Whereas trains tend to operate in a one-dimensional environment (except at switches and crossings, where many problems occur), and planes tend to operate in a three-dimensional environment, ships for the most part operate in a two-dimensional space—except for swells and sinking. Nevertheless, many of the types of control problems experienced with trains and planes also appear in ship control.

2.6.1 **Ship Problems**

Here are a few examples of problems with ships.

Tempest Puget, or The Sound and the Ferries. In the 1980s, there were at least a dozen dock crashes in the Puget Sound ferry system (the largest such system in the United States) that were attributable to on-board computer failures. The damages for one crash alone (September 12, 1986) cost an estimated $750,000 in repairs to the Whidbey Island dock. The $17 million mid-sized Issaquah ferries (100 cars, 1200 passengers) came on board in 1980 with the slogan "Computerized propeller systems make the ferries more fuel efficient." The state sued the ferry builder (the now bankrupt Marine Power & Equipment of Seattle), which agreed to pay $7 million over 10 years. The state's recommendation was to spend an extra $3 million cutting the six ferries over to *manual controls*.[63]

It may seem disappointing that the fix was to bypass the computer systems rather than to make them work. Nevertheless, accepting reality is clearly a good idea. Although they did not have a gift horse in whose mouth to look, perhaps Seattle still believes in the truth ferry.

The *QE2* hits a shoal. In August 1992, the ocean liner *Queen Elizabeth 2* had its hull damaged while cruising off the island of Cuttyhunk, not far from Martha's Vineyard, Massachusetts. The nautical charts had not been updated since they were made in 1939, and showed a shoal at 39 feet in the midst of deeper waters. The ship's draw was supposedly 32 feet, although it was reported in the *Vineyard Gazette* that the ship may have been traveling faster than normal, which would have increased its draw. The entire area has been known as a dangerous one for ships for centuries. Nevertheless, the *QE2* was in a standard navigation channel, heading for New York. Felicity Barringer in *The New York Times* noted that "at least

two of the ship's three electronic navigational systems were operating at the time" of the accident. Divers later found the rocks and
paint chips from the *QE2*. What is the technology connection? Reliance on old data? Inability of the detection equipment? Failure of
technology by itself was not the cause. The pilot was a local-area
expert.[64]

Exxon Valdez. The *Exxon Valdez* accident in early April 1989 was apparently the result of an erroneous autopilot setting and human
negligence. The crash onto Bligh Reef and subsequent oil spill (the
worst in U.S. history) were blamed alternatively on the captain (who
was absent and allegedly drunk), the third mate, the helmsman,
and the "system"—Exxon's bottom line. Further assessment of the
blame is considered in Section 8.2. (See *SEN 14*, 5.)

Sensitive coral reef ruined by reverse-logic steering? Zdravko Beran, the
captain of a ship that ran aground in 1989 on an environmentally
sensitive live coral reef off the Fort Jefferson National Monument
in Florida, attributed the accident to a confused officer and to a
bad user interface. Apparently, an officer, Zvonko Baric, incorrectly
changed course because the steering mechanism on the ship operated in the opposite fashion from most such controls. Irrespective of whether the control system was computer based, this case
demonstrates dramatically the potential dangers of inconsistent or
nonstandard user interfaces (contributed by Jim Helman, in *SEN*
15, 1).

Submarine sinks the trawler *Antares*. Four Scottish fishermen were killed
when a submarine hit a Scottish trawler, *Antares*, in the Firth of
Clyde. The submarine commander claimed that the submarine's
computer had indicated a 3-mile separation between the vessels.[65]

Ship lists despite computer-controlled ballast tanks. The *Dona Karen*
Marie, a fish-processing ship lying in a Seattle drydock, was listing
toward port on August 4, 1992, until an engineer came to attempt
to correct the problem. His adjustment resulted in the ship leveling,
and then listing to starboard. A problem in the computer control of
the ballast tanks was blamed.[66]

2.6.2 Summary of Ship Problems

Table 2.6 provides a brief summary of the causes of the cited
problems. (The abbreviations and symbols are given in Table 1.1.)
Again, the cases considered exhibit considerable diversity of

TABLE 2.6 Summary of ship problems

| | Source of the Problems | | | | | | | | |
Case	Req def	Sys des	HW impl	SW impl	Sys use	HW malf	Envir	Anal-ysis	Evol, maint
Puget Sound	●	○	○	○	○	?	○		★!!
QE2	?				?	?	○		○
Exxon Valdez					●		○		
Coral reef		○		●	●		○		
Antares		?	?	?	○	?	○		
Drydock		?	?	?			○		

causes and effects. Operator problems are evident in the *Exxon Valdez* and coral-reef cases, although in the latter case the system interface contributed. System design and implementation issues were clearly implicated in the Puget Sound ferry problems. In the majority of cited cases, uncertainties remain as to the exact nature of the causes (as indicated by the proliferation of question marks in the table).

2.7   **Control-System Safety**

This section considers various problems in computer-related control systems used in specific applications, such as chemical processes, elevators, retractable stadium domes, and drawbridges. In many of these cases, the requirements for reliability and safety failed to be met. Closely related cases involving robotic systems are considered separately in Section 2.8.

2.7.1   **Chemical Processes**

Various problems in chemical plants have involved computers.

Union Carbide: I thought you told me that could not happen here! After the December 3, 1984, chemical leak of methyl isocyanate that killed at least 2000 people at a Union Carbide plant in Bhopal, India, various spokespeople for Union Carbide said it could not possibly happen at the sister plant in South Charleston, West Virginia. On March 7, 1985, the West Virginia plant had a leak of 5700 pounds of a mixture that included about 100 pounds of poisonous mesityl oxide, a bigger leak than had ever occurred previously at that plant (there were no deaths). Although neither Bhopal nor the West Virginia case was computer related, both illustrate a common head-in-the-sand problem, sometimes also known as "nothing can go wrong [click] go wrong [click] go wrong . . . ."

Union Carbide: Another toxic leak due to a database problem. In August 1985, another Union Carbide leak (causing 135 injuries) resulted from a computer program that was not yet programmed to recognize aldicarb oxime, compounded by human error when the operator misinterpreted the results of the program to imply the presence of methyl isocyanate (as in Bhopal). A 20-minute delay in notifying the county emergency authorities exacerbated the problem.[67]

British watchdog systems bark their shins. Watchdog equipment is often used to monitor chemical plants for the occurrence of undesirable events. Two cases are identified here, and numbered for reference in Table 2.7 at the end of the section.

1. In one case, a failure in the watchdog circuitry caused valves to be opened at the wrong time; several tons of hot liquid were spilled.[68]
2. In another case, a pump and pipelines were used for different purposes in handling methanol, but switching from one mode to another resulted in spillage. Apparently, the watchdog was not designed to monitor mode switching.[69]

Dutch chemical plant explodes due to typing error. At a Dutch chemical factory, a heavy explosion caused the death of 3 firefighters of the factory fire brigade, and injured 11 workers, including 4 firefighters. The severe damage was estimated at several tens of millions NL guilders; fragments from the explosion were found at a distance of 1 kilometer. The accident was the result of a typing error made by a laboratory worker in preparing a recipe. Instead of tank 632, he typed tank 634. Tank 632 contained resin feed classic (UN-1268), normally used in the batch process. Tank 634 contained dicyclopentadiene (DCDP). The operator, employed for only 3 months and still in training, forgot to check whether the tank contents were consistent with the recipe, and thus filled the reactor with the wrong chemicals. The fire brigade was called by an overheat alarm before the explosion, but was apparently unprepared for the particular chemical reaction. In court, a judge ruled that the management of the company had paid insufficient attention to safety, and the company was fined 220,000 NL Guilders.[70]

2.7.2 **Openings and Closings, Ups and Downs**

The next group of cases involves doors, elevators, roofs, draw-bridges, and other entities controlled by computer.

Computer-room door kills woman. A South African woman was killed on December 27, 1988, in a freak computer-room accident. The death occurred when 1.5-ton steel doors closed on the woman as she stood in their path but out of sight of optical sensors intended to detect obstructions. The accident took place at the computer facilities of Liberty Life in Johannesburg as the 23-year-old woman was handing a document to a colleague in the course of her employment.[71]

Elevator deaths in Ottawa. On April 1, 1989, a 13-year-old girl was killed by the doors of an Ottawa elevator (which had been serviced just hours before). At the end of May 1989, another person was killed after having been caught in the doors while entering the elevator (again serviced just hours before) and being dragged along. Both problems were apparently due to a flaw in the interlock circuits that permitted the elevator to move with only one door closed. Subsequent investigation showed that the flaw had been reported by the manufacturer (Otis) in 1978, along with a one-wire fix. The building then changed ownership in 1980, the maintenance company changed in 1988, and the fix was never installed — until after the second accident. Furthermore, no maintenance records were kept.[72]

Olympic stadium roof tears. The roof of the Olympic Stadium in Montreal developed tears during different tests of the automatic retracting and closing mechanism, one case occurring on September 8, 1989. In another case, a faulty winch apparently placed uneven tension on the roof. The roof was 12 years late, and its cost all by itself reportedly was equal to that of a completely covered stadium.[73]

SkyDome, Release 0.0. In summer 1989, the 54,000-seat Toronto Sky-Dome became the world's largest stadium with a retractable roof using rigid segments. (Melbourne already had a similar one, seating only 15,000.) However, the roof was able to operate at only one-third speed, taking 1 hour to open, because the computer programs to work it were not ready.[74] Michael Wagner reported that an architect client of his claimed that the stress from repeated openings and closings had been seriously miscalculated, and that three or four times a year would be possible, rather than the estimated 30 or 40, as otherwise the system would be overly stressed. (The problems now seem to have been largely overcome.)

Computer glitch causes Fresno water mains to rupture. A computer-based system controlling 106 water pumps and wells and 877 miles of pipes in Fresno, California, crashed three times within 1.5 hours on November 14, 1988. The malfunction was attributed to a burglar alarm in one of the pumps that sent confusing signals to the computer system, temporarily shutting down the pumps. The automatic restart that shifted to manual control sent water pressure levels up to 75 pounds per square inch (instead of 40 to 45) through the pipes, rupturing water mains (particularly the older ones) and damaging 50 residential plumbing systems. It also triggered 24 automatic fire alarms. The manual default settings were apparently improper.[75]

Drawbridge opens without warning in rush-hour traffic. The Evergreen Point Floating Bridge in Seattle opened unexpectedly on December 22, 1989. Cars crashed into the rising span, killing one driver and injuring five others in the morning rush hour. Subsequent analysis discovered a screw driven into one wire and a short in another wire. The two shorted wires, one on the east drawspan and one on the west drawspan, combined to send current around safety systems and to lift the west section of the drawspan.[76]

Drawbridge controls halt traffic. The computer that controls the Route 37 drawbridge in Dover, Delaware, failed on August 29, 1992, preventing the barrier gates from reopening for 1 hour on a hot afternoon. The manual controls to override the computer system also did not work.[77]

Bit-dropping causes boulder-dropping. A cement factory had a state-of-the-art 8080-based process-control system controlling the conveyors and the rock crusher used in making cement. Apparently defective MOSTEK RAM (random-access memory) chips tended to drop bits (in the absence of error-detecting or -correcting codes), which on this occasion caused the second of a series of three conveyors to switch off, which in turn stacked up a large pile of boulders (about 6 to 8 feet in diameter) at the top of the conveyor (about 80 feet up) until they fell off, crushing several cars in the parking lot and damaging a building.[78]

TABLE 2.7 Summary of control-system problems

	Source of the Problems								
Case	Req def	Sys des	HW impl	SW impl	Sys use	HW malf	Envir	Anal-ysis	Evol, maint
Aldicarb				•	•		○		
Watchdog	2•	○			○	1•	○		
Dutch plant					•		○		
Door kills		○	•				○		
Elevators		○				○	○		•
Olympic Std.		•				○	○	○	
SkyDome	○	○	○	•			○	○	
Fresno		•	○		○	○	○		
Seattle		•				○	○		○
Dover						•	○		?
Boulders		•				○	○		

2.7.3 Summary of Control-System Problems

Table 2.7 provides a brief summary of the causes of the cited problems. (The abbreviations and symbols are given in Table 1.1.)

In these cases, the primary causes are quite diverse, with all but two columns of the table represented by at least one case (•). Human errors played a smaller role than did system problems (including both hardware and software), in both design and implementation. Not surprisingly, the physical environment contributed in every case, as a secondary cause.

2.8 Robotics and Safety

We introduce this section by considering Asimov's Laws of Robotics. Most of Isaac Asimov's robot-related science fiction observes his Three Laws of Robotics [4]. His final novel [5] adds a Zeroth Law, to establish a precedence over the other laws. The four laws are as follows, in their presumed order, and adapted for consistency (by means of the parenthesized emendations that presumably would have been specified by Asimov had he made the prepending of the Zeroth Law explicit).

- Law 0. A robot may not harm humanity as a whole.
- Law 1. A robot may not injure a human being or, through inaction, allow a human being to come to harm (except where it would conflict with the Zeroth Law).
- Law 2. A robot must obey the orders given it by human beings, except where such orders conflict with (the Zeroth Law or) the First Law.
- Law 3. A robot must protect its own existence unless such protection conflicts with (the Zeroth Law or) the First or Second Law.

Asimov's Laws of Robotics serve well as an aid in writing science fiction (see *The Robots of Dawn*); they also provide a first approximation (albeit simplistic) of a set of requirements for designers of robotic systems. Thus, for example, the First Law would force greater attention to be paid to fail-safe mechanisms.

2.8.1 Robotic Safety

Robots are finding increasingly wide use. Here are a few cases in which human safety was an issue and robots did not live up to expectations.

Death in Japan caused by industrial robot. A worker was killed by an industrial robot on July 4, 1981, in the Kawasaki Heavy Industries plant in Hyogo, Japan. The robot was designed by Unimation in Connecticut, and was manufactured under a licensing arrangement by Kawasaki. Kenji Urata "was pinned by the robot's claw against a machine for processing automobile gears after entering an off-limits area to repair an[other] apparently malfunctioning robot." Opening a fence surrounding the robot would have shut off its power supply, but instead the worker jumped over the fence and set the machine on manual control. One report[79] implied that the man was actually pinned by the second robot, which was delivering parts for the production-line activity. Subsequent reports noted possibly as many as 19 more robot-related deaths in Japan (*SEN 11*, 1), six of which were later suspected of being triggered by stray electromagnetic interference affecting the robots (*SEN 12*, 3).

Death in Michigan caused by robot. The national Centers for Disease Control in Atlanta reported "the first documented case of a robot-related fatality in the United States." Working in a restricted area with automated die-casting machinery on July 21, 1984, a Michigan man was pinned between the back end of a robot and a steel pole. He suffered cardiac arrest and died 5 days later.[80]

Risks of automated guided vehicles: ALCOA worker killed. A 24-year-old Madisonville, Tennessee, electrician employed by ALCOA died on September 8, 1990, at the University of Texas Hospital following an accident at ALCOA's North Plant. He had been working on an overhead crane that was not operating when the crane's tray grab (the part that hangs down and lifts trays of coils of aluminum sheet) was struck by the top of a coil being transported at ground level by an automated guided vehicle. The impact caused the crane to move toward him, and he was crushed between an access platform on the crane and the personnel lift he had used to reach the crane.[81]

Roboflops. Ron Cain noted two close calls in his welding lab. In one case, an error in a 68000 processor caused an extraneous transfer to a robot `move` routine, accidentally destroying a small jack. In another, some drive-motor cards in a Cincinnati-Milacron unit failed, causing two robot joints to jerk wildly. In each case, manual use of the `kill` button was able to stop the action. Ron added that these cases were "worth keeping in mind the next time you stand near a robot."[82]

Robotic waiter runs amok. In Edinburgh, Scotland, a robot was dressed in a black hat and bow tie, supposedly helping to serve wine in a restaurant. During its first hour on the job, it knocked over furniture, frightened customers, and spilled a glass of wine. Eventually its head fell into a customer's lap. When it appeared in court the next day (responding to unspecified charges—presumably disturbing the peace), it was still out of control.[83]

Robotic aide stumbles at Stanford Hospital. At Stanford University Hospital, Cookie, one of three robots (the other two are Flash and Maxwell) designed to help deliver patients' meals, X-ray films, equipment, and documents, veered off course (after performing its meal delivery), and fell down a set of stairs. The cause of the malfunction was not specified. The robots are no longer delivering food to patients, because the food was too often cold by the time it arrived.[84]

Rambling robot disrupts NBC evening news broadcast. On a Saturday evening, while anchoring a weekend news program, Connie Chung was reading an urgent story about the Middle East. Suddenly, she began to disappear from the screen as the camera moved away from her and ran into the stage manager. The usual camera operators had been replaced by a robotic camera crew in an NBC cost-cutting move (three robots at a cost of "less than $1 million together").[85]

Budd Company robot accidentally dissolves its own electronics. A Budd Company assembly robot was programmed to apply a complex bead of fluid adhesive, but the robot "ignored the glue, picked up a fistful of highly active solvent, and shot itself in its electronics-packed chest." Its electronics were disabled.[86]

Tempo AnDante? No, not moving at all. A robot (Dante) descending for exploration inside the Mount Erebus volcano had its fiber-optic control cable snap only 21 feet from the top of the volcano, immobilizing the robot.[87] A new effort by a team at Carnegie-Mellon University is underway to have Dante descend into the Mount Spurr Volcano in Alaska, using wireless communications.[88]

2.8.2 Summary of Robotic Problems

Table 2.8 provides a brief summary of the causes of the cited problems. (The abbreviations and symbols are given in Table 1.1.) Numerous questions remain unanswered at this time.

Hardware malfunction occurred in several cases, suggesting that inadequate attention was paid to fault tolerance. In other cases, some sort of system problem was evident, but whether it was in hardware or software is not known.

TABLE 2.8 Summary of robotics-system problems

	Source of the Problems								
Case	Req def	Sys des	HW impl	SW impl	Sys use	HW malf	Envir	Anal-ysis	Evol, maint
Kawasaki					●		○		
Michigan					○		○		
ALCOA				?	●		○		
68000						●			
Milacron						●			
Waiter		?	?	?		?			
Hospital			?	?		?	?		
Camera robot			?	?		?	?		
Budd robot			?	?		?	?		
Dante						●	○		

2.9 **Medical Health and Safety**

Microprocessors, minicomputers, and large-scale computers are increasingly being used in medical applications. Various computer-related accidents related to medical and health issues are considered here.

2.9.1 **Therac-25**

The most prominently reported risk-related cases in medical electronics were undoubtedly those involving the Therac-25, a computer-based electron-accelerator radiation-therapy system. The Therac-25 was involved in six known accidents, including three deaths directly attributable to radiation overdoses (with one additional death presumably from terminal cancer rather than radiation).

This section is based on a thorough investigation of the Therac-25 by Nancy Leveson and Clark Turner [83]. Their study took several years of detective work and analysis of a mass of documentation. Their results are particularly important, because many of the previous media accounts and papers have been incomplete, misleading, or just plain wrong.

Eleven Therac-25 systems were installed, five in the United States, six in Canada. Six accidents involved massive overdoses between 1985 and 1987, when the machines were finally recalled:

- Marietta, Georgia, June 3, 1985. A 61-year-old woman received severe radiation burns from 15,000 to 20,000 rads (whereas the normal dose was 200 rads). She lost shoulder and arm functionality. Breast removal was required because of the burns.

- Hamilton, Ontario, Canada, July 26, 1985. A 40-year-old woman received between 13,000 and 17,000 rads in treatment of cervical cancer, and would have required a hip replacement as a result of the overdose — except that she died of cancer on November 3, 1985.

- Yakima, Washington, December 1985. A woman received an overdose that caused erythema (abnormal redness) on her right hip.

- Tyler, Texas, March 21, 1986. A man received between 16,500 and 25,000 rads in less than 1 second, over an area of about 1 centimeter. He lost the use of his left arm, and died from complications of the overdose 5 months later.

- Tyler, Texas, April 11, 1986. A man received at least 4000 rads in the right temporal lobe of his brain. The patient died on May 1, 1986, as a result of the overdose.

- Yakima, Washington, January 1987. A patient received somewhere between 8000 and 10,000 rads (instead of the prescribed 86 rads). The patient died in April 1987 from complications of the overdose.

Blame was placed at various times on operator error, software failure, and poor interface design. The identification of the software and interface problems was a harrowing process, particularly because tests after each accident indicated that nothing was wrong. In particular, three flaws were identified. One was the ability of the operator to edit a command line to change the state of the machine such that the execution of the radiation commands took place before the machine state had been completely changed (that is, to low-intensity operation). The second flaw involved the safety checks inadvertently being bypassed whenever a particular 6-bit program counter reached zero (once every 64 times). The third problem was that certain hardware safety interlocks in the Therac-20 (which was not computer controlled) had been removed from the Therac-25, because those interlocks were supposed to be done in software.

The detailed analysis of Leveson and Turner is quite revealing. A quote from the end of [83] is appropriate here:

> Most previous accounts of the Therac-25 accidents have blamed them on software error and stopped there. This is not very useful and, in fact, can be misleading and dangerous: If we are to prevent such accidents in the future, we must dig deeper. Most accidents involving complex technology are caused by a combination of organizational, managerial, technical and, sometimes, sociological or political factors; preventing accidents requires paying attention to *all* the root causes, not just the precipitating event in a particular circumstance.
>
> Accidents are unlikely to occur in exactly the same way again. If we patch only the symptoms and ignore the deeper underlying causes or we fix only the specific cause of one accident, we are unlikely to have much effect on future accidents. The series of accidents involving the Therac-25 is a good example of exactly this problem: Fixing each individual software flaw as it was found did not solve the safety problems of the device. Virtually all complex software will behave in an unexpected or undesired fashion under some conditions (there will always be another software 'bug'). Instead, accidents need to be understood with respect to the complex factors involved and changes made to eliminate or reduce the underlying

root causes and contributing factors that increase the likelihood of resulting loss associated with accidents.

Although these particular accidents occurred in software controlling medical devices, the lessons to be learned apply to all types of systems where computers are controlling dangerous devices. In our experience, the same types of mistakes are being made in non-medical systems. We must learn from our mistakes so that they are not repeated.

These conclusions are relevant throughout this book.

2.9.2 Other Medical Health Problems

The Therac-25 is the most widely known of the computer-related medical problems. However, several others are noteworthy.

Zaragoza overdoses. The Sagitar-35 linear accelerator in the hospital in Zaragoza, Spain, may have exposed as many as 24 patients to serious radiation overdoses over a period of 10 days. At least 3 people died from the excessive radiation. Apparently, this machine has no computer control, but was left in a faulty state following repair of an earlier fault (*SEN 16*, 2).

North Staffordshire underdoses. Nearly 1000 cancer patients in the United Kingdom were given radiation doses between 10 percent and 30 percent less than prescribed over a period of 10 years. The error was attributed to a physicist who introduced an unnecessary correction factor when the planning computer was originally installed in 1982 (*SEN 17*, 2).

Plug-compatible electrocutions. A 4-year-old girl was electrocuted when a nurse accidentally plugged the heart-monitoring line into an electrical outlet at Children's Hospital in Seattle, Washington (Associated Press, December 4, 1986; *SEN 12*, 1). Seven years later, the *same* problem recurred. A 12-day-old baby in a Chicago hospital was electrocuted when the heart-monitor cables attached to electrodes on his chest were plugged directly into a power source instead of into the heart-monitor system.[89] (See Challenge 2.1.)

Risks in pacemakers. Three cases are considered here and numbered for reference in Table 2.9 at the end of the section. (1) A 62-year-old man "being treated for arthritis with microwave heating died abruptly during the treatment. Interference from the therapeutic microwaves had reset his pacemaker, driving his already injured heart to beat 214 times a minute. It couldn't do it."[90] (2) Another man died when his pacemaker was reset by a retail-store antitheft device (*SEN 10*, 2). (3) In a third case, a doctor accidentally set a patient's pacemaker into an inoperative state while attempting to reset it (see *SEN 11*, 1, 9, reported by Nancy Leveson from a discussion with someone at the Food and Drug Administration).[91]

Defibrillators. Doctors were warned about surgically implanted cardio-verter-defibrillators that can be deactivated by strong magnets such as are found in stereo speakers (*SEN 14*, 5).

Other interference problems. There was a report of a hospital in London where alarms were repeatedly triggered by walkie-talkies operating in the police band (440 to 470 MHz). At another hospital, a respirator failed because of interference from a portable radio (*SEN 14*, 6). Further problems involving interference are considered in Section 5.5.

Side effects of radiation and environmental contamination. Electromagnetic radiation from various sources, including video display terminals (VDTs), has long been considered a potential source of health-related problems.[92] Dermatological problems have been associated with VDT use, including rosacea, acne, seborrheic dermatitis, and poikiloderma of Civatte. (See *SEN 13*, 4 for references.) Deterioration of eye focusing is reported (*SEN 13*, 4). Higher miscarriage rates among women working in computer-chip manufacturing have been noted (*SEN 12*, 2).

Other health risks of using computers. Various stress-related problems are associated with computer use, including carpal tunnel syndrome and ulnar nerve syndrome, as well as stress resulting from increased noise, apparently especially noticeable in women (*SEN 15*, 5). There was also a report of a Digital Equipment Corporation DEC 11/45 computer falling on a man's foot (Anthony A. Datri in *SEN 12*, 4).

Risks in medical databases. A woman in Düsseldorf, Germany, told the court that she had been erroneously informed that her test results showed she had incurable syphillis and had passed it on to her daughter and son. As a result, she strangled her 15-year-old daughter and attempted to kill her son and herself. She was acquitted. The insurance company said the medical information had been based on a computer error—which could have been a lame excuse for human error![93]

Software developed by Family Practitioner Services in Exeter, England, failed to identify high-risk groups of women being screened for cervical and breast cancer.[94]

Other automated hospital aids. Walter Reed Army Medical Center reportedly spent $1.6 billion on a new computer system intended to streamline its health-care delivery. That system apparently bungled pharmacy orders, patient-care records, and doctors' orders. There were complaints that the access to narcotics was not properly controlled. In addition, doctors complained that their workloads had increased dramatically because of the computer system (*SEN 17, 3*).[95]

A physician reported that a 99-year-old man in the emergency room had a highly abnormal white-blood-cell count, which the computer reported to be within normal limits. The computer was reporting values for a infant child, having figured that the year of birth, entered as *89*, was 1989, not 1889.[96]

London Ambulance Service. As many as 20 deaths may be attributable to the London Ambulance Service's inability to dispatch ambulances in response to emergencies. After severe difficulties in system development, including repeated test failures, the system was finally placed in operation. The system then collapsed completely, including worst-case delays of 11 hours. "An overcomplicated system and incomplete training for control staff and ambulance crews are the likely causes of the collapse of London's computerised ambulance dispatch service . . . . One software company says that the London Ambulance Service (LAS) underestimated the pressure placed on staff at the control center, and that it makes working there 'like a wartime action room.' "[97]

Emergency dispatch problems. Numerous problems with emergency telephone lines have been reported, including the death of a 5-year-old boy due to the failure of the 911 computer-terminal operator in San Francisco (*SEN 12, 2*), and the death of a man because the system truncated the last digit in his street number. A woman in Norfolk, Virginia, died while waiting over $1/2$ hour for an ambulance to be dispatched; the delay was blamed on the software developer's failure to install a message-tracking program (*SEN 16, 1*). In Chicago, a computer program rejected the calling telephone number at its correct address because the address of the previous possessor of that telephone number was also listed. Two people died in the fire (*SEN 17, 1*).

TABLE 2.9 Summary of health and safety problems

	Source of the Problems								
Case	Req def	Sys des	HW impl	SW impl	Sys use	HW malf	Envir	Anal-ysis	Evol, maint
Therac-25	o	o	●	●	●		o	o	o
Zaragoza					o	o	o		●
N.Staff'shire		●		o	o				
Electrocution	o	o	o		●		o		
Pacemakers	(o)	(o)	(o)		3●		1,2●		
Radiation					o	?	o		
Düsseldorf				?	?	?			

2.9.3   Summary of Medical Health Problems

Table 2.9 provides a brief summary of the causes of the cited problems. (The abbreviations and symbols are given in Table 1.1.)

System use was implicated in one way or another in each of these cases. In the Therac-25 accidents, it is clear that a range of factors contributed, including various system problems. The argument has been made that the people who died or were injured because of excessive radiation were terminally ill patients anyway, so the failure was not really that important. However, that argument should never be used to justify bad software practice and poorly designed system interfaces.

The first electrocution caused by a heart-monitoring device was the result of a bad mistake. The second similar electrocution is certainly disheartening, indicating a serious lack of awareness. (See Challenge C2.1 at the end of the chapter.)

The pacemaker problems are typical of both repetitiveness and diversity within a single type of device. The first case involved electromagnetic interference from a therapy device within the purview of the medical facility. The second case involved interference from an antitheft device, with no warning of potential effects. However, the basic problem was the same—namely, that pacemakers may be affected by interference. The third case resulted from a doctor's mistake using an interface that was not fail-safe. The three cases together suggest that these devices deserve greater care in development and operation.[98]

2.10 **Electrical Power**

This section considers difficulties in power systems, both nuclear and conventional. The causes and effects both vary widely.

2.10.1 **Nuclear Power**

Nuclear-power systems require exceedingly critical reliability to maintain stability. Computer systems are being used in various automatic shutdown systems — for example, by Ontario Hydro — and in control systems as well. Nevertheless, the nuclear-power industry could make better use of computers — at least in reporting and analysis of status information — in avoiding problems such as those noted here.

Early nuclear-power problems. To indicate the extent of nuclear-power problems, we give here a terse chronology of the more significant early nuclear-power accidents.[99]

- December 2, 1952, Chalk River, Canada. One million gallons of radioactive water built up, and took 6 months to clean up. Human error was blamed.

- November 1955, EBR-1 experimental breeder, Idaho Falls. A misshapen-rod mishap was blamed on human error.

- October 7 to 10, 1957, Windscale Pile 1, on the English coast of the Irish Sea. This case was at the time the largest known release of radioactive gases (20,000 curies of iodine). Fire broke out. One-half million gallons of milk had to be destroyed. The plant was permanently shut down.

- Winter 1957–58, Kyshtym, USSR. Radiation contamination ranged over a 400-mile radius. Cities were subsequently removed from Soviet maps. Details are apparently still not available.

- May 23, 1958, Chalk River, Canada, again. A defective rod overheated during removal. Another long cleanup ensued.

- July 24, 1959, Santa Susana, California. A leakage occurred and was contained, although 12 of 43 fuel elements melted.

- January 3, 1961, SL-1 Idaho Falls (military, experimental). Three people were killed when fuel rods were mistakenly removed.

- October 5, 1966, Enrico Fermi, Michigan. A malfunction melted part of the core, although the damage was contained. The plant was closed in 1972.

- June 5, 1970, Dresden II in Morris, Illinois. A meter gave a false signal. The release of iodine was 100 times what was permissible, although the leakage was contained.

- November 19, 1971, Monticello, Minnesota. Fifty-thousand gallons of radioactive waste spilled into the Mississippi River, some of which got into the St. Paul water supply.
- March 22, 1975, Brown's Ferry, Decatur, Alabama. Insulation caught fire, and disabled safety equipment. The cleanup cost $150 million.
- March 28, 1979, Three Mile Island II, Pennsylvania. The NRC said that the situation was "within 1 hour of catastrophic meltdown." There were four equipment malfunctions, human errors, and inadequate control monitors. (This case is considered further, after this enumeration.)
- February 11, 1981, Sequoyah I, Tennessee. Eight workers were contaminated when 110,000 gallons of radioactive coolant leaked.
- January 25, 1982, Ginna plant, Rochester, New York. A steam-generator tube ruptured.
- February 22 and 25, 1983, Salem I, New Jersey. The automatic shutdown system failed twice, but manual shutdown was successful.
- April 19, 1984, Sequoyah I, again. A radiation leak was contained.
- June 9, 1985, Davis-Besse, Oak Harbor, Ohio. A number of pieces of equipment failed, and at least one wrong button was pushed by an operator. Auxiliary pumps saved the day. (This case is considered further, later in this section.)
- Several months after Davis-Besse, a nuclear plant in San Onofre, California, experienced violent shaking in the reactor piping when five check valves failed. There was a leak of radioactive steam, and damage to the pipe surrounds resulted.

Three Mile Island 2: Dangers of assuming too much. The temperature of the fuel rods at Three Mile Island II increased from the normal 600 degrees to over 4000 degrees during the accident on March 28, 1979, partially destroying the fuel rods. The instruments to measure core temperatures were not standard equipment in reactors. Thermocouples had been installed to measure the temperature as part of an experiment on core performance, and were capable of measuring high temperatures. However, whenever the temperature rose above 700 degrees, the system had been programmed to produce a string of question marks on the printer — rather than the measured temperature.[100] Furthermore, *intended* rather than *actual* valve settings were displayed. (The venting of tritium-contaminated water and removal of radioactive waste to the Hanford waste-disposal site were not completed until August 12, 1993.)

Davis-Besse nuclear-power plant. The Davis-Besse nuclear-power plant had an emergency shutdown on June 9, 1985. A report[101] included the following quote:

> Davis-Besse came as close to a meltdown as any U.S. nuclear plant since the Three Mile Island accident of 1979. Faced with a loss of water to cool the reactor and the improbable breakdown of *fourteen* [emphasis added] separate components, operators performed a rescue mission noted both for skill and human foible: They pushed wrong buttons, leaped down steep stairs, wended their way through a maze of locked chambers and finally saved the day . . . by muscling free the valves and plugging fuses into a small, manually operated pump not designed for emergency use.

The lack of a backup pump had been identified much earlier as an intolerable risk, but was met with "prior power-company foot dragging and bureaucratic wrangling."

Nuclear Regulatory Commission documents compiled in a Public Citizen report reveal that over 20,000 mishaps occurred in the United States between the 1979 meltdown at Three Mile Island and early 1986; at least 1000 of these were considered to be "particularly significant." (In addition, there were large radiation emissions from Hanford in its early days that were not considered as dangerous at the time. It was only afterward, when the maximum permitted levels were reduced by two orders of magnitude, that the danger of the routine emissions was realized. The cancer rate in that area is now four times normal.)[102]

Soviet Navy. There were at least 12 serious radiation accidents in the Soviet Union's atomic-powered Navy prior to 1986, including these:[103]

- 1966 or 1967. The Icebreaker *Lenin* had a reactor meltdown, killing approximately 30 people.
- 1966. A radiation leak in the reactor shielding of a nuclear submarine near Polyarnyy caused untold deaths.
- April 11, 1970. There was an unspecified casualty resulting from the nuclear propulsion system of an attack submarine.
- Late 1970s. A prototype Alfa-class submarine experienced a meltdown of the core, resulting in many deaths.
- December 1972. A radiation leakage resulted from a nuclear torpedo.
- August 1979. The propulsion system failed in a missile submarine.
- September 1981. The rupture of a nuclear reactor system in a submarine resulted in an unspecified number of deaths.

Chernobyl. The Chernobyl disaster of April 27, 1986, apparently surprised a lot of people who previously had soft-pedaled risks inherent in nuclear-power plants. At least 92,000 people were evacuated from the surrounding area, and 250,000 children were sent off to summer camp early. High radiation levels were detected in people, animals, meat, produce, dairy products, and so on, within the Soviet Union and in Italy, France, Germany, and Scandinavia, among other countries. The town of Chernobyl has been essentially dismantled. Thirty-one deaths were noted at the time, although the death toll continues to mount. Vladimir Chernousenko, the director of the exclusion zone, has estimated that there have been nearly 10,000 deaths among the clean-up crew. At least 0.5 million people have been contaminated, including 229,000 in the clean-up crew alone—roughly 8500 of whom were dead as of early 1991.[104]

Some details have been provided by the official Soviet report, confirming what was suggested by early statements that an experiment went awry:

> The Soviet Union was conducting experiments to check systems at Chernobyl's fourth nuclear reactor when a sudden surge of power touched off the explosion. . . . Soviet officials have said that the explosion happened when heat output of the reactor suddenly went from 6 or 7 percent to 50 percent of the plant's capacity in 10 seconds. The power had been reduced for a prolonged period in preparation for a routine shutdown. . . . "We planned to hold some experiments, research work, when the reactor was on this level," Sidorenko [deputy chairman of the State Committee for Nuclear Safety] said [May 21, 1986]. "The accident took place at the stage of experimental research work."[105]

The official Soviet report says that four different safety systems were all turned off so that researchers could conduct an experiment on the viability of emergency power for cooling—including the emergency cooling system, the power-regulating system, and the automatic shutdown system. The report primarily blames human errors—only one-fourth of the control rods were inserted properly (there were not enough, and they were not deep enough), and too much coolant was added.[106]

A subsequent report from the Soviet Foreign Ministry[107] indicated that the experiments had been intended to show how long Chernobyl 4 could continue to produce electricity in spite of an unexpected shutdown. They were testing to see whether turbine generators could provide enough power to keep the cooling systems going for up to 45 minutes. Incidentally, Chernobyl 3 shared various resources with Chernobyl 4, and consequently its reopening was also affected. (Chernobyl 1 was restarted on September 30, 1986.)

The Chernobyl reactors were intrinsically difficult to operate and to control adequately — they represent an early design that uses graphite (which is flammable) to trap neutrons in producing the desired chain reaction, and uses water as a coolant. However, if the computer controls are inadequate, and the reactor process inherently unstable, the problems lie much deeper in the process than with the operators. Various American scientists were cited as saying that "most Soviet reactors were so difficult to operate and so complex in design that mistakes were more likely than with other reactor designs."[108]

Human error blamed for Soviet nuclear-plant problems. Human error caused 20 of the 59 shutdowns at Soviet nuclear-power plants in the first 6 months of 1991 (*Trud*, July 24, 1991). "It is not the first time that we have to admit the obvious lack of elementary safety culture in running reactors," Anatoly Mazlov, the government's head of nuclear safety, said. Mazlov reported that Soviet nuclear-power plants worked at only 67-percent capacity during that 6-month period.[109]

In *RISKS*, Tom Blinn noted that the Soviet nuclear engineer and scientist Medvedev's book on the Chernobyl disaster reported on the root causes — basically, human error. Ken Mayer cautioned against blaming people when the human interface is poorly designed. His theme recurs in many cases throughout.

Distributed system reliability: Risks of common-fault modes. Jack Anderson[110] contrasted Chernobyl with the nuclear-power situation in the United States, giving another example of the it-couldn't-happen-here syndrome. (See also *SEN 11*, 3.)

> We have learned that, since the hideous accident in the Ukraine, the Nuclear Regulatory Commission staff called in the inspectors and informed them that new, more lenient interpretations of the fire-safety regulations had been approved by the commissioners over the inspectors' vehement protests. . . . Incredibly, the new guidelines let nuclear-plant operators sidestep the protection of redundant control systems by planning fire safety for the first set of controls only. The guidelines permit partial fire barriers between the first control

system and the backup system, which can be in the same room. This means that a fire could short-circuit both systems.

Flaw in the earthquake-simulation model *Shock II* closes five nuclear plants. Following the discovery of a program error in a simulation program used to design nuclear reactors to withstand earthquakes, five nuclear-power plants were shut down in March 1979: Duquesne Light's Shippingport (Pennsylvania), Wiscasset (Maine), James Fitzpatrick (Scriba, New York), and two at Surry (Virginia). Three types of problems are worth noting here—program bugs (in simulations, analyses, real-time control, and operating systems), fundamental inaccuracies in the underlying requirements and models, and the intrinsic gullibility of the computer neophyte— including administrators, engineers, and laypersons.

The programmed model relating to prediction of effects of earthquakes on nuclear-power plants is known as *Shock II*. The results of the program were found to differ widely from previous results— and there were indications that the results were not even superficially reproducible! (Actually, only *one* subroutine was implicated! Apparently, the arithmetic sum of a set of numbers was taken, instead of the sum of the absolute values. The fix was to take the square root of the sum of the squares—such deep mathematical physics!) The reported conclusion reached on discovery of the errors was that the five reactors might not actually survive an earthquake of the specified strength, contrary to what had been asserted previously. Government regulations require reactors to be able to withstand an earthquake as strong as the strongest ever recorded in the area. All four states have had significant earthquakes in recorded history, although they have had only minor ones in recent years.

Accurate live testing of reactors for earthquake damage is difficult in the absence of live earthquakes (but is very dangerous in their presence). Thus, the burden falls on the testing of the computer model as a concept, and then on the testing of the programs that implement it. (At least, that would seem to be good software methodology!). The model for the five reactors is used by the Boston firm that designed the plants, Stone and Webster. The relevant part of the model deals with the strength and structural support of pipes and valves in the cooling systems. A problem was initially discovered in the secondary cooling system at the Shippingport plant. Recalculations showed stresses far in excess of allowable tolerances.

As a result, the model underwent further analysis, and changes were made to the reactors to try to correct the situation. However, this incident brought to light two key factors in critical systems— namely, the correctness of computer programs and the appropriateness of the underlying requirements. As the use of computers increases in the design and operation of life-critical environments and systems, the problem posed by these factors will become both more widespread and more important.

There are many difficulties in modeling such activities. Usually, a set of mathematical equations exists that approximately constitutes the model. However, various programming decisions and other assumptions must often be made in implementing a model, some of which may reveal a fundamental incompleteness of the model. Thus, after a while, the program tends to define the model rather than the other way around. At present, validating such a model is itself a highly nonintuitive and nonformal process. A complete nonprocedural formal specification of the model would be helpful, but that approach has only begun to be taken recently in shutdown systems.[111]

Crystal River, Florida. A short circuit in the controls caused the coolant temperature to be misread in the Crystal River nuclear plant in Florida. Detecting an apparent drop in temperature, the computer system sped up the core reaction. This overheated the reactor, causing an automatic shutdown. The pressure relief valve was opened (and mistakenly left open) under computer control. As a result, the high-pressure injection was turned on, flooding the primary coolant loop. A valve stuck, and 43,000 gallons of radioactive water poured onto the floor of the reactor building. Finally an operator realized what had happened, and closed the relief valve.[112]

Nuclear computer-safety fears for Sizewell B. Software engineers close to the design of the software intended to protect the Sizewell B nuclear reactor from serious accidents expressed fears that the system is too complex to check, and have suggested that the system be scrapped. Sizewell B is the first nuclear-power station in the United Kingdom to rely heavily on computers in its primary protection system. A computer-controlled safety system was seen as superior to one operated by people because it would diminish the risk of human error. But Nuclear Electric told *The Independent* that the system for Sizewell B, based on 300 to 400 microprocessors, is made up of modules that constitute more than 100,000 lines of code.[113]

Sellafield safety problems. Britain's nuclear watchdog has launched a full-scale investigation into the safety of computer software at nuclear installations, following an incident at the Sellafield reprocessing plant in which computer error caused radiation safety doors to be opened accidentally.[114]

The £240-million Sellafield plant was expected to help British Nuclear Fuels to return waste to the country of origin. The plant encases high-level waste in glass blocks for transport and storage, using a process that is known as *vitrification.*

In mid-September 1991, a bug in the computer program that controlled the plant caused radiation-protection doors to open prematurely while highly radioactive material was still inside one chamber. Nobody was exposed to radiation and the plant has since been shut down, but the incident rang alarm bells within the nuclear inspectorate. The inspectorate originally judged as acceptable the computer software that controls safety—partly because the software consisted of only a limited amount of computer code. However, the computer program was later amended with a software patch that is thought to have caused the doors to open too soon.

Software error at Bruce nuclear station. A computer software error caused thousands of liters of radioactive water to be released at the Bruce nuclear station at Kincardine, near Owen Sound in Canada. The reactor remained down for at least 6 weeks.[115]

PWR reactor system "abandoned owing to technical problems." Electricité de France (EDF) decided in principle to abandon the Controbloc P20 decentralized plant supervisory computer system developed by Cegelec for their N4 Pressurized Water Reactor (PWR) series, because of major development difficulties.[116]

Neutron reactor lands in hot water. A nuclear reactor at one of Europe's leading physics research centers was shut down by French safety authorities following the discovery that it had been running at 10 percent over its permitted power output for almost 20 years, ever since it came into operation in the early 1970s. The extra power went unnoticed because the instrument used to measure the output of the reactor at the Institut Laue-Langevin (ILL) at Grenoble in France was calibrated with ordinary water, whereas the reactor uses heavy water.[117]

Trojan horse in Lithuanian atomic power plant. A worker in a nuclear-power plant in Ignalina, Lithuania, attempted to plant a Trojan horse in the nonnuclear part of the reactor controls. His intent was to be paid for repairing the damage, but his efforts were detected and were undone by plant managers.[118] (Many other cases of malicious Trojan horse activities are given in Chapter 5; this one is included here to illustrate that some reliability problems are attributable to malicious causes.)

Nine Mile Point 2. The Nine Mile Point 2 nuclear-power plant near Oswego, New York, has had various problems. The Nuclear Regulatory Commission noted that Nine Mile Point's two reactors "ranked among the worst of the 111 licensed nuclear reactors in the United States."[119] Two relevant cases are included here and numbered for reference in Table 2.10 at the end of the section.

1. *NMP-2 reactor knocked offline by two-way radio in control room.* The up-again down-again Nine Mile Point 2 was back on line on April 25, 1989, following a shutdown over the weekend of April 22 and 23 that "shouldn't have happened," according to a federal official. An employee accidentally keyed a hand-held two-way radio near circuitry for the turbine-generator monitoring system Saturday night. The transmission shut down the system, which in turn triggered an automatic shutdown of the entire facility. A section chief of the NRC region 1 office said that he had never heard of a similar accident, but that most plants are sensitive and there are strict rules to prevent such an occurrence. Replacement fuel costs $350,000 per day when the 1080 MW plant is down. The plant had been up less than 1 week after an earlier shutdown caused by corrosion and loose wiring in a meter.[120]

2. *NMP-2 reactor shut down by a power surge.* Nine Mile Point 2 was shut down again on August 13, 1991, because of a transformer failure. A site area emergency was declared for only the third time in American history, although it was reported that there was "no danger" (*SEN 16*, 4).

2.10.2 **Conventional Power**

Nonnuclear power systems are also increasingly computer controlled. The first three cases involve propagation effects reminiscent of the 1980 ARPAnet collapse and the 1990 AT&T long-distance slowdown.

The northeastern U.S. blackout. The great northeast power blackout in the late 1960s was blamed on a power-level threshold having been set too low and then being exceeded, even though the operating conditions were still realistic. (There was also a lack of adequate isolation among the different power grids, because such a propagation effect had never before occurred on that scale.)

Blackout on west coast blamed on computer error. The power failure that blacked out millions of utility customers in 10 western states for up to an hour on October 2, 1984, was traced to a computer error in an Oregon substation. Equipment in Malin, Oregon, misread a power loss from a Pacific Gas and Electric line. The computer system thus thought that the electrical loss on a 2500-kilovolt link between Oregon and California was twice as big as it actually was, somehow setting off a network chain reaction. This event was apparently considered to be a routine occurrence that the computer system should have handled with no difficulty rather than propagating.[121] It is intriguing that electrical power-grid isolation may actually prevent such occurrences from happening electrically, but this example of the computer-based propagation of a bogus event signal is similar to the ARPAnet collapse (Section 2.1).

Los Angeles earthquake affects the Pacific Northwest. The Los Angeles earthquake of January 17, 1994, knocked out power to the entire Los Angeles basin. Grid interdependencies caused power outages as far away as Alberta and Wyoming; in Idaho, 150,000 people were without power for 3 hours.[122]

Ottawa power failure. A brief fire at Ottawa Hydro's Slater Street station on the morning of August 7, 1986, resulted in a loss of power to a substantial section of the downtown area. Even after 48 hours of work, sections of the city were still without power, causing officials to reexamine their long-accepted system-reliability standards.

> Ottawa Hydro engineering manager Gordon Donaldson said "the system is built to be 99.99 percent reliable . . . now we will be looking at going to another standard of reliability—99.999 percent." He also said that the cost would be huge—many times the $10 million cost of the Slater Street station—and Hydro customers may not be prepared to accept the cost . . . . The Slater station is the biggest and was considered the most reliable of the 12 across the city. It has three units, each of which is capable of carrying the whole system in an emergency. But all three were knocked out. . . . The culprit, an Ontario Hydro control board [called a "soupy board"] that monitors

the equipment at the substation, didn't even have anything directly to do with providing power to the thousands of people who work and live in the area. . . . its job is to make the system safer, cheaper and more reliable . . . . The board is considered so reliable that it doesn't have its own backup equipment. [!]

Automatic teller machines (ATMs) as far as 100 miles distant from Ottawa were knocked out of commission—the central computer that controls them was in the area of outage. Many traffic signals were out for days, as were a number of businesses.

The economic costs of the power failure were expected to be in the millions of dollars. Recalling the aftereffects of the evening power failure in the northeastern United States, it was deemed unlikely that the Ottawa birthrate would increase. As columnist Charles Lynch noted: "The Ottawa power failure took place during the breakfast hour, not normally a time when Ottawans are being polite to one another, let alone intimate."[123]

The Chicago Loop single point of failure. On April 13, 1992, Chicago experienced the closest thing to the "Chicago Fire" this century. The 40 to 60 miles of century-old freight tunnels underneath the Chicago Loop (the main downtown area) were flooded. The flooding appears to have been caused by a newly installed bridge piling that breached the tunnel where it passes under the Chicago River. When built, these tunnels were used for transporting coal, newsprint, and many other items on an electric railway.

The risks to computing were and are significant. Although no longer used to transport freight, these tunnels are now used as conduits for communication cables that connect together the city's main business district. Even more damaging, the tunnels connect the basements of numerous buildings that were flooded. These flooded basements are home to telephone and electrical equipment, most of which was disabled for days. The loss to the city was expected to exceed $1 billion. Indeed, the city of Chicago had a single weak link.[124]

Computers go nuts for insurgent squirrel. A squirrel caused a short-circuit in a transformer, causing a power surge in Providence, Rhode Island, on October 29, 1986. The surge affected numerous computers, although the backup transformer prevented a power outage.[125]

More kamikaze squirrels. There have been at least three times in my years at SRI International (since 1971) that a squirrel blacked out the entire institute. After the second squirrelcide (which downed my laboratory's primary computer system for 4 days), SRI established a cogeneration plant that was supposed to guarantee uninterruptible power, with appropriate isolation between the standby generators and the local power utility. As usual, nothing is guaranteed. That the "no-single-point-of-failure" power system had a single point of failure was demonstrated on May 29, 1989, during the Memorial Day holiday, by the feet of a squirrel who managed to short out the isolation point. The power was off for approximately 9 hours, and many computers remained down after that—some with their monitors burned out.[126]

Raccoons, power, and cold-fusion experiments. A raccoon electrocuted itself at the University of Utah, causing a 20-second power outage that resulted in a loss of data on the computers being used by Fleischmann and Pons in trying to verify their cold-fusion experiments. Raccoons managed to cripple the Jet Propulsion Laboratory more than once in the past. The latest one survived, and went on to became a local celebrity.[127] Evidently, animals pose a threat to installations with single-point-of-failure power systems.

2.10.3   Summary of Electrical-Power Problems

Table 2.10 provides a brief summary of the causes of the cited problems. (The abbreviations and symbols are given in Table 1.1.)

This table is one of the densest in the chapter, with many problems relating to inadequacies in system design, implementation, and use. There are risks inherent in systems that require significant training of operators and constant vigilance under circumstances when normally nothing goes wrong. Problems in analysis (particularly in the *Shock II* simulation model and the Grenoble case) and evolution and maintenance are also implicated. The environmental peculiarities of nuclear and conventional power systems contribute to the overall effects of each problem as well—including the single-point failure modes attributable to squirrels and a raccoon.

2.11 Computer Calendar Clocks

In this section, we consider time- and date-related problems. To emphasize the intrinsic nature of calendar-clock problems and how they depend on computer representations of dates and times, we

TABLE 2.10 Summary of electrical-power problems

| | Source of the Problems | | | | | | | | |
Case	Req def	Sys des	HW impl	SW impl	Sys use	HW malf	Envir	Anal- ysis	Evol, maint
Early nuclear	(o)	(o)	(o)	(o)	o	(o)	o	(o)	(o)
TMI-2		o	●	o	●		o	o	o
Davis-Besse		?	o		●★	o	o	o	o
Soviet Navy		(o)	(o)		(o)	(o)	o		
Chernobyl	o	o	o		●	o	o	o	o
Other Soviet	(o)	(o)	(o)	(o)	(o)	(o)	(o)	(o)	(o)
Shock II	●	o	o	●	o		o	●	o
Crystal River		o	o	o	o	●	o	o	?
Sizewell B	o	o		o			o	o	o
Sellafield	o	o		●	o		o	o	o
Bruce		o	o	●	o		o	o	o
French PWR		o	o		o		o	o	o
Grenoble		o			o		o	●	o
Ignalina					misuse		o	★	★
9-Mile Pt 2	o	o	o		o	2●	1●	o	o
Northeast	o				●		o		
West Coast				●			o		
Northwest		o					●		
Ottawa	o	o	o		o		●	o	o
Chicago		o	o		o		●	o	o
RI squirrel		o	o			o	●		
SRI squirrels		o	o			o	●		
Utah raccoon		o	o			o	●		

use (in this section only) a mathematically natural format for clock-related dates: *year-month-day*. This format illustrates the natural numerical order in which carries propagate (upward) from seconds to minutes to hours to days to months to years, and it serves to underlie the nature of those cases in which carries and overflows are not properly handled. Note that the American representation of *month-day-year* and the European representation of *day-month-year* are both mathematically unnatural, although the latter is at least logically ordered. In addition, there are often ambiguities between and within the two forms, as in *11/12/98,* which could be

November 12 or 11 December; furthermore, the year could be 1898 or 1998, for example. We can expect many new ambiguities when we reach *1/1/00* and *1/2/00*.

2.11.1 Dependence on Clocks

We consider first a few problems related to dependence on computer clocks.

Dependence on remote clocks. In Colorado Springs, one child was killed and another was injured at a traffic crossing; the computer controlling the street crossing did not properly receive the time transmitted by the atomic clock in Boulder, which affected the system's ability to vary the controls according to the school schedule. In all, 22 school crossings were affected (*SEN 14*, 2).

SRI's Computer Science Laboratory computer system once used a then-common eleven-clock averaging algorithm to reset the local clock automatically on reboot after a crash. Unfortunately, at the moment of reboot, a clock at the University of Maryland was off by 12 years, based on which the CSL clock was initialized to be off by 15 months. (Yes, the *new* algorithms now discard extreme values, and rely on systems with more dependable clocks.)

Byzantine clocks. Algorithms for making a reliable clock out of less reliable clocks are potentially nontrivial. The old three-clock algorithms (such as taking the median of three values) break down if one clock can report different values to its neighbors at any one time—whether maliciously or accidentally. In that case, it can be shown that four clocks are both necessary and sufficient. Furthermore, if n clocks can be potentially untrustworthy, then $3n+1$ clocks are required to provide a **Byzantine clock**—namely, one that can withstand arbitrary errors in any n clocks [70, 142].

Year ambiguities. In 1992, Mary Bandar received an invitation to attend a kindergarten in Winona, Minnesota, along with others born in '88. However, Mary was 104 at the time. The person making the database query had typed 1988, but the software kept only the last two digits (as noted by Ed Ravin in *SEN 18*, 3, A-3).

G.C. Blodgett's auto-insurance rate tripled when he turned 101; he was the computer program's first driver over 100, and his age was interpreted as 1, which fit into the program's definition of a teenager—namely, someone under 20 (noted by Lee Breisacher in *SEN 12*, 1, 19).

In Section 2.9 we observed the case of the almost-100-year-old man whose white-blood-cell count was interpreted as normal because the program interpreted his birthyear (input *89*) as *1989* rather than as *1889* (*SEN 15*, 2). This kind of problem will certainly be exacerbated as we approach and pass the turn of the century, and as more people become centenarians.

2.11.2 Dates and Times

We next consider problems relating specifically to calendar-clock arithmetic.

Overflows. The number $32{,}768 = 2^{15}$ has caused all sorts of grief that resulted from the overflow of a 16-bit word. A Washington, D.C., hospital computer system collapsed on *1989 Sep 19*, 2^{15} days after *1900 Jan 01*, forcing a lengthy period of manual operation. Brian Randell reported that the University of Newcastle upon Tyne, England, had a Michigan Terminal System (MTS) that crashed on *1989 Nov 16*, 2^{15} days after *1900 Mar 01*. Five hours later, MTS installations on the U.S. east coast died, and so on across the country—an example of a genuine (but unintentional) distributed time bomb.

John McLeod noted that COBOL uses a two-character date field, and warned about having money in the bank on *1999 Dec 31* at midnight. Robert I. Eachus noted that the Ada `time_of_year` field blows up after 2099, and MS-DOS bellies up on *2048 Jan 01*.

Don Stokes noted that Tandem CLX clocks struck out on *1992 Nov 1* at 3 P.M. in New Zealand, normally the first time zone to be hit, where the program deficiency attacked Westpac's automatic teller machines and electronic funds transfer point-of-sale terminals (EFTPOSs). For each of the next 4 hours thereafter, similar problems appeared in succeeding time zones, until a microcode bug could be identified and a fix reported. Thus, the difficulties were overcome before they could reach Europe. In some cases, the date was converted back to December 1983, although the bug affected different applications in different ways. Some locations in later time zones avoided 3 P.M. by shifting past it; others set their clocks back 2 years. Fortunately, the day was a Sunday, which decreased the effect.

The *linux* term program, which allows simultaneous multiple sessions over a single modem dialup connection, died worldwide on *1993 Oct 26.* The cause of an overflow was an integer variable defined as int rather than unsigned int.[128]

Year-end roundup. The Pennsylvania Wild Card Lotto computer system failed on *1990 Jan 01.* The winners of the lottery could not be determined until the software had been patched, 3 days later.

Summer Time, and the livin' is queasy. The U.S. House of Representatives passed a bill in April 1989 that would have delayed the end of Pacific daylight time in presidential election years until after the November election, with the intent of narrowing the gap between when the predictions from the rest of the continental United States start pouring in and when the polls close in California. The bill was never signed, but the option of "US/Pacific-New" was inserted into Unix systems to be used in the event it passed. As a consequence, several administrators on the west coast chose that option, and their systems failed to make the conversion to Pacific standard time on *1992 Oct 26 00:00* (*SEN 18,* 1).

The end-April 1993 cutover to summer time in Germany resulted in a steel production line allowing molten ingots to cool for 1 hour less than intended. To simplify programming, a German steel producer derived its internal computer clock readings from the Braunschweig radio time signal, which went from 1:59 A.M. to 3:00 A.M. in 1 minute. When the process controller thought the cooling time had expired (1 hour too early), his resulting actions splattered still-molten steel, damaging part of the facility.[129]

On the same night, the Bavarian police computer system stopped working at 3:00 A.M., blocking access to all of its databases (Debora Weber-Wulff, in *SEN 18,* 3, A-4).

Arithmetic errors. John Knight found an item in the October 1990 Continental Airlines magazine, while flying home from the 1990 Las Cruces safety workshop. The note described how the airline rented aircraft by the entire day, even if the plane was used only for a few hours. The billing for rentals was consistently 1 day too little, because the billing program merely subtracted the begin and end dates. This example exhibits the classical *off-by-one* error, which is a common type of programming mistake.

Nonportable software. The National Airspace Package, a program developed in the United States for modeling controlled airspace, failed to work when it was tried in the United Kingdom—the program had ignored longitudes east of Greenwich.[130]

2.11.3 **Leap-Year Problems**

Astoundingly, each leap-year or leap-second brings a new set of problems.

Leaping forward. John Knight reported that a Shuttle launch scheduled to cross the end-of-year 1989 was delayed, to avoid the software risks of both the year-end rollover and a leap-second correction that took place at the same time.

Not-making ends meat! Shortly after *1988 Feb 29*, the Xtra supermarket was fined $1000 for having meat around 1 day too long, because the computer program did not make the adjustment for leap-year.

Leap-day 1992. The date of *1992 Feb 29* brought its own collection of problems. The following episodes are worth relating, all of which stem from 1992 and were described in *SEN 17, 2, 10-12.*

Paul Eggert's contribution for International Software Calendar Bug Day observed that Prime Computer's MAGSAV failed at midnight on leap-day. However, Prime's 800 number is not answered on Saturdays, so they probably did not get as many complaints as might have occurred on a weekday. G.M. Lack noted that MAGSAV probably failed on leap-day because it tried to increment the year by one to set a tape label expiration date, and the resulting nonexistent date *1993 Feb 29* threw it for a loop.

Jaap Akkerhuis reported that Imail caused systems to crash worldwide on leap-day 1992, because the mail handlers did not recognize the date.

Roger H. Goun reported that the PC MS-DOS mail system UUPC/extended hung the PC on leap-day 1992.

Drew Derbyshire, the author of UUPC, traced the problem to a bug in the mktime() library function in Borland C++ 2.0, which converts a time to calendar format. Drew demonstrated that mktime() will hang a PC on leap-day, and reported the problem to Borland. As distributed, UUPC is compiled with Borland C++ 2.0, though source code is available for do-it-yourselfers .... Drew tried to warn UUPC users by mail after discovering the problem on Saturday. Ironically, many did not get the message until Sunday or Monday, when they found their PCs hung in uupoll.

Rhys Weatherley noted that a Windows 3.0 newsreader using Borland C++ 2.0 locked up, due to a bug in mktime converting to Unix date/time formats, although the problem may have been due to the run-time library.

Douglas W. Jones noted that all liquor licenses in Iowa expired on *1992 Feb 28*, and the new licenses were not in force until *1992 Mar 1*. The state announced that this gap was due to a computer error and promised not to enforce the law on leap-day for establishments caught in the interim. (I suppose there might have been a headline somewhere such as "A glitch in time shaves fine.")

Tsutomu Shimomura parked on leap-day at the San Diego off-airport parking lot, and was given a `time_in` ticket dated *1992 Feb· 30*; returning on *1992 Mar 6*, he was presented with a demand for $3771 (for 342 days @ $11/day and 9 hours @ $1/hour). It is intriguing to contemplate why the computer program used *1991 Mar 30* as the `time in`; it apparently kept the 30, but propagated a carry from Feb to Mar!

It ain't over 'til it's over. A leap-year bug in an ATM program did not hit until midnight on *1992 Dec 31*, causing several thousand ASB regional bank customer transactions to be rejected. Each magnetic stripe was corrupted during the period from midnight to 10 A.M., and anyone trying a *second* transaction was blocked.[131] The same phenomenon also was reported for 1500 TSB regional bank customers in Taranaki, from midnight until after noon.[132] Both banks used National Cash Register (NCR) ATM systems. This case was another example of New Zealand bringing in the new day first— serving as the king's taster for clock problems (Conrad Bullock, in *SEN 18, 2,* 11)—as in the Tandem Westpac case noted previously. NCR got a fix out fairly quickly, limiting the effect further west.

2.11.4 Summary of Clock Problems

Table 2.11 provides a highly simplified summary of the causes of the cited problems. It suggests simply that all of the potential sources of difficulty have manifested themselves. (The abbreviations and symbols are given in Table 1.1.)

TABLE 2.11 Summary of clock and date problems

| | Source of the Problems | | | | | | | | |
Case	Req def	Sys des	HW impl	SW impl	Sys use	HW malf	Envir	Anal- ysis	Evol, maint
Date and time cases	(o)	(o)	(o)	(o)	(o)	(o)	(o)	(o)	(o)

Many of these problems stem from the absence of a requirement that the system be able to continue to work in the more distant future, and from the presence of short-sighted programming practice.

As elsewhere, there is a serious lack of system sense and consistent software practice with respect to date and time arithmetic. Obvious problems created by limitations on leap-year and date–time representations tend not to be anticipated adequately. Perhaps no one ever dreamed that FORTRAN and COBOL would still be around into the next century. The lessons of this section seem to be widely ignored. New systems continue to fall victim to old and well-known problems.

You might think that the leap-day problems would be anticipated adequately by now. Getting clock arithmetic correct might seem to be a conceptually simple task—which is perhaps why it is not taken seriously enough. But even if earlier leap-year problems were caught in older systems, they continue to recur in newer systems. So, every 4 years, we encounter new problems, giving us 4 more years to develop new software with old leap-year bugs, and perhaps even to find some creative new bugs![133]

Many computer programmers are concerned about the coming millenium, and speculations on what might happen are rampant. There are many lurking problems, some of which are suggested here.

The maximum-field-value problem would seem to be obvious enough that it would have been better anticipated; however, it keeps recurring. Distributed system clocks are a potential source of serious difficulties, as illustrated by the synchronization problem that caused postponement of the first Shuttle launch (Section 2.2.1). Defensive design is particularly appropriate.

Planning for the future is always important. It is high time that we looked far ahead. We still have time to think about the millenial problems, analyzing existing programs and developing standard algorithms that can help us to avoid alarming consequences. Events on *2000 Jan 01* should indeed be interesting, particularly because 2000 will be a leap-year, following the rule that 100-multiples are *not* leap-years—except for the 400-multiples. Because there were no clock and date programs in 1900, problems caused by this particular rule may not arise until 2100 (or 2400).

2.12 **Computing Errors**

We conclude this collection of reliability problems with a few miscellaneous software and hardware cases relating to unexpected computational results.

Floating-point accuracy. A fascinating article by Jean-Francois Colonna[134] observes that five *algebraically equivalent* computational formulae for computing Verhulst dynamics based on the iterative equation

$$X_n = (R+1)X_{n-1} - RX_{n-1}^2$$

produce wildly different results even for fairly innocuous values of R and n. The paper considers five corresponding programs in C, each run on both IBM ES9000 and IBM RS6000, with $R = 3$ and $X_1 = 0.5$. Although the results are quite close to each other for values of X_{40}, they differ by a factor of over 1000 for the smallest and largest value of X_{60}. The same rather startling effect occurs for other programming languages and for other machines.

Risks of FORTRAN in German. Bertrand Meyer (*SEN 17*, 1) related that some FORTRAN compilers permit writing to a unit as well as to a device. Writing to unit 6 gives standard output, whereas writing to device 6 overwrites the disk. Apparently many German-speaking programmers (for whom both "unit" and "device" are translated as Einheit) were victimized by undesired disk deletions.

Bugs in Intel 486 and AMD 29000 RISC chips. Compaq discovered a flaw in the trigonometric functions when testing the new Intel 486 chip. This flaw was corrected in later versions. Three flaws were also detected in a version of the Advanced Micro Devices 32-bit RISC processor 29000, although workarounds were available (*SEN 15*, 1).

Harvard Mark I. A wiring mistake in the Harvard Mark I lay dormant for many years until it was finally detected. This case is discussed in Section 4.1.

2.13 **Summary of the Chapter**

The range of problems relating to reliability is incredibly diverse, even within each type of causal factor summarized by the tables. Referring back to the causes itemized in Section 1.2, almost all of the basic types of problems arising in system development (Section 1.2.1) and in operation and use (Section 1.2.2) are represented in this chapter. Two cases of malicious misuse are included (see Tables 2.4 and 2.10), although that class of causes is the primary subject of Chapters 3 and 5. Similarly, the effects observed in the cases discussed in this chapter encompass many of the effects noted in Section 1.3.

In general, it is a mistake to attempt to oversimplify the identification of the relevant modes of causality, partly because they occur so diversely and partly because each application area has its own peculiarities—but also because multiple factors are so often involved. (The issue of assigning blame is reconsidered in Section 9.1.)

The differences among causes and effects that vary according to the application area are illustrated throughout the chapter. People are a significant factor in many of the cases. There are numerous cases of system problems relating to software and hardware, as well as to environmental problems. The other causalities included in the section-ending table columns are also amply represented.

In principle, many techniques exist whose consistent use might have avoided the problems noted in this chapter (such as those summarized in Table 7.2). In practice, however, it is difficult to eliminate all such problems, as discussed in Chapter 7.

As we discuss in Section 4.1, reliability is a weak-link problem. Although a system may be designed such that it has far fewer weak links than it would if it were not designed defensively, the presence of residual vulnerabilities seems to be unavoidable. In some cases, it may take multiple causative factors to trigger a serious effect; however, the cases discussed in this chapter suggest that such a combination of factors may indeed occur. (This point is amplified in Chapter 4.1.)

John Gall's *Systemantics: How Systems Work and Especially How They Fail* [46] has several suggestions from 1975 that are still relevant here:

- In general, systems work poorly or not at all.
- New systems mean new problems.
- Complex systems usually operate in failure mode.
- When a fail-safe system fails, it fails by failing to fail safe.

Challenges

C2.1 Consider the electrocutions of heart-monitor patients noted in Section 2.9.2. What is the simplest countermeasure you can think of that would completely prevent further recurrences? What is the most realistic solution you can think of? Are they the same?

C2.2 For any event summarized in this chapter (other than that mentioned in C2.1), speculate on how the causative factors could have been avoided or substantially reduced in severity. Perfect hindsight is permitted. (Reading the rest of the book may help you to reduce the amount of speculation that you need to apply in some cases. However, this exercise is intended as an anticipatory analysis.)

C2.3 Similarities between the 1980 ARPAnet collapse and the 1990 AT&T long-distance slowdown have been noted in Section 2.1. Identify and discuss three other pairs of problems noted in this chapter for which identical or almost-identical modalities caused similar results.

C2.4 Design a simple alarm system that will continue to work despite the loss of electrical power *or* the loss of standby battery power *or* malfunction of a single sensor whose sole purpose is to detect the situation for which the alarm is expected to trigger. (You may use multiple sensors.) Try to identify circumstances under which your design might fail to operate properly. Can you overcome those vulnerabilities? Are there any single-point sources of failure?

CHAPTER 3 Security Vulnerabilities

Caveat emptor.
(Let the buyer beware.)

THIS CHAPTER CONSIDERS security vulnerabilities. It examines some of the characteristic system flaws that can be exploited. It also discusses a few remarkable cases of system flaws. Chapter 5 presents specific examples of cases in which such vulnerabilities have been exploited or have otherwise caused problems.

The informal definition of security given in Section 1.1 implies freedom from undesirable events, including malicious and accidental misuse. In the computer sense, undesirable events might also include the results of hardware malfunctions. In this natural usage, **security** would be an all-inclusive term spanning many computer-system risks. In common technical usage, however, **computer security** and **communication security** generally refer to protection against human misuse, and exclude protection against malfunctions. Two particularly important security-related challenges concern assuring confidentiality and maintaining integrity. A third involves maintaining system availability despite threats from malicious or accidental system misuse. Chapter 4 demonstrates the close coupling between reliability and security concepts; many of the techniques for achieving one contribute to enhancing the other. The following security-related terms are used here:

- **Confidentiality** (or secrecy) means that information is protected from unintended disclosure. Computer-system mechanisms and policies attempt to enforce secrecy—for example, to protect individual rights of privacy or national defense. The system does not accidentally divulge sensitive information, and is resistant to attempts to gain access to such information.

- **Integrity** means literally that a resource is maintained in an unimpaired condition, or that there is a firm adherence to a specification (such as requirements or a code of values). In the computer sense, **system integrity** means that a system and its system data are maintained in a (sufficiently) correct and consistent condition, whereas (user) **data integrity** means that (user) data entities are so maintained. In this sense, the danger of losing integrity is clearly a security concern. Integrity could be related to unintended disclosure (in that nonrelease is a property to be maintained), but is generally viewed more as being protection against unintended modification. From the inside of a system, integrity involves ensuring **internal consistency.** From an overall perspective, integrity also includes **external consistency;** that is, the internals of the system accurately reflect the outside world. Related to external consistency are notions such as the legality of what is done within the system and the compatibility with external standards. Integrity in the larger sense also involves human judgments.

- **Availability** means that systems, data, and other resources are usable when needed, despite subsystem outages and environmental disruptions. From a reliability point of view, availability is generally enhanced through the constructive use of redundancy, including alternative approaches and various archive-and-retrieval mechanisms. From a security point of view, availability is enhanced through measures to prevent malicious denials of service.

- **Timeliness** is relevant particularly in real-time systems that must satisfy certain urgency requirements, and is concerned with ensuring that necessary resources are available quickly enough when needed. It is thus a special and somewhat more stringent case of availability. In certain critical systems, timeliness must be treated as a security property—particularly when it must be maintained despite malicious system attacks.

Once again, there is considerable overlap among these different terms. Also important are requirements for human safety and for overall survivability of the application, both of which depend on the satisfaction of requirements relating to reliability and security:

- **System survivability** is concerned with the ability to continue to make resources available, despite adverse circumstances including hardware malfunctions, software flaws, malicious user activities, and environmental hazards such as electronic interference.

- **Human safety** is concerned with the well-being of individuals, as well as of groups of people. In the present context, it refers to ensuring the

safety of anyone who is in some way dependent on the satisfactory behavior of systems and on the proper use of technology. Human safety
with respect to the entire application may depend on system survivability, as well as on system reliability and security.

There is clearly overlap among the meanings of these terms. In
the sense that they all involve protection against dangers, they all
are components of security. In the sense that protection against
dangers involves maintenance of some particular condition, they
might all be considered as components of integrity. In the sense
that the system should behave predictably at all times, they are
all components of reliability. Various reliability issues are clearly
also included as a part of security, although many other reliability
issues are usually considered independently. Ultimately, however,
security, integrity, and reliability are closely related. Any or all of
these concepts may be constituent requirements in a particular application, and the failure to maintain any one of them may compromise the ability to maintain the others. Consequently, we do not
seek sharp distinctions among these terms; we prefer to use them
more or less intuitively.

The term **dependable computing** is sometimes used to imply
that the system will do what is expected with high assurance, under
essentially all realistic circumstances. Dependability is related to
trustworthiness, which is a measure of trust that can reasonably
be placed in a particular system or subsystem. Trustworthiness is
distinct from **trust**, which is the degree to which someone has faith
that a resource is indeed trustworthy, whether or not that resource
is actually trustworthy.

3.1 **Security Vulnerabilities and Misuse Types**

Security vulnerabilities can arise in three different ways, representing three fundamental gaps between what is desired and what can
be achieved. Each of these gaps provides a potential for security
misuse.

First, a **technological gap** exists between what a computer system is actually *capable of enforcing* (for example, by means of its
access controls and user authentication) and what it is *expected to
enforce* (for example, its policies for data confidentiality, data integrity, system integrity, and availability). This technological gap
includes deficiencies in both hardware and software (for systems

and communications), as well as in system administration, configuration, and operation. Discretionary access controls (DACs) give
a user the ability to specify the types of access to individual resources that are considered to be authorized. Common examples
of discretionary controls are the user/group/world permissions of
Unix systems and the access-control lists of Multics. These controls are intended to limit access, but are generally incapable of enforcing copy protection. Attempts to constrain propagation through
discretionary copy controls tend to be ineffective. Mandatory access controls (MACs) are typically established by system administrators, and cannot be altered by users; they can help to restrict
the propagation of copies. The best-known example is multilevel
security, which is intended to prohibit the flow of information in
the direction of decreasing information sensitivity. Flawed operating systems may permit violations of the intended policy. Unreliable
hardware may cause a system to transform itself into one with unforeseen and unacceptable modes of behavior. This gap between
access that is intended and access that is actually authorized represents a serious opportunity for misuse by authorized users. Ideally, if there were no such gap, misuse by authorized users would
be a less severe problem.

Second, a **sociotechnical gap** exists between *computer system
policies* and *social policies* such as computer-related crime laws,
privacy laws, and codes of ethics. This sociotechnical gap arises
when the socially expected norms are not consistent with or are
not implementable in terms of the computer system policies. For
example, issues of *intent* are not addressed by computer security
policies, but are relevant to social policies. Intent is also poorly
covered by existing "computer crime" laws.

Finally, a **social gap** exists between *social policies* and *actual
human behavior.* This social gap arises when people do not act according to what is expected of them. For example, authorized users
may easily diverge from the desired social policies; malicious penetrators do not even pretend to adhere to the social norms.

The technological gap can be narrowed by carefully designed,
correctly implemented, and properly administered computer systems and networks that are meaningfully secure, at least to the
extent of protecting against known vulnerabilities. For example,
those systems that satisfy specific criteria (see Section 7.8.1) have
a significant advantage with respect to security over those systems
that do not satisfy such criteria. The sociotechnical gap can be

narrowed by well-defined and socially enforceable social policies, although computer enforcement still depends on narrowing the technological gap. The social gap can be narrowed to some extent by a narrowing of the first two gaps, with some additional help from educational processes. Malicious misuse of computer systems can never be prevented completely, particularly when perpetrated by authorized users. Ultimately, the burden must rest on more secure computer systems and networks, on more enlightened management and responsible employees and users, and sensible social policies. Monitoring and user accountability are also important.

Computer misuse can take many forms. Various classes of misuse are summarized in Figure 3.1 and Table 3.1. For visual simplicity, the figure is approximated as a simple tree. However, it actually represents a system of descriptors, rather than a taxonomy in the usual sense, in that a given misuse may involve multiple techniques within several classes.

The order of categorization depicted is roughly from the physical world to the hardware to the software, and from unauthorized use to misuse of authority. The first class includes external misuses that can take place without any access to the computer system. The second class concerns hardware misuse, and generally requires involvement with the computer system itself. Two examples in this second class are eavesdropping and interference (usually electronic or electromagnetic, but optical and other forms are also possible). The third class includes masquerading in a variety of forms. The fourth includes the establishment of deferred misuse—for example, the creation and enabling of a Trojan horse (as opposed to subsequent misuse that accompanies the actual execution of the Trojan horse—which may show up in other classes at a later time) or other forms of pest programs discussed in Section 3.2. The fifth class involves bypass of authorization, possibly enabling a user to appear to be authorized—or not to appear at all (for example, to be invisible to the audit trails). The remaining classes involve active and passive misuse of resources, inaction that might result in misuse, and misuse that helps in carrying out additional misuses (such as preparation for an attack on another system, or use of a computer in a criminal enterprise).

The main downward-sloping right diagonal path in Figure 3.1 indicates typical steps and modes of intended use of computer systems. The leftward branches all involve misuse; the rightward branches represent potentially acceptable use—until a left-

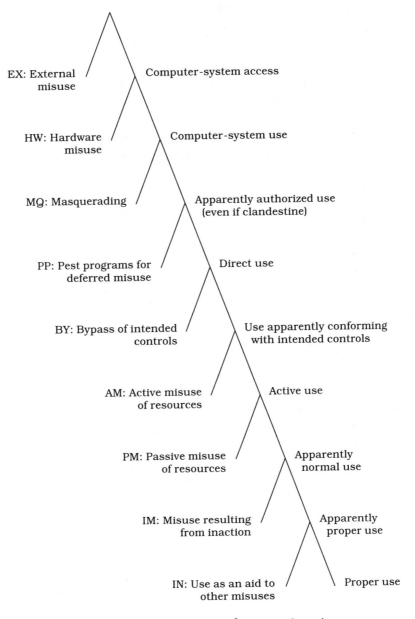

FIGURE 3.1 Classes of techniques for computer misuse
Adapted from P.G. Neumann and D.B. Parker, "A summary of computer misuse
techniques," Twelfth National Computer Security Conference, Baltimore, 1989.

TABLE 3.1 Types of computer misuse

Mode	Misuse type
External (EX)	
1. Visual spying	Observing of keystrokes or screens
2. Misrepresentation	Deceiving operators and users
3. Physical scavenging	Dumpster-diving for printout
Hardware misuse (HW)	
4. Logical scavenging	Examining discarded/stolen media
5. Eavesdropping	Intercepting electronic or other data
6. Interference	Jamming, electronic or otherwise
7. Physical attack	Damaging or modifying equipment, power
8. Physical removal	Removing equipment and storage media
Masquerading (MQ)	
9. Impersonation	Using false identities external to computer systems
10. Piggybacking attacks	Usurping communication lines, workstations
11. Spoofing attacks	Using playback, creating bogus nodes and systems
12. Network weaving	Masking physical whereabouts or routing
Pest programs (PP)	Setting up opportunities for further misuse
13. Trojan horse attacks	Implanting malicious code, sending letter bombs
14. Logic bombs	Setting time or event bombs (a form of Trojan horse)
15. Malevolent worms	Acquiring distributed resources
16. Virus attacks	Attaching to programs and replicating
Bypasses (BY)	Avoiding authentication and authority
17. Trapdoor attacks	Utilizing existing flaws; see Table 3.2
18. Authorization attacks	Password cracking, hacking tokens
Active misuse (AM)	Writing, using, with apparent authorization
19. Basic active misuse	Creating, modifying, using, denying service, entering false or misleading data
20. Incremental attacks	Using salami attacks
21. Denials of service	Perpetrating saturation attacks
Passive misuse (PM)	Reading, with apparent authorization
22. Browsing	Making random or selective searches
23. Inference, aggregation	Exploiting database inferences and traffic analysis
24. Covert channels	Exploiting covert channels or other data leakage
Inactive misuse (IM/25)	Willfully failing to perform expected duties, or committing errors of omission
Indirect misuse (IN/26)	Preparing for subsequent misuses, as in off-line preencryptive matching, factoring large numbers to obtain private keys, autodialer scanning

Adapted from P.G. Neumann and D.B. Parker, "A summary of computer misuse techniques," Twelfth National Computer Security Conference, Baltimore, 1989.

ward branch is taken. (Each labeled mode of usage along the main-diagonal intended-usage line is generally the antithesis of the corresponding leftward misuse branch.) Every leftward branch represents a class of vulnerabilities that must be defended against — that is, detected, avoided, or recovered from. The means for prevention, deterrence, avoidance, detection, and recovery typically differ from one branch to the next. (Even inaction may imply misuse, although no abusive act of commission may have occurred.)

The two classes of misuse types that are of main interest here are *preplanned pest programs,* such as Trojan horses, viruses, and worms (with effects including time bombs, logic bombs, and general havoc), and *bypasses of authority* (trapdoor exploitations and authorization attacks). These classes are discussed next. Several other forms are important in the present context, and are also considered.

3.2   Pest Programs and Deferred Effects

Various types of malicious attacks employ the insertion of code that can result in subsequent malicious effects; these are collectively referred to as *pest programs.* Pest-program attacks involve the creation, planting, and arming of software using methods such as Trojan horses, logic bombs, time bombs, letter bombs, viruses, and malicious worms. Generically, many of these are subcases of Trojan horse attacks.

3.2.1   Pest Programs in General

This section considers pest programs in general computer systems. Section 3.2.2 considers personal-computer viruses.

- A **Trojan horse** is an entity (typically but not always a program) that contains code or something interpretable as code, which when executed can have undesired effects (such as the clandestine copying of data or the disabling of the computer system).
- A **logic bomb** is a Trojan horse in which the attack is detonated by the occurrence of some specified logical event, such as the first subsequent login by a particular user.
- A **time bomb** is a logic bomb in which the attack is detonated by the occurrence of some specified time-related logical event, such as the next time the computer date reaches Friday the Thirteenth.
- A **letter bomb** is a peculiar type of Trojan horse attack whereby the

harmful agent is not contained in a program, but rather is hidden in a piece of electronic mail or data; it typically contains characters, control characters, or escape sequences squirreled away in the text such that its malicious activities are triggered only when it is read in a particular way. For example, it might be harmless if read as a file, but would be destructive if read as a piece of electronic mail. This kind of attack can be prevented if the relevant system programs are defensive enough to filter out the offending characters. However, if the system permits the transit of such characters, the letter bomb would be able to exploit that flaw and thus to be triggered.

- A **virus** is in essence a Trojan horse with the ability to propagate itself iteratively and thus to contaminate other systems. There is a lack of clarity in terminology concerning viruses, with two different sets of usage: one for strict-sense viruses, another for personal-computer viruses. A **strict-sense virus**, as defined by Cohen [27] is a program that alters other programs to include a copy of itself. A **personal-computer virus** is similar, except that its propagation from one system to another is typically the result of human inadvertence or obliviousness. Viruses often employ the effects of a Trojan horse attack, and the Trojan horse effects often depend on trapdoors that either are already present or are created for the occasion. Strict-sense viruses are generally Trojan horses that are self-propagating without any necessity of human intervention (although people may inadvertently facilitate the spread). Personal-computer viruses are usually Trojan horses that are propagated primarily by human actions such as moving a floppy disk from one system to another. Personal-computer viruses are rampant, and represent a serious long-term problem (see Section 3.2.2). On the other hand, strict-sense viruses (that attach themselves to other programs and propagate without human aid) are a rare phenomenon — none are known to have been perpetrated maliciously, although a few have been created experimentally.

- A **worm** is a program that is distributed into computational segments that can execute remotely. It may be malicious, or may be used constructively — for example, to provide extensive multiprocessing, as in the case of the early 1980s experiments by Shoch and Hupp at Xerox PARC [155].

The setting up of pest programs may actually employ misuses of other classes, such as bypasses or misuse of authority, or may be planted via completely normal use, as in a letter bomb. The subsequent execution of the deferred misuses may also rely on further misuse methods. Alternatively, execution may involve the occurrence of some logical event (for example, a particular date and time or a logical condition), or may rely on the curiosity, innocence, or normal behavior of the victim. Indeed, because a Trojan horse typically executes with the privileges of its victim, its execution may require no further privileges. For example, a Trojan horse program might find itself authorized to delete all the victim's files.

A comparison of pest-program attacks with other modes of security misuse is given in Section 3.6.

3.2.2   Personal-Computer Viruses

Personal-computer viruses may attack in a variety of ways, including corruption of the boot sector, hard-disk partition tables, or main memory. They may alter or lock up files, crash the system, and cause delays and other denials of service. These viruses take advantage of the fact that there is no significant security or system integrity in the system software. In practice, personal-computer virus infection is frequently caused by contaminated diagnostic programs or otherwise infected floppy disks. See Section 5.1 for further discussion of virus attacks.

3.3   Bypass of Intended Controls

This section begins with a discussion of bypass vulnerabilities, and then considers a particularly important subset typified by password vulnerabilities, along with the corresponding types of attacks that can exploit these vulnerabilities.

3.3.1   Trapdoors

A **trapdoor** is an entry path that is not normally expected to be used. In some cases, its existence is accidental and is unknown to the system developers; in other cases, it is intentionally implanted during development or maintenance. Trapdoors and other system flaws often enable controls to be bypassed. Bypass of controls may involve circumvention of existing controls, or modification of those controls, or improper acquisition of otherwise-denied authority, presumably with the intent to misuse the acquired access rights subsequently. Common modes of unauthorized access result from system and usage flaws (for example, trapdoors that permit devious access paths) such as the following (see [105], with subtended references to earlier work by Bisbey, Carlstedt, Hollingworth, Popek, and other researchers), summarized in Table 3.2.

TABLE 3.2 Types of trapdoor attacks

Subtype	Mode of attack (within type 17 in Table 3.1)
a	Improper identification and authentication
b	Improper initialization and allocation
c	Improper finalization (termination and deallocation)
d	Improper authentication and validation
e	Naming flaws, confusions, and aliases
f	Improper encapsulation, such as accessible internals
g	Asynchronous flaws, such as atomicity anomalies
h	Other logic errors

Inadequate identification, authentication, and authorization of users, tasks, and systems. Lack of checking for identity and inadequate authentication are common sources of problems. System spoofing attacks may result, in which one system component masquerades as another. The debug option of sendmail and the .rhosts file exploited by the Internet Worm [138, 150, 159] are examples (see Section 5.1.1). For example, the .rhost mechanism enables logins from elsewhere without any authentication being required — a truly generous concept when enabled. These exploitations also represent cases in which there was an absence of required authority. (Password-related trapdoors are noted separately after this itemization.)

Improper initialization. Many bypasses are enabled by improper initialization, including improper initial domain selection or improper choice of security parameters; improper partitioning, as in implicit or hidden sharing of privileged data; and embedded operating-system parameters in application memory space. If the initial state is not secure, then everything that follows is in doubt. System configuration, bootload, initialization, and system reinitialization following reconfiguration are all serious sources of vulnerabilities, although often carried out independently of the standard system controls.

Improper finalization. Even if the initialization is sound, the completion may not be. Problems include incompletely handled aborts, accessible vestiges of deallocated resources (residues), incomplete external device disconnects, and other exits that do not properly clean up after themselves. In many systems, deletion is effected by the setting of a *deleted* flag, although the information is still present and is accessible to system programmers and to hardware maintenance personnel (for example). A particularly insidious flaw of this type has existed in several popular operating systems, including in TENEX, permitting accidental piggybacking (tailgating) when a user's communication line suffers an interruption; the next user who happens to be assigned the same login port is simply attached to the still active user job. Several examples of accidental data residues are noted in Section 5.2.

Incomplete or inconsistent authentication and validation. User authentication, system authentication, and other forms of validation are often a source of bypasses. Causes include improper argument validation, type checking, and bounds checks; failure to prevent permissions, quotas, and other programmed limits from being exceeded; and bypasses or misplacement of control. The missing bounds check in `gets` exploited by the `finger` attack used in the Internet Worm is a good example. Authentication problems are considered in detail in Section 3.3.2.

Improper naming. Naming is a common source of difficulties (for example, see Section 6.5), particularly in creating bypasses. Typical system problems include aliases (for example, multiple names with inconsistent effects that depend on the choice of name), search-path anomalies, and other context-dependent effects (same name, but with different effects, depending on the directories or operating-system versions).

Improper encapsulation. Proper encapsulation involves protecting the internals of a system or subsystem to make them inaccessible from the outside. Encapsulation problems that cause bypasses include a lack of information hiding, accessibility of internal data structures, alterability of audit trails, midprocess control transfers, and hidden or undocumented side effects.

Sequencing problems. The order in which events occur and the overlap among different events that may occur simultaneously introduce serious security bypass problems, as well as serious reliability problems, especially in highly distributed systems. Problems include incomplete atomicity or sequentialization, as in faulty interrupt or error handling; flawed asynchronous functionality, such as permitting undesired changes to be made between the time of validation and the time of use; and incorrect serialization, resulting in harmful nondeterministic behavior, such as critical race conditions and other asynchronous side effects. A **race condition** is a situation in which the outcome is dependent on internal timing considerations. It is **critical** if something else depending on that outcome may be affected by its nondeterminism; it is **noncritical** otherwise. The so-called **time-of-check to time-of-use (TOCT-TOU)** problem illustrates inadequate atomicity, inadequate encapsulation, and incomplete validation; an example is the situation in which, after validation is performed on the arguments of a call by reference, it is then possible for the caller to change the arguments.

Other logic errors. There are other diverse cases leading to bypass problems—for example, inverted logic (such as a missing not operation), conditions or outcomes not properly matched with branches, and wild transfers of control (especially if undocumented).

Tailgating may occur accidentally when a user is attached randomly to an improperly deactivated resource, such as a port through which a process is still logged in but to which the original user of the process is no longer attached (as in the TENEX problem noted previously). Unintended access may also result from other trapdoor attacks, logical scavenging (for example, reading a scratch tape before writing on it), and asynchronous attacks (for example, incomplete atomic transactions and TOCTTOU discrepancies). For example, trapdoors in the implementation of encryption can permit unanticipated access to unencrypted information.

3.3.2   Authentication and Authorization Vulnerabilities

Password attacks. Password attacks are one of the most important classes of authentication attacks, and are particularly insidious because of the ubiquity of passwords. Some of the diversity among password attacks is illustrated in the following paragraphs.

Exhaustive trial-and-error attacks. Enumerating all possible passwords was sometimes possible in the early days of time-sharing systems, but is now much less likely to succeed because of limits on the number of tries and auditing of failed login attempts.

Guessing of passwords. Guessing is typically done based on commonly used strings of characters (such as dictionary words and proper names) or strings that might have some logical association with an individual under attack (such as initials, spouse's name, dog's name, and social-security number). It is amazing how often this approach succeeds.

Capture of unencrypted passwords. Passwords are often available in an unencrypted form, in storage, as they are being typed, or in transit (via local or global net, or by trapdoors such as the Unix feature of using /dev/mem to read all of memory). For example, the Ethernet permits *promiscuous mode* sniffing of everything that traverses the local network; it is relatively easy to scan for commands that are always followed by passwords, such as local and remote logins.

Derivation of passwords. Certain systems or administrators constrain passwords to be algorithmically generated; in such cases, the algorithms themselves may be used to shorten the search. Occasionally, inference combined with a short-cut search algorithm can be used, as in the TENEX connect flaw, where the password comparison was done sequentially, one character at a time; in that case, it was possible to determine whether the first character was correctly guessed by observing page fault activity on the next serially checked password character, and then repeating the process for the next character—using a match-and-shift approach. Another attack, which appears to be increasing in popularity, is the *preencryptive dictionary attack*, as described by Morris and Thompson [96] and exploited in the Internet Worm. That attack requires capturing the encrypted password file, and then encrypting each entry in a dictionary of candidate words until a match is found. (It is possible to hinder this attack somewhat in some systems by making the encrypted password file unreadable by ordinary users, as in the case of a completely encapsulated shadow password file that is ostensibly accessible to only the login program and the administrators. However, usurpation of administrator privileges can then lead to compromise.)

Existence of universal passwords. In rare cases, a design or implementation flaw can result in the possibility of universal passwords, similar to skeleton keys that open a wide range of locks. For example, there has been at least one case in which it was possible to generate would-be passwords that satisfy the login procedure for every system with that login implementation, without any knowledge of valid passwords. In that case, a missing bounds check permitted an intentionally overly long password consisting of a random sequence followed by its encrypted form to overwrite the stored encrypted password, which defeated the password-checking program [179]). This rather surprising case is considered in greater detail in Section 3.7.

Absence of passwords. In certain cases, trapdoors exist that require no passwords at all. For example, the .rhost tables enable unauthenticated logins from any of the designated systems. Furthermore, some Unix remote shell (rsh) command implementations permit unauthenticated remote logins from a similarly named but bogus foreign user. The philosophy of a single universal login authentication for a particular user that is valid throughout all parts of a distributed system and — worse yet — throughout a network of networks represents an enormous vulnerability, because one compromise anywhere can result in extensive damage throughout. (In the context of this book, the verb *to compromise* and the noun *compromise* are used in the pejorative sense to include penetrations, subversions, intentional and accidental misuse, and other forms of deviations from expected or desired system behavior. The primary usage is that of compromising something such as a system, process, or file, although the notion of compromising oneself is also possible — for example, by accidentally introducing a system flaw or invoking a Trojan horse. To avoid confusion, we do not use *compromise* here in the sense of a mutual agreement.)

Nonatomic password checking. Years ago, there were cases of applications in which the password checking could be subverted by a judiciously timed interrupt during the authentication process. The scenario typically involved attempting to log in with a legitimate user name and an incorrect password, then interrupting, and miraculously discovering oneself logged in. This was a problem with several early higher-layer authenticators.

Editing the password file. If the password file is not properly protected against writing, and is not properly encapsulated, it may be possible to edit the password file and to insert a bogus but viable user identifier and (encrypted) password of your own choosing, or to install your own variant password file from a remote login.

Trojan horsing the system. Trojan horses may be used to subvert the password checking — for example, by insertion of a trapdoor into an authorization program within the security perimeter. The classical example is the C-compiler Trojan horse described by Thompson [167], in which a modification to the C compiler caused the next recompilation of the Unix login routine to have a trapdoor. This case is noted in Section 3.7. (Trojan horses may also capture passwords when typed or transmitted, as in the second item in this list.)

The variations within this class are amazingly rich. Although the attack types noted previously are particularly dangerous for fixed, reusable passwords, there are also comparable attack techniques for more sophisticated authentication schemes, such as challenge–response schemes, token authenticators, and other authenticators based on public-key encryption. Even if one-time token authenticators are used for authentication at a remote authentication server, the presence of multiple decentralized servers can permit playback of a captured authenticator within the time window (typically on the order of three 30-second intervals), resulting in almost instantaneous penetrations at all the *other* servers.

There are many guidelines for password management, but most of them can be subverted if the passwords are exposed. Even if callback schemes are used in an attempt to ensure that a dial-up user is actually in the specified place, callback can be defeated by remotely programmable call forwarding. Techniques for overcoming these vulnerabilities are considered in Section 7.9.2.

3.4 **Resource Misuse**

In addition to the two forms of malicious attacks (pest programs and bypasses) already discussed, there are various forms of attack relating to the misuse of conferred or acquired authority. Indeed, these are the most common forms of attack in some environments.

3.4.1 **Active Misuse of Resources**

Active misuse of apparently conferred authority generally alters the state of the system or changes data. Examples include misuse of administrative privileges or superuser privileges; changes in access-control parameters to enable other misuses of authority; harmful data alteration and false data entry; denials of service (including saturation, delay, or prolongation of service); the somewhat exotic **salami attacks** in which numerous small pieces (possibly using roundoff) are collected (for example, for personal or corporate gain); and aggressive covert-channel exploitation. A **covert channel** is a means of signaling without using explicit read–write and other normal channels for information flow; signaling through covert channels is typically in violation of the intent of the security policy. Covert storage channels tend to involve the ability to detect the state of shared resources, whereas covert timing channels tend to involve the ability to detect temporal behavior. For example, a highly constrained user might be able to signal 1 bit of information to an unconstrained user on the basis of whether

or not a particular implicitly shared resource is exhausted, perhaps requiring some inference to detect that event. If it is possible
to signal 1 bit reliably, then it is usually possible to signal at a
higher bandwidth. If it is possible to signal only unreliably, then
error-correcting coding can be used. (See Section 4.1.) Note that
the apparently conferred authority may have been obtained surrep-
titiously, but otherwise appears as legitimate use.

3.4.2   Passive Misuse of Resources

Passive misuse of apparently conferred authority generally results in reading information without altering any data and without altering the system (with the exception of audit-trail and status
data). Passive misuse includes browsing (without specific targets in
mind), searching for specific patterns, aggregating data items to derive information that is more sensitive than are the individual items
(for example, see [84]), and drawing inferences. An example that
can employ both aggregation and inference is provided by traffic
analysis that is able to derive information without any access to
the data. In addition, it is sometimes possible to derive inferences
from a covert channel even in the absence of a malicious program
or malicious user that is signaling intentionally.

These passive misuses typically have no appreciable effect on the
objects used or on the state of the system (except, of course, for
the execution of computer instructions and possibly resulting audit
data). They do not need to involve unauthorized use of services and
storage. Note that certain events that superficially might appear to
be passive misuse may in fact result in active misuse—for example,
through time-dependent side effects.

3.5   Other Attack Methods

Several other attack methods are worth noting here in greater detail—namely, the techniques numbered 1 through 12 in Table 3.1,
collected into general categories as follows:

External misuse. Generally nontechnological and unobserved,
external misuse is physically removed from computer and communication facilities. It has no directly observable effects on the
systems and is usually undetectable by the computer security systems; however, it may lead to subsequent technological attacks.
Examples include visual spying (for example, remote observation

of typed keystrokes or screen images), physical scavenging (for example, collection of waste paper or other externally accessible computer media such as discards—so-called **dumpster diving**), and various forms of deception (for example, misrepresentation of oneself or of reality) external to the computer systems and telecommunications.

Hardware misuse. There are two types of **hardware misuse**, passive and active. **Passive hardware misuse** tends to have no (immediate) side effects on hardware or software behavior, and includes logical scavenging (such as examination of discarded computer media) and electronic or other types of eavesdropping that intercept signals, generally unbeknownst to the victims. Eavesdropping may be carried out remotely (for example, by picking up emanations) or locally (for example, by planting a spy-tap device in a terminal, workstation, mainframe, or other hardware-software subsystem). **Active hardware misuse** generally has noticeable effects, and includes theft of computing equipment and physical storage media; hardware modifications, such as internally planted Trojan horse hardware devices; interference (electromagnetic, optical, or other); physical attacks on equipment and media, such as interruption of or tampering with power supplies or cooling. These activities have direct effects on the computer systems (for example, internal state changes or denials of service).

Masquerading. Masquerading attacks include impersonation of the identity of some other individual or computer subject; spoofing attacks that take advantage of successful impersonation; piggybacking attacks that gain physical access to communication lines or workstations; playback attacks that merely repeat captured or fabricated communications; and network weaving that masks physical whereabouts and routing via both telephone and computer networks, as practiced by the Wily Hackers [162, 163]. Playback attacks might typically involve replay of a previously used message or preplay of a not-yet used message. In general, masquerading activities often appear to be indistinguishable from legitimate activity.

Inaction. The penultimate case in Table 3.1 involves misuse through inaction, in which a user, operator, administrator, maintenance person, or perhaps surrogate fails to take an action, either intentionally or accidentally. Such cases may logically be considered as degenerate cases of misuse, but are listed separately because they may have quite different origins.

Indirect attacks. The final case in Table 3.1 involves system use as an indirect aid in carrying out subsequent actions. Familiar examples include performing a dictionary attack on an encrypted password file (that is, attempting to identify dictionary words used as passwords, and possibly using a separate machine to make detection of this activity more difficult [96]); factoring of extremely large numbers, as in attempting to break a public-key encryption mechanism such as the Rivest-Shamir-Adleman (RSA) algorithm [137], whose strength depends on a product of two large primes being difficult to factor; and scanning successive telephone numbers in an attempt to identify modems that might be attacked subsequently.

3.6 Comparison of the Attack Methods

Misuse of authority is of considerable concern here because it can be exploited in either the installation or the execution of malicious code, and because it represents a major threat modality. In general, attempts to install and execute malicious code may employ a combination of the methods discussed in Sections 3.2 through 3.5. For example, the Wily Hackers [162, 163] exploited trapdoors, masquerading, Trojan horses to capture passwords, and misuse of (acquired) authority. The Internet Worm [138, 150, 159] attacked four different trapdoors, as discussed in Section 5.1.1.

The most basic pest-program problem is the Trojan horse. The installation of a Trojan horse often exploits system vulnerabilities, which permit penetration by either unauthorized or authorized users. Furthermore, when they are executed, Trojan horses may exploit other vulnerabilities such as trapdoors. In addition, Trojan horses may cause the installation of new trapdoors. Thus, there can be a strong interrelationship between Trojan horses and trapdoors. Time bombs and logic bombs are special cases of Trojan horses. Letter bombs are messages that act as Trojan horses, containing bogus or interpretively executable data.

The Internet Worm provides a graphic illustration of how vulnerable some systems are to a variety of attacks. It is interesting that, even though some of those vulnerabilities were fixed or reduced, equally horrible vulnerabilities still remain today. (Resolution of the terminology war over whether the Internet Worm was a worm or a virus depends on which set of definitions is used.)

3.7 **Classical Security Vulnerabilities**

Many security flaws have been discovered in computer operating systems and application programs. In several cases, the flaws have been corrected or the resultant threats reduced. However, discovery of new flaws is generally running ahead of the elimination of old ones.

We consider here a few particularly noteworthy security flaws.

The C-compiler Trojan horse. A now-classical Trojan horse involved a modification to the object code of the C compiler such that, when the login program was next compiled, a trapdoor would be placed in the object code of login [167]. No changes were made either to the source code of the compiler or to the source code of the login routine. Furthermore, the Trojan horse was persistent, in that it would survive future recompilations. Thus, it might be called a **stealth** Trojan horse, because there were almost no visible signs of its existence, even after the login trapdoor had been enabled. This case was, in fact, perpetrated by the developers of Unix to demonstrate its feasibility and the potential power of a compiler Trojan horse and not as a malicious attack. But it is an extremely important case because of what it demonstrated.

A master-password trapdoor. Young and McHugh [179] (*SEN 12,* 3) describe an astounding flaw in the implementation of a password-checking algorithm that permitted bogus overly long master passwords to break into every system that used that login program, irrespective of what the real passwords actually were and despite the fact that the passwords were stored in an encrypted form. The flaw, shown in Figure 3.2, was subtle. It involved the absence of strong typing and bounds checking on the field in the data structure used to store the user-provided password (field b in the figure). As a result, typing an overly long bogus password overwrote the next field (field c in the figure), which supposedly contained the encrypted form of the expected password. By choosing the second half of the overly long sequence to be the encrypted form of the first half, the attacker was able to induce the system to believe that the bogus password was correct.

Undocumented extra argument bypasses security. Sun's login program for the 386i had an argument that bypassed authentication, installed for convenience. Discovery and abuse of that argument

```
Internal Data Structure              The Password-Checking Algorithm
= = = = = = = = = = = = = = = =      = = = = = = = = = = = = = = = = = =
a. User login name                   1. USER TYPES login name --> a
b. User-typed PW                     2. Stored encrypted PW --> c
c. Stored encrypted PW               3. USER TYPES PW --> b
d. Encrypted form of typed PW        4. Encrypt user typed PW --> d
                                     5. Compare c and d


        Step 1.     3.       2.           4.
        -----------------------------------------
          Store | Store | Stored     | Encrypted
          login | typed | encrypted  | typed
          name  | PW    | PW         | PW
          = = = = = = = = = = = = = = = = = = = = =
          |  a  |   b   |    c       |   d     |
          = = = = = = = = = = = = = = = = = = = = =
           Step 5 compares c and d.


The Master-Password Attack              The Perfect Match!
= = = = = = = = = = = = = = = = =       --------------------------
EMEMY CHOOSES a string --- "opqrst".    |  a  |   b   |c   |d      |
ENEMY ENCRYPTS string, gets "uvwxyz"    --------------------------
1. ENEMY TYPES any legitimate user name,
     which is entered into field a.     1.|Name|       |       |       |
2. The stored encrypted PW goes into c. 2.|Name|       |ghijkl|       |
3. ENEMY types PW "opqrstuvwxyz" ---
     which is entered into b (and c!).  3.|Name|opqrst|uvwxyz|       |
4. Field b is encrypted and stored in d.4.|Name|opqrst|uvwxyz|uvwxyz|
5. Surprise!  Fields c and d match.     5.           uvwxyz=uvwxyz
```

FIGURE 3.2 Master-password flaw and attack (PW = password)

would have allowed anyone to become omnipotent as root (*SEN 14*, 5).

Integer divide breaks security. Sun Microsystems announced and fixed a bug in September 1991: "A security vulnerability exists in the integer division on the SPARC architecture that can be used to gain root privileges." (This case is included in the on-line reportage from Sun as Sun Bug ID 1069072; the fix is Sun Patch ID 100376-01.)

Flaws in hardware or in applications. There are numerous security flaws that appear not in an operating system but rather in the application or, in some cases, in the hardware. Infrared-reprogrammable parking meters are vulnerable to attack by simulating the appropriate signals (*SEN 15*, 5). Cellular telephones are vulnerable to radio-frequency monitoring and tampering with identifiers. Several of the Reduced Instruction Set Computer (RISC) architectures can be crashed from user mode (*SEN 15*, 5). Hitachi Data Systems has the ability to download microcode dynamically to a running system; unfortunately, so do penetrators (*SEN 16*, 2). There was also a report of an intelligent system console terminal that was always logged in, for which certain function keys could be remotely reprogrammed, providing a Trojan horse superuser attack that could execute any desired commands and that could not be disabled (Douglas Thomson, *SEN 16*, 4).

3.8 **Avoidance of Security Vulnerabilities**

Subtle differences in the types of malicious code are relatively unimportant, and often counterproductive. Rather than try to make fine distinctions, we must attempt to defend against all the malicious-code types systematically, within a common approach that is capable of addressing the underlying problems. The techniques for an integrated approach to combatting malicious code necessarily cover the entire spectrum, except possibly for certain vulnerabilities that can be ruled out completely—for example, because of constraints in the operating environment, such as if all system access is via hard-wired lines to physically controlled terminals. Thus, multipurpose defenses are more effective in the long term than are defenses aimed at only particular attacks. Besides, the attack methods tend to shift with the defenses. For these reasons, it is not surprising that the defensive techniques in the system-evaluation criteria are, for the most part, all helpful in combatting malicious code and trapdoor attacks, or that the set of techniques necessary for preventing malicious code is closely related to the techniques necessary for avoiding trapdoors. The weak-link nature of the security problem suggests a close coupling between the two types of attack.

Malicious-code attacks such as Trojan horses and viruses are not covered adequately by the existing system-evaluation criteria. The existence of malicious code would typically not show up in a system design, except possibly for *accidental* Trojan horses (an exceedingly rare breed). Trojan horses remain a problem even in the most advanced systems.

There are differences among the different types of malicious-code problems, but it is the similarities and the overlaps that are most important. Any successful defense must recognize both the differences and the similarities, and must accommodate both. In addition, as noted in Chapter 4, the similarities between security and reliability are such that it is essential to consider both together — while handling them separately where that is convenient. That approach is considered further in Chapter 7, where the role of software engineering is discussed (in Section 7.8).

To avoid such vulnerabilities, and eventually to reduce the security risks, we need better security in operating systems (for mainframes, workstations, and personal computers), database management systems, and application systems, plus better informed system administrators and users. Techniques for improving system security are also discussed in Chapter 7.

3.9 Summary of the Chapter

Security vulnerabilities are ubiquitous, and are intrinsically impossible to avoid completely. The range of vulnerabilities is considerable, as illustrated in Figure 3.1 and Table 3.1. Some of those vulnerabilities are due to inadequate systems, weak hardware protection, and flawed operating systems; personal computers are particularly vulnerable if used in open environments. Other vulnerabilities are due to weaknesses in operations and use. Certain vulnerabilities may be unimportant in restrictive environments, as in the case of systems with no outside connectivity. Misuse by trusted insiders may or may not be a problem in any particular application. Thus, analyzing the threats and risks is necessary before deciding how serious the various vulnerabilities are.

Awareness of the spectrum of vulnerabilities and the concomitant risks can help us to reduce the vulnerabilities in any particular system or network, and can pinpoint where the use of techniques for defensive design and operation would be most effective.[1]

Challenges

C3.1   Vulnerabilities are often hidden from general view — for example, because computer-system vendors do not wish to advertise their system deficiencies, or because users are not sufficiently aware of the vulnerabilities. Such vulnerabilities, however, often are well known to communities that are interested in exploiting them, such as malicious hackers or professional thieves. Occasionally, the vulnerabilities are known to system administrators, although these people are sometimes the last to find out. Ask at least two knowledgeable system administrators how vulnerable they think their systems are to attack; you should not be surprised to get a spectrum of answers ranging from everything is fine to total disgruntlement with a system that is hopelessly nonsecure. (The truth is somewhere in between, even for sensibly managed systems.) Try to explain any divergence of viewpoints expressed by your interviewees, in terms of perceived vulnerabilities, threats, and risks. (You might also wish to consider the apparent knowledge, experience, truthfulness, and forthrightness of the people whom you questioned.)

C3.2   Consider a preencryptive dictionary attack on passwords. Suppose that you know that all passwords for a particular system are constrained to be of the form abcdef, where abc and def represent distinct lower-case three-letter English-language dictionary words. (For simplicity, you may assume that there are 50 such three-letter words.) How would the constrained password attack compare with an exhaustive search of all six-letter character strings? How does the constrained password attack compare with an attack using English-language words of not more than six letters? (For simplicity, assume that there are 7000 such words in the dictionary.) Readers of other languages may substitute their own languages. This challenge is intended only to illustrate the significant reduction in password-cracking effort that can result if it is known that password generation is subject to constraints.

C3.3   Describe two password-scheme vulnerabilities other than those listed in Section 3.3.2. You may include nontechnological vulnerabilities.

C3.4   For your favorite system, search for the 26 types of vulnerabilities described in this chapter. (If you attempt to demonstrate the existence of some of these vulnerabilities, please remember that this book does not recommend your exploiting such vulnerabilities without explicit authorization; you might wind up with a felony conviction. Furthermore, the defense that "no authorization was required" may not work.)

CHAPTER 4

Causes and Effects

*The causes and the effects
are not always
distinguishable.*

IN SECTION 4.1, WE CONSIDER the nature of causative factors associated with risks, including the roles of weak links and multiple simultaneously acting causes. In Section 4.2, we examine the distinctions and similarities between accidental and intentional causes.

4.1 Weak Links and Multiple Causes

A **weak link** in a system is a point at which a failure or an attack can render the system incapable of continuing to satisfy its requirements (for security, integrity, reliability, survivability, or whatever). As in a chain, in which loss of a single link destroys the entire chain, a weak link can represent the potential for a disaster triggered at a single point. We seek to design reliable systems and secure systems with no (single-point) weak links. However, it is also desirable to protect against multiple causes, because we can never guarantee that only single failures or attacks will occur at any one time.

The cable cuts in Chicago, the New York area, and White Plains noted in Section 2.1 involved single-point weak links whose severance resulted in major consequences because of correlated effects. The *RISKS* archives contain many other cases in which a single event appeared to be sufficient to trigger a disaster. In many of those cases, however, it was actually the confluence of several events that led to the triggered problem, as in the case of a Trojan horse written by one person, planted by another, and accidentally triggered by a third. In some of those cases involving multiple causes, the causative events were independent, whereas in other cases they were interrelated. This section discusses some of the underlying causes and their effects, and ways in which the causes can be interrelated.[1]

4.1.1 Single-Event Causes

We begin with a few cases of single weak links.

Cable cuts with widespread effects. The severance of the cable near White Plains, New York, that disconnected New England from the ARPAnet in 1986 (see Section 2.1) can be viewed as a single-point failure with respect to the cable, but as a highly correlated set of seven events with respect to the seven supposedly independent links. Whereas the intent of the ARPAnet configuration was clearly to provide multipath redundancy, the implementation was not faithful to the intent of the design and transformed a redundant design into one that was vulnerable to a single-point weakness. The Chicago and New York cable cuts (also noted in Section 2.1) further illustrate multiple correlated effects with respect to the abstraction of individual telephone calls or logical links, but with a single weak-link event at the level of the physical implementation (that is, the cable). In general, events at a particular layer of abstraction may seem to be unrelated, whereas they are interrelated at lower layers.

DC-10 crash blamed on failed indicator. An American Airlines DC-10 crashed because its stall-warning indicator failed. However, the weak-link cause was that the power supposedly driving the warning device was expected to come from the engine that had failed (*SEN 11*, 5).

Other cases. Referring to cases introduced in Section 2.2.2, the Atlas-Agena (missing hyphen), *Mariner I* (missing overbar in a handwritten equation), *Aries* (wrong resistor), *Gemini V* (incorrect programming short-cut), and *Phobos 1* (missing character) all resulted from human error. It is clear that a minor human error can cause inordinate effects.

Digital versus analog technologies. In general, the technology related to digital computers is substantively different from that of continuous mechanical systems. In mechanical systems, a small fault is usually transformed into a small error. In computer systems, the alteration of a single bit may be enough to cause devastation. The purpose of fault-tolerant computing, discussed in Section 7.7, is to prevent such far-reaching effects resulting from single causes.

4.1.2   Independent Multiple Causes

Next, we consider several examples that were caused (or at least reported to be caused) by independent events. In the first case, three analyses were all *independently wrong!*

Independent tests err harmoniously. In the Handley–Page Victor aircraft, three independent test methods were used to analyze the tailplane stability. Each of the three tests had an error, but coincidentally they all came up with roughly the same numbers—each wrong. This case is considered in greater detail in Section 7.5, during a discussion of the role of modeling and simulation (*SEN 11*, 2, 12, April 1986, plus erratum in *SEN 11*, 3, 25, July 1986).

Davis-Besse nuclear-power plant. The Davis-Besse nuclear-power plant emergency shutdown in June 1985 (noted in Section 2.10) involved the loss of cooling water, the breakdown of *14* separate components, and multiple human errors.[2]

Three Mile Island 2. The Three Mile Island near-meltdown (noted in Section 2.10) involved at least four equipment failures and a design flaw that prevented the correct temperature from being identified, plus serious misjudgment.

Simultaneous multiple disk failures down Toronto Stock Exchange. Even though the Tandem primary and backup computers both operated in the desired nonstop mode, three different and apparently independent disk-drive failures prevented the required data access and caused the Toronto Stock Exchange to shut down for 3 hours on August 16, 1989. (See *SEN 14*, 6, 8-9, Oct 1989.)

In each of these cases, a combination of supposedly independent circumstances was required. Several other coincidental cases are noted elsewhere, such as the multiple problems with the San Francisco BART and Muni Metro systems all occurring on December 9, 1986 (Section 2.5), and lightning striking twice in the same place (see Section 5.5.2).

4.1.3   **Correlated Multiple Causes**

In this subsection, we recall several cases from Chapter 2 in which multiple causes were involved, but in which there were correlations among the different causes.

The 1980 ARPAnet collapse, revisited. The four-hour collapse of the ARPAnet [139], which was noted in Section 2.1, required the confluence of four events: the absence of parity checking in memory (an implementation deficiency — parity checking existed in network communications); a flawed garbage-collection algorithm (a design oversimplification); and the concurrent existence of two bogus versions of a status message (resulting from dropped bits) and the legitimate message. These problems seem independent in origin, except that the two bit droppings might have been due to the same transient hardware memory problem. However, they were clearly interrelated in triggering the consequences.

The 1990 AT&T system runaway, revisited. The AT&T problem noted in Section 2.1 involved the confluence of several events: despite extensive testing before installation, the inability to detect an obscure load- and time-dependent flaw in the switch-recovery software; the presence of the same flaw in the recovery software of every switching system of that type; an untolerated hardware fault mode that caused a switch to crash and recover; because the recovery occurred during a period of heavy telephone traffic, neighboring switches that were unable to adjust to the resumption of activity from the first switch (due to the presence of two signals from the first previously dormant switch within about 10 milliseconds, which triggered the obscure flaw); and the triggering of the same effect in other switches, and later again in the first switch, propagating repeatedly throughout the network. (The effect finally died out when the load dwindled.)

In each of these two cases, there were triggering events (two different status words with dropped bits and a hardware crash, respectively) initiating global effects. However, the startling consequences depended on other factors as well.

Shuttle *Columbia* return delayed. As noted in Section 2.2.1, the shuttle mission STS-9 lost multiple computers in succession at the beginning of reentry, delaying the reentry. However, one loose piece of solder may have been responsible for all of the different processor failures.

Discovery **landing-gear design ignored the possibility of simultaneous failures.** The shuttle *Discovery* had landing-gear problems when returning to earth on April 19, 1985. One of the main wheel sets locked, and then another—blowing out one tire and shredding another. The Aerospace Safety Advisory Panel warned in January 1982 that the "design is such that should a tire fail, its mate (almost certainly) would also fail—a potential hazard." Indeed, both right tires had problems at the same time. Further, the ASAP again warned in January 1983 that "the landing gear tires and brakes have proven to be marginal and constitute a possible hazard to the shuttle." (All three of the earlier ASAP recommendations had been ignored.)[3]

Simultaneous engine failures. The case of the Transamerica Airlines DC-8/73 that had three of its four engines fail at the same time is noted in Section 2.4. In this case, there was a highly correlated common cause, although not one that would normally be considered as a weak link.

Topaz in the rough. An extraordinary case occurred at Digital Equipment Corporation's System Research Center in Palo Alto, California, on February 16, 1990, when the internal research environment Topaz became unusable. The in-house distributed name service at first seemed to be the culprit, but prolonged system difficulties were all attributable to a remarkable confluence of other interacting events. The description of this case by John DeTreville [36] is a classic, and is recommended as essential reading for system developers.

Patriot missiles. As noted in Section 2.3, the Patriot missile problems can be attributed to a variety of causes, including the clock problem and the nonadherence to the 14-hour maximum duty cycle. But those two causes are correlated, in that the latter would not necessarily have been a problem if the clock problem had not existed.

Common flaws in n-version programming. The concept known as *n-version programming* is the notion of having different programs written independently from the same specification, and then executing them in parallel, with conflicts resolved by majority voting. Brilliant and colleagues [16] have shown that, even when the different versions appear to be independent, these versions may exhibit common fault modes or have logically related flaws. In one startling case, two separately programmed versions of a more carefully developed and verified program were both wrong; because the other two programs coincidentally happened to be consistent with each other, they were able to outvote the correct version, as described by Brunelle and Eckhardt [18].

Two wrongs make a right (sometimes). Multiple faults can be self-canceling under certain conditions. Two somewhat obscure wiring errors (perhaps attributable to a single confusion) remained undetected for many years in the pioneering Harvard Mark I electromechanical computer in the 1940s. Each decimal memory register consisted of 23 10-position stepping switches, plus a sign switch. Registers were used dually as memory locations and as adders. The wires into (and out of) the least significant two digits of the last register were crossed, so that the least significant position was actually the second-to-least position, and vice versa, with respect to memory. No errors were detected for many years during which that register was presumably used for memory only, such as in the computation of tables of Bessel functions of the nth kind; the error on read-in corrected itself on read-out. The problem finally manifested itself on the $(n+1)$st set of tables when that register was used as an adder and the carry went into the wrong position. The problem was detected only because it was standard practice in those days to take repeated differences of successive computed values of the resulting tables; for example, kth differences of kth-order polynomials should be constant. The differencing was done by hand, using *very old* adding machines.

There are other examples as well, such as loss of nonredundant power sources in otherwise redundant systems, and replicated program variables (parameters) derived from a common source, as in the case of pilots entering erroneous data once and then being able to copy the input instead of having to reenter it. Further cases are considered in Section 5.5; they relate specifically to accidental denials of service.

4.1.4 **Reflections on Weak Links**

Networked systems provide an opportunity for identical flaws to exist throughout. In the case of the ARPAnet collapse, each node had identical software, and used the same overly permissive garbage-collection algorithm. In the case of the AT&T blockage, each switch had the identical flawed recovery software. In the case of the Internet Worm [35, 57, 138, 150, 159] discussed in Section 3.1 and 5.1.1, the worm threaded its way through the same flaws wherever they existed on similar systems throughout the ARPAnet and Milnet. The commonality of mechanism throughout a network or distributed system provides an opportunity for fault modes and security vulnerabilities that are pervasive.

One of the lessons of this section is that, when a persistent failure occurs, even though it may not yet be critical, the nature of the reliability (and security) problem has changed and the risks must be reevaluated. Indeed, if seemingly noncritical problems are ignored, the risks may tend to escalate dramatically. When further faults occur subsequently, the results can be disastrous. Consequently, individual faults should be repaired as rapidly as possible commensurate with the increased risks.

4.2 Accidental versus Intentional Causes

This section considers the potential distinctions between events that are caused accidentally and those that are caused intentionally. We see that weak links may cause serious problems in both cases.

A system may fail to do what was expected of it because of intentional misuse or unintended factors. Intentional system misbehavior may be caused by individuals or teams, acting in a variety of roles such as requirements specifiers, designers, implementers, maintainers, operators, users, and external agents, taking advantage of vulnerabilities such as those enumerated in Section 3.1. Accidental system misbehavior may be caused by the same variety of people plus innocent bystanders, as well as by external events not caused by people (for example, "acts of God"). Types of problems and their accompanying risks are suggested in Sections 1.2 and 1.3.

We next consider the similarities and differences between intentionally caused problems and unintentionally caused ones.

4.2.1   Accidents That Could Have Been Triggered Intentionally

If an event can happen accidentally, it often could be caused intentionally.

Where existing systems have suffered accidental calamities, similar or identical disasters might have been caused intentionally, either by authorized users or by penetrators exploiting security vulnerabilities. Examples of past accidental events follow:

The 1980 ARPAnet collapse. The ARPAnet collapse discussed in Sections 2.1 and 4.1 required a confluence of a hardware-implementation weakness (the lack of parity checking in memory) and a weak software garbage-collection algorithm, and was triggered by hardware faults in memory. The global shutdown was clearly an unintentional problem. However, given the hardware weakness and the software weakness, this fault mode could have been triggered intentionally by the malicious insertion into the network of two or more bogus status messages, which would have had the identical effect. (See [139].)

The 1986 ARPAnet Northeast disconnect. The ARPAnet severance of New England from the rest of the network, discussed in Section 2.1, was caused by a backhoe cutting seven supposedly independent links, all in the same conduit. Knowledge of such a commonality in a more critical network could lead to an attractive target for a malicious perpetrator. Similar conclusions can be drawn about the many other cable cuts noted in Section 2.1.

The 1990 AT&T collapse. The collapse of the AT&T long-distance network depended on the existence of flawed switch-recovery software in each of the switches. The global slowdown was triggered accidentally by a crash of a single switch. However, a maliciously caused crash of a single switch would have produced exactly the same results, perhaps exploiting external development and maintenance routes into the switch controllers. This example illustrates the interrelations between reliability and security threats.

The 1988 Internet Worm. Inherent weaknesses in system software (finger), passwords (for example, vulnerability to dictionary-word preencryptive password attacks) and networking software (the sendmail debug option and .rhosts tables) resulted in severe degradation of Berkeley Unix systems attached to the ARPAnet and Milnet. Although the penetrations were intentional (but not malicious), the rampant proliferation within each attacked system was accidental. However, it is now clear that far worse consequences could have been caused intentionally by a malicious attack exploiting those vulnerabilities. This case is discussed in greater detail in Section 3.1 and [138, 150, 159].)

Chernobyl, 1986. Intentional Chernobyl-like disasters could be triggered by utility operators or disgruntled employees, particularly in control systems in which shutting off the safety controls is an administrative option. In some control systems for other applications, there are remote access paths for diagnosis and maintenance whose misuse could result in similarly serious disasters.

Interference. Various cases of electronic, electromagnetic, and other forms of accidental interference have been observed, and are noted in Section 5.5. Many of those could have been done intentionally. Indeed, several cases of malicious interference are noted in Section 5.4. Some of these have involved intentional piggybacking onto and spoofing of existing facilities, such as has occurred in several up-link cable-TV satellite takeovers.

Accidental security problems. Numerous accidental security violations such as the unintended broadcasting of a password file can also lead to serious reliability and integrity problems. Accidental security problems are considered in Section 5.2. Many of these could have been caused intentionally.

4.2.2   Potential Malicious Acts That Could Also Be Triggered Accidentally

If an event can be caused intentionally, it often could happen accidentally (even if less feasibly).

Some intentional perpetrations may require combinatoric or sequential events, or possibly multiperson collusions. In cases requiring complex circumstances, the feasibility of accidental occurrence generally is less than for the same circumstances to occur intentionally. However, for simple events, the accidental feasibility is more comparable to the intentional feasibility. Examples of potential malicious acts follow.

Intentional deletion. On a logged-in Unix keyboard, a malicious passerby could type rm * (rm is an abbreviation for remove, and the asterisk denotes any name in the current directory); as the result (when completed by a carriage return), every file in the directory would be deleted. A legitimate user of the same directory might accidentally type the same sequence of keystrokes. Alternatively, that user might attempt to delete all files whose names end with the number 8, by intending to type rm *8 but instead typing rm *9 by mistake and then attempting to delete the 9 but instead hitting the terminating carriage return in an effort to press the *delete* key. (The *delete* key and the *carriage-return* key are adjacent on many keyboards.)

Covert activities. Intentional planting of Trojan horses and exploitation of covert channels are examples of covert threats. The likelihood of an equivalent coherent event happening accidentally seems far-fetched in general. However, the triggering of an already planted Trojan horse (as opposed to its implanting) is usually an accidental event, done by an unsuspecting person or by a normal computer-system activity. Such accidental triggering of an intentionally planted pest program bridges the gap between the two types of activity. Furthermore, personal-computer viruses have accidentally been included in vendor software deliveries on several occasions.

Malicously caused outages. Milnet and other similar networks can be intentionally crashed by subverting the network control. This type of vulnerability existed for many years in the old ARPAnet, in which the nodes (Interface Message Processors, or IMPs) were maintained by Bolt, Beranek and Newman (BBN) from Cambridge, Massachusetts, using the network itself for remote debug access and for downloading new software. Subverting the network control would have been relatively easy, although — to the best of my knowledge — this vulnerability was never attacked. Malicious remote downloading of bogus node software that subsequently prevented remote downloading would be a particularly nasty form of this attack. Such a collapse would seem to be relatively unlikely to occur accidentally. However, a trapdoor that was intentionally installed could be triggered accidentally. For example, a trapdoor is sometimes installed for constructive emergency use in debugging or maintenance (although that is a dangerous practice). Section 5.1.2 gives examples of pest programs that were installed for malicious purposes, such as subsequent attempts at blackmail or employment to repair the problem; those programs also could have been triggered accidentally. In addition, penetration of telephone network-control systems has also occurred, and may have resulted in outages.

4.3 Summary of the Chapter

Considerable commonality exists between reliability and security. Both are weak-link phenomena. For example, certain security measures may be desirable to hinder malicious penetrators, but do relatively little to reduce hardware and software faults. Certain reliability measures may be desirable to provide hardware fault tolerance, but do not increase security. On the other hand, properly chosen system architectural approaches and good software-engineering practice can enhance both security and reliability. Thus, it is highly advantageous to consider both reliability and security within a common framework, along with other properties such as application survivability and application safety.

From the anecdotal evidence, there are clearly similarities among certain of the causes of accidental and intentional events. However, some accidents would have been difficult to trigger intentionally, and some malicious acts would have been difficult to reproduce accidentally. There are no essential functional differences between accidental and intentional threats, with respect to their potential effects; the consequences may be similar — or indeed the same. However, there are some differences in the techniques for addressing the different threats. The obvious conclusion is that we must anticipate both accidental and intentional types of user and system behavior; neither can be ignored.

In many cases of system disasters, whether accidentally or intentionally caused, a confluence of multiple events was involved that resulted in significant deviations from expected system behavior. This phenomenon is discussed in Section 4.1, although that discussion centers on unintentional events — that is, cases of unreliability. The discussion is immediately extensible to intentional misuse — that is, to violations of the intended security or integrity.

- Some accidental system problems that seemed attributable to single weak links were actually due to multiple events (independent or correlated). The 1980 ARPAnet collapse is an example.

- Some system problems that seemed attributable to multiple events were actually due to single weak links. The 1986 ARPAnet Northeast disconnect noted in Section 2.1 is an example. Many of these cases also could have been triggered by a single malicious act.

- Some system problems that seemed attributable to independent events were in reality caused by correlated events. The 1980 ARPAnet collapse noted in Section 2.1 illustrates this correlation, as does the case in which two separately programmed versions of a thoroughly developed module exhibited a common flaw that permitted them to outvote the correct version [18].

Thus, it becomes imperative for system designers to anticipate the occurrence of multiple deleterious events, whether accidentally or intentionally caused, and to anticipate problems of both reliability and security. Problems that are seemingly completely unrelated to security may nevertheless have security implications. Examples — such as the Sun integer divide that could be used to gain root privileges, noted in Section 3.7 — are scattered throughout this book.

A system cannot be secure unless it is adequately reliable, and cannot be either reliable or available if it is not adequately secure. There are many further references to system reliability (see Chapter 2) and to system security (see Chapters 3 and 5). However, there is only sparse literature on the subject of systems that must be both reliable and secure.[4]

Challenges

C4.1   Identify how security and reliability interact, in hardware, in system software, in applications, and in environments transcending computer and communication systems. Include confidentiality, integrity, and availability among your security requirements.

C4.2   Pick a system with which you are familiar. Find and describe its main weak links with respect to any of the sources of risks in Section 1.2.

C4.3   Reconsider your design for Challenge C2.4. Having read this chapter, can you find additional sources of failure, including multiple weak links?

CHAPTER 5

Security and Integrity Problems

*Security used to be
an inconvenience sometimes,
but now it is a necessity
all the time.*

MARTINA NAVRATILOVA,
AFTER THE STABBING OF
MONICA SELES BY A FAN
OF STEFFI GRAF, 1993

WE NEXT CONSIDER A VARIETY OF PROBLEMS relating to system security, including confidentiality, integrity, and availability, among other requirements. In Section 5.1, we examine various malicious and other purposeful computer misuses that relate to security and integrity. In subsequent sections, we examine security accidents (Section 5.2) and computer misuse as it relates to applications — including spoofs (Section 5.3), denials of service (Sections 5.4 and 5.5), financial misuse and accidents (Sections 5.6 and 5.7), electronic voting (Section 5.8), and incarceration of inmates (Section 5.9). Privacy issues are deferred until Chapter 6.

5.1 Intentional Misuse

Every system has vulnerabilities.
Every system can be compromised.

There have been many widely publicized cases of computer misuse, including attacks by the West German Wily Hackers, various computer-based credit-card and telephone frauds, increasingly many types and instances of viruses in personal computers, and the Internet Worm. A few perpetrators have received jail sentences.

Just a few of the most interesting cases of malicious computer misuse are noted here. Many others are given in the on-line *Risks Forum* (see Appendix A) and the quarterly issues of *Software Engineering Notes* — for example, see [113].

5.1.1 Misuse by Nonauthorized or Unexpected Users

A few representative cases of misuse are included in this section.

The Internet Worm. Late on the evening of November 2, 1988, a program was released that spread itself iteratively across Berkeley Unix systems throughout the Internet (the logical extension of what used to be the ARPAnet, encompassing many other networks) [35, 57, 138, 150, 159]. The worm program exploited three different trapdoors: the debug option of sendmail, gets (used in the implementation of finger), and remote logins exploiting .rhost files. It also made a somewhat gratuitous attempt to use a few hundred passwords previously obtained by selected preencryptive matching attacks. The result was a self-propagating worm with viruslike infection abilities that was able to copy itself into many systems and then to run. It moved from system to system, entering by whichever of these flaws it found first.

The Internet Worm provides an example of the intentional propagation of effects from system to system throughout a network (but, as noted in Section 4.2, the proliferation within each system was not intended); access to one system was used iteratively to gain access to other systems. Although multiple weak links were exploited, there was essentially only one agent that was causing the iterative propagation, and the four weak links were the same throughout.

The perpetrator, Robert Tappan Morris, was indicted on a felony count, and found guilty. He was sentenced to community service with a fine of $10,000 (*SEN 14*, 6; *15*, 3; *16*, 2). At his trial, Morris testified that about 50 percent of his time in developing the worm had been devoted to preventing it from proliferating within any given system, while trying to maintain its presence in case a copy was detected and deleted.

The Internet Worm's exploitation of sendmail, finger, and .rhosts required *no* authorization! Debate over whether Morris exceeded authority is therefore somewhat moot.

Seldom has the computer community been so divided by one incident. In the final analysis, there seem to be relatively widespread moderate sentiments that the Worm was a badly conceived experiment that should never have been attempted, and that the sentence of its creator was essentially fair—neither meting out excessive punishment nor failing to provide a deterrent to would-be emulators. But many diverse positions have also been expressed. On one side are people who think that Morris should have received an extensive jail term, or perhaps should have been barred from the computer profession for life, or that companies willing to employ him should be boycotted. On the other side are people who think that Morris became a sacrificial lamb to his country in demonstrating a diverse collection of flaws that have long cried out for greater recognition, or that he was an accidental whistleblower whose most serious mistake was a programming error that enabled the Worm to replicate out of control *within* each penetrated system, contrary to what he had intended. Then there are people who think that the ARPAnet was a sandbox anyway, whose main original reason for existence was to conduct experiments with networking! Incidentally, once it was evident that the Worm had run amok, Morris asked a friend to post a message explaining the Worm and how to provide an antidote. Unfortunately, that message did not spread widely because of the network congestion; even worse, the Department of Defense Milnet authorities cut that network off from the rest of the Internet, so that Milnet system administrators were in the dark as to the problem and its potential remediation. Doug McIlroy [89] expressed concerns that many of the potential lessons may have gone unnoted. "Those who repudiate only the final misdeed implicitly absolve the prior lapses in ethics and oversight that made the worm fiasco possible. They signal that you can get away with building, promoting, distributing, and selling deceitful software as long as you are not caught exploiting it." The debate still continues, while similar risks persist.

West German cracking activities. West German crackers planted Trojan horses, attacked NASA systems, and exploited flaws in a new operating-system release. A perpetrator was arrested in Paris. After detecting breakins at the Lawrence Berkeley Laboratory, Cliff Stoll expended considerable effort to track down one of the perpetrators, Markus Hess [162, 163]. Hess and the others were also accused of computer espionage for the the Soviet spy agency, the KGB. Three of the Wily Hackers were indicted on espionage charges, and received mild convictions for espionage but none for the system attacks.[1]

Dutch crackers. The Netherlands, which previously had not been particularly active in arresting people for malicious hacking, took two young men into custody on January 27, 1992. They were charged with forgery (changing files), racketeering (masquerading), and vandalism, with a motive of "fanatical hobbyism."[2]

"Mad Hacker" jailed. Nicholas Whiteley (self-styled as the "Mad Hacker") was sentenced on June 7, 1990, to 4 months in jail for malicious damage to property (tapes), perhaps because the British Computer Misuse Act was not in effect until August 29, 1990, and would not cover his computer-breakin activities. His appeal failed (*SEN 15*, 5; *16*, 2).

Cracking NASA. Richard G. Wittman of Colorado was accused of two felonies in cracking into NASA computers and of five misdemeanors for interfering with government operations. He was sentenced to a 3-year probation period and to mental health treatment (*SEN 17*, 1; *17*, 3).

Other breakins. There were numerous other reports of arrests for break-ins. Nine high-school students in Pennsylvania were arrested along with other U.S. students for breaking into computers and for obtaining millions of dollars worth of goods and services using credit-card numbers gained through telephone taps. In the same week in July 1987, two other people were arrested for breakins at Stanford and Berkeley (*SEN 12*, 4).

Australian activities. Three Australians were indicted for breaking into and tampering with Internet computers in the United States and with other computers in Australia.[3] Another was fined $750 for unauthorized access (*SEN 15*, 3). A 20-year-old computer-science student was charged with unauthorized access and with 47 counts of misusing the Australian telephone system for unauthorized computer access to U.S. computers (*SEN 16*, 4).

Wollon-gong but not forgotten. A support engineer who had her employment with the Wollongong Group of Palo Alto, California, terminated for "nonperformance" in November 1987 subsequently used her password (which surprisingly was still valid 2 months later) to offload proprietary source code.[4]

"Terminus." Computer consultant Leonard Rose pleaded guilty to federal felony wire-fraud charges for stealing Unix source code. He was also accused of having distributed a Trojan horse program that would allow him to gain unauthorized system access.[5]

Telephone phreaking and related misuse. From the early days of tone generators to spoof the coin-box bongs for nickels, dimes, and quarters, to "blue boxes" that emit appropriate internal operator tones, to credit-card scams and computer penetrations that enable free telephone calls, the telephone phreakers have been notably successful over the years. Recently, law enforcement has been a little more active in prosecuting the phreakers. An 11-count federal indictment accused five metropolitan New York City youths of computer tampering and fraud, wire fraud, wiretapping, and conspiracy related to misuse of telephones, computers, and credit (*SEN 17*, 4). Various other indictments have also been reported (for example, *SEN 15*, 3). Telephone-system penetrations have taken place, involving misuse of switching systems and information systems. Herbert Zinn ("Shadow Hawk") was accused of breaking into AT&T and government computer systems, and of stealing software (*SEN 12*, 4; *14*, 2). Kevin Mitnick was arrested when he was 17 for breaking into Pacific Bell computer systems and switches, altering telephone bills, and stealing data. He was arrested 8 years later for breaking into a Digital Equipment Computer, stealing a computer security system, and making free long-distance telephone calls.[6] There are numerous other cases as well.

Cellular-telephone fraud. Capturing and replaying cellular-telephone identifiers to avoid charges is amazingly simple, and is increasingly popular. The identifying electronic serial numbers (ESNs) can be acquired by using scanners; the stolen ESNs are implanted in "cloned" cellular telephones whose call charges are then billed to the unknowing victim of the stolen ESN. In one early example, 18 people were arrested for altering cellular mobile telephones (*SEN 12*, 2). The problem of cellular-telephone fraud has become significantly more severe in recent years, and the losses are now on the order of $0.5 billion each year.

Prestel. A British reporter was given a demonstration of how to penetrate British Telecom's Prestel Information Service. He was shown what appeared to read Prince Philip's electronic mailbox (which was actually a dummy) and watched a financial market database being altered (again, possibly a demo version). The event was widely reported.[7] The subsequent prosecution was the first such case in Britain (*SEN 11*, 3), but the conviction was reversed by the Appeal Court and the House of Lords (*SEN 13*, 3).

TV or not TV. A television editor who had been hired away from another station was charged with unlawfully entering his former employer's computer system. He had originally helped to create the system's security (*SEN 14*, 2).

Fox Television discovered that their computers had been penetrated by a journalist who had gotten access to sensitive files (*SEN 15*, 3).

Debit-card copying. There have been reports of the magnetic strips on public-transit fare cards (for example, for the Metro in Washington, D.C., and for the San Francisco Bay Area Rapid Transit, BART) being copied repeatedly onto cards with almost no remaining value. Even though the information is encrypted, the copy/playback attack works.

Database misuse. A 14-year-old boy from Fresno, California, used "secret" (!) access codes obtained from an on-line bulletin board, and accessed the TRW credit information system, from which he acquired credit-card numbers, with which he charged at least $11,000 worth of merchandise (*SEN 15*, 1). A 12-year-old boy from Grosse Ile, Michigan, was arrested for tapping into TRW credit files and posting credit-card numbers on electronic bulletin boards (*SEN 15*, 3). Another 14-year-old from Prairie Village, Kansas, browsed through confidential files of at least 200 companies, and was also able to access an Air Force satellite-positioning system (*SEN 14*, 6). The ease with which such database accesses can be accomplished suggests the expression "child's play."

Voice-mail cracking. The Certified Grocers of California (CerGro) had their voice-mail system cracked. Two hundred voice-mailboxes were reprogrammed for illicit purposes, including a database for stolen credit-card numbers, cocaine prices, and prostitution (*SEN 13*, 4). The Houston City Hall voice-mail system had been configured with no passwords required; someone rerouted confidential voice-mail messages to nonintended recipients (*SEN 16*, 4).

Trial by BBoard. In the aftermath of an article he wrote on malicious hacking activities, *Newsweek* reporter Richard Sandza was subjected to an electronic bulletin-board trial (in absentia, of course), and pronounced guilty. Consequently, the retribution involved someone accessing the TRW credit database to gain and post Sandza's credit-card numbers. As a result, $1100 in merchandise was charged to him, and his home computer was crashed remotely via his unlisted telephone number (*SEN 10*, 1).

Politicians' computers get hit. In their Washington, D.C., offices, Republican U.S. Representatives Zschau and McCain each had computer systems penetrated via dialup lines, with letters to constituents deleted and addresses deleted from mailing lists (*SEN 11*, 2). In New

Jersey, a Republican state legislature staffer admitted breaking into the Democrats' computer and obtaining thousands of documents (*SEN 16*, 1). Information on about 17,000 of Ross Perot's supporters disappeared from a campaign computer, although it was not known for sure whether the deletion was done maliciously or inadvertently (*SEN 17*, 4).

Student grade fraud. In various cases, students have gained access to computers to change their course grades, at Stanford around 1960 and, in more recent cases, in Alaska, Columbia University, and the University of Georgia (*SEN 8*, 5; *16*, 3).

5.1.2   Pest-Program Exploitations

There have been many instances of Trojan horses, including time bombs, logic bombs, and personal-computer virus attacks. Indeed, new strains of viruses are continuing to emerge at an alarming rate.

Trojan Horse Exploitations

A few of the more interesting cases involving Trojan horses are included here.

Trojan dog. Richard Streeter of CBS, Inc., downloaded onto his PC a bulletin-board program that was advertised as providing enhanced graphics. Instead, the program wiped out all of his files and displayed "Arf! Arf! Got You!" on his screen.[8]

Trojan turkey. A program passed around the ARPAnet reportedly drew a nice picture of a turkey on your screen when you compiled and ran it. The program also deleted all unprotected files (*SEN 13*, 3).

Password-catching Trojan horses. Beginning in fall 1993, Trojan horses appeared in the network software of numerous Internet computers. In particular, `telnet`, a program that permits logins to and from remote sites, was altered so that it could capture all passwords presented to it. This type of attack is an increasingly serious threat, and is ongoing.[9]

In the PC-VAN network joining NEC PC9800 computers in Japan, user passwords were captured by a Trojan horse and recorded in a cryptographic form that could later be decrypted by the attacker (*SEN 13*, 4).

Emergency system Trojan horsed. A former employee maliciously modified the software of the Community Alert Network installed in New York and in San Jose, California. The software did not fail until it was needed in response to a chemical leak at Chevron's refinery in Richmond, California. The emergency system was then down for 10 hours (*SEN 17*, 4).

Beware of smart telephones. A scam was detected involving third-party pay telephones that could capture and record credit-card numbers for later illegal reuse (*SEN 16*, 3). This type of Trojan horse attack is also seen in a teller-machine fraud noted in Section 5.6.

Time-Bomb and Logic-Bomb Exploitations

Several specific forms of Trojan horses are considered next—namely, a few cases of intentionally inserted Trojan horse attacks involving time bombs or logic bombs. Several of these cases involved attempted blackmail or extortion.

General Dynamics logic bomb. A programmer, Michael John Lauffenberger, was convicted of logic bombing General Dynamics' Atlas rocket database. He had quit his job, but was hoping to be rehired at a premium when the time bomb went off, because he thought he would be the only one who could fix it. It was discovered accidentally by another programmer.[10]

New York insurance database logic bomb. While working as a consultant to a New York City law firm to upgrade its medical-payments database system, Donald R. Lewis planted a logic bomb intended to crash the system when presented with a claim numbered 56789. The law firm paid him an extra $7000 to do the repair job (removing a conditional statement from the program), but then must have discovered what happened, because the bottom line was that he had to pay them back the $25,000 he had gotten for the entire job (*SEN 17*, 4).

Time bomb deletes brokerage records. Donald Gene Burleson was prosecuted on felony charges for planting a time bomb that, shortly after he was fired, deleted more than 168,000 brokerage records of USPA & IRA in Fort Worth, Texas. He was convicted and fined (2 to 10 years, up to $5000).[11]

Logic bomb in Lithuanian nuclear-power plant. Section 2.10 notes the case of a power-plant employee who installed a pest program in the control software, hoping to be paid to repair the damage.

Typesetter disables employer's system? A British freelance printer was accused of taking revenge on a company that refused to pay him £2000 by locking up their computer with a password only he knew.

The company eventually went bankrupt and sued him. He denied the charges.[12]

Pandair logic bomb. A contract programmer, James McMahon, was accused of planting logic bombs in a Pandair Freight system in the United Kingdom. One locked up terminals, and the other was set to wipe out memory. However, he was cleared of all charges for insufficient evidence (*SEN 13*, 1; *13*, 2).

Viruses

There are many different types of viruses, and a continual emergence of variants. The number of distinct personal-computer virus strains increased from five at the beginning of 1988 to over 1000 early in 1992, and has continued to grow dramatically since then; numbers over 2000 were commonly cited by mid-1993. The increase in the number of virus strains and the growth of the antivirus industry are both enormous.

Self-modifying (**polymorphic**) viruses and stealth viruses are emerging that can conceal their existence in a variety of ways, including by distributing themselves in smaller pieces.

Personal-computer viruses would be much less of a problem if the personal-computer operating systems had any serious security that could permit the operating system to protect itself against viruses. Note that a virus executes as though it were the legitimate user of the system, and thus is simultaneously a masquerader and a Trojan horse operating with whatever privileges the user has (that is, normally omnipotent!).

The on-line *RISKS* archives tracked many of the early reports of personal-computer viruses. However, it rapidly became clear that continuing to do so would be a losing battle. Fortunately, at about that time, the VIRUS-L newsgroup appeared (known as comp.virus on USENET—see Appendix A).[13]

We list here only a few of the highlights of the virus phenomenon.

Jerusalem Virus attacks. A strain of the Jerusalem (a.k.a. Israeli) virus that triggers each Friday the Thirteenth infected the U.S. Government Printing Office (*SEN 15*, 2). On Friday the Thirteenth of April, 1990, there were attacks all over China, which was also plagued by attacks on government computers in more than 90 departments in September of 1991 (*SEN 15*, 2; *15*, 3). The World Bank was attacked in the same month (*SEN 16*, 4).

"Clearing up" the Italian judiciary. The Gp 1 virus was found throughout many Italian judicial computer systems. Its effect was to award the maximum security clearance to uncleared users (*SEN 17*, 3).

The AIDS Trojan horse. Joseph Popp allegedly mailed more than 20,000 floppy disks from the "PC Cyborg Corp" that supposedly contained information on AIDS, but actually had a Trojan horse, which when executed demanded £200 Sterling to eradicate the pest program (*SEN 15*, 1). Popp was subsequently extradited from the United States to Britain and accused on 11 charges, including attempted blackmail of medical institutes (*SEN 17*, 2).

Contaminated products. One of the stranger aspects of viral propagation is that several of the products designed to detect and remove viruses were themselves contaminated, resulting in further contaminations when they were used. Recorded instances included a contaminated antiviral program called flushot, which itself contained a Trojan horse. In addition, Leading Edge shipped 6000 IBM-compatible personal-computer systems with the Michelangelo virus, which wipes the hard disk on the artist's birthday, March 6. Intel shipped 800 copies of infected LANSpool 3.01 computer network software, also infected with Michelangelo. DaVinci Systems shipped 900 copies of eMAIL 2.0 demonstration disks that were infected with Michelangelo. Prior to the birthday, Norton released a free utility to detect Michelangelo; unfortunately, it had undocumented "features" that could wipe anything after the first partition. On the birthday, various Michelangelo attacks were reported, in New Zealand, Australia, Japan, China, Poland, Germany, South Africa, and Canada. There were also some instances in the United States, although the enormous media hype that preceded the day may well have raised the levels of awareness sufficiently to minimize further damage. Novell accidentally shipped a self-masking "stealth" Stoned III virus to as many as 3800 of its customers (*SEN 17*, 2). The Jerusalem virus noted previously was found in a commercial release of game software (*SEN 15*, 3). Appendix 9 of Ferbrache [44] lists 17 distinct vendor-software packages that were contaminated in the shrinkwrap. MSDOS, Macintosh, Atari, and Amiga viruses are included in the list.

Even a bogus scare can cause troubles. A Friday the Thirteenth attack on the SunOS system was widely rumored on the day before to have been planted by a disgruntled employee of Sun Microsystems. The rumor had almost no substance (there had actually been a clock-related bug fix). However, some of the panic caused one installation to set the clock back so that Friday would appear to be Thursday — and its screenblank program then had to wait 24 hours before it could check for further activity (*SEN 13*, 3).

5.1.3   Misuse by Authorized Personnel

In various cases, misuse has been perpetrated by a user with some authorized access, possibly exploiting system vulnerabilities to gain additional access as well.

Insider frauds. Computer-based financial frauds committed by insiders are included in Section 5.6. Election frauds are discussed in Section 5.8.

Insider misuse of databases. Examples of insider misuse relating to privacy violations in law-enforcement and government databases are given in Section 6.2. There have also been reports of insiders altering law-enforcement databases to delete references to citations and arrest warrants.

Evidence tampering. The ease with which fingerprint evidence can be faked is demonstrated by a New York State Police scandal in which, over a period of 10 years from 1982 to 1992, all five investigators in the identification unit of Troop C in Sidney, New York, were implicated in repeated cases of evidence tampering, particularly to provide incriminating "evidence" where none existed. They were responsible for investigations in five upstate counties. Various prison sentences were meted out.[14]

Digital evidence is also subject to tampering, as illustrated by the novel and movie, *Rising Sun.* Even if great care is exerted to protect the integrity of digitally recorded images, those images can be altered with relative ease by appropriate insiders. The same is true of electronic mail, as noted in Section 5.3. On the other hand, such alterations can be used constructively, as in the editing of facial expressions to produce the proper smiles on the Tyrannosaurus Rex in *Jurassic Park* and the removal of a pageturner's hand from a video of a Yo-Yo Ma performance.

5.1.4   Other Cases

An enumeration of computer security problems is never complete. Here are two miscellaneous types.

Theft of computers. Several cases of stolen computers have been noted, including potential misuse of data. In one strange case, a thief purloined the computer of a tax preparer, but later returned the floppy disks (*SEN 13*, 3).

Inference. In many cases, information that is not directly accessible to users—whether or not they are authorized—can be inferred, by logical inference or by exploitation of covert channels (see Section 3.4). An example is provided by someone taking a test who noticed a reverse symmetry in the emerging answers; by intuiting that the mask used to score the first half of the test would also be used for the second half when the mask was turned over and upside down, the test taker was able to guess correctly the answers to the questions he had not yet answered, and to detect incorrect answers where there was a mismatch in those already answered (*SEN 16*, 3). (Other examples of inference possibilities are given in Challenges C5.2 and C5.3 at the end of the chapter.)

5.1.5   Comments on Intentional Misuse

The increased prevalence of breakins, misuse by insiders, and personal-computer viruses may be considered a symptom of problems to come. Computer systems and networks often do not enforce sufficient security, and, in many cases, they are intrinsically vulnerable. The existing laws are not adequately applicable. (What do "access" and "authorized access" mean?) Ethical teachings are desirable, but may not have much effect on determined misusers, especially in a society in which fraud and creative malpractices are commonplace—and are even considered as successes by some people.

Easy access is not a virtue in systems in which critical functionality (for example, life preserving) can be compromised. Security technology has been advancing in recent years. However, attack techniques have escalated accordingly—somewhat similar to strains of bacteria that continually mutate to develop immunity to new antibiotics. Preencryptive dictionary attacks on password files described in 1979 by Bob Morris and Ken Thompson [96] have been used, for example, in penetrations of U.S. computers from Australia and Europe and within the United States. Other password weaknesses are also being exploited. Electronic capture of vital information is becoming easier.

The security provided by many computer systems is fundamentally flawed. In some cases, valid security techniques exist but are not being used properly. We need hardware and software systems that can hinder misuse by insiders as well as by penetrators. People are the ultimate problem. Despite improving technology, serious risks remain.

Although cases of security penetrations and misuses by authorized users continue, many such cases remain unreported while further vulnerabilities lurk—waiting to be abused. Some of the deeper implications of the overall security problem remain obscured from general view.

5.2 Security Accidents

In addition to security problems caused by malicious misuse, we also consider accidental security problems, such as the following.

The password file and the message of the day were interchanged. One day in the early 1960s on the MIT Compatible Time-Sharing System (CTSS), the entire unencrypted password file appeared as the message of the day whenever anyone logged in. This mishap was the result of two different people using the same editor in the same directory, one editing the password file and the other editing the message-of-the-day file, with the editor program using fixed names for the temporary files. The original design had made the implicit assumption that the editor would never be used more than once at the same time in the same directory. See [96, 28] and a note from F.J. Corbató in *SEN 15*, 2, who added this insight: "The tale has at least two morals: First, design bugs are often subtle and occur by evolution with early assumptions being forgotten as new features or uses are added to systems. Second, even system programmers make mistakes so that prudent system management must be based on expecting errors and not on perfection."

Discovery **software exposure.** In the preparations at Rockwell International for the shuttle *Discovery*'s return on August 22, 1988, the protection provided by IBM's access-control facility RACF was accidentally disabled, leaving the software capable of being modified by programmers who were not supposed to access the system except in "browse" mode. Changes to the software could have been made either accidentally or intentionally at that time (*SEN 13, 3*).

Incomplete deletions and other residues. The *RISKS* archives include quite a few cases of information residues resulting from improper deletion of data. The Air Force sold off more than 1200 surplus digital tapes and almost 2000 analog tapes, many with sensitive data that had not been erased. Five out of the seven installations investigated had inadvertently released tapes with secret data.[15] The confidential files of a federal prosecutor in Lexington, Kentucky, remained on disks of a broken computer that were sold off for $45 to a dealer in used government equipment. The data included sealed federal indictments and employee personal data. Because the machine was broken, normal deletion did not work and magnetic erasure had been attempted (*SEN 15*, 5). A similar case involved FBI data (*SEN 16*, 3). A British military laptop was stolen, containing "extremely sensitive" information on the Gulf War operations (*SEN 16*, 2). Because many systems perform deletion by setting a *deleted* flag or removing a pointer, rather than by actually doing the physical deletion of the data, this problem is much more widespread than is generally realized.

Damning residues. Whether such residues are good or bad may depend on who you are. For example, White House backup computer files remained undeleted after the Irangate saga (*SEN 12*, 2). A similar case involved Brazilian president Fernando Collor de Mello (*SEN 18*, 1, 7). The residual presence of Gulf War battle plans provided incriminating evidence in a case involving the theft of $70,000 worth of computers (*SEN 17*, 4).

After-effects from residues. In a further twist, a New Zealand man bought old disks from Citibank that apparently contained residual details of overseas accounts and money-laundering activities. His death under mysterious circumstances was suspected to be linked to his possession of the damaging data (*SEN 18*, 1, 13).

5.3   **Spoofs and Pranks**

This section considers a few mischievous spoofs and pranks.[16]

5.3.1   **Electronic-Mail Spoofs**

There have been several now-classical cases of April Fools' Day electronic mail (E-mail). Of particular note are the ground-breaking

1984 message allegedly from Chernenko and the 1988 message allegedly from Gene Spafford. (Perhaps leap years are special?)

Chernenko. The 1984 Chernenko Spoof announced that the USSR had joined the Internet world, and looked forward to open discussions and peaceful coexistence. (The message is shown in Figure 5.1, with the header information slightly simplified.) The USENET return path for the message ended with moskvax!kremvax!chernenko; the original address information also contained *cia* and *nsa*, to add to the humor. Piet Beertema, the creator of the spoof, had rigged the mailer tables so that not only did the outgoing mail have the bogus address, but also responding mail was delivered to him. Perhaps most fascinating was the collection of responses that ensued. Some people took the message as genuine, and were either indignant at its content or joyously supportive. Others recognized the spoof, and typically expressed either delight or hostility (for example, indignation at the rampant misuse of network resources). (See *SEN 9*, 4, 6-8, for Piet's description of the event and the responses he received.)

Spafford. The 1988 Spafford Spoof was a serious discussion on how to recognize April Fools' Day messages — for example, a date of April 1, a time of 00:00:00, subtle "mispellings," use of nonexistent sites and/or Russian computer names such as kremvax or moscvax (sic), funky message IDs, and names of "well-known" people. There were also warnings of impending risks and a discussion of the dangers of bogus messages. Attentive reading of the message (Figure 5.2) shows that each of the proffered warning signs is present in the message itself, suggesting that the message was a self-referential hoax.[17] Although not publicly acknowledged at the time, the perpetrator was Chuq von Rospach.

An Aporkryphal Tail? E-mail tends to spread widely around the Internet. Figure 5.3 illustrates the question of whether a particular piece of E-mail is genuine, and whether its sender is authentic.

In this example, every litter bit counts. This item appears to be bogus — although nicely hammed up. IPFRC was not a known site address (noted by Michael Wagner), recalling Chernenko@moskvax. Furthermore, reference to "pig" instead of "hog" is highly suspect, according to "Billy Bob" Somsky. Perhaps my SRI colleagues and I can help get to the bottom of this story. As part of a system for detecting and analyzing anomalies, we have developed a Security

```
Relay-Version: version B 2.10 beta 3/9/83; site sdcrdcf.UUCP
Posting-Version: version B 2.10.1 4/1/83 (SU840401); site
kremvax.UUCP
Path: sdcrdcf!hplabs!hao!seismo!harpo!decvax!mcvax!moskvax!
kremvax!chernenko
From: chernenko@@kremvax.UUCP (K. Chernenko)
Newsgroups: net.general,eunet.general,net.politics,eunet.politics
Subject: USSR on Usenet
Message-ID: <0001@@kremvax.UUCP>
Date: Sun, 1-Apr-84 08:02:52 PST
Posted: Sun Apr  1 08:02:52 1984
Date-Received: Tue, 3-Apr-84 00:39:45 PST
Organization: MIIA, Moscow
```

Well, today, 840401, this is at last the Socialist Union of
Soviet Republics joining the Usenet network and saying hallo to
everybody.

One reason for us to join this network has been to have a means of
having an open discussion forum with the American and European
people and making clear to them our strong efforts towards attaining peaceful coexistence between the people of the Soviet
Union and those of the United States and Europe.

We have been informed that on this network many people have given
strong anti-Russian opinions, but we believe they have been misguided by their leaders, especially the American administration,
who is seeking for war and domination of the world. By well in-
forming those people from our side we hope to have a possibility
to make clear to them our intentions and ideas.

Some of those in the Western world, who believe in the truth of
what we say have made possible our entry on this network; to them
we are very grateful. We hereby invite you to freely give your
comments and opinions.

```
Here are the data for our backbone site:
Name: moskvax
Organization: Moscow Institute for International Affairs
Contact: K. Chernenko
Phone: +7 095 840401
Postal-Address: Moscow, Soviet Union
Electronic-Address: mcvax!moskvax!kremvax!chernenko
News/Mail: mcvax kremvax kgbvax
```

And now, let's open a flask of Vodka and have a drink on our entry
on this network. So: NA ZDAROVJE!

```
K. Chernenko, Moscow, USSR
...decvax,philabs!mcvax!moskvax!kremvax!chernenko
```

FIGURE 5.1 Chernenko Spoof

Path: mcvax!uunet!seismo!sundc!pitstop!sun!moscvax!perdue!spaf
From: spaf@@cs.purdue.EDU (Gene Spafford)
Subject: Warning: April Fools Time again (forged messages on the
loose!)
Date: 1 Apr 88 00:00:00 GMT
Organization: Dept. of Computer Sciences, Purdue Univ.

Warning: April 1 is rapidly approaching, and with it comes a USENET
tradition. On April Fools day comes a series of forged, tongue-in-
cheek messages, either from non-existent sites or using the name of
a Well Known USENET person. In general, these messages are harmless
and meant as a joke, and people who respond to these messages without
thinking, either by flaming or otherwise responding, generally end up
looking rather silly when the forgery is exposed.

So, for the next couple of weeks, if you see a message that seems completely out of line or is otherwise unusual, think twice before posting
a followup or responding to it; it's very likely a forgery.

There are a few ways of checking to see if a message is a forgery.
These aren't foolproof, but since most forgery posters want people to
figure it out, they will allow you to track down the vast majority of
forgeries:

* Russian computers. For historic reasons most forged messages have as
  part of their Path: a non-existent (we think!) russian computer,
  either kremvax or moscvax. Other possibilities are nsacyber or
  wobegon. Please note, however, that walldrug is a real site and
  isn't a forgery.
* Posted dates. Almost invariably, the date of the posting is forged
  to be April 1.
* Funky Message-ID. Subtle hints are often lodged into the Message-Id,
  as that field is more or less an unparsed text string and can contain random information. Common values include pi, the phone number
  of the red phone in the white house, and the name of the forger's
  parrot.
* Subtle mispellings. Look for subtle misspellings of the host names
  in the Path: field when a message is forged in the name of a Big
  Name USENET person. This is done so that the person being forged
  actually gets a chance to see the message and wonder when he
  actually posted it.

Forged messages, of course, are not to be condoned. But they happen,
and it's important for people on the net not to overreact. They happen
at this time every year, and the forger generally gets [his/her] kick
from watching the novice users take the posting seriously and try to
flame their tails off. If we can keep a level head and not react to
these postings, they'll taper off rather quickly and we can return to
the normal state of affairs: chaos.

Thanks for your support. Gene Spafford

FIGURE 5.2 Spafford Spoof

```
Date: Mon, 14 Sep 87 23:41:57 CDT ...
Sender: BITNIC LINKFAIL List <LINKFAIL@bitnic.bitnet>
From: ZEKE@ipfrcvm
Subject: IPFRCVM downtime
To: LOCAL DISTRIBUTION <LINKFAIL-LOCAL@omnigate.clarkson.edu>

IPFRCVM --- Iowa Pig Farm Research Center will be down tomorrow from
20:00--23:00 for system maintenance.  Since we are an end node, nobody
will be affected except for us.

It turns out that one of our sows got in through a hole in the wall and
had her litter of piglets under our raised floor.  The operator on duty
got quite a scare when he heard a number of squeals.  He assumed we had
some massive head crashes and powered down the CPU.  Since the squeals
continued, we traced it to a corner under our raised floors.  We will
be off the air tonight so that we can power down again and get the sow
and her piglets out from under the floor.

Zeke --- System Grunt, IPFRC
```

FIGURE 5.3 Pig-farm E-mail (Zeke)

Officer User Interface, known as SOUI, which might have been of help in bringing in the sow.

Various conclusions are relevant here. E-mail spoofs are still relatively easy to perpetrate in some systems — for example, using trapdoors or overly powerful privileges to insert bogus from addresses or to alter existing messages. Authentication of mail can be achieved by addition of cryptographic integrity seals [66], but they have not yet become widely used. Some spoofs could be dangerous if people were to take them seriously. However, explicitly clueing in the audience tends to spoil the fun on the more obvious and less harmful spoofs.

5.3.2 Pranks with Electronic Displays

We include two cases of tampering with electronically controlled public displays.

A Rose Bowl Weevil. Students at the California Institute of Technology are famous for their high-tech pranks. Here is a relevant example that affected the 1984 Rose Bowl Game.[18] The victimized organizing committee might be called the lesser of weevils, that is, bowl weevils.

For a CalTech course named Experimental Projects in Electrical Circuits, Dan Kegel and Ted Williams devised a scheme to take over the Rose Bowl scoreboard for the 1984 Rose Bowl game between UCLA and Illinois. This project was sanctioned in the abstract by their professor, although he apparently did not know until just before the game that the Rose Bowl scoreboard had been selected as the target.

Situated 2 miles away from the stadium, they used a radio link to a microcomputer that piggybacked onto the scoreboard control circuits, enabling them to control the scoreboard. Their initial messages ("GO CIT!" and a graphic of the CalTech beaver) went largely unnoticed, so in the final quarter they changed the team names to CalTech and MIT. Unable to figure out what was happening, officials shut down the scoreboard, with CalTech leading MIT 38 to 9.

Newspapers of March 27, 1984, reported that the two CalTech seniors had pleaded *nolo contendere* to a misdemeanor trespassing charge and were fined $330 each. Their explanation was broadcast around the Internet, as shown in Figure 5.4. The City Prosecutor claimed that the actual damages to the scoreboard were $4200, but that the city had found a temporary way to fix it.

Electronic information-board spoofed. The intended message on a display board at Connecticut and L Street NW in Washington, D.C., was superseded by an offensive bogus message, which flashed five times in 25 minutes. No one among the operations staff seemed to know how the bogus display could have been perpetrated. No one took credit for it, and no one was able to identify the perpetrator(s) (*SEN 15*, 1).

5.3.3   Risky Spoof-Like Scams

Although closely related in their causes, cases with more evil intent and more serious effects have occurred, and are considered in other parts of this book because they cannot be classified as spoofs or pranks. Two serious cases involving impersonations of air-traffic controllers are noted in Section 2.4.2. Several scams are considered in Section 5.9 relating specifically to prison escapes, one of which involves a bogus E-mail message. There have also been a variety of scams in which users were requested by E-mail or other communications to give their passwords or to change their passwords temporarily to a given string, allegedly in the interests of catching a would-be thief or system breaker or detecting a security flaw (*SEN 16*, 3).

We installed a device to take over control of the Rose Bowl scoreboard weeks before the actual game without the knowledge of any CalTech staff or faculty. Our only modification to their equipment was a splice in the cable to the scoreboard where we attached our microprocessor. During the game, we placed several messages such as ''Go CalTech!'' on the scoreboard. The frustrated stadium officials responded by turning off the power to the scoreboard before the game was over. There was no malfunction of either the stadium computer or our device.

In the days following the game, we contacted the Rose Bowl officials and offered to remove our device and to explain how we had gained control. This offer was ignored by the Rose Bowl officials and the city of Pasadena. Unfortunately, the Rose Bowl officials did not understand that our project had made no modifications to their computer, as we would have told them. They needlessly spent $1200 in shipping costs to have it checked out. There was, of course, no damage and hence no repairs necessary to either their computer or scoreboard. All that really had to be done was to unplug a connector we had installed. The figure of $4000 printed by newspapers was an exaggerated estimate from the start.

Weeks later the City Prosecutor of Pasadena, against the recommendation of the Mayor and the City Council, charged us with four misdemeanors. We read this news on the front page of the Los Angeles Times five days before we received actual notification by mail from the city clerk. When articles questioning the city's sense of humor appeared in local papers, he tried to defend his actions by writing to local newspapers. Apparently the city did not consider this appropriate; his office, previously independent, has since been placed under the authority of the City Attorney.

In cooperation with the city of Pasadena, CalTech agreed to share half the amount needlessly spent by the Rose Bowl on their computer. This amount of $660 was paid by CalTech to the Rose Bowl. It was mentioned in court, and the newspapers erroneously reported it as a fine to us as individuals. The City Prosecutor dropped every charge against us, except for the insignificant ''loitering in a public place after midnight.'' We pleaded no contest to this charge, and there was no sentence. It was agreed that this also will shortly be dropped from our record.

We have been surprised by the amount of attention which several newspapers and television stations have given to these events regarding the Rose Bowl. We have been disappointed that there have been several misconceptions and misquotes conveyed to the public. We hope that with more serious matters, journalists will take more care to report stories accurately and to avoid sensationalism.

Conclusion: Don't believe everything you read in newspapers.

FIGURE 5.4 Rose Bowl scoreboard takeover (Kegel and Williams)

The hypothesis that we will *confirm* other intelligent life is
even more intriguing than the hypothesis that there *is* other
intelligent life. I am sad to report that the former hypothesis is
more likely to fail than the latter. The reason is told by this
little story:

Once upon a long time ago, there was a civilization whose individual
members communicated by broadcast transmissions, first voice, later
radio. As they increased their broadcasts' power, they became concerned about eavesdroppers. To guard their privacy, they invented a
method of enciphering their transmissions. So advanced became their
ciphers that an observer could not distinguish their transmissions
from pure white noise. This civilization lived to a ripe old age in
peaceful privacy.

A hundred million years later, another civilization began to wonder
if they were alone in the universe. Their great mathematicians proved
that the probability of being alone is zero. And so they built
powerful antennas to receive the transmissions of their distant
brothers. For years they listened; all they picked up was pure white
noise. Eventually they concluded they were alone in the universe,
and they took down the antennas.

FIGURE 5.5 Intelligent life in space (Peter J. Denning)

5.3.4   **Risks of Minimizing Entropy**

A reverse danger exists—namely, that a message dated April
First really is genuine, but that it appears to be so bogus or so
commonplace that no one believes it. This danger represents a form
of **wolf–wolf** syndrome. The following case might be an example.

In his President's Letter in the *Communications of the ACM*, December 1981, Peter Denning debunked the prediction that other
intelligent life would be confirmed during 1982 (as claimed by some
researchers involved in the search for extraterrestrial intelligence).
Denning's statement is reproduced in Figure 5.5.

In the April 1991 *Inside Risks* column of the *CACM*, we noted
that we had just learned that researchers at a major NASA center claimed to have confirmed extraterrestrial intelligence. They
told us that the key is to couple Denning's contention (that intelligent transmissions are hidden in pure white noise) with the
well-known statistical fact that, whereas some real noise is *approximately* white, none is *purely* white. The researchers found a beam
of pure white noise coming from the direction of Alpha Centauri.
Cryptologists told us they do not hold much hope that they will

decipher the signal successfully, citing a theorem that a perfectly unbreakable encoding process produces a signal that appears to be pure white noise.

5.3.5 Defensive Spoofs

Trojan-horse spoofs have also been used for defensive purposes. Here are two examples.

Cable freeloaders caught by free offer. Continental Cablevision of Hartford offered viewers a free T-shirt during the broadcast of the Holyfield–Bowe fight on November 14, 1992. However, the offer and its free telephone number were seen by only those people using illegal decoders; 140 freeloaders called the 800 number within minutes of the ad's broadcast. Continental sent the callers T-shirts by certified, return-receipt mail, with a follow-up letter reminding them of the federal law (fines up to $10,000) and demanding a $2000 fine.[19]

Cadsoft detects illegal programs. Cadsoft offered a free demonstration program that stealthily searched the hard disk for the use of illegal copies—which were seriously cutting into their business. Whenever the program found any, it invited the user to print out and return a voucher for a free handbook. About 400 users responded, and received in return a letter from the company's lawyers, who sought to collect at least 6000 deutschmarks from each of them. Employees of IBM, Philips, and German federal offices were among them, innocent or not.[20]

5.4 Intentional Denials of Service

Recognizing that intentional and unintentional problems may be closely related, we next consider denials of service that were caused maliciously—in addition to those caused by pest programs noted in Section 5.1. Denials of service that occurred accidentally (that is, nonmaliciously) are discussed in Section 5.5.[21]

Satellite TV interference and spoofing. A Home Box Office program was preempted in April 1986 by someone identifying himself as "Captain Midnight," who overwhelmed the programmed movie (*The Falcon and the Snowman*)[22] with his own message protesting HBO's scrambling. The spoofing lasted for about 5 minutes (*SEN 11*, 3;

SEN 11, 5; Associated Press, April 27, 1986). The intruder was later identified and apprehended.[23]

Similar interruptions of regular programming have occurred several times since, including a bogus program being inserted into the Playboy Channel (*SEN 12*, 4; *SEN 16*, 1), and a pirate broadcast that took over WGN-TV and WTTW in Chicago (*SEN 14*, 2). Video pirates also disrupted a Los Angeles cable broadcast of the 1989 Super Bowl (*SEN 14*, 2).

Newspaper advertisement altered. A coffee advertisement in the Italian newspaper *La Notte* was sabotaged, exploiting the lack of user authentication in the paper's computer system. The Italian word for coffee was replaced with an Italian four-letter word. The following day, a crossword puzzle and the horoscope were similarly modified (*SEN 17*, 1).

Sabotage of Encyclopaedia Britannica database. An ex-employee, disgruntled about being fired, changed words in the text of the 1988 edition in preparation — for example, substituting "Allah" for "Jesus Christ"; the alterations were caught before publication (*SEN 11*, 5).

Analyst locks out others. In a dispute over alleged wrongdoings of his superiors, the Washington, D.C., finance analyst changed the password on the city's computer and refused to share it. The Deputy Mayor (who was himself under investigation by a federal grand jury at the time) called him "a nerd and an imbecile" (*SEN 11*, 2).

Insurance computer taken hostage. The former chief financial officer of an insurance company, Golden Eagle Group Ltd, installed a password known only to himself and froze out operations. He demanded a personal computer that he claimed was his, his final paycheck, a letter of reference, and a $100 fee — presumably for revealing the password (*SEN 12*, 3).

Town's data deleted. All of the computer-based financial records of Prescott Valley, Arizona, were wiped out, just before the new year's budget was about to be prepared. Sabotage was strongly suspected (*SEN 12*, 2).

Company data deleted. A former cost estimator for Southeastern Color Lithographers in Athens, Georgia, was convicted of destroying billing and accounting data on a Xenix system, based on an audit trail linking the delete commands to his terminal — but not necessarily to him! The employer claimed damages of $400,000 in lost business and downtime.[24]

Bogus cable chips zapped. Denials of service may also be used constructively. American Cablevision of Queens, New York, had its revenge on users of illegally installed chips. It created a signal that zapped just the bogus chips, and then waited to catch 317 customers who called to complain that their screens had gone dark (*SEN 16*, 3).

Bringing the system down. Each computer system seems to have its own ways of being crashed. In the early days, people sought to find new ways to crash systems—although this effort was certainly antisocial. (The artificial intelligence folks at MIT solved this problem by installing a crash command, which neatly removed the challenge.) The MIT Compatible Time-Sharing System (CTSS) in the 1960s was brought to its knees by a command file (runcom, like a Unix shell script) that recursively invoked itself. Each recursion created a new saved file, and a hitherto undetected bug in the system permitted the saved files to exhaust the disk space. (This incident was reported in *SEN 13*, 3 by Tom van Vleck—who with Noel Morris diagnosed and fixed the problem.)

5.5 Unintentional Denials of Service

Outages have been caused (for example) by improper system design, programming, and maintenance, and "acts of God"—although almost always with underlying human causes (a theme that is discussed in Section 9.1). Vulnerabilities in many other existing systems could also result in serious loss of system survivability. This section considers various cases of accidental denials of service, along with a few related events.

5.5.1 Hardware, Software, and Communications Problems

We first consider computer and communication systems with *survivability* requirements—that is, systems that are expected to continue to perform adequately in the face of various kinds of adversity. Fault-tolerant and nonstop (for example, Tandem) systems are designed to survive specific types of hardware malfunctions. Secure systems are intended to withstand certain types of misuse—such as malicious denial-of-service attacks that can impair functional survivability or diminish performance. Survivable systems may need to be both fault tolerant and secure—for example, if the perceived threats include hardware malfunction, malicious misuse, power failures, and electromagnetic (or other) interference.

There may be critical hard real-time requirements as well, in which stringent time deadlines must be met.

We summarize several illustrative past problems that suggest the pervasive nature of the survivability problem; there are many diverse causes and potential effects.

The 1980 ARPAnet collapse. The 1980 ARPAnet collapse resulted in a network-wide 4-hour total outage, as discussed in Section 2.1, due to both hardware and software problems

Various telephone cable cuts. Cable cuts resulted in long-term outages, as noted in Section 2.1, including the 1986 isolation of New England from the rest of the ARPAnet and shutdowns of airports.

The 1990 AT&T slowdown. The 1990 AT&T slowdown resulted in an 9-hour collapse of long-distance services, as discussed in Section 2.1, due primarily to a flawed software implementation of the crash-recovery algorithm.

Phobos. The Soviet *Phobos 1* probe was doomed by a faulty software update, which caused a loss of solar orientation, which in turn resulted in irrevocable discharge of the solar batteries. *Phobos 2* encountered a similar fate when the automatic antenna reorientation failed, causing a permanent loss of communications (*SEN*, *13*, 4; *SEN 14*, 6).

Automobile-traffic control. Section 2.11.2 notes the case in which a child was killed and another injured when computer-controlled traffic lights failed at 22 school crossings in Colorado Springs, Colorado — because of the failure of radio communications in receiving the time from an atomic clock. Other traffic problems were also reported, for example, one in Orlando, Florida, where cabling was left undone after a system upgrade (*SEN 14*, 1), a second due to a centralized single-computer outage in Lakewood, Colorado (*SEN 15*, 2), and a third in Austin, Texas, due to an untested upgrade (*SEN 15*, 3).

Automated teller machines. There have been numerous reports of automated teller machines (ATMs) accidentally gobbling up perfectly legitimate ATM cards (*SEN 9*, 2; *10*, 2; *10*, 3; *10*, 5; *12*, 2; *12*, 4), as well as cases of entire bank ATM operations being shut down by system malfunctions (*SEN 14*, 1; *14*, 2).

Business shutdowns. The archives include reports of numerous business outages, including gas stations and fast-food stores (*SEN 11*, 5; *12*, 1). A newly opened supermarket in Aylesford was closed because a breakdown in its centralized computer prevented the bar-code scanners from working at all 32 checkout stations (*SEN 17*, 1).

Hi-tech theater controls. In 1985, the computer-controlled stage turn-table for the musical *Grind* ground to a halt 30 minutes into the first act in Baltimore. The star of the show, Ben Vereen, gave an extemporaneous speech on how he felt about "the new mechanized world we live in" (*SEN 10*, 2).

The rotating stage for the American premiere of *Les Miserables* failed 30 minutes into the matinee performance on December 28, 1986, at Kennedy Center in Washington, D.C., necessitating $120,000 in ticket refunds (plus parking refunds as well) for the matinee and the evening performance because of "glitches in the . . . controls." The turntable could be operated only at full speed, which was much too fast to be safe (*SEN 12*, 2).

The opening performance of *The Who's Tommy* in Boston on December 1, 1993, had to be canceled because the computers controlling the high-tech musical did not function properly after the trip from the previous week's performances in Louisville.[25]

The Amsterdam Stopera (a combined town hall and music theater) had installed a modern computer-controlled door system. Unfortunately, the doors did not work properly, and people were locked inside (Piet van Oostrum in *SEN 14*, 1).

In a somewhat less dramatic case, the Theatre Royal in Newcastle installed a new ticket-reservation system in time for the Royal Shakespeare Company's visit. The system was down for several days, and *no tickets could be sold.* Yes, there was no backup (as noted by Robert Stroud in *SEN 12*, 2).

DBMS failure kills giraffes. The air-cargo database management system at the Amsterdam air cargo terminal failed completely. According to Ken Bosworth of Information Resources Development, it took several days and several dead giraffes before the problem was solved.[26]

Coke Phone Home. Telephone records of a city building in Fayetteville, North Carolina, supposedly unoccupied on nights and weekends, showed hundreds of telephone calls from two extensions in January 1985. Because all the calls were to the local Coca Cola Bottling Company, it was clear that the Coke machines were trying to contact their headquarters—which was eventually traced to a program bug (*SEN 10*, 2). In 1992, Peter Scott reported on someone with the 82nd Airborne assigned to an office at Fort Bragg. When the telephone was plugged in, it began to ring incessantly; the calls were traced to a Coke machine whose default telephone number (perhaps in a different area code) had never been changed (*SEN 17*, 2).

Library catalogs. The New York Public Library lost the computer-based reference numbers for thousands of books when information was transferred from one computer to another. Apparently, there was no backup (*SEN 12*, 4). Chuck Weinstock noted an electrical failure that shut down the computer center at Carnegie-Mellon University for a few days; the library was out of business—because their catalogs existed only in on-line form (*SEN 12*, 2).

The Monitor and the Merry Mac? This case actually involves IBM PCs, but might be applicable to Macs as well. John B. Nagle observed that it is possible to burn out a monochrome monitor under software control, simply by stopping the horizontal sweep (*SEN 13*, 3).

5.5.2   Ambient Interference

Interference from electronic or other signals is a nasty problem, because it is difficult to prevent and is difficult to diagnose when it does occur.

Tomahawk. On August 2, 1986, a Tomahawk missile suddenly made a soft landing in the middle of an apparently successful launch. The abort sequence had accidentally been triggered as a result of a mysterious bit dropping. "Cosmic radiation" was one hypothesis. (On December 8, 1985, a Tomahawk cruise missile launch crashed because its midcourse program had been accidentally erased on loading.) (See *SEN 11*, 2; *11*, 5; *12*, 1.)

Black Hawk. In tests, radio waves triggered a complete hydraulic failure of a UH-60 Black Hawk helicopter, effectively generating false electronic commands. (Twenty-two people were killed in five Black Hawk crashes before shielding was added to the electronic controls. Subsequently, Black Hawks were not permitted to fly near about 100 transmitters throughout the world (*SEN, 13*, 1; *15*, 1).

The *Sheffield* radar was jammed by its own communications. There were various erroneous reports about the cause of the *Sheffield* sinking during the Falklands War, which killed 20 crew members on May 4, 1982. Initial reports suggested the French-made Exocet missile fired by an Argentine plane was not on the list of enemy missiles, and therefore was not expected to be used against the British. That explanation was then denied by the British Minister of Defence,

Peter Blaker. A later report[27] contributed by Martin Minow indicated that the electronic antimissile defenses on the British frigate *Sheffield* were either jammed or turned off during the attack because of attempted communications between the captain and naval headquarters. The ship's transmitter was on the same frequency as the homing radar of the Exocet (*SEN 11*, 3).

Cosmic rays and the *Challenger*. The communication channel capacity of the space shuttle *Challenger* was cut in half for about 14 hours on October 8, 1984, due to "a heavy cosmic burst of radiation." The "cosmic hit" erased part of the memory of the stationary-orbit Tracking and Data Relay Satellite (TDRS). Communications were resumed after TDRS was reprogrammed from the ground. An earlier report on a study by J.F. Ziegler at IBM and W.A. Lanford at Yale University showed that densities in 1980 chip technology were such that about one system error per week could be attributable to cosmic-ray interference at the electron level. As altitude increases, the likelihood increases. As chip density increases, the likelihood increases. (See *SEN 10*, 1.)

Incidentally, the first TDRS experienced interference from extraneous radio transmissions. This problem was intrinsic to the design. The discovery resulted in cancellation of the March 7, 1985, liftoff of the shuttle *Challenger*, which was intended to place a second TDRS in orbit.[28]

Other interference in air and space. Other cases are worth noting, such as the sunspot activity that affected the computers and altered Skylab's orbit in 1979 (*SEN, 13*, 4), and the Atlas-Centaur whose program was altered by lightning (*SEN, 12*, 3;*15*, 1), noted in Section 2.2.2. Osaka International Airport's radar screens were jammed by electromagnetic interference from a television aerial booster (*SEN 12*, 3). A Boeing 707 struck by lightning over Elkton, Maryland, in 1963 is noted in Section 2.4. The interference problems during the 1986 raid on Libya are noted in Section 2.3. In a strange case, a cellular telephone in someone's luggage in the cargo hold of a commercial airliner was reported to have received a telephone call whose emitted radio-frequency signals apparently triggered a fire alarm in the hold (*SEN 14*, 6, reported on August 15, 1989). The apparent discovery of a pulsar in 1989 was later attributed to interference from a television camera (*SEN 16*, 3). (Although that case of interference did not result in a denial of service in the usual sense, there was a consequent denial of the pulsar's existence.) There have been bans on in-flight use of computers with mouse devices (*SEN 17, 3*), and more recently bans on hand-held cellular telephones, because of perceived interference with navigational systems (*RISKS 14, 33*, February 18, 1993).[29]

Lightning wallops rockets. Lightning hit the rocket launch pad at the NASA launch facility at Wallops Island, Virginia, on June 10, 1987, igniting three small rockets and accidentally launching two of them on their preplanned trajectories. Somewhat ironically, the rockets were scheduled to have been launched to study the effects of night-time thunderstorms (*SEN 12, 3*).

Lightning strikes twice. On July 31, 1988, lightning struck the drawbridge between Vineyard Haven and Oak Bluffs on Martha's Vineyard, Massachusetts, paralyzing the three-phase controls and then ricocheting into the elevated transformer. As a result, 40 sailboats and tall powerboats were locked into the Lagoon Pond for almost 3 days. (That weekend was the one when the ferry *Islander* ripped a hole in its belly when it ran aground, and had to be taken out of service for many weeks; 500 cars were backlogged that day alone.) A previous lightning strike, only 3 weeks before, had closed the same drawbridge for 24 hours.[30]

Mining equipment. A miner was killed when two pieces of equipment were accidentally set to be controlled by the same frequency. The miner was knocked off a ledge by the unintended machine, a scoop tram (*SEN 14, 5*).

Big Mac attacked. McDonald's experienced a strange interference problem; electrical appliances (toasters) and time keeping were affected. As a result of the special timers introduced for McMuffin products, time clocks were gaining 2 to 4 hours each day, inflating employees' paychecks accordingly. The new toasters' voltage-control circuits were inducing voltage spikes in the power line, disrupting the clocks—which were driven by the same power circuit. McDonald's had installed over 5000 toasters before the problem was diagnosed. Bogus food orders were also emerging, such as 11 hamburgers, 11 fries, and 11 cokes, replicating the items of previous orders. This duplication wreaked havoc with the inventory and financial systems as well. In a separate McProblem, interference from new higher-power local police radios caused McDonald's cash drawers to open.[31]

Garage doors for openers. Years ago, signals from Sputnik, the first Soviet orbiter, opened and closed garage doors as it went overhead.

When President Reagan's airborne command plane (an E-4B, a
modified 747) was parked at March Air Force Base, thousands of
remote-control garage-door openers in the San Bernardino (California) area failed, apparently due to jamming from the plane's radio
transmissions (Associated Press, April 4, 1986).

In 1987, the U.S. Army installation at Fort Detrich jammed garage-door remote controls near Frederick, Maryland (*SEN 13*, 1).

In 1989, garage doors in the Mt. Diablo area in California were
disabled by temporary transmissions between the Alameda Naval
Air Station and a Navy ship (*SEN 14*, 5). (Thus, each of the three
main U.S. military services were culprits!)

Nuclear-power plants. The Nine Mile Point 2 nuclear reactor in Oswego,
New York, was knocked off-line by a transmission from a two-way
radio in the control room, because the radio signals were picked up
by the turbine-generator monitoring system; this interference triggered an automatic shutdown (*SEN 14*, 5). A similar event occurred
at least twice 4 years later at the Palo nuclear-power plant in Iowa
(*SEN 18*, 1, 12).

Sunspots in Quebec. On March 13, 1989 (the unlucky Friday the Thirteenth fell on a Monday that month, as Pogo might have noted),
intense solar activity knocked out a remote substation, resulting in
6 million people in Canada's Quebec province being without electricity for almost 12 hours (*SEN 14*, 5).

Interference in hospitals. Edward Ranzenbach reported that, on a visit
to a local hospital intensive-care unit, he noticed a respirator repeatedly triggering an alarm and having to be manually reset. He
noted that this problem occurred each time there was traffic on his
portable radio around 800 megahertz. Such radios are now banned
from that hospital (*SEN 14*, 6).

Risks in pacemakers. In Section 2.9, we note the case of the 62-year-old
man being given microwave therapy for arthritis, and dying after
microwave interference reset his pacemaker to 214 beats a minute.
We also cite the case of a man who died when his pacemaker was
reset by a retail-store antitheft device.

Interference in the theater. During a performance of *A Chorus Line* at-
tended by President Ford, a Secret Service man received a call
on his walkie-talkie. His push-to-talk switch wiped out the CMOS

memory of the lighting board, plunging the entire theater into darkness (*SEN 12*, 2).

Sir Andrew Lloyd Webber's $5-million musical *Sunset Boulevard* had its London opening delayed 13 days because the elaborate scenery kept shifting unexpectedly on the Adelphi Theater stage. The cause was discovered by the composer himself when he was visiting the theater. "I made a call on my mobile telephone, and the set moved. I made a second call and it moved again." Hydraulic valves controlling the sets were triggered by the telephone transmissions.[32] (This was a real setback!)

Hats off for Johnny Carson! On August 31, 1989, Johnny Carson did an impression of Abe Lincoln as a budding young stand-up comic, wearing a 2-foot top-hat. The end of the skit involved triggering a radio-controlled device that blew the hat upward off his head. A long delay arose during the taping of the show when the hat kept blowing off Johnny's head backstage before his entrance. His technicians figured out that radio-frequency interference from nearby kids with remote-control robot cars kept triggering the hat. The obvious solution was to get the kids to stop transmitting during the skit. Honest, Abe had some good lines, but Johnny's hair-raising gimmick top-hatted them all (*SEN 14*, 6).

Interference with robots. Section 2.8 notes at least six deaths in Japan attributed to robots affected by stray electromagnetic interference.

Clocks run too fast. The village of Castle Donnington, Leicestershire, United Kingdom, installed new street-lighting systems with automatic timers that caused certain types of alarm clocks to race ahead. Mark Huth noted that the older clocks with red (light-emitting diode) displays count the cycles in the AC power, whereas the newer clocks with green (electroluminescent) displays count the cycles generated by a quartz crystal oscillator isolated from the power line by a DC power supply.[33]

Automobile microprocessor interference. There have been numerous reports on microprocessor-controlled automobile control systems being sensitive to electromagnetic interference, particularly from nearby citizen's-band transmitters. Effects have included the sudden speeding up of cars on automatic cruise control (*SEN 11*, 1).

Visible and invisible light. In the late 1970s, the BBC was filming a documentary in the U.S. Library of Congress. Howard Berkowitz reported that, occasionally, all of the computer tape drives would stop, rewind, and unload, and that the operating system would crash. The cause was traced to electronic flashes used for still pictures, which triggered the end-of-tape sensors (*SEN 12*, 4). Dan Klein reported on ultraviolet erasable electronically programmable read-only memory (EPROMs) being susceptible to photographic flashes (*SEN 14*, 1).

Power anomalies. The scoreboard clock kept failing during a Seattle–Denver National Basketball Association game. The problem was eventually traced to reporters having hooked up their portable computers to the same circuit that the scoreboard was using (*SEN 13*, 3). Lindsay Marshall reported that the computer room at the University of Newcastle upon Tyne lost all power when a circuit breaker blew at 13:50 P.M. on July 23, 1986, just as the television coverage for the Royal Wedding ended (*SEN 11*, 5). Other strangely coincidental events, such as plumbing floods during commercial breaks in television spectaculars and the dramatic increase in the birth rate 9 months after the Northeast power blackout, also have been reported.

Other interference cases. There have been various additional reports of strange system behavior in which stray electromagnetic or cosmic radiation was suspected, but was not always confirmed as the cause. Railway switches were allegedly triggered by video-game machines. Train doors opened in transit between stations. In Japan in 1986, 42 people were killed when two crashproof rollercoasters collided, with electromagnetic interference apparently the cause. An F-16 bomb dropped on rural West Georgia on May 4, 1988, was thought to have been triggered by stray signals (*SEN 14*, 5). The Air Force's PAVE PAWS radar has reportedly triggered airplane ejection seats and fire extinguishers (*SEN 15*, 1). The B-1B (stealth) bomber had electronic countermeasures that jammed its own signals (*SEN 14*, 2). Such episodes are particularly scary when the cause cannot be confirmed unequivocally, in which case recurrences are harder to prevent.

5.5.3   Other Environmental Factors

The physical world around us also contributes a variety of other effects.

Barometer up, planes down. Barometric pressure reached 31.85 inches at Northway, Alaska, on February 1, 1989, then the highest reading ever recorded in North America and the third highest in the world. (Temperatures were reported unofficially at −82 degrees Fahrenheit; the official weather bureau thermometer gave up at −80.) Because most aircraft altimeters could not provide accurate readings, the FAA grounded all air traffic that would require instrument approaches.[34]

Fires and floods. The fire and the ensuing water damage in Hinsdale, Illinois, on May 8, 1988, seriously affected computers and communications throughout the area; 35,000 telephone subscribers were out of operation and a new telephone switch had to be brought in to replace the old one. At least 300 ATMs were inoperative. Car telephones became hot items for conducting commerce (*SEN 13*, 3).

The Minneapolis Federal Reserve Bank flooded when an air-cooling pipe burst. A serious security vulnerability was opened up during the backup operation (*SEN 16*, 3).

Other fires have had a variety of devastating effects, including the May 1988 Dreyers Ice Cream plant fire in which the entire collection of secret formulae for ice-cream flavors was lost. It came at a terrible time; the flavor team had not yet completed its plan to have computer backups on everything, just in case (*SEN 13*, 3).

Snow. The snow-laden roof of a computer center collapsed in Clifton, New Jersey, on March 13, 1993. As a result, 5000 ATMs throughout the United States were shut down. The preplanned backup site for that computer center was unable to take over the operation because it was already doing emergency processing for computer systems that had been affected by the World Trade Center bombing the month before (*SEN 18*, 3, A-4).

Air conditioning. Dave Horsfall reported from Australia that a noisy air-conditioning system was seriously disrupting a council meeting, so the mayor ordered it shut off. Of course, no one remembered to turn it on again; by the next morning, one of the computers had been cooked (*SEN 13*, 4).

5.5.4 Prevention of Denials of Service

Attempting to attain any level of guaranteed service is a fundamental problem in real-time control systems, communication systems, medical systems, and many other types of applications. In particular, with their a priori emphasis on alternate routing, both the ARPAnet and the AT&T network in the past represented outstanding examples of highly survivable systems. The fault modes that caused the 1980 and 1990 collapses were unanticipated.

The generalized form of nondenial of service—that is, survivability—clearly encompasses many requirements such as security (prevention of penetration and misuse), reliability, availability, and real-time responsiveness; assuring it necessitates extreme care in development and operation, including care even greater than that required for systems that must be merely secure or fault tolerant.

5.6 Financial Fraud by Computer

Pursuing the duality between intentional and unintentional events, we next turn to financial problems. In this section, we consider financial fraud, both successful and thwarted. In Section 5.7, we consider accidental losses.

5.6.1 Perpetrated Fraud

Public reports include only a fraction of the known cases of fraud; private reports suggest that many others have occurred. This section gives a few cases that are acknowledged.

Volkswagen scam. Volkswagen lost almost $260 million as the result of an insider scam that created phony currency-exchange transactions and then covered them with real transactions a few days later, pocketing the float as the exchange rate was changing (*SEN 12*, 2, 4). This case is an example of a salami attack—albeit with a lot of big slices. Four insiders and one outsider were subsequently convicted, with the maximum jail sentence being 6 years, so their efforts were not entirely successful!

ATM fraud. Losses from ATMs are numerous. The *RISKS* archives include a $350,000 theft that bypassed both user authentication and withdrawal limits, $140,000 lost over a weekend because of exploitations of a software bug, $86,000 stolen via fabricated cards and espied personal identifying numbers (PINs), $63,900 obtained via the combination of a stolen card and an ATM program error, and various smaller scams.

Bogus ATM captures PINs. Alan Scott Pace, 30, and Gerald Harvey Greenfield, 50, were arrested on charges of credit-card fraud, wire fraud, interstate transportation of stolen property, and conspiracy to commit a felony. Mr. Greenfield was also charged with bank fraud. They had planted a bogus ATM in the Buckland Hills Mall in Manchester, Connecticut, which captured account numbers and PINs from the unsuspecting customers, whose requests were then rejected (although there were reports that the machine might have occasionally given out some money just to appear legitimate). They then fabricated bogus bank cards using the account numbers and PINs that their Trojan-horse ATM had captured. Their arrest on June 29, 1993, was based on routine films of their having used genuine ATMs from which they allegedly withdrew more than $100,000. Also seized were software, three handguns, bank-network stickers, a police scanner, credit cards and passports, and equipment to make the phony bank cards.[35]

New Hampshire subsequently informed Connecticut that Pace was wanted in New Hampshire for a string of nine jewelry scams in 1987. He had been under indictment in 1989 for running a bogus jewelry store, but never showed up for arraignment.[36]

Bogus transactions. First National Bank of Chicago had $70 million in bogus transactions transferred out of client accounts. One transaction exceeded permissible limits, but the insiders managed to intercept the telephone request for manual authorization. However, that transaction then overdrew the Merrill–Lynch account, which resulted in the scam being detected. Seven men were indicted, and all the money was recovered (*SEN 13*, 3, 10).

Two people used direct-access facilities to transfer BFr 245 million from Belgian BNP accounts to their own accounts in other banks, through an apparent breach in the bank's security. The transactions were detected by a series of audits, and the funds were recovered (*SEN 19*, 1, 6-7).

A 23-year-old employee of Ceska Sporitelna, the Czech Republic's biggest savings bank, transferred 35 million crowns ($1.19 million) from various accounts over 8 months. He wrote his own software to do the transfers, but only after warning the bank officials of their weak computer security. The theft was not detected until he withdrew almost one-half of the money; he was arrested as he was stuffing the money into a briefcase (*SEN 19*, 1, 7).

Diversion of funds. At the University of Texas, an employee used a dean's password to divert $16,200 over a 1-year period. He awarded fellowship stipends to students who were not eligible. The diversion was detected when a student wrote to the dean of recruiting to thank the dean for his generosity (*SEN 17*, 3).

Other frauds. Other frauds include a collaborative scam that acquired 50 million frequent-flier miles, an individual effort that gained 1.7 million miles, a collaborative effort involving millions of dollars worth of bogus airline tickets, and a bank computer-system employee who snuck in an order to Brinks to deliver 44 kilograms of gold to a remote site, collected the gold, and then disappeared.

Detective detected. A Pinkerton's detective-agency employee embezzled $1 million by transferring the funds to her own account and to accounts of two fictitious companies. This and another scam applying for refunds from false tax returns were detected after the employee left Pinkerton's. At the time that this case was reported, she was facing up to 30 years imprisonment and huge fines (*SEN 16*, 4). The *RISKS* archives do not include the final disposition of the case.

5.6.2   Thwarted Attempts

Attempts that were not successful also frequently remain unreported. Here are a few cases that managed to surface.

Bogus transfer requests. The First Interstate Bank of California came within a whisker of losing $70 million as the result of a bogus request to transfer funds over the automated clearinghouse network. The request came via computer tape, accompanied by phony authorization forms. It was detected and canceled only because it overdrew the debited account (*SEN 17*, 3).

The Union Bank of Switzerland received a seemingly legitimate request to transfer $54.1 million (82 million Swiss francs). The automatic processing was serendipitously disrupted by a computer system failure, requiring a manual check—which uncovered the attempted fraud. Three men were arrested (*SEN 13*, 3, 10).

Bogus lottery ticket. The Pennsylvania state lottery was presented with a winning lottery ticket worth $15.2 million that had been printed *after* the drawing by someone who had browsed through the on-line file of still-valid unclaimed winning combinations. The scam was detected because the ticket had been printed on card stock that differed from that of the legitimate ticket (*SEN 13*, 3, 11).

Gambling fraud. In 1983, a multiple slot-machine progressive payoff had reached $1.7 million at Harrah's Tahoe. The details remain sketchy, but it appears that a group of insiders figured out how to rig the microchip to trigger the payoff. The group tried to get a collaborator to collect, but he panicked when confronted with photographers, and the scam was exposed (*SEN 8,* 5).

Two-person authorization of bogus transfers. On Christmas Eve 1987, a Dutch bank employee made two bogus computer-based transfers to a Swiss account, for $8.4 million and $6.7 million. Each required two-person authorization, which was no obstacle because the employee knew someone else's password. The first transaction was successful. The second one failed accidentally (due to a "technical malfunction"), and was noted the following working day. Suspicions led to the arrest of the employee (*SEN 13,* 2, 5).

Counterfeit ATM cards. An ATM-card counterfeiting scam planned to make bogus cards with a stolen card encoder, having obtained over 7700 names and PINs from a bank database. An informant tipped off the Secret Service before the planned mass cashin, which could have netted millions of dollars (*SEN 14,* 2, 16).

Disappearing checks. An innovation in check fraud that is only marginally technology related involves the use of a chemical that causes bogus checks to disintegrate shortly after being deposited (*SEN 14,* 1, 16).

In general, computer misuse is getting more sophisticated, keeping pace with improvements in computer security. Nontrivial authentication (for example, more sophisticated than fixed passwords) can hinder outsiders, although systems with open networking and dialup lines are potentially more vulnerable to penetrations than are systems with no possible outside access. Authentication within a system or network among supposedly trusted components is vital, but often lacking. Fraud by insiders remains a problem in many commercial environments (often not even requiring technology, as in the U.S. savings and loan fiasco, now estimated to exceed $1.5 trillion in apparent losses). High-tech insider fraud can be difficult to prevent if it blends in with legitimate transactions.

Most of the thwarted attempts noted here were foiled only by chance, a situation that is not reassuring—particularly because more cautious perpetrators might have been successful. We do not know the extent of successful frauds. Financial institutions tend not to report them, fearing losses in customer confidence and escalations in insurance premiums. This lack of reporting leaves us wondering how many successful cases have *not* been detected, or have been detected but not reported. More comprehensive system security, authentication (of users and systems), accountability, auditing, and real-time detectability would help somewhat. More honest reporting by corporations and governmental bodies would help to reveal the true extent of the problems, and would be beneficial to all of us in the long term. In any event, computer-aided fraud will continue. The higher the stakes in terms of funds available for scamming or skimming, the greater the incentives for committing computer-aided financial crimes.

5.7 Accidental Financial Losses

In the previous section, we considered intentional computer-aided financial fraud. In this section, we consider accidental financial mishaps; some of these were subsequently reversible, whereas others entailed irrevocable losses.

5.7.1   Cases of Accidental Financial Loss

The following cases exhibit amazing diversity; they are listed roughly in order of decreasing loss.

My BoNY loss, she spilleth! [37] One of the most dramatic examples was the $32 billion overdraft experienced by the Bank of New York (BoNY) as the result of the overflow of a 16-bit counter that went unchecked. (Most of the other counters were 32 bits wide.) BoNY was unable to process the incoming credits from security transfers, while the New York Federal Reserve automatically debited BoNY's cash account. BoNY had to borrow $24 billion to cover itself for 1 day (until the software was fixed), the interest on which was about $5 million. Many customers were also affected by the delayed transaction completions (*SEN 11*, 1, 3–7).

Making Rupee! Due to a bank error in the current exchange rate, an Australian man was able to purchase Sri Lankan rupees for (Australian) $104,500, and then to sell them to another bank the next day for $440,258. (The first bank's computer had displayed the Central Pacific franc rate in the rupee position.) Because of the circumstances surrounding the bank's error, a judge ruled that the man had acted without intended fraud, and could keep his windfall of $335,758 (*SEN 12*, 4, 10).

Racetrack losses. "A series of computer malfunctions" was blamed for the Los Alamitos racetrack losing $26,000 in excess payouts when the final results were posted incorrectly (*SEN 16, 2*; 5).

Bank generosity. A Norwegian bank cashpoint computer system (ATM) consistently dispersed 10 times the amount requested. Many people joyously joined the queues as the word spread (*SEN 15, 3*, 7).

Replicated payments. A software flaw caused a bank in the United Kingdom to duplicate every transfer payment request, for a period of half an hour, totaling over £2000 million (or 2 billion British pounds as counted in the United States). Even though the bank claimed to have recovered all of the funds, Brian Randell speculated on possible lost interest — with a potential maximum around £0.5 million a day (*SEN 15, 1*, 5-6).

Replicated transactions. During a test of its computers, the Federal Reserve Bank accidentally reran 1000 transactions from the previous working day, transferring $2 billion to 19 different financial institutions. However, the error was caught quickly and no losses were incurred (*SEN 11, 2*, 9).

Replicated transfers. Udo Voges reported on a bank in Munich that accidentally mounted the wrong tape, redoing all the monthly transfers that had already been processed at the end of the month. The repeated transfers were later reversed (*SEN 14, 2*, 9).

Hot wire transfer. A high-flying wire-transfer organization had one group that dealt in multiples of one-thousand, while another group dealt with actual amounts. The inevitable result was that a $500 thousand Federal Reserve transaction was converted into $500 million — although the unusually large transaction was questioned manually and then reversed (anonymously contributed to *SEN 10, 3*, 9-10 by someone in that organization).

Winning lottery tickets bought after closing. Software was blamed for allowing six winning tickets to be purchased *after* the New England Tri-State lottery drawing was announced. The flaw was caught before payouts were made (*SEN 16, 1*, 19).

5.7.2 Prevention of Financial Losses

Preventing financial losses involves defending against intentional and accidental events. Some systems do well against one mode, but not against the other. The cases cited here and in the previous section suggest that there are risks in both modes. Although different techniques may be involved, the manifestations of these two modes of loss have much in common. Generalizing the system design and operational practice somewhat can permit coordinated detection and prevention of both cases. Indeed, there are losses that occurred accidentally that could have been caused with malicious intent, and a few others that were intentionally caused that could have occurred accidentally, as suggested in Chapter 4. The distinction between the two modes of loss is in general blurred, and it is wisest to anticipate both modes.

Controls for authentication (of users and systems), system integrity (for example, prevention of accidental or malicious system alterations), and database integrity (for example, external consistency with the real world, as well as internal consistency within the computer systems) are particularly important. The Clark–Wilson model [25] for application integrity is appropriate, embodying both good accounting practice and good software-engineering practice. It can be used profitably in conjunction with well-conceived approaches for increased system security, to help prevent both intentional and accidental losses. Many of the problems cited in this section and the previous section could have been prevented, or detected, or at least minimized, with a combination of good system design, enforcement of authentication and finer-grain access controls, and sensible administrative controls. However, some systems will always be susceptible to insider fraud, and systems with intentionally wide-open connectivity and remote users will always have some susceptibility to outsider fraud.

5.8   Risks in Computer-Based Elections

Errors and alleged fraud in computer-based elections have been recurring *Risks Forum* themes. The state of the computing art continues to be primitive. Punch-card systems are seriously flawed and easily tampered with, but are still in widespread use. Direct recording equipment is also suspect, with no ballots, no guaranteed audit trails, and no real assurances that votes cast are properly recorded and processed. Computer-based elections are being run or considered in many countries, including some countries notorious for past riggings. The risks discussed here exist worldwide.

5.8.1   Erroneous Election Results, Presumably Accidental

Computer-related errors occur with alarming frequency in elections. In 1989, there were reports of uncounted votes in Toronto and doubly counted votes in Virginia and in Durham, North Carolina. Even the U.S. Congress had difficulties when 435 Representatives tallied 595 votes on a Strategic Defense Initiative measure. An election in Yonkers, New York, was reversed because of the presence of leftover test data that accumulated into the totals. Alabama and Georgia also reported irregularities. After a series of mishaps, Toronto has abandoned computer-based elections altogether. Most of these cases were attributed to "human error" rather than to "computer error," and were presumably due to operators and not to programmers; however, in the absence of dependable accountability, who can tell?

In 1992, there were numerous further goofs. In Yamhill County, Oregon, votes for the District Attorney candidates were reversed. Because the computer program assumed the candidates were in alphabetical order, a two-to-one landslide went to the wrong candidate (at least until the error was caught).

In Ventura County, California, yes and no votes were reversed on all the state propositions, although the resulting errors did not alter the statewide outcomes.

Ray Todd Stevens reported on voting machines that were misaligned so that it was possible to vote for Bush but not for Clinton. (A voting official said that "they only deal with the totals and it would all average out.")

5.8.2   Election Fraud

If wrong results can occur accidentally, they can also happen intentionally. Rigging has been suspected in various elections. In other cases, fraud might easily have taken place. Numerous experts have attested to the ease with which close elections could be rigged. However, lawsuits have been unsuccessful, particularly given the absence of trustworthy audit trails.

The opportunities for rigging elections are manifold, including the installation of trapdoors and Trojan horses — child's play for vendors and knowledgeable election officials. Checks and balances are mostly placebos, and are easily subverted. Incidentally, Ken Thompson's oft-cited Turing address [167] noted in Section 3.3.2 reminds us that tampering can occur even without any source-code changes; thus, code examination is not sufficient to guarantee the absence of Trojan horses.

For many years in Michigan, manual system overrides were necessary to complete the processing of noncomputer-based precincts, according to Lawrence Kestenbaum.

Doug Hardie cited a personal experience in observing a flagrant case of manual intervention with a punched-card voting system at San Jose State University—albeit in only a small election. (He also had a cute comment on the linguistic distinction between the election machine being *fixed* and its being *repaired.*)

In the St. Petersburg, Florida, mayoral election on March 23, 1993, some computer printouts "released inadvertently by election officials showed 1429 votes had been cast in Precinct 194 [which has *zero* registered voters], raising questions of vote tampering." This anomaly was explained as a compilation of "summary votes" that were legitimate but that had been erroneously allocated in copying the results from one computer system to another. Coincidentally (?), the margin of victory was 1425 votes. A subsequent recount seemed to agree with the original totals.[38] On the other hand, controversy continued for months afterward. By the way, a consistent Trojan horse somewhere in the process would of course give reproducible results; the concurrence of a recount is by itself not enough.

In addition to various cases of fraud having been alleged in the use of electronic voting systems (see, for example, Ronnie Dugger's *New Yorker* article [39]), paper-ballot systems are of course vulnerable as well. A recent example involves Costilla County in Colorado, where absentee ballots have been voted for ineligible voters (friends, relatives, and dead persons) as far back as 1984, and have been decisive. However, that hardly seems like news here. The conclusion is that, in principle, all voting systems are easy to rig—given appropriate access to whatever it takes (computer systems, bogus paper ballots, and so on). Trojan horses can in essence be arbitrarily subtle.

John Board at Duke University expressed surprise that it took more than 1 day for the doubling of votes to be detected in eight Durham precincts. Lorenzo Strigini reported in November 1989 on a read-ahead synchronization glitch and an operator pushing for speedier results, which together caused the computer program to declare the wrong winner in a city election in Rome, Italy (*SEN 15,* 1). Many of us have wondered how often errors or frauds have remained undetected.

5.8.3 **Reduction of Risks in Elections**

The U.S. Congress has the constitutional power to set mandatory standards for federal elections, but has not yet acted. Existing standards for designing, testing, certifying, and operating computer-based vote-counting systems are inadequate and voluntary, and provide few hard constraints, almost no accountability, and no independent expert evaluations. Vendors can hide behind a mask of secrecy with regard to their proprietary programs and practice, especially in the absence of controls. Poor software engineering is thus easy to hide. Local election officials are typically not sufficiently computer-literate to understand the risks. In many cases, the vendors run the elections. (See [144].)

Providing sufficient assurances for computer-based election integrity is an extremely difficult problem. Serious risks will always remain, and some elections will be compromised. The alternative of counting paper ballots by hand is not promising, and is not likely to be any less subvertible. But we must question more forcefully whether computer-based elections are really worth the risks. If they are, we must determine how to impose more meaningful constraints. Section 7.9 considers what might be done to avoid some of the problems discussed here.[39]

5.9 **Jail Security**

Iron type bars and silicon chips do not a prison make.

This section summarizes a collection of technology-based problems related to prison and jail security. Several of these cases involved scams that permitted inmates to escape. Section 6.5 notes a different type of law-enforcement problem relating to false imprisonments that resulted from naming problems and mistaken identities.

Jailed drug kingpin freed by bogus E-mail. An alleged cocaine dealer, William Londono, was released from Los Angeles County Jail on August 25, 1987, on the basis of an E-mail message that had apparently been fabricated by someone with access to the jail's computer system. About 70 people had legitimate access to the system, but it was not known whether the perpetrator was an insider or an outside masquerader. However, Londono's release appeared to have insider accomplices; for example, he and his street clothes were missing, and his departure was not discovered for 6 days! This case followed two previous escapes from the same jail involving inmates switching identification wristbands.[40]

Jailbreak by fax. Jean Paul Barrett, a convicted forger serving a 33-year term, was released from a Tucson, Arizona, jail on December 13, 1991, after a forged fax had been received ordering his release. A legitimate fax had been altered to bear his name.[41]

Seven inmates escaped in Santa Fe. While the prison computer control system was down on July 4, 1987, in Santa Fe, New Mexico, a prisoner kidnapped a guard, shot another, commandeered the control center, and released six other prisoners. All seven went through an emergency door on the roof, pole-vaulted over a barbed-wire prison fence, and disappeared. The guard tower was being staffed only during daylight hours "because of financial restrictions."[42] (It was subsequently staffed 24 hours a day.) The prison computer-control system was reportedly down at the time, and would otherwise have monitored the motion detectors and thereby prevented the escape! Apparently, the monitoring software had been disabled because of too many false alarms. (See a report by James Lujan in *SEN 12*, 4, which noted that only one of the seven escapees had been apprehended.)

Woman escapes from Oregon jail. Diane Downs, a convicted murderer of some notoriety (she shot her three children, killing one, allegedly to rid herself of the responsibility for them), escaped from the medium-security Oregon women's prison on July 11, 1987. While in the recreation yard, she scaled two fences and walked away. Budget money was tight, so there was no guard assigned to watch inmates in the yard; instead, the jail depended on an alarm system in the outer fence. The alarm did go off, but no one paid attention to it because it had been going off every day, usually because of strong winds or birds. (See *SEN 12*, 4, reported by Andrew Klossner.) Both this and the previous case remind us of the boy who cried "wolf!" When a system gives so many false alerts, it is time to do something to improve the false-positive discrimination.

Dutch computer system sets criminals free, arrests innocent people. One day after a new Dutch computer system was installed at the Central Investigation Information Department (CRI) in The Hague in the Netherlands, it began to behave strangely. Criminals were set free, and innocent people were arrested. The computer system was taken out of service. Unfortunately, the backup system had been decommissioned. The vendor blamed the police for using the system incorrectly.[43]

Computer breakin for jail breakout. A computer breakin was used in an attempted jail breakout in the Santa Clara County jail in California. A prison inmate gained access to the on-line prison information system and managed to alter the data for his release date, from December 31 to December 5. (He wanted to be home for Christmas.) However, the alteration was detected by a suspicious deputy comparing the on-line entry with manual records, after the inmate had bragged about how he was going to get out early.[44]

Faulty locks delay prison opening. A new El Dorado County jail could not be opened for some weeks because the computer-controlled cell doors would not lock. The vendor was charged a daily penalty of $1250.[45]

San Joaquin County jail doors unlocked. On the evening of December 27, 1992, the new San Joaquin (California) County jail computer system automagically unlocked all of the cell doors in a high-risk area, with a highly audible series of loud clicks, releasing about 120 potentially dangerous inmates who were being held in an "administrative segregation pod." Fortunately, the pod was itself isolated by other doors that remained locked. The glitch was attributed to a spurious signal from the *incoder card*, whose responsibilities include opening those doors in emergencies.[46]

Pickable high-tech locks. Less than 1 year after the opening of the supposedly escape-proof Pelican Bay State Prison near Crescent City, California, inmates learned how to pop open the pneumatic cell doors at will. A similar system in the Santa Rita Jail in Alameda County was also found to be pickable.[47]

Oklahoma power outage freezes jail doors. Oklahoma County opened a new jail in November 1991, with a comprehensive new computer system developed in Colorado. Toward the end of February 1993, the software failed, leaving each of the doors in a state that could not be changed manually. Some prisoners remained locked in their cells, some doors remained wide open. Twenty-two jailers were trapped in a control room for an entire shift when the computer system shut down due to a 5-minute power outage. An attempted fix 4 days later failed.[48]

5.10 **Summary of the Chapter**

This chapter considers several of the more illustrative security problems, the intent being to help you gain a greater appreciation for the range of vulnerabilities presented in Chapter 3 and the ways in which those vulnerabilities have been and can be exploited. Such an appreciation is essential to preventing the occurrence of similar problems in the future, in existing systems as well as in new systems.

Table 5.1 provides a brief summary of the causes of the problems cited in this chapter. The abbreviations and symbols are as in Table 1.1. The column heads include a column headed *Misuse*, indicating explicit willful system misuse, as opposed to other problems arising in the course of normal system use.

TABLE 5.1 Summary of security problems and their causes

	Source of the Problems									
Case	Req def	Sys des	HW impl	SW impl	Sys use	Mis- use	HW malf	Envir	Anal- ysis	Evol, maint
Internet Worm	o	●		o	o	●			o	o
Crackers	o	●	(o)	o	o	●				
Phone phreaking	o	●	o	o	o	●		o		
Trojan horses	o	●	(o)	o	o	●				
PC viruses	o	●	(o)	o	o	●				
CTSS PW file	o	o		●	o					o
Discovery				●						o
Residues					o			o		●
Rose Bowl	o				o	●		o		
Other spoofs	o	o		o		●				
Service denials:										
Malicious	(o)	(o)		(o)		●				
Accidental	(o)	(o)		(o)	(o)	o	(o)	(o)		(o)
Financial losses:										
Frauds	(o)	(o)		(o)	(o)	●				
Accidents	(o)	(o)	(o)	(o)	(o)	●	(o)			(o)
Voting	(o)	(o)	(o)	(o)	(o)	(o)	(o)	(o)	(o)	(o)
Jail problems	(o)	(o)	(o)	(o)	(o)	(o)	(o)	(o)		

Each of the first five cases in the table indirectly reflects pervasive inadequacies throughout system development and operation, although the direct cause is external system misuse. For example, in the case of personal-computer viruses, the unwitting victim is the importer of the virus (typically, via floppy disk) and sometimes is its trigger; the original source of the virus may be long ago and far away. However, the existence of the virus on a given system relies on the inability of the personal-computer operating system to protect itself against itself; that flaw may alternatively be attributed to unspecified requirements, poor system design, weak software implementation, and, in some cases, inadequate hardware.

The situation has improved only somewhat since the Internet Worm, which demonstrated how vulnerable a certain class of systems (Berkeley Unix) was at that time. Today's computer systems and networks are still generally vulnerable to attack, externally by penetrators and internally by supposedly authorized users. Many of the classical vulnerabilities of Chapter 3 are still present, in one guise or another.

Designing systems and networks that are secure and reliable is a difficult task, and requires an overall system perspective, as suggested in Chapter 4. Many techniques that could be used are known in the research and prototype development communities, but those techniques have been relatively slow to reach the commercial marketplace and thence common use. Some of these techniques are considered further in Chapter 7, along with criteria and other desiderata for secure and reliable systems. The criteria outlined in Section 5.8 give a cursory indication of the breadth of scope required for one particular application area, but those criteria are, in most cases, generally applicable to many other types of applications. Considerable experience is also required to operate and administer those systems and networks.

In certain applications, it is possible to seal off a system from outside users; however, the circumstances in which that is practical are generally co-opted by pressing needs for increased interconnectivity and interoperability. For example, the need for remote maintenance of telephone switching systems requires that telephone switch controllers be available remotely. For many years, it was relatively easy for outsiders to penetrate the telephone system via the maintenance interfaces. Recent incorporation of user authentication that does not rely on fixed passwords has slowed down the frequency of attack.

Even if security were to be considerably improved to combat intentional misuse, Sections 5.2, 5.5, and 5.7 suggest that accidental misuse by authorized users and unexpected events related to modes of system unreliability would continue to undermine security.[49]

Challenges

Warning: As noted at the end of Chapter 3, carrying out experimental attacks on computer and communication systems is not recommended; it could result in felony or misdemeanor charges, the resultant need to pay serious lawyers' fees, and a first-hand opportunity to study the use of computer systems in jails. Nevertheless, anyone involved in designing and implementing a system, or merely in using a system, should expand his or her horizons by trying to anticipate the types of problems described in this chapter. It may surprise you to discover how many such attacks could be perpetrated on systems that you believe are sound.

C5.1   Do you believe the statement at the beginning of Section 5.1, that every system can be compromised? Defend your conclusion.

C5.2   What inferences can you draw from the following information? Salaries associated with individuals are stored in a database, but are not accessible to unprivileged users. However, a query exists that provides the average salary of an arbitrary collection of named individuals, as long as more than 10 people are included. Can you, as an unprivileged user, derive the salaries of every individual? If you can, describe how. If you cannot, what would you require to do so?

C5.3   A particular directory is protected so that *wildcarding* is not permitted; that is, `ls *` or its equivalent does not provide a listing of the directory entries. However, *escape completion* is permitted. That is, if an initial character string of an entry name is long enough to determine the following characters uniquely, then, if that string is typed followed by an `escape` character, the system will provide the rest of the characters in the entry name; for example, typing `ls ris` followed by an `escape` character would result in the system completing the command line as, say, `ls risks`, if no other entry name were to begin with `ris` . Can you obtain a list of the entire set of directory entry names — that is, the equivalent of `ls *`? If you can, describe how. If you cannot, explain why not.

C5.4   The telephone book for Agency X is classified; in particular, the list of employees' names is classified, as is the association of names with telephone numbers. The main switchboard number is publicly known.

In some cases, a switchboard operator will give you the number and connect you, if you know the name of an individual. In other cases, a computer-automated touchtone service may field your call. In either case, how might you obtain a list of names and numbers?

C5.5   In Challenge C5.4, suppose that the operator will not give you the telephone number for a named individual, but will connect you. Suppose that direct in-dialing is also possible, bypassing the switchboard. Can you obtain a list of names? Can you obtain the associated numbers? Explain your answers.

C5.6   Analyze two arguments for and two against the reporting of cases of system misuse that have violated security. Are these arguments the same as those for and against the reporting of known or newly detected system vulnerabilities? Why? Is the discussion of types of vulnerabilities in Chapter 3 consistent with your analysis? Explain your answer.

C5.7   Reconsider your design of the simple alarm system in C2.4, knowing what you now know about security and the vulnerabilities detected in C4.3. Add security features to your design to make it resistant to malicious attacks, such as attempts to cut the primary power or the backup-battery wires. Identify circumstances under which your design might fail to operate properly, including both single-point and multiple-source failure modes.

CHAPTER 6

Threats to Privacy and Well-Being

*If you don't defend your
rights, you lose them—
by attrition.*

LAWRENCE FERLINGHETTI[1]

WE NEXT CONSIDER a variety of problems relating to violations of personal privacy and threats to general well-being.

6.1 Needs for Privacy Protection

Few social issues seem to attract more interest in the computer profession than does privacy.

Perhaps this interest is not surprising. The tie between public safety and privacy protection is well known in the *RISKS* world. And the ACM Code of Professional Conduct urges each ACM member to "consider the health, privacy and general welfare of the public in his [or her] work."[2] In fact, in the late 1960s and early 1970s, the ACM played a leading role in promoting privacy protection. In 1973, a government advisory committee, chaired by ACM member Willis Ware, produced a landmark report that provided the foundation for the Privacy Act of 1974.[3] However, translating concern for privacy into effective public policy these days is not an easy task. There's plenty of skepticism about politics, and scientists and engineers tend to keep their distance. But when computer professionals do get involved, good results can occur.[4]

Section 6.1 originally appeared as an *Inside Risks* column, *CACM, 35*, 4, 164, April 1992, and was written by **Marc Rotenberg**, while he was Director of the Washington Office of Computer Professionals for Social Responsibility. He is now with the Electronic Privacy Information Center. He chairs the ACM Committee on Scientific Freedom and Human Rights.

181

NCIC. In 1989, the FBI agreed not to pursue several features proposed for the National Crime Information Center upgrade (NCIC-2000) that an expert panel had concluded could create serious privacy and security problems.[5]

Lotus Marketplace Households. In 1990, Equifax and Lotus withdrew Marketplace Households, a direct-marketing product containing names and addresses from credit files, with estimated incomes for 120 million consumers. When problems with the "opt-out" procedure, the security scheme, and the potential misuses of personal data were aired in widely distributed network newsgroups (including *RISKS*), Lotus received more than 30,000 requests for removal from the database, which evidently helped to persuade them to drop the product.[6]

Calling-Number Identification. In 1991, many state public-utility commissions heard testimony from computer and telecommunications experts and decided that safeguards would be necessary for the proposed Calling-Number IDentification service (CNID, sometimes mistakenly referred to as Caller ID). The recent history of CNID is particularly interesting. Members of Computer Professionals for Social Responsibility (CPSR) and others came up with several innovative ideas that caught the attention of the public utility commissions and the telephone companies.

In California, Jeff Johnson recommended that the CNID service be redesigned so that the caller's identity, and not the number of the calling line, would be transferred to the call recipient. Challenging the popular name for the service, Jeff pointed out that "Caller ID" provided only a string of numbers and said that, understandably, most people would rather know *who* is calling. The Administrative Law Judge in California agreed and decided that the CNID service was not in the public interest. Pacific Bell eventually withdrew the service, but now offers Callback, which permits the recipient of a call to return the most recent call—without disclosing the originating telephone number. Other states now provide CNID.

In Massachusetts, Ronni Rosenberg and Coralee Whitcomb testified before the Department of Public Utilities that callers should be able to decide when to release their telephone numbers, and callees should be able to decide when to accept a call. They also pointed out that Call Trace would be preferable to CNID for handling harassing calls. The DPU required both per-call and per-line blocking.

In Oregon, the Public Utilities Commission endorsed CPSR member Erik Nilsson's proposal to provide free per-line blocking to all telephone users via a ballot. In a case with harrowing testimony on the effects CNID can have on women's safety, the PUC proposed a new Random False Identity Service, which would mask the caller's telephone number — for example, to protect domestic violence shelters and volunteers.

In Vermont, CPSR suggested to the Public Service Board that those telephone subscribers with unlisted numbers were certainly entitled to have the disclosure of their numbers protected. The PSB agreed and recommended per-line blocking.

Some valuable new services may result from these CNID hearings, and many serious privacy problems will be avoided. Still, there are many opportunities for technical input on the policy front. One of the surprising conclusions of a recent Congressional report is that it is not "technologically possible" to block the delivery of CNID information to an 800 or 900 number. This finding would no doubt come as a surprise to the operator of 1-900-STOPPER, who provides just such a service to thousands of customers. And it might disappoint Thomas Alva Edison, who once said, "What man makes with his hands, he can control with his head."

In the next few years, there will be important policy questions about the protection of medical records, the use of the social-security number (SSN), and the sale of transactional data. The protection of network communications — particularly records of individual messages — will be especially important.

6.2 Privacy Violations

If you can read this, we wasted 50 billion dollars.
  BUMPER STICKER ON THE STEALTH BOMBER,
  QUIPPED BY ART LETTERMAN, JULY 27, 1993

The foregoing chapters include various cases with privacy implications. The malicious security misuses of Section 5.1 represent many violations of data confidentiality supposedly enforced by system and network security, including database accesses, telephone tapping, and other communication interceptions — in some cases involving credit-card fraud and other subsequent illegal acts. There are also the accidental losses of confidentiality noted in Section 5.2. In considering violations of individual and corporate rights, we also must address rights other than privacy. For example, if election results are significantly different from what they should have been — through accident or malice — the rights of citizens have clearly been violated, although it may not be clear exactly which rights, simply because rights are often muddled by societal interpretation. (See Section 5.8.)

In this section, we consider a few of the many additional cases relating specifically to violations of individual rights and misuses of database information.

DMV records lead killer to victim. California Division of Motor Vehicle (DMV) records have in the past been relatively easy to access. On July 18, 1989, actress Rebecca Schaeffer was murdered by an obsessed fan who tracked down her home address through DMV records (via an Arizona private investigator). In response, Governor George Deukmejian directed the DMV to restrict release of information, to protect individual privacy and safety. (The DMV had 41 million requests in 1988, most seemingly business related.) New rules took place on October 1, 1989, and require bulk users to register and sign restrictive agreements; the rules also impose a 10-day delay on the response in certain cases. The new practice of notifying the driver when an individual request is made will thus give the driver a little warning before the record is mailed out. (DMV information is all part of the public record, but the home addresses of certain drivers — judges and law-enforcement officers, for example — are supposedly not to be released. Whether they are actually on-line but suppressed by the system is another matter.) (See *SEN 14*, 6.)

Arizona murder based on internal data misuse. A former Arizona law-enforcement officer used information obtained from three individuals in three different law-enforcement agencies to track down his estranged girlfriend; he then murdered her. After an investigation, the printouts provided by the three individuals were discovered, and the individuals were identified, prosecuted, and convicted. In another case, a law-enforcement operative in Pennsylvania ran background database searches for her drug-dealing boyfriend to check on whether prospective clients were actually undercover drug agents.[7]

Other insider misuse of law-enforcement and governmental databases. Several reports have cited cases of law-enforcement personnel misusing access. For example, 45 Los Angeles police officers were

cited during the period 1989 to 1992 for using department computers to run background checks for personal reasons (*SEN 18,*
1, 21).

A Metro-North Commuter Railroad police chief was indicted for
misusing a confidential New York State police database, although
he claimed that his actions conformed with standard procedure
(*SEN 13,* 4).

An unidentified employee of the Anaheim Police Department
apparently misused his access to the DMV computer system to
obtain the home address of a man who had been targeted by anti-
abortionists. This led to the man's house in Tustin, California,
being picketed in February 1993. "It taught me I can't trust anyone," he said. "When you find out the perpetrators of harassment
were helped by the Anaheim Police Department, you wonder where
does it stop." Under state law, unauthorized disclosure of DMV
records is a misdemeanor with penalties up to 1 year in jail plus a
fine of $5000 (*SEN 18,* 3, A-12).

Three British police officers were given suspended sentences for
misusing the Police National Computer to obtain personal information for private detectives (*SEN 14,* 2).

Eighteen private investigators and Social Security Administration (SSA) employees in nine states were charged on December 18,
1991, with buying and selling confidential data from SSA and FBI
computers, including earnings histories and criminal records (*SEN
17,* 2).

The Inspector General of Health and Human Services reported
that their office cited $15 million in penalties in over 2500 cases
of abuse of privileges (*SEN 18,* 1, 21). One particularly flagrant
case involved Nationwide Electronic Tracking (NET), a company in
Tampa, Florida, which was able to access government databases
(including IRS, SSA, and NCIC) rapidly by using a network of insiders. Eleven of the 14 indicted pleaded guilty to 30 counts of
conspiracy, unauthorized disclosure of tax information, theft and
conversion of government property (records), aiding and abetting a
crime, bribery of public officials, making false official statements,
and fraudulent access to government computers.[8]

Cellular telephone eavesdropping. An article by John Flinn[9] included the
following examples of cellular snooping.

- A supposedly private conference call among San Francisco Mayor
Jordan, real-estate magnate Walter Shorenstein, and several others

discussing the then-not-public withdrawal of George Shinn from the effort to save the San Francisco Giants was *broadcast* on a television frequency.

- "On the first day of the Soviet coup against Mikhail Gorbachev . . . , a scanner buff overheard Vice President Dan Quayle making a call from Air Force Two to Senator John Danforth about the unfolding crisis."

- "In New Hampshire, an anti-nuclear activist picked up calls made from the control room at the Seabrook nuclear plant, including one real-life Homer Simpson saying, 'I've got a bad feeling about these valves.'"

- A Green Bay Packer football player was overheard calling a male escort service and making explicit requests.

- A 23-minute conversation allegedly between Princess Diana and a man who called her "my darling Squidge" was taped by a retired bank manager in Oxford, and transcribed in *The Sun.* (The woman allegedly referred to the Royal Family as "this ****ing family.") The transcript of that conversation has now been widely circulated.

Bork bill. Seeking something incriminating, the *City Paper* in Washington, D.C., acquired the video rental records of Judge Robert Bork when he was a Supreme Court nominee. (They discovered he liked mysteries.) As a result, the Video Privacy Protection Act of 1988 (S. 2710, known as the Bork bill) was passed, controlling access to video records, including their sales to direct marketers.

Private NBC memo divulged. Bryant Gumbel of NBC's "Today" show was asked by the show's Executive Producer to evaluate the staff. Gumbel's supposedly private memo somehow was given to a reporter, who published it in *NY Newsday.*[10]

E-mail privacy invasions. Belgian Prime Minister Wilfried Martens discovered that his E-mail had been routinely read for several months by someone using his password (*SEN 14*, 1). An agent of the Internal Revenue Service was accused of giving a defendant tax data on the judges, jurors, and others involved in the defendant's trial (*SEN 16*, 3). In 1986, Oliver North was reported to have sent the following message to his aide Ronald Sable: "Oh Lord, I lost the slip and broke one of the high heels. Forgive please. Will return the wig Monday."[11] (Ollie is a well-known spoofster, so who knows?)

Stolen doctors' computers lead to blackmail concerns. At least 20 thefts of doctors' computers were reported in the United Kingdom, and others are suspected (because such thefts do not have to be reported). Perhaps the motive was merely theft of equipment, but the systems contained sensitive data that could be used for blackmail or defamation (*SEN 18*, 1, 22).

Equifax credit records misused by Dayton ring. Thirty people were caught using an Equifax password to sell off credit-card numbers, credit records, and bill-payment histories (*SEN 17*, 2).

Risks of erroneous data. The credit bureau subsidiary of TRW (rarely called Thompson, Ramo, Wooldridge) settled a lawsuit with the Federal Trade Commission and 19 states, having been accused of violating consumer privacy and making reporting errors that harmed the credit ratings of thousands of consumers. The settlement required TRW to make improvements in its business practices and to pay $300,000 to the states to cover the legal fees.[12]

Other lawsuits. Epson America, Inc., was sued for invasion of privacy for tapping messages transmitted between their Hewlett-Packard computer system and an external MCI E-mail service (*SEN 15*, 5).

Two former employees of Nissan Motor Corp. USA sued Nissan, claiming they had been fired illegally by a manager who had eavesdropped on their E-mail and had found a message critical of him (*SEN 16*, 2).

A Washington State employee sued the state for reading his supposedly private E-mail to see if he was misusing the system for private purposes (*SEN 16*, 2).

Proctor & Gamble. Proctor & Gamble discovered confidential corporate information in an article by Alecia Swasy in the *Wall Street Journal*. They attempted to find the source of the leak by obtaining a court order to have Cincinnati Bell provide records of many millions of calls by 650,000 subscribers in the local area code, over a period of more than three months. Those records were then scanned for calls to Swasy's home or office telephone number (*SEN 16*, 4). This process narrowed the suspects down to one former P&G manager, who was interrogated. Apparently no charges were filed—because in fact no law had been broken [164].

Escrowed Encryption Standard, SKIPJACK, Clipper, and Capstone. Extensive discussion arose over the U.S. government's intentions of providing a classified algorithm, known as SKIPJACK, to be used in the Clipper Chip for encrypting and decrypting telephonic communications, while enabling authorized organizations to wiretap despite the encryption—but presumably only with a court-obtained warrant that enables access to a pair of SKIPJACK keys, which are normally stored in separate escrow repositories. Concern centered on the subvertibility of the escrowed keys and the potential for clandestine trapdoors. The approach is also suspect because its intended purpose can be circumvented by uses of private encryption facilities, which has led to speculation that the government might seek to outlaw private uses of cryptography. Capstone is the corresponding algorithm for digital computer communications.[13]

Matt Blaze of AT&T Bell Laboratories has demonstrated an attack that potentially could be used to defeat the ability of law enforcement to decrypt communications [10].

An analysis of U.S. crypto policy is provided by an ACM study group report [73], a summary of which is given in [74].

Accidental privacy losses. Kevyn Collins-Thompson reported to *RISKS* that he received a piece of rejected mail returned to him as undelivered. The only problem was that he was not the original sender. The message began, "My dearest Janice: At last, we have a method of nonverbal communication which is completely private" (*SEN 14*, 1).

Apparently because 2.2 million people showed up for the traditional New York city parade for the 1986 "World Champion" New York Mets baseball team, there was not enough stock-market ticker tape to shower on the parade, so computer printouts of brokerage-house transaction records were used as well (*SEN 12*, 1).

A San Diego school had its payroll printouts accidentally wind up as Christmas gift-wrap paper in a local store (*SEN 12*, 2).

The San Francisco Public Defender's computer database was (allegedly accidentally) set up so that it was readable by the police. As many as 100 cases could have been compromised, but it is not known whether any actually were (*SEN 10*, 2).

The Australian government accidentally sent letters to about 6000 households with explicit financial details about other households. Because the letters had correct data on the front and incorrect data on the reverse side, an alignment error was suspected (*SEN 17*, 2)—that is, an off-by-one error.

A baby-monitoring system provided microphones around the house to monitor baby noises. However, it also broadcast every sound throughout the neighborhood (*SEN 13*, 1).

6.3 **Prevention of Privacy Abuses**

If you don't want someone to know what you are doing, don't do it.
OLD CHINESE SAYING, NOTED BY DAVE PARNAS

The foregoing collection of cases leaves us with a general question: Under what circumstances should there be an expectation of privacy? Congress has ruled that there is no expectation of privacy in cellular telephones and portable telephones, which radiate their signals widely in an unencrypted form. However, there seems to be an expectation of privacy in a computer database, especially if the computer system requires a password for initial access. On the other hand, Sections 3.3.2 and 5.1 demonstrate that passwords themselves do not provide a very secure basis for authentication.

First, your system administrator or anyone with appropriate privileges may be able to read everything even without normal access to your accounts—legally or otherwise. Worse yet, in a realistic sense, there are many ways for insiders and outsiders to break the system security. Therefore, if you want data, programs, or text to be really private, do not store them in a computer that can be accessed remotely. Otherwise, there are essentially no ironclad ways of guaranteeing your privacy. Laws that make privacy violations illegal cannot prevent violations; they can only possibly deter violations. If computer security is inadequate or personnel are untrustworthy, there is no hope for privacy. The risks of misuse must be considered before storing anything in computer databases.

Privacy problems tend to arise in the social gap and in the sociotechnical gap noted at the beginning of Section 3.1. There are intrinsic limitations on what can be enforced by technological security controls. However, the use of encryption in communications can greatly reduce the likelihood of message interception. Within computer systems, access controls and user authentication can clearly help somewhat in restricting access to systems and to information. Mandatory access controls (such as multilevel security noted in Chapter 7) can help to limit the flow of information to within a class of processes and individuals operating at a particular clearance level. Discretionary access controls generally cannot do that, and thus are intrinsically risky in the preservation of privacy. If privacy is an overriding concern, the use of computer databases is inherently risky, and it may be wiser to avoid automation in the first place—a possible conclusion that might be reached in the example of the federal witness-protection program noted in Challenge C6.2 at the end of the chapter.

6.4 **Annoyances in Life, Death, and Taxes**

In addition to privacy problems related to computers, there are mundane ways in which computers and their handlers have made people's lives more difficult. We consider several such cases here.

6.4.1 **Yes, But I'm Not Dead!**

Computer databases have created the mistaken impression that someone was dead, with various consequences.

Checks bounced. Forman Brown (at 85 years of age) wrote in the *Los Angeles Times* (noted by Debbie Estrin) that his bank was rejecting his checks with a deceased stamp, the Social Security Administration had stopped depositing checks into his account, and Medicare objected to paying bills 6 months after his alleged death. His death had been erroneously recorded (*SEN 11*, 3).

Refund blocked. Judi Sommer in Vancouver (at 40 years of age) was prevented from receiving a tax refund from Revenue Canada, which insisted she was dead. Her social insurance number had been inadvertently reported, instead of her deceased mother's (*SEN 13*, 4).

Vietnam Memorial errors. Fourteen Americans had their names mistakenly carved in granite on the Vietnam Memorial in Washington, D.C., among the 58,175 listed as missing or dead. At least one was attributed to the input of a wrong number. (A 0.024 percent error rate is small enough for government work?) (See *SEN 16*, 2.)

But what if you really are dead? The death of a reclusive 51-year-old Dutch man was masked for 6 months because all of his bills were being paid automatically.[14] The 1990 death of an elderly Swedish woman went unnoticed for 3 years for the same reason.[15]

6.4.2 **Billing and Skewing**

Here are a few cases that involve financial mistakes attributable to automated processes.

Satellite delays disrupt ATM transaction. A Vancouver woman visiting Honolulu attempted to withdraw $1100 (Canadian) from her home bank using an ATM, which was controlled by a computer in New Jersey. The satellite delays combined with a flaw in the supposedly atomic transaction protocol resulted in her account being debited without her getting the money. On seeing her monthly statement, she accused her fiancé of theft, and had him apprehended. It took another month to sort it all out (*SEN 12*, 1).

Electrifying bills. A Tampa couple was billed $4,062,599.57 for 1 month's electricity, with an offer to pay in "budget" monthly installments. The blame was placed on a computer operator. The correct bill was for $146.76 (*SEN 13*, 4).

Faye Starman was billed $6.3 million, instead of $63, for electricity, after an input error attributed to a utility company employee's unfamiliarity with a new computer system (*SEN 16*, 1).

Water you waiting for? Malcolm Graham had a 1-month water bill for $22,000, for just under 10 million gallons. A replacement meter had been improperly set, causing the computer program to interpret the difference between readings as diluvial water usage (*SEN 16*, 4).

The barcode is worse than the bite. Customers in Pleasant Grove, Utah, had their water shut off after a new billing system was introduced. The barcodes on the envelopes had not been changed, and the envelopes were misdirected.

David Brinkley billed mistakenly. David Brinkley was mistakenly sent a tax bill for $0.10 by the District of Columbia, along with a nasty warning that he would owe $2,137 in penalties and interest if he did not pay. He paid the $0.10 bill, but mentioned it in his ABC network news program. Tax officials later blamed the bill on a "mathematical audit error" (*SEN 12*, 4).

IRS overbilling. Dickie Ann Conn was found in arrears by the IRS for $67,714 in back taxes. She was then sent a bill for more than $1 billion (including penalties). The IRS later admitted an error in the interest computation (*SEN 16*, 2).

Tax-preparation glitches. The MacInTax program for the 1991 tax year failed to pick up the other income (for example, from 1099-Misc) when a previously saved tax data file was being recomputed.

John Pettitt reported on a PC-based tax-preparation error that required him to pay $36,800 too much in estimated 1992 federal taxes. The program neglected to deduct his state tax and ignored a foreign-tax credit in calculating the alternative minimum tax. The errors were detected when his final tax form was prepared (the bug had been fixed by then), but he had to pay $700 in interest (*SEN 18*, 3, A-6).

Catalectic dachshunds. Hundreds of cat owners in Chicago were billed $5 for failure to register their dachshunds. The pet-vaccination database had been crosslinked with the license database in an attempt to identify unlicensed pets, and "DHC" had been used as a code for both Domestic House Cat and Dachshund (*SEN 12*, 3).

6.4.3　The Computer Is Always Right?

Some computer-related errors are difficult to overcome, because of what might be called autoinertia. Others are simply inconvenient.

The judge can't budge. In a skating competition, the United Kingdom's premiere skater Joanne Conway was accidentally given a rating of 4.2 instead of 5.2. The judge immediately detected the keying error, but the computer system interface and competition rules do not permit any corrections. The only recourse would have been an official appeal, which was deemed unnecessary in view of her final placement (*SEN 17*, 2).

Blank blanks fifth grader. A Florida fifth grader's computer-based sixth-grade placement-test score was zero. Despite protests, the student was forced to repeat fifth grade. Six weeks into the new school year, manual rescoring of the test detected an extra blank between the student's first and last names that had led to the zero score (*SEN 12*, 2).

False arrests. False arrests and other mixups due to computer-data name confusions are noted in Section 6.5; they are particularly nasty instances of computer-related annoyance.

Risks of automated documentation aids. Strange problems have been created by computer-based documentation systems such as editors, spelling checkers and correctors, and automatic hyphenation. We summarize briefly several cases from the *RISKS* archives. An author had written a novel whose main character was named David; the author decided at the last minute to globally change that name to Jeff, and unsuspectingly wound up with a reference to *Michelangelo's Jeff*. The letter *B* was substituted for a family name in a medical study; when it was subsequently decided that the full name (Blenkinsop) could be used, the global edit led to *Hepatitis Blenkinsop*.[16]

Spelling correctors often suggest inappropriate corrections. In various instances, *Mafia enforcer* was transformed into *Mafia in-*

former, payout into *peyote,* and *back in the black* into *back in the AfroAmerican*—the last one in a politically correct newspaper environment. Mary Shafer noted that DECMate II transforms *NASA* into *NAUSEA.* Scott Siege noted that the spelling checker for a Unix system failed to recognize the word *Unix,* and that a checker for the Apple MacIntosh suggested that *Laserwriter* be changed to *Laserjet* (which is Apple's printer).

Here are a few inventive hyphenations that I have encountered:

| Many many- | works- | times- | Emac- | SeaV- | viola- | male- |
| ears | tation | tamp | stool | iew [86] | tion | factors |

6.4.4   Fried Green Automatoes

Even the restaurant business is becoming highly automated, and susceptible to difficulties.

Beef with restaurant's hi-tech computer. Yigal Arens reported on a restaurant in Los Angeles at which he and his family had ordered steaks on the rare side. During a 2-minute power failure, the waiters lit candles. When the steaks arrived, they were seriously overdone. Yigal was told that the power failure had blacked out the restaurant computer's memory (*SEN 12,* 2) as well as the steaks. This report does seem to be in keeping with a new line of high-tech excuses (namely, "the computer ate my homework," rather than "the dog ate it").

Octopusillanimousness after computer-based menu substitutions. The restaurant at the Sydney Opera House had the usual startup problems. Three people ordered river trout. Some minutes later, an embarrassed waiter told them: "Sorry, we put the trout through the cash register, and it came out in the kitchen as octopus." The diners settled for octopus.[17] Obviously the wrong "menu" popped up on the screen! Or were they out of trout and pulling somebody's leg—not the octopus's—and using the computer as an excuse? A subsequent cartoon highlighted this situation, with the waiter saying, "Everyone is getting the fettucine today; our computer is down."

6.4.5   Frustration Abounds

These examples may seem relatively unimportant in the grander scheme of things—for example, contrasted with life-critical control systems whose malfunction or misuse could kill hundreds or even millions of people. However, many people have had similar frustrating experiences, some of which have seriously threatened their sense of personal well-being. The nuisance factor is insidious, and deserves to be recognized as a problem in its own right; it is pervasive, it is commonly discounted as insignificant, and it exemplifies a basic inattention to human needs. Moreover, it is often symptomatic of greater risks.

6.5 What's in a Name?

To prevent our name being stolen and misused again, we don't have a name. Anybody who thinks he's guessed the name and tries to pass himself off as an initiate . . . reveals that he is a fraud.
     HAGBARD CELINE[18]

This section considers cases in which names and identifiers were the cause of problems, serious or otherwise.

6.5.1   Identity Problems

All sorts of problems are attributable to the use of identifiers, resulting from wrong names, multiple names (aliases), ambiguous names, confused names, forgotten names, impersonations and other unauthenticated identities, and, in some cases, the absence of identifiers altogether. Mere knowledge of a name or identifier can lead to harmful acts against an individual. All of these risks arise in computer-related systems and in life situations, often in combination with one another.

Misuse of fingerprint system. Martin Lee Dement spent 2 years in Los Angeles County Jail, because of botched use of the then-new California Automated Latent Print System. Manual check of another suspect's prints finally cleared him (*SEN 14*, 6).

Evidence to the contrary. Joseph O. Robertson was arrested, extradited, and confined to a state mental facility for 17 months, despite available mug shots and fingerprints that subsequently exonerated him (*SEN 14*, 5).

Beware of imitations. After Terry Dean Rogan lost his wallet (which contained his driver's license and credit cards), someone impersonating Rogan committed two murders and two robberies, which resulted in a warrant being placed in the National Crime Information Center (NCIC) database. Rogan was arrested five times in 14 months, despite trying to get the NCIC records corrected after he discovered the problem on his first arrest. He eventually sued and won $55,000 from the Los Angeles police.[19]

Richard Sklar was apprehended three times on computer checks because of the activities of a masquerader (*SEN 14*, 2).

Clinton Rumrill III has had credit-card and traffic problems resulting in civil and criminal charges against him. A childhood "friend" was impersonating him by using his name and social-security number. Police are aware of the problem, but their computers believe that the two are actually the same person. Rumrill was told that the easiest solution would be for him to change his name and SSN.[20]

San Francisco attorney Charles Sentman Crompton II was plagued by an impostor who had used his name, address, and SSN to establish charge accounts, to rent an apartment, and to get a driver's license. This activity resulted in $3000 in bills. The impostor was arrested numerous times, including for car theft, and each time gave Crompton's identity. Crompton was given the phony driver's license when the impostor dropped it fleeing from a suspicious clerk. He forwarded a copy of it to the DMV, explaining the situation, and asked for a new license — with a different identifying number. Unfortunately, the DMV mailed the new license to the impostor, further compounding the problem.[21]

Beware of name similarities. Sheila Jackson Stossier was arrested, jailed, and given a computer arrest record with an alias for her married name, because of an NCIC hit on an outstanding warrant for someone named Shirley Jackson (*SEN 10*, 3).

Donny Ray Boone spent 41 days in jail in Florida because of a confusion with a similarly named individual (Bone?), as reported by "The Osgood File" on CBS, July 20, 1993.

In Montreal, two people named Steven Reid had the same birthday, with expected consequences. Lt. Gerard Blouin of the Montreal Police stated, "It's up to him to change his name somehow. If he can modify his name, just by adding a middle initial or something, it would help him."[22] (It probably would not help enough, we suspect.)

Two Neil Fosters in the Boston area had similar appearances. The wrong one was apprehended after a query on the database produced a match on incomplete information, with unfortunate consequences (*SEN 15*, 2).

Two people named Shirley Jones had different birthdays, heights (6 inches apart) and weights (70 pounds apart). The wrong one was arrested despite the obvious disparities, while the real suspect was already in jail (*SEN 10*, 3).

Different people with the same SSN. Anne Marie O'Connor and Ann Marie O'Connor in the New York City area unknowingly shared the same SSN. They also looked similar, and both had birthdays in September. This situation was discovered only when one of them was dunned for back taxes on their combined incomes! (See *SEN 13*, 2.)

Two men in New York named James Edward Taylor shared the same birthday, birth state, and SSN. This situation was first detected in 1965, but had still not been corrected when reported in 1973 (*SEN 15*, 2).

Blue Cross blew across its crossing blues. New York's Blue Cross computer system was unable to distinguish two hospital patients with the same gender and birth date, and created awful billing and payment problems as a result of twins and triplets being treated by the same doctor on the same date. Considerable annoyance resulted for patients, parents, and doctors (*SEN 17*, 3).

Bogus licenses. A masquerader obtained a bogus "duplicate" driver's license for Teresa Stover from the DMV branch in Bailey's Crossroads, Virginia, which was then parlayed into $30,000 in credit-card charges. The same DMV branch was discovered to have issued thousands of bogus licenses, allegedly for only a nominal bribe (*SEN 16*, 3).

SSN misuse. Felonies for stealing, selling, or otherwise misusing SSNs are on the rise in the United States. For example, someone discovered that 12 people were fraudulently using her SSN, another person found that someone using her SSN had obtained 16 credit cards in her name and had charged $10,000, and a third discovered that her unemployment benefits had already been collected by five other people![23]

Identifiers in general. Many different types of problems can arise from supposedly unique identifiers (SUIDs), such as license plates and SSNs, not so much because of the existence of those identifiers, but rather because of the numerous possibilities for their accidental or intentional misuse. Examples include an agency improperly assigning an identifier, a masquerader fraudulently obtaining one, or someone making queries that cross-link disparate databases or otherwise gaining access to information from which information and inferences can be drawn.

Imposition of stricter administrative requirements and judicial penalties might help to ensure the quality of computer-database entries, with respect to both correctness and timeliness of information. False identifications could be reduced if positive matches are never based on partial information without further confirmation. Similarly, negative identifications could be achieved in cases where the wrong person has been apprehended, simply by insisting on a confirmation based on complete information. For example, more thorough forms of low-ambiguity authentication such as biometrics (fingerprints and other fairly unique physical characteristics) can also reduce the probability of false identification, and should be required when lives are at stake.

There are serious risks associated with relying on supposedly unique identifiers, some of which are noted here. Whereas SSNs and other SUIDs are potentially wonderful for avoiding false *identification* (but break down in cases of multiply used or bogus SUIDs), they are useless for *authentication*. Unfortunately, these two fundamentally different functions are too often confused. Finally, more stringent policies need to be established and uniformly enforced regarding the use of databases and identifiers — especially across different systems.[24]

6.5.2   **Name-and-Address Problems**

Numerous cases have been reported of computer-generated letters with absurd name interpretations. Table 6.1 summarizes a few of the more amusing.[25] In other reported cases, mail addressed to *SWITZERLAND* was routed to a nonexistent town in North Dakota, Switzerla ND, and mail to *WEST GERMANY* was sent to West Germa NY. (Mark Brader suggested *DEUTSCHLA ND* might have gotten similar treatment.) The "Etalfried Wedd" case (derived from the firm name of Friedman, Wedd, et al.) came with a letter offering the recipient a preapproved loan for $750. Mike Kelley followed up that incident with a marvelous parody (*SEN 15*, 5, 3) in which "Etalfried" indignantly complained about the paltriness of the amount, and was later offered an unsecured cash loan for $250,000! The

TABLE 6.1 A few mistaken salutations

Actual Identity	Addressee	Greeting (Dear)
Georgia-Pacific Corporation	Georgia P. Corporati	Ms. Corporati
Bradley University	Mrs. Bradley Un, IV	Mrs. Un
James R. Maynard III		Mr. Iii
Lambda Chi Alpha	Alpha, Lambda C.	
Undergraduate Lounge		Mr. Ung Lounge
Lord X		Mr. Lord
St. Peter's College	Saint Peter S. College	Saint College
Department of Computer Science		Mr. Science
Friedman Wedd, et al.		Etalfried Wedd
Julian Thomas Apt. B 6		Mr. 6
Goleta Valley Cycling Club	Goleta V. Club	Mr. Club

story ends with Etalfried finally getting an unsecured cash loan of $3.4 billion and retiring to "elegant and commodious surroundings on the sea in a small and remote South American country."

6.6 **Use of Names as Identifiers**

A name is a name is a name, even if it is also an identifier.
(APOLOGIES TO GERTRUDE STEIN.)

A wide variety of databases track information about individuals. Difficulties arise when the wrong person's records are retrieved, when two people's records are commingled, or when one individual appears repetitively in a database, stored under different names. One contributing factor is the use of people's names as identifiers. A debate on this topic within the Internet *RISKS* community produced numerous responses. A terse summary follows, although the issues are far too complex to be addressed fully.[26]

- Names serve two functions:
    1. Cultural and self-image
    2. Societal identification
Separating these functions simplifies the discussion.

Section 6.6 originally appeared as an *Inside Risks* column, *CACM, 36,* 4, 154, April 1993, written by **Donald Norman**. He is former chairman of the Department of Cognitive Science at the University of California, San Diego. He is now an Apple Fellow at Apple Computer, Inc., in Cupertino, California.

- Societal identification leads to issues of privacy. Privacy is a complex, culturally based notion: What one individual considers intensely personal, another might consider public business.
- Three different concerns about personal records are often confused:
    1. Reliability and accuracy
    2. Misuse
    3. Privacy

Names are critically important for an individual's or family's self-image and cultural values. For many societies, artificially imposed names, no matter how well intentioned and gently enforced, would not work (although some nations do enforce culturally permitted names, and some take steps to reduce name confusions). Names serve so many functions that, despite the convenience, we should probably not use names as the means of access to critical records: Doing so leads to too much confusion for which there is no easy remedy.

Several *RISKS* respondents suggested that we should separate the self-image, self-identity function of the name from that of societal identification. Then, we must devise some other means of identification for society. The identifier should also be a humane one, easy to use and requiring little or no learning. Several identifiers might be used: a simple one for noncritical usage, and more complex ones (possibly redundant and encrypted) for critical items.

6.6.1   Universal Identification

Unique identifiers are needed for legitimate societal functions (for example, licensing, voting, social-security benefits, income tax). Names, even when coupled with birth date or other personal items are still too easily confused (for example, 25 percent of Koreans have the last name Kim). If names cannot serve as reliable identifiers, what can? How can we develop a unique identification scheme that addresses the problems of accuracy, misuse, and privacy? Considerable discussion was devoted to this topic. Many correspondents urged separate identifications for separate purposes to minimize the chance for misuse. One interesting fact that surfaced is that the U.S. social-security number is not a good personal identifier for technical reasons: Only nine digits to register 250 million people. There are no check-digits, and there is such a dense packing of the encoding that random guesses or errors of data entry or memory can access a legitimate account.

6.6.2   **Reliability and Accuracy**

We rely on databases for credit ratings, police checks, medical records, and other transactions. All too often the records are erroneous — for example, because they were input with incomplete or fallacious information, or because they are the combined records of different individuals. Problems of this type are frequent and well known. The solutions will not be easy, and no complete answers were forthcoming in this on-line discussion.

6.6.3   **Misuse and Privacy**

Part of the privacy issue comes from the potential for misuse; another part arises because people sometimes demand a right to privacy. The first question to be addressed is why is there a concern. One problem is that, in the United States, we do not practice what we preach. We claim that we have religious, political, sexual, and racial freedom, but we do not. If we really had that freedom, then maybe we would not need so much privacy. Regardless of what the laws state, people's lives would become intolerable if others knew certain information. Democratic voting policies for political candidates illustrate the point. Why secret ballots? Is it because people are ashamed of their votes, because some would prefer to say one thing in public and act another way in private, or because of the fear of pressure being applied to individuals if their voting patterns could be established? The answer is probably "all of the above." Similar situations arise in all aspects of life.

The debate about the use of personal names as identifiers helped to elucidate the complex social and technical problems associated with large databases. There is probably no single solution to all the issues, but the discussion illustrates yet another area where the technology of computer science must be applied with judicious concern for the rights and customs of individuals and societies.

6.7   **Summary of the Chapter**

Privacy protection can be helped somewhat by computer-system access controls and user authentication, but it is ultimately at risk for both technological and nontechnological reasons. Abuses of privacy are insidious, because they can happen to anyone and their

TABLE 6.2 Summary of threats to privacy and well-being, and their causes

Case	Source of the Problems									
	Req def	Sys des	HW impl	SW impl	Sys use	Mis-use	HW malf	Envir	Anal-ysis	Evol, maint
R. Schaeffer					○	●				
Arizona murder					○	●				
Insider misuse		(○)				●				
Cellular telephones	○	●	○		(○)	●				
Bryant Gumbel						●				
E-mail misuses	○					●				
Satellite delay				●				○		
Billing problems				○	○					
Tax preparation				○	○					
ID problems	(○)	(○)		(○)	(○)	(○)		(○)	(○)	(○)

effects can significantly alter the course of a person's life — as in the case of Rebecca Schaeffer (Section 6.2).

This chapter presents a diverse collection of problems relating to privacy violations, frustrations, and other personal difficulties caused by computer systems and by the people who depend on those systems; not surprisingly, the causes are themselves diverse. Table 6.2 provides a brief summary of the causes of the cited problems. The abbreviations and symbols are as in Table 1.1. The "misuse" column is included, as in Chapter 5.

Privacy violations have resulted from the misuse of databases and communication systems, as well as from inadvertent disclosure of sensitive information. The risks of privacy problems tend to increase in scope and magnitude as databases are increasingly linked together and as communications become a fundamental part of our lives, interconnecting telephones, fax machines, interactive video systems, and computers — without adequate security.

Many of the causes of privacy abuse stem from inadequate system security, the absence of differentiated user privileges (all-or-nothing is the general default), and inherent ambiguities. However, the most insidious cases involve misuse or inadvertent use by individuals — whether or not those people have authorized system access. There are various potential motivations for abuse of rights, including espionage, financial gain (as in the sale of credit- or criminal-history information), curiosity, and revenge. In two of the cases cited here, lives have been lost as a result.

Numerous other cases are noted that resulted in annoyance but not necessarily in losses of privacy or infringement of rights. In the cited cases that include annoyance, billing problems, and name confusions, improper system use and poor human judgment are often implicated. In several cases, software inadequacies are also a contributing factor.[27]

Challenges

C6.1   Given security controls that can protect data elements at an arbitrary granularity on a per-user basis and authentication controls that can, with extremely high probability, ensure the correctness of a user's identity, what risks to privacy still exist? What might you do about them?

C6.2   Suppose that you are being protected under the federal witness-protection program for having testified in a trial against the perpetrators of the most heinous and well-funded crime of the century. You have been given a new identity and a new life. Knowing what you know about system security and reliability, are there circumstances and constraints under which you would be willing to entrust your true identity and your current whereabouts to a computer database system? If so, what are they? Do you think you could design such a system whose operation would be sufficiently trustworthy? Would you have to trust all of the people who might have access to that system? Would you be willing to trust those people?

C6.3   Consider the cases in this chapter in which a unique identifier was the direct cause of a problem, as well as those cases in which the use of such an identifier could have eliminated a problem. Is the use of the social-security number or other universal identifier inherently dangerous? If the SSN were used only as stipulated by U.S. law, would another number have to be created? Can you think of other alternatives? What conclusions can you draw? What recommendations can you make? What residual problems would there be?

C6.4   Consider the use of automatic vehicle identification techniques that would enable automated toll gates to charge a fee without the driver having to slow down or that would enable speeders to be ticketed automatically. What risks can you foresee? What measures might be taken to minimize those risks? Do you think this is a good idea?

CHAPTER 7

A System-Oriented Perspective

The serious problems of life are never fully solved. If ever they should appear to be so, it is a sure sign that something has been lost. The meaning and purpose of a problem seem to lie not in its solution but in our working at it incessantly.

C.G. JUNG

7.1 The Not-So-Accidental Holist: A System View

Think of the small as large and the few as many.
LAO TSE, *TAO TE CHING, 63*[1]

We consider here the importance of an overall systems viewpoint in avoiding computer-related risks. A **system** is a regularly interacting or interdependent group of items forming a unified whole. In computer systems, one person's components may be another person's system, and one person's system may in turn be one of another person's components. That is, each layer of abstraction may have its own concept of a system. We speak of a memory system, a multiprocessor system, a distributed system, a multisystem system, a networked system, and so on. A system design can most effectively be considered *as a unified whole* when it is possible to analyze the interdependent subsystems individually, and then to evaluate, reason about, and test the behavior of the entire system based on the interactions among the subsystems. This system view is particularly true of distributed systems that mask the presence of distributed storage, processing, and control. At each layer of abstraction, it is desirable to design (sub)systems that are context-free; in reality, however, there may be subtle interactions that must be accommodated — particularly those involving the operating environment.

One of the problems that we encounter throughout research, development, and indeed life is that we tend to compartmentalize our endeavors, with individuals becoming specialists in relatively narrow areas, with the result that they often fail to see the bigger picture. There is a great need at certain crucial times in many system developments to bring together the different communities, such as people who fully understand hardware, software, networks, and the intended applications, as well as people who understand the importance of the human interface. In too many cases, these folks have not communicated with one another, resulting in system glitches that illustrate **Conway's Law**:

> The organization of a system directly imitates the organization of the people developing the system.

For example, weaknesses in human communication typically beget analogous weaknesses in computer communication in corresponding system manifestations. This problem can be particularly severe in distributed systems in which various components have been developed by different people. In many cases, it is only *after* the occurrence of an accident or system failure that there is awareness of certain hitherto invisible system interactions and of the latent flaws that these interactions may trigger.

7.1.1   **Risks of Nonholistic Views**

The cases enumerated here include many in which a failure to consider the whole system resulted directly or indirectly in serious consequences.

Absence of end-to-end testing. In the development of the Hubble Space Telescope, no overall system tests were performed—only subassembly tests were done, and they succeeded because they satisfied an erroneous monitoring program that tolerated a 1-millimeter error in the polishing process. In addition to mirror imperfections, there were also sensors that were misdirected because of a wrong sign on the precession relating to star data, the motion of the second antenna was limited by a misplaced cable, and the motion of the first antenna was limited by a software mistake.[2] In a remarkable and successful rescue effort, the astronauts aboard the shuttle *Endeavour* (STS-61) (launched on December 2, 1993) were able to replace a damaged solar panel with new solar arrays, replace two sets of faulty gyroscopes, and install corrective mirrors to improve the precision. Finally, correcting a misaligned antenna resolved what earlier had appeared to be a computer-system problem.

Multiple causes. Both the 1980 ARPAnet collapse and the 1990 AT&T long-distance slowdown (discussed in Section 2.1) involved a confluence of hardware and software problems that had not been adequately anticipated. Further telephone problems in June 1991 continued to demonstrate the intrinsic difficulties in making highly distributed systems robust *and* efficient.

Multiprocessor incompatibilities. In the first shuttle launch, the 2-day launch delay (Section 2.2.1) resulted from a multicomputer clock synchronization problem that could not be detected locally.

Security problems. Many system and network penetrations (Section 5.1) have resulted from a lack of a suitable system perspective on the part of developers, administrators, and users.

Environmental influences. The *Challenger* disaster and many other cases (including the squirrelcides of Section 2.10) remind us that the physical environment is a vital part of the system.

Poor human interfaces. See Section 7.2 for a discussion of how the interfaces for users, operators, and maintenance personnel can be particularly critical.

7.1.2   Introduction to a System Perspective

There is a pressing need to integrate what is known about different disciplines. In some cases it is vital to accommodate different requirements, such as reliability, availability, confidentiality, integrity, human safety, real-time performance, and massive throughput, and to do so simultaneously and dependably. We recognize that sometimes these requirements are in conflict with one another, in which case sound engineering judgments become essential. In such cases, development methodologies, design languages, and good programming practices cannot overcome the need for sage individuals with a suitably holistic system perspective. These concepts are explored further in the remainder of this chapter.

7.2 **Putting Your Best Interface Forward**

Human interfaces to computer-based systems have been a source of serious difficulties. Blame for resulting disasters has often fallen on users, operators, and maintainers, but can generally be traced back at least in part to the original system developers. Problems can arise on both input and output. Some interfaces are oversimplified, whereas others are overly complex and difficult to use; many contain high-risk ambiguities. Each of these situations has led to harmful system behavior, with several cases revisited here.

Accident-prone conventions. We noted in Section 5.7 a high-rolling group that always dealt with wire transfers in multiples of thousands, whereas the other groups within the same organization used the actual amount, the result being a $500,000 Federal Reserve transaction converted into $500,000,000 (*SEN 10*, 3, 9-10).

That case is reminiscent of when the shuttle *Discovery* (STS-18) was positioned upside down in attempting to conduct a Star Wars–type laser-beam missile-defense experiment. The computer system had been given the number +10,023, with the expectation that a mirror would be positioned (downward) toward a point +10,023 feet above sea level—that is, at a laser beam on top of Mona Kea; however, the input was supposed to be in nautical miles, so that the mirror was actually aimed upward (*SEN 10*, 3, 10).

Unintended interface puns. Ambiguities in the human interface are common. The next two cases illustrate harmful input sequences that might be called *computer puns,* because each has a double meaning, depending on context.[3]

BRAVO editor. Jim Horning reported on a lurking danger in getting into edit mode in Xerox PARC's pioneering WYSIWYG (What You See Is What You Get) editor BRAVO. If the user accidentally typed edit when the BRAVO was already in edit mode, BRAVO interpreted the character sequence edit as "Everything Deleted Insert t" and did exactly as instructed—it transformed the contents of the file into the single letter t. After the first two characters, it was still possible to undo the ed; however, once the i was typed, the only remaining fallback was to replay the recorded keystroke log from the beginning of the editing session (except for the edit sequence) against the still-unaltered original file. (This type of recovery would not have been possible in many other systems.)

Univac line editor. A similar example was reported to me by Norman Cohen of SofTech. He had been entering text using the University of Maryland line editor on the Univac 1100 for an hour or two, when he entered two lines that resulted in the entire file being wiped out. The first line contained exactly 80 characters (demarcated by a final carriage return); the second line began with the word about.

> Because the first line was exactly 80 characters long, the terminal handler inserted its own carriage return just before mine, but I started typing the second line before the generated carriage return reached the terminal. When I finished entering the second line, a series of queued output lines poured out of the terminal. It seems that, having received the carriage return generated by the terminal handler, the editor interpreted my carriage return as a request to return from input mode to edit mode. In edit mode, the editor processed the second line by interpreting the first three letters as an abbreviation for abort and refusing to be bothered by the rest of the line. Had the editing session been interrupted by a system crash, an autosave feature would have saved all but the last 0 to 20 lines I had entered. However, the editor treated the abort request as a deliberate action on my part, and nothing was saved.

Complicated interfaces. The Iranian Airbus shot down by the *Vincennes* was being tracked by an Aegis system, whose complicated user interface was determined to be a contributing cause (see Section 2.3). The *Stark's* inability to cope with the Iraqi Exocets was also partly attributable to the human-machine interface (*SEN 12*, 3, 4). Lack of familiarity with a new interface replacing a conventional throttle may have contributed to the 1989 crash of a 737-400 on an underpowered takeoff from LaGuardia Airport in New York (*SEN 15,* 1). Three Mile Island and Chernobyl are further examples of complicated interfaces that contributed to disasters.

Flaky interfaces. Automatic speech recognition and handwriting recognition are intrinsically unreliable when used for purposes of contextual understanding rather than just for user identification. Variations in dialect among different people and variations in speech by the same person both tend to make speech recognition difficult. Handwriting recognition is similarly risky. The handwriting interface to Apple's Newton was described by Ken Siegman[4] as being flaky, slow, poorer for left-handed writers, and strictly limited to a 10,000-word dictionary. Ken (whose name Newton interpreted as "Rick 5 Jeffries") cited the following firsthand example: "Hello, this is Ken, writing this message to test the fax on Newton. So far it's useless." The result he got was this: "Hello, thisis ken irrit nj to test the fax on xiewwtoz. Sofar itf lervgelj." Similar examples have been noted elsewhere, including in the Doonesbury comic strip.

Nonatomic transactions. Section 2.9.1 discusses the Therac-25, a therapeutic linear accelerator in which a supposedly atomic transaction had an unsafe intermediate state that should have been prevented by the hardware and the software. In addition, the command language presented an extremely low and error-prone level of abstraction. (The temporary fix of removing the key cap from the edit key on the Therac-25 control console was clearly an attempt to hinder low-level operator-command hacking, but ducked the deeper issues.)

Dehumanizing the loop. In fly-by-wire aircraft in which critical operations are completely controlled by computer, there is no longer sufficient time for pilots to respond in emergencies. In such cases, leaving the human in the loop could be dangerous. However, taking the human completely out of the loop can also be dangerous, especially if there are unrecognized flaws in the computer system or if the environment presents operating conditions that had not been anticipated adequately by the designers.

Much more care needs to be devoted to human-visible machine interfaces. In general, interface design must be considered as a fundamental part of the overall system design. Superficially, explicit prompting and confirmation can be helpful, with insistence on self-defining inputs and outputs where ambiguities might otherwise arise. Some interfaces are intrinsically risky, however, and patching up the interface may only increase the risks. Consistent use of abstraction, information hiding, parameterization, and other aspects of good software-engineering practice should be applied to human interfaces as well as internally, throughout system design and development. Peter Denning suggested that some of the best interface design work has been done by teams consisting of experts in the domain, experts in graphics, and experts in computation, as in the "cockpit of the future" project at NASA Ames.

A possible moral is that you have to know when to scrub your interface; in some cases, cosmetic palliatives are inadequate, and a better interface and system design would be preferable.

Newer systems have lurking dangers comparable to earlier systems, but with even more global effects. In user interfaces, there are many cases in which a slight error in a command had devastating consequences. In software, commands typed in one window or in one directory may have radically different effects in other contexts. Programs are often not written carefully enough to be independent of environmental irregularities and of less-than-perfect users. Search paths provide all sorts of opportunities for similar computer puns (including the triggering of Trojan horses). Accidental deletion is still a common problem, although many systems and applications provide a form of *undelete* operation that can reverse the effects of a *delete* operation, until the occurrence of a particular time or event, at which point the deletion becomes permanent. In hardware, various flaws in chip designs have persisted into delivery.

I offer a few observations relating to human-machine interfaces.

- Although systems, languages, and user interfaces have changed dramatically, and we have learned much from experience, similar problems continue to arise—often in new guises.

- Designers of human interfaces should spend much more time anticipating human foibles.

- Manual confirmations of unusual commands, crosschecking, and making backups are ancient techniques, but still helpful.

- Computers do not generally recognize, understand, or appreciate puns and other ambiguities.[5]

7.3 Distributed Systems

A distributed system is one in which the failure of a computer you didn't even know existed can render your own computer unusable.
LESLIE LAMPORT

As we evolve more and more toward distributed systems, we must recognize that certain design decisions must be fundamentally altered, and in particular that we must not rely on weak-link centralized servers.[6]

In this section, we summarize briefly problems that are generic to computer systems. Of particular interest are those problems that are intensified by the development and use of **distributed systems,** in which there may be geographical dispersion of hardware, logical distribution of control among coordinating computers, and both logical and physical distribution of data. Various requirements are considered collectively, to emphasize the interactions among them. A generalized notion of **trustworthiness** is used to imply system dependability with respect to whichever set of requirements is to be enforced. Thus, we speak of the trustworthinessof a system, of a subsystem, or of people who are expected to live up to certain assumptions about their behavior.

Distributed systems obviously have great intuitive appeal. People can have greater control over their own facilities. Workstations and computing engines can be integrated to provide enormous computing power. Systems can be configured to provide hardware fault tolerance, reliable communications, high availability, and physical isolation where desired. The benefits of central file servers can still be achieved. However, the simplicity of those arguments sweeps under the rug serious problems of security and controllability that arise when the sharing of data and distributed processing are permitted.

Generic threats to the security of computer systems and networks (such as those enumerated in Section 3.1) are particularly relevant to distributed systems. The requirements of confidentiality, integrity, and prevention of denials of service are the same as for centralized systems, but distributed data and control tend to make global enforcement more difficult.

The analysis of trustworthiness can be significantly more complicated for a distributed system than for centralized systems, although in principle the concepts are the same. Heterogeneous resources and mixed degrees of user and system trustworthiness are characteristically sources of difficulty.

7.3.1   Risks in Distributed Systems

We next identify various potential problem areas in distributed systems.

Untrustworthy computer systems. In a distributed system, it is not always clear what hidden dependencies exist, and which of those involve dependence on less trustworthy systems and networks. In general, it is difficult to avoid such potentially risky dependencies, unless either all components are equally trustworthy or their relative trustworthiness is somehow made explicit and is respected throughout. Trustworthiness must include adequate system security, system integrity, availability, and protection against denials of service. Vulnerabilities in any one system or its network software may lead to penetrations, Trojan horses, or virus attacks on other systems, such as the Internet Worm's exploitation of send-mail, fingerd, and the .rhosts remote logins, discussed in Section 5.1. Unintentional or unpredicted behavior may also have serious side effects. Of particular importance here are mutually suspicious systems, in which neither can be sure of the trustworthiness of the other; such systems require special care to guard against a wide range of threats.

Untrustworthy networks and communications. Distributed systems are particularly vulnerable to network unreliability and inadequate communication security, both internally and externally. Even with constructive redundancy, breakdowns in communications can isolate subsystems. An example was the 1986 case when New England was cut off from the ARPAnet, because all seven supposedly independent trunk lines went through the same physical conduit—which was severed. Unencrypted local networks and long-haul networks may give rise to loss of confidentiality and integrity, as well as compromised authentication (for example, password capture). Use of "promiscuous" mode in the Ethernet permits eavesdropping on all local network communications, including passwords, authenticators, and other interesting information. In many systems and networks, passwords are transmitted in unencrypted form, in some cases worldwide. Even in the presence of encryption, it may be possible to replay encrypted authenticators unless they are constructively made nonreusable—for example, cryptographically based **one-time tokens** that incorporate a timestamp to prevent replay attacks.

Untrustworthy users. Distributed systems are particularly vulnerable to users erroneously presumed to be trustworthy or infallible. This problem exists in centralized systems, but can be exacerbated by geographic remoteness and apparent logical independence in distributed systems. Undesirable activities include not only malicious misuse but also accidental misuse.

Identification and authentication. It is often difficult to know the identity of a remote user, user surrogate, or system, particularly in distributed heterogeneous environments. Providing assurances that an identity is genuine—**authentication**—becomes utterly fundamental to distributed systems. The term **user surrogate** implies something acting on behalf of a user, directly or indirectly, such as a user process or a daemon process that runs independently of particular users. In some cases, an entire system can act as a user surrogate.

A related authentication problem involves **nonrepudiation**— that is, providing assurances of genuineness such that a seemingly authentic but possibly forged message cannot subsequently be claimed to be a forgery. Some authentication systems are not strong enough to provide assurances of nonrepudiation.

In addition, distributed systems exacerbate the need for different system components to be able to authenticate one another. For example, an authentication server must be able to authenticate those system components that communicate with it for access requests. Furthermore, the various system components must be able to authenticate the authentication server when updating a user's authorizations. Techniques such as public-key cryptography hold promise in this area, for example, for distribution of **one-time shared keys** (sometimes misnamed secret keys!) This problem is made still more difficult by the need for alternative authentication servers, because a single centralized authentication server is vulnerable to denial of service attacks and accidental outages. Adding still further complexity with multiple servers is the need to keep them consistent in spite of network outages and malicious attacks. Techniques for enhancing authentication are given in Section 7.9.2.

Distributed data. There are many benefits of **distributed data,** including the high availability of data despite system and network outages. This can be achieved by making constructive use of redundant or less recent multiple versions, and by avoiding dependence on less accessible or less reliable sites. These benefits are countered by the problems of consistency and concurrency control, which escalate substantially in widely distributed systems. **Data integrity** is a potential problem in the presence of untrustworthy sites. **Communication confidentiality** may also be a problem, along with **covert channels** (see Section 3.4)—that is, storage channels or timing channels indirectly permitting signaling between cooperating processes, despite direct communications being forbidden.

Fault tolerance and robust algorithms in distributed control. Distributed systems present opportunities for greater algorithmic robustness,   particularly   in   response   to   unexpected behavior. However, the increased complexity may result in less stability unless carefully controlled. Simplifying assumptions can make algorithms less complex, but also less able to cope with real-

istic events. The absence of assumptions about what events must
be protected against leads to complex algorithms (for example,
Byzantine algorithms that can withstand arbitrary combinations
of faults, termed **Byzantine faults** [70]). (A Byzantine clock algorithm is noted in Section 2.11.2.) Byzantine algorithms tend to
require extensive confirmations, or time delays, or both. Short-
sighted solutions are often risky. A middle ground is needed that
is both realistic and practical. In some cases, it is the management
of the redundancy itself that is the cause of difficulties, as in the
New York area airport shutdowns due to the AT&T internal power
problems on September 17, 1991, noted in Section 2.1.[7]

Backup and recovery. Distributed control and distributed data
both exacerbate the problems of recovering from complex fault
modes; in a highly distributed system, complete consistency is
usually not globally possible, and thus local consistency must
suffice. Preserving consistent distributed versions is complicated
by the need to protect recent versions and redundant copies from
compromise and from subsystem outages. Recovery systems that
attempt to overcome system failures are inherently difficult to test
adequately, as demonstrated by the AT&T problem of January 15,
1990, noted in Section 2.1.

Optimization, high throughput, and enormous parallelism.
Highly parallel systems (with perhaps thousands of processors executing simultaneously) present opportunities for increased performance. However, short-cuts in software-engineering practice may
result in optimizations that increase the risks in the long run. Furthermore, the very-high-performance hardware architectures have
in general ignored security problems to achieve that performance.

Distributed auditing. Distributed control among heterogeneous
systems or among homogeneous systems with different administrative organizations can complicate the problems of audit-trail
collection (that is, **monitoring**) and audit-trail analysis (that is,
auditing). In the absence of a suitably global perspective, dis-
ruptive activity may go undetected far longer than it would with
centralized auditing, simply because events across different system components are difficult to correlate. Careful cooperation is
required to ensure that real-time or retrospective analysis can identify the people, processes, and systems involved, without violating
confidentiality and privacy requirements.

System administration and use. Distributed control introduces new complexities for system operation. In the absence of

centralized control, there is typically no one entity that knows what the global state of the system is, who its users are, what their physical locations are, what the system configurations are, what system components are connected to which networks, what access may be available to gateways, and what possibilities exist for remote accessibility from systems on other networks. Thus, there may be a poorer ability to provide management of the resources. Similarly, users are typically less aware of other people who may have access to the user's resources and consequently are not sufficiently aware of the vulnerabilities.

Nonlocal side effects. Small effects in one portion of a distributed system can propagate unexpectedly. Hidden fault modes or other vulnerabilities may be lurking, or may be introduced by program changes to a system that has worked properly in the past, even if thought to have no weak links. Three examples of this phenomenon are provided by the first shuttle synchronization failure (Section 2.2.1), the ARPAnet collapse of 1980, and the AT&T collapse of 1990 (Section 2.1).

7.3.2   Distributed Systems as Systems

In each of these areas, the problems are quite broad with respect to, for example, security, integrity, reliability, availability, performance, system configuration control, and administration. External penetrations and misuses by authorized users are part of the problem, as are attainment of confidentiality, integrity, adequacy of service, and sufficient anticipation of accidental events and accidental misuse. System configuration, maintenance, and general evolution add to each of these problems.

Many people believe that distributed systems can make life easier for system developers and users alike. But the risks of hidden pitfalls are significant. Implicit trust may unknowingly be conferred on parts of a system that are inadequately reliable, secure, safe, and so on; people are also error prone. The close resemblance between the 1990 AT&T saturation and the 1980 ARPAnet collapse suggests that intrinsic problems still remain and are likely to recur in different guises.

There is widespread consensus that such events can and will continue to happen, particularly because of the role of people. Reflecting on the telephone outages, Jim Horning somewhat ironically recalled the Congressional testimony of Sol Buchsbaum of

AT&T Bell Laboratories, who asserted that a large, robust, and resilient Strategic Defense Initiative (Star Wars) system could be designed and implemented, because it could use the demonstrably sound techniques found in the U.S. public telecommunications network. There was much debate over whether the saturation was a programming-language problem or a programmer problem. Bill Murray stressed the AT&T outage as a *system* problem rather than just a *software* problem. He also warned of gratuitous automation. Jonathan I. Kamens quoted Edwin A. Irland, who had noted that "failure to recover from simplex faults is usually a significant source of total outage time." Gene Spafford warned of increasing technoterrorism in such events being caused intentionally. Lively discussion went on for over 1 month.

Jim Horning added that the 1990 telephone system failure bears a close resemblance to the December 1981 failure of an experimental distributed system, Grapevine. In both cases, the persistence of the recovery code itself caused each node to crash again whenever recovery was attempted. One of the ironics of the Grapevine incident was that it occurred while the principals were presenting Grapevine to the ACM Symposium on Operating Systems Principles [149].

In our modern times, distributed systems need not have so many weak links. There are typically all sorts of hidden dependencies— such as on password servers, file servers, name servers, system logs, and lock managers—whose malfunctions can cause pervasive disturbances. Caveh Jalali noted how timeouts were nested in Sun/OS, ensuring total blockage under certain circumstances. In the research community and in the Tandem world, we know how to reduce drastically the dependence on weak links. It is time that developers of distributed operating systems got the message: Distributed systems are a step forward only if they cannot be totally disabled by simple server failures; ideally, they should be able to survive single failures.

A stand-alone personal computer or totally centralized system works just fine as long as that system is up. The corresponding situation in distributed systems is that a system works wonderfully as long as every component you depend on is working properly. But the likelihood of success is even lower in distributed systems, unless weak links have been avoided by good system design. The problems of designing robust distributed systems are not conceptually difficult, but nevertheless present significant challenges.

7.4 **Woes of System Development**

Confront the difficult while it is still easy;
accomplish the great task by a series of small acts.
  LAO TSE, *TAO TE CHING*, 63[8]

Complex computer systems are rarely developed on time, within budget, and up to spec. Here are just a few examples from the *RISKS* archives that suggest how pervasive the problems are. In most cases, details are not readily available regarding what went wrong.

London Stock Exchange Taurus. The London Stock Exchange spent £400 million in the development of Taurus, an automated stock-transaction system. The entire project was scuttled after it became clear that the system was unlikely ever to satisfy its requirements; its complexity had grown beyond manageability. Much of the criticism centered on the system security and the system integration. The chief executive of the exchange resigned.[9]

Virginia child-support system. The state of Virginia acquired a new system for distributing child-support checks, but experienced massive delays, confusion, lost checks, delayed payments, and improper seizure of tax refunds. Operations costs were expected to be triple the original estimates.[10]

Bank of America MasterNet. Bank of America spent $23 million on an initial 5-year development of MasterNet, a new computer-based trust accounting and reporting system. After abandoning the old system, BoA spent $60 million more trying to make the new system work—and finally gave up. Departed customer accounts may have exceeded billions of dollars.[11]

Allstate Insurance automation. In 1982 Allstate Insurance began to build an $8 million computer to automate its business, with Electronic Data Systems providing software. The supposedly 5-year project continued until at least 1993, with a cost approaching $100 million.

Richmond utility system. In 1984 the city of Richmond, Virginia, hired the accounting firm of Arthur Young to develop a $1.2 million billing and information system for its water and gas utilities. After spending almost $1 million, Richmond canceled the contract for nondelivery. Arthur Young retaliated with a $2-million breach of contract suit.

Business Men's Assurance. Business Men's Assurance began a 1-year project in 1985 to build a $0.5 million system to help minimize the risk of buying insurance policies held by major insurers. After spending $2 million, the completion date was slipped to 1990.

Oklahoma compensation system. The state of Oklahoma hired a major accounting firm in 1983 to design a $0.5 million system to handle its workers' compensation claims. Two years and more than $2 million later, the system still did not exist. It was finally finished in 1987, for nearly $4 million.

Blue Cross and Blue Shield. Blue Cross and Blue Shield United of Wisconsin hired EDS in late 1983 to build a $200 million computer system. The system was delivered on time in 18 months, but it did not work correctly; it issued $60 million in overpayments and duplicate checks. By the time it was finished in 1987, Blue Cross had lost 35,000 policyholders.

Surface Mining. The U.S. Office of Surface Mining spent $15 million on a computer system intended to prevent violators of stripmine laws from getting new permits. The system could not keep identities straight, and the Government Accounting Office (GAO) called it a failure.[12]

L.A. property-tax billing. Thousands of Los Angeles County homeowners were billed retroactively for up to $15,000 in additional property taxes, resulting from a 1988 glitch in an $18 million computer system that was subsequently rewritten from scratch. In addition, the county was unable to collect $10 million that it was owed in taxes.[13]

Pentagon modernization. Modernization of a Pentagon computer system used for general data processing was running $1 billion over budget and far behind schedule. The congressional report released about this system says that Pentagon computer systems have experienced "runaway costs and years of schedule delays while providing little capability." Charles A. Bowsher, the head of the General Accounting Office, said that problems with the Pentagon's accounting system may impede efforts to reduce spending in the Department of Defense because of inaccuracies in the data used to manage the department.[14]

B-1 bomber. The B-1 bomber required an additional $1 billion to improve its ineffective air-defense software, but software problems prevented it from achieving its goals.

Satellite Tracking Control Facility. The software for the modernization of the Satellite Tracking Control Facility was reportedly about 7 years behind schedule, was about $300 million over budget, and provided less capability than required.

NORAD modernization. The modernization of the software at NORAD headquarters was running $250 million over budget and years late.

ASPJ. The Airborne Self-Protection Jammer (ASPJ), an electronic air-defense system installed in over 2000 Navy fighters and attack planes, was $1 billion over budget, 4 years behind schedule, and only "marginally operationally effective and marginally operationally suitable."

Software schedules. General Bernard Randolph, commander of the Air Force Systems Command: "We have a perfect record on software schedules — we have never made one yet and we are always making excuses."

C-17. The C-17 cargo plane being built by McDonnell Douglas had a $500 million overrun because of problems in its avionics software. A GAO report noted that there were 19 on-board computers, 80 microprocessors, and 6 different programming languages. It stated that "The C-17 is a good example of how *not* to approach software development when procuring a major weapons system."[15] The cost-dispute settlement required the government to pay $348 million and McDonnell Douglas to cover $454 million, although a subsequent GAO report delivered to Congress on April 19, 1994, concluded that the actual out-of-pocket cost to the contractor was only $46 million.

The software development process itself. An important report by James Paul and Simon Gregory[16] takes to task the **waterfall model** (which encompasses the entire system-development cycle) and the system- and software-procurement process. "Software is now the choke point in large systems . . . . Government policies on everything from budgeting to intellectual property rights have congealed over time in a manner almost perfectly designed to thwart the development of quality software," James Paul told *Science*, "The federal procurement system is like a software system with bugs."[17]

7.5 Modeling and Simulation

*The less we understand a phenomenon, the more variables we require
to explain it.*
LEWIS BRANSCOMB

Analysis based on system modeling and simulation is always tricky.
When it catches a horrendous bug that would have undermined
system behavior, it is invaluable. When it fails to detect such a bug,
it is a potential source of disaster, especially if its apparent success
promotes false credibility. The *RISKS* archives include examples of
both types.

7.5.1 Simulation Testing Successful in Debug

We begin with several cases in which simulation uncovered flaws
in a design or a program before any bad effects could occur.

F-16 flipover. Section 2.3 notes two bugs that were caught in simulation — the F-16 program bug that caused the virtual airplane to flip
over whenever it crossed the equator, and the F-16 that flew upside
down because the program deadlocked over whether to roll to the
left or to the right.

Shuttle STS-2 abort problem. Preparing for the second shuttle mission,
the astronauts in simulation testing attempted to abort and return to their simulated earth during a particular orbit. They subsequently changed their minds and tried to abort the abort. When
they then decided to abort the mission after all on the next orbit,
the program got into a two-instruction loop. Apparently the designers had not anticipated that anyone would ever abort *twice* on the
same flight (*SEN 8,* 3, Jul 1983).

Nuclear simulations. Difficulties with the Shock II model are noted in
Section 2.10; they necessitated the closure of five nuclear plants.

7.5.2 Simulation Missed Flaw, Live Testing Found It

We consider next a case in which simulation failed to detect a
flaw that was later uncovered by full-scale testing.

Titan IV SRB explosion. On April 1, 1991, a Titan IV upgraded solid
rocket booster (SRB) blew up on the test stand at Edwards Air Force
Base. The program director noted that extensive three-dimensional
computer simulations of the motor's firing dynamics did not reveal subtle factors that apparently contributed to failure. He added

that full-scale testing was essential precisely because computer analyses cannot accurately predict all nuances of the rocket motor dynamics.[18]

7.5.3   Modeling, Simulation, or Testing Failed

Further cases illustrate problems that could not be detected by modeling, simulation, or testing.

Handley-Page Victor aircraft crash. The Handley-Page Victor aircraft tailplane flutter problem is mentioned in Section 4.1. Each of three independent test methods used in flutter analysis had an error, but coincidentally all came up with seemingly consistent results, each wrong, but for a different reason. First, a wind-tunnel model had an error relating to wing stiffness and flutter; second, the results of a resonance test were erroneously accommodated in the aerodynamic equations; third, low-speed flight tests were incorrectly extrapolated. This congruence of results led to the conclusion that there was no tailplane flutter problem at any attainable speed. The tailplane broke off during the first flight test, killing the crew. (See *SEN 11*, 2, 12, plus erratum in *11*, 3, 25.)

Electra body failures. Structural failures of the Electra aircraft were apparently due to simulation having omitted a dynamic effect (gyroscopic coupling) that had never been significant in piston-engined planes (*SEN 11*, 5).

Northwest Airlines crash. The crash of Northwest Flight 255 that killed 156 people in 1987 is discussed in Section 2.4. There was a later report that the flight simulator behaved differently from the aircraft. In particular, the warning indicator for the MD-80 aircraft went off as expected in the simulator, but did not do so in the planes. (The FAA's fix for that was to change the simulator rather than the aircraft, because the warning system was considered "nonessential."[19]

Colorado River flooding. In the late spring of 1983, there was serious flooding from the Colorado River. Too much water had been held back prior to spring thaws. There were six deaths, with damages costing millions of dollars. The problem was traced to a bug in the computer program that had modeled the flood process and predicted how much water should be stored. The implications were that any one or all of the model, the program, and the data could have been faulty.[20]

Salt Lake City shopping mall roof collapses. The collapse of the Salt Lake City shopping mall involved an incorrect model, tests that ignored the extreme conditions, and some bad assumptions. The roof caved in after the first big snowfall of the season — fortunately, before the mall was opened to the public (noted by Brad Davis in *SEN 11*, 5).

Hartford Civic Center roof collapse. The collapse of the Hartford Civic Center Coliseum's 2.4-acre roof under heavy ice and snow on January 18, 1978, apparently resulted from the wrong model being selected for beam connection in the simulation program. *After* the collapse, the program was rerun with the correct model — and the results were precisely what had actually occurred.[21]

Stars and Stripes skids the grease. In losing the America's Cup, the racing boat *Stars and Stripes* was victimized by problems in computer modeling and tank testing of scale models. Three iterations of modeling and tank-testing on supposedly improved designs yielded results that were degrading rather than improving. This counter-productivity led to a startling discovery: The simulation program accidentally included a digital filter left over from an earlier oil-platform test.[22]

7.5.4   **Perspective**

Analysis and testing based on modeling and simulation are typically dependent on the accuracy of assumptions, parameters, and programs. We must be suspicious of every detail throughout the overall system engineering. Even end-to-end testing of an entire system is not enough. In discussing the Electra simulation problem, Jim Horning summed up: "Simulations are only as good as the assumptions on which they are based." In fact, they may not even be that good. Rebecca Mercuri noted that "It is the illusion that the *virtual* is *real* and that the *system* is an *expert* that creates a false sense of confidence." The roles of modeling, simulation, and testing all must be considered accordingly.

7.6   **Coping with Complexity**

Seek simplicity and distrust it.
ALFRED NORTH WHITEHEAD

Everything should be made as simple as possible, but no simpler.
ALBERT EINSTEIN

7.6.1   **Factors Affecting Complexity**

Coping with complexity is a serious problem in system development, operation, maintenance, and use.[23] Here are some relevant observations.

Complexity is in the eye of the beholder. Some people have serious difficulties managing intrinsic complexity, especially in coping with reality. Others thrive on creating monstrous systems where simpler ones would do. Between these extremes are a chosen few whose instincts, experience, and training permit them to manage complexity with relative ease.

There are some people who believe they could successfully create enormously complex, dependable systems meeting arbitrarily stringent requirements (such as in the early conceptions of Star Wars), in the face of copious evidence that very large system-development projects are rife with serious shortcomings and are subject to all sorts of inadequately anticipated events. For the naïve and the optimists, *complexity is the eye of the hurricane.* Everything seems to be calm, until the development progresses sufficiently far or until something must be changed, with consequent unanticipated disasters.

Complexity will also be increasingly in the eye of the law. If a computer system is implicated in deaths or property loss, the defense may ultimately depend on whether generally accepted system-engineering practices were in use. If a computer audit trail seems to implicate someone as a perpetrator of inside misuse, the defense may depend on whether that audit trail could have been altered. Strangely, the legal implications may encourage generally poor practice rather than better practice.

Complexity is often viewed in the eye of the technologist. Complexity must not be considered solely as a technological problem. It must be regarded in a broader perspective that includes social, economic, and world-political issues. Again, Star Wars comes to mind. The need for global awareness may seem unfortunate to the manager who wishes to circumscribe his responsibilities starkly, but such awareness is absolutely essential. In many cases, complexity is out of control because of nontechnological problems, to which management may be a major contributor. In other cases, the technology itself is not able to overcome the other problems.

Complexity is ubiquitous. Complexity means different things to different people. We use an intuitive notion of "complex" here, roughly equivalent to what we normally think of as "complicated" — difficult to analyze, understand, or explain. We eschew numerical measures that might appear to quantify complexity but that can themselves be risky if they are institutionalized to the point that design decisions are made on the basis of those measures rather than on that of sound judgment.

Complexity has diverse causes. Certain applications are intrinsically complex, no matter how you look at them. Stringent real-time constraints, distributed control, and concurrent execution tend to add complexity in certain ways, but can alternatively be used as forcing functions that demand a conceptual simplicity of the overall system. Systems with elaborate user interfaces are often complex. In a classical tradeoff, the user interface may be simplified at the expense of internal system complexity, or the system may be simplified at the expense of much greater human interaction; however, each of these efforts is likely to be counterproductive unless a suitable balance is struck. Measures to increase reliability (for example, fault tolerance and recovery) can add significant complexity to an otherwise simple system, particularly if the system seriously attempts to anticipate all realistic exception conditions that might somehow arise. In some systems, the code responsible for fault and error handling outweighs everything else. Software tools may create further complexity in their attempts to control it. Overall, complexity tends to grow faster than the size of the system, under any meaningful definition of complexity.

Complexity tends to increase. Combatting complexity is made increasingly difficult by continual demands for larger and more elaborate systems, extensions of existing systems into areas that push the limits of the technology or the limits of the approach, and demands for increased interoperability by linking disparate systems into heterogeneous distributed systems and networks.

Complexity is difficult to control. The development of complex systems is always a challenge, with many obstacles: The requirements are often ill-defined and poorly understood; the interfaces to other subsystems and to the rest of the world are ill-defined; the design is specified (if at all) only after the implementation is mostly well underway; the schedules are often unrealistic and driven by external events; the developers are not ideally matched to the tasks at hand; the funding is inadequate, and so on.

A common simplistic rejoinder is that we can avoid these obstacles simply by "doing it right in the first place." Unfortunately, the obstacles tend to be pervasive and not easy to avoid, even with wonderful technology and gifted people. The principles of good system development are not easy to employ wisely. Experience shows that motherhood cannot be taken lightly if it is to be done right.

7.6.2   Structural Approaches to Managing Complexity

In light of the existing software practice, it is appropriate to consider constructive approaches to the development of complex systems. We discuss techniques for structuring both the development effort and the system design itself, with significant potential returns on investment, mentally, financially, managerially, and practically.

Constructive Approaches

There are many approaches to controlling complexity. First, there is enormous payoff from good management, especially if aided by software-engineering and system-engineering techniques that help to structure the system design and the development effort. In addition, there are great benefits from being able to reuse software and hardware components that have been carefully developed and evaluated. Standards for interfaces, development techniques, programming languages, and tools all may have benefits. To the extent that the mechanisms are demonstrably sound and firmly established, software functionality can migrate into hardware. Also helpful are tools that help to structure the entire development cycle (including requirements, specifications, programming, reviews, walkthroughs, testing, and formal analysis), whether they support the management process or the development itself. For example, it would be helpful to obtain projective views of a system design from differing perspectives, such as from the vantage point of the networking or storage management. Even techniques that merely enable managers to ask more sensible questions can be beneficial. However, managers and technologists must both beware of overendowing tools with supposedly magical Wizard-of-Oz–like powers.

Various approaches have been discussed for structuring the design of a complex system, including those in Dijkstra [37], Parnas [122] and Neumann [107]. (See also [103] for a systems-oriented overview.) Useful techniques include partitioning and modularization, hierarchical abstraction, abstract data types and object-oriented design, strong typing, encapsulation and information hiding, functional isolation, decoupling of policy and mechanism, separation of privileges, allocation of least privilege, and virtualization (such as the invisibility of physical locations, concurrency, replication, hardware fault tolerance, backup, recovery, and distribution of control and data). These techniques are revisited in Section 7.8 in the context of software engineering. There can be significant benefits from the use of higher-level (more abstract) languages in which to express requirements, designs, and implementations, although the existing languages all seem far from ideal. Also of value as structuring concepts are **multilevel security** (MLS) (for example, no adverse flow of information with respect to sensitivity of information) and **multilevel integrity** (MLI) (for example, no dependence on less trusted entities). In addition, **formal methods** (such as specifications based on mathematical logic and reasoning based on mathematical theorem proving) have potential for addressing requirements, specifications, programs, and hardware, possibly including selected formal analyses of consistency or correctness for particularly important properties and components.

Dependence

Among all of the techniques for managing complexity, perhaps the most poorly understood and yet potentially most valuable are those relating to the structuring of a system—for example, into layers of abstraction or into mutually suspicious cooperating subsystems. Parnas [124] defines and discusses the mathematical relation in which one component **depends for its correctness on** another component. (He also discusses other hierarchical relationships, although the depends-on relation is the most important here.) If one component depends on another, then there need to be adequate assurances that the depended-on component is adequately trustworthy, or else that its misbehavior would not be harmful. With some care, it is possible to develop trustworthy systems using untrustworthy components, as is the case in fault-tolerant systems. Malicious misbehavior, correlated faults, collusion, and other more obscure modes of misbehavior are referred to as **Byzantine** fault modes.

Whether Byzantine or more conventional modes are addressed, whenever one component must depend for its correctness on another component, the dependencies must be carefully controlled, respecting varying degrees of trustworthiness inherent in the different components. **Correctness** may be defined in terms of requirements such as confidentiality, system and data integrity, availability, and performance. The layers of abstraction can profitably reflect the different degrees of criticality of the properties that each layer enforces.

It may be useful to extend the depends-on relation to encompass multilevel integrity (for example, Biba [9]). With such an extension, a component would — to a first approximation — *depend on only those other components that are considered at least as trustworthy;* in reality, there are typically various cases in which it is necessary to deviate from that strict policy, and in those cases it is necessary that the management of those exceptions themselves be done in a trustworthy way. In some circumstances, the exceptions are so predominant or so nonhierarchical that they become the rule.[24]

Trusted Computing Bases

The security community has evolved a notion of a **trusted computing base** (TCB), which completely controls all use of its own operations, and which cannot be tampered with.[25] It encapsulates all of its operations, mediating all security-relevant accesses. In distributed systems, a trusted server may be thought of as a TCB for the objects, access to which it mediates.

The essence of trusted computing bases is that security-relevant components are separated from security-irrelevant components, which do not need to be trusted with respect to security. Having made that separation, design effort and analysis for security can focus on the TCB.

The TCB notion may be extended usefully to other properties of complex systems in general. For example, a TCB may be trusted to enforce fundamental properties such as multilevel security or multilevel integrity, and also high-availability processing, basic safety properties, financial soundness of an enterprise, or simply doing the right thing. The Clark–Wilson application integrity properties [25] represent a model for the sound behavior of a transaction-oriented system; an application system ensuring those properties could be a TCB with respect to those properties; however, ensuring those properties in turn requires that the underlying operating system, database-management system, and so on, cannot be compromised.

Structuring a system hierarchically according to dependence on its components according to their trustworthiness can help significantly in managing complexity. This approach is particularly vital in the design of distributed systems, in which some components may be of unknown trustworthiness.

System Engineering

The overall perspective of **system engineering** is essential for managing complexity. The risks are widely distributed throughout development and operation. Potentially every supposedly minor change could have serious consequences unless the system design and development methodology reflect the decoupling of cause and effect, the need to provide incremental closure on each change (for example, Moriconi and Winkler [95]), and the need for discipline throughout the development process.

Efforts to combat complexity must address not only software but also hardware issues, environmental factors, and the workings of potentially all the people involved as requirements definers, designers, specifiers, implementers, users, administrators, and malefactors, any of whom might wittingly or unwittingly undermine the work of others.

Unfortunately, some of the biggest problems confronting computer system developers stem from the paucity of real and useful systems that have successfully been methodologically developed and carefully documented. Few efforts provide explicit lessons as to how best to manage requirements, the design, the implementation, and the entire development process. Seldom do we find a system development whose design decisions were well documented, individually justified, and subsequently evaluated — explaining how the decisions were arrived at and how effective they were. Clearly, however painful it may be to carry out such an effort, the rewards could be significant.

7.7 Techniques for Increasing Reliability

The most likely way for the world to be destroyed, most experts agree, is by accident. That's where we come in; we're computer professionals. We cause accidents.

NATHANIEL BORENSTEIN [15]

An enormous range of techniques exists for increasing system reliability and achieving fault tolerance. Each technique makes assumptions about the potential faults that need to be accommodated, and then attempts to cover those faults adequately. The simplest assumptions involve transient errors that will occur occasionally and then disappear; in such cases, error detection and retry may be adequate. On the other end of the spectrum are the assumptions of essentially unrestrictive failure modes, namely, the Byzantine failures [70]. Transcending Byzantine fault modes generally requires complicated algorithms. As an example, a Byzantine clock is noted in Section 2.11, composed of $3n+1$ constituent clocks such that the overall clock will remain within its prescribed accuracy despite arbitrary (accidental or malicious) failures of any n of the constituent clocks.

Fault tolerance. Fault tolerance involves designing a system or subsystem such that, even if certain types of faults occur, a failure will not occur. Many techniques have been used to improve reliability and specifically to provide fault tolerance. These techniques include forward error recovery and backward error recovery, existing at various layers of abstraction in hardware or in software.

Forward error recovery. Forward error recovery implies detecting an error and going onward in time, attempting to overcome the effects of the faults that may have caused the errors. It includes the constructive use of redundancy. For example, error-correcting codes may be used to correct faults in memory, errors in communications, or even errors in arithmetic operations. Sufficient extra information is provided so that the desired information can be reconstructed. Forward recovery also includes hardware-instruction retry, which often is used to overcome transient faults in processing. Forward recovery may involve taking alternative measures in the absence of certain resources. However, the presence of faults can often be masked completely. Results are not made available until correction has been accomplished.

Backward error recovery. Backward error recovery implies detecting an error and returning to an earlier time or system state, whether or not the effects have been observed externally or have otherwise propagated. It includes the use of error-detecting codes, where a fault or error is detected and some alternative action is taken. It also includes rollback to an earlier version of data or an earlier state of the system. It may include fail-safe and fail-stop modes in which degraded performance or less complete functional behavior may occur. The presence of faults is not masked in some cases — for example, when a garbled message is received and a retry is requested.

7.7.1   Error-Detecting and Error-Correcting Codes

We can illustrate the need to avoid weak links by considering the use of error-detecting and error-correcting codes [128, 135], whether for transmission, for storage, or for processing operations (as in the case of codes capable of correcting arithmetic errors). The **Hamming distance** [56] between two equally long binary words is the number of positions in which those words differ. The minimum Hamming distance of a code is the smallest distance between arbitrary pairs of code words. As we see below, if the minimum Hamming distance is $d = 2e + 1$, then e independent errors can be corrected.

First, consider uncorrelated errors in which a binary digit (**bit**) position is altered from 0 to 1 or from 1 to 0. The addition of a parity check bit, so that there is an even number of 1 bits among all of the bit positions, results in the ability to detect any one arbitrary bit position in error. Such a code has minimum Hamming distance 2. Any single-bit alteration converts a word with an even number of 1 bits into a word with an odd number of 1 bits, which is immediately recognized as erroneous.

A code with minimum Hamming distance 4 can correct single errors and also detect arbitrary double errors. This ability is illustrated in Table 7.1 with a trivial 4-bit code consisting of two code words, 0000 and 1111. The presence of an error in a single-bit position is clearly detectable as an apparent single error. The presence of errors in two bit positions is clearly recognizable as an apparent double error. However, the presence of errors in three bit positions of one code word would appear to be a single error in the other code word; if the code were used for single-error correction, the received code word would be miscorrected as though it were a single error. Somewhat more insidiously, quadruple errors would appear to be correct messages, with no error indication. Thus, if triple or quadruple errors are at all likely, it would be desirable to use a code with a larger Hamming distance, or else to find a more reliable communication medium.

TABLE 7.1 A trivial 4-bit code with Hamming distance 4

Code Word	Correct and Incorrect Interpretations
0 0 0 0	Presumed correct representation of **A** (but could be a 4-bit error of **B**)
0 0 0 1	1-bit error of **A**, or 3-bit error of **B**
0 0 1 1	2-bit error of **A**, or 2-bit error of **B**
0 1 1 1	1-bit error of **B**, or 3-bit error of **A**
1 1 1 1	Presumed correct representation of **B** (but could be a 4-bit error of **A**)

Suppose that a code has a minimum Hamming distance of 7. Such a code could be used to correct up to triple errors, or to correct up to double errors and to detect up to quadruple errors, or to correct single errors and to detect up to quintuple errors, or simply to detect sextuple errors. The choice of how to use such a code needs to be made with knowledge of the expected errors. The choice of which code to use also depends on the nature of the expected errors. Deeper knowledge of the entire system is also required, to ascertain the potential damage if the actual errors exceed the capability of the code.

Suppose that the errors are likely to be correlated—for example, that they tend to occur within consecutive bursts during transmission. In such cases, it is possible to use burst-detecting and burst-correcting codes, as long as the burst length is not *too* long. However, if the noise characteristics of the communication (or storage) medium are high, or if the risks of the consequences of exceeding the fault-tolerance coverage are too great, then physical replication may be desirable—in addition to coding. Alternatively, error detection and retry using an alternative path provide both temporal and spatial redundancy for increased communication reliability, assuming that real-time requirements do not preclude such an approach—as in the case of communications with distant spacecraft.

7.7.2 Applicability and Limitations of Reliability Techniques

In a typical application, each system layer depends on the functionality of lower layers and employs reliability techniques appro-

TABLE 7.2 Reliability threats and fault-tolerance techniques

Layer	Threats	Fault-Tolerance Mechanisms
Applications	Environment, hardware (HW), software (SW)	Application-specific redundancy and rollback
Systems	Outages	System isolation, data security, system integrity
Databases	Data errors	Atomic transactions and safe updates, complete transaction histories, backup
Networks	Transmission errors	Reliable controllers; safe asynchrony and handshaking; alternative routing; error-detecting and error-correcting codes
Processes	HW/SW faults	Alternative computations, rollback
Files	Media errors	Replication of critical data on different media and sites; archiving, backup, retrieval
Processors	HW faults	Instruction retry; error-correcting codes in memory and processing; replication; multiple processors and memories

priate to that layer. The association of such techniques with the threats at different layers is illustrated in Table 7.2. In essence, this table suggests that the implementation at any layer should be designed such that the layer can be largely responsible for its own reliability, that it may constructively depend on and take advantage of lower-layer techniques, and that higher-layer actions may have to be taken in the event that fault tolerance or recovery cannot be effected at the particular layer.

Despite efforts to increase reliability, there is always the potential for circumstances in which those efforts break down — for example, in the face of massive faults or subsystem outage or of faults that exceed the coverage of the fault tolerance.

Techniques for achieving hardware-fault tolerance and software recovery are widespread in the literature, and many of those techniques have made their way into commercial off-the-shelf computer systems.[26]

7.8 Techniques for Software Development

Developing complex systems that must satisfy stringent requirements for reliability, security, human safety, or other forms of application correctness, such as the ability to manage money soundly, requires an extremely principled approach to system development, well beyond what is traditionally experienced in general programming practice. Such an approach is needed especially when the systems are highly dispersed physically or when the control and accountability are distributed. System engineering and software engineering are in essence approaches that seek to manage complexity. However, they must not be invoked blindly because they present pitfalls when applied to complex systems.

7.8.1   System-Engineering and Software-Engineering Practice

As noted in Section 7.1, the need for an overall system perspective is fundamental to the development of secure and reliable systems making extensive use of computers and communications. Beginning with system conceptualization and carrying through requirements definition, design, specification, implementation, and on into system configuration and initialization, maintenance, and long-term system evolution, it is essential never to lose sight of that overall perspective. In addition, continued evaluation is meaningful throughout the development (and redevelopment) process, with respect to the concepts, requirements, design, specification, implementation, and ensuing evolution. Part of that evaluation involves assessing the extent to which the desired criteria have been met.

Good system-engineering and software-engineering practice can add significantly to such system developments. As we can observe from the attack methods enumerated in Section 3.1, many characteristic security-vulnerability exploitations result directly because of poor system and software engineering; such opportunistic attacks occur particularly in trapdoor attacks and other ways of defeating authorization mechanisms, and in both active and passive forms of misuse. Similarly, modes of unreliable system behavior often arise because of poor engineering practice. Unfortunately, many past and existing software system-development efforts — operating systems, database-management systems, and applications — have failed to take adequate advantage of good engineering practice, particularly those systems with stringent requirements for security, reliability, and safety.

Being weak-link phenomena, security, reliability, and human safety depend on sound practice throughout the entire development process. Although human errors made in the early stages of development can sometimes be caught in later stages, those errors that are *not* caught are typically the most insidious. Thus, each stage noted in the following discussion is important in its own right in the development of reliable, secure, high-performance systems. For each stage, illustrations are included of problems that might have been avoided, referring specifically to incidents discussed in preceding chapters.

Concept formation. Developers must wrestle from the outset with the real goals of the intended system, application, or (in some cases) the entire enterprise, and must anticipate which system problems will potentially be critical later in the development. Sometimes, problems arise because a system is expected to perform a service that could not realistically be implemented, as in the case of the original Star Wars concept. In some cases, design and implementation complications arise because of overspecificity in the original concept, and prevent the development of a system that might have more general applicability. Serious effort must be expended at the outset of a development to ensure that the system conceptualization is sound, realistic, effective, and efficiently implementable. The personal-computer operating-system industry provides a horrible example of a short-sighted concept, where it was never realized that an operating system sometimes needs to be able to protect itself.

Criteria for system evaluation. Explicit criteria need to be established consensually in advance, providing realistic constraints that systems and system developments must satisfy, and against which the completed systems can be evaluated. Various criteria exist for secure systems, such as the U.S. Department of Defense Trusted Computer Security Evaluation Criteria (TCSEC) — for example, the Orange Book [101] and Red Book [100], and the European and Canadian guidelines, as well the many U.S. National Institute of Standards and Technology federal information processing standards on security. A set of criteria for evaluating system safety is in use in the United Kingdom [169, 170].

Requirements definition. The people and organizations that develop system requirements must anticipate all of those problems that should already have become evident in concept formation, as well as other problems that arise in design and implementation. The result should provide specific and realistic requirements for the resulting systems, as well as requirements for the development process itself. As noted throughout this book, developers must address not only the security requirements but also those requirements that interact with security, such as reliability, throughput, real-time performance, and reusability. Fundamental mistakes in requirements definition tend to permeate the entire development effort, even if caught later on. Serious effort must be expended to ensure that the requirements are sound and consistent with the overall system conceptualization. Whenever security is encapsulated into a kernel or trusted computing base, care must be taken to characterize the privileged exceptions. With respect to the security requirements, and to some of the other requirements that interact with security such as reliability and performance, formal definitions of those requirements can be helpful in smoking out ambiguities and inconsistencies in the requirements. A priori requirements definition is vital within a total systems context (for example, see [104]), but is nevertheless often given inadequate attention. Requirements should include aspects of security and reliability, but should also declare what is needed with regard to the human interface, ease of use, generality, flexibility, efficiency, portability, maintainability, evolvability, and any other issues that might later come home to roost if not specified adequately. Whether or not the Patriot requirements for only 14-hour consecutive operation were appropriate, they were not respected by the operational practice. (On the other hand, the clock-drift problem was the result of serious underengineering, and apparently undermined even operations within the 14-hour window.)

System design. The system-design process is typically the source of many system flaws. Particularly annoying are those flaws that remain undetected, because they can be difficult and expensive to fix—especially if they are detected much later. Practical design issues include deciding on the extent to which a system can be built out of already existing or easily modifiable components. Design issues in the large include deciding on the nature of distribution to be used (control, data, etc.), the extent to which the system needs to be fault tolerant and which types of reliability techniques should be employed, the type of communication mechanisms (interprocess communication, message passing, and remote procedure calls), system structuring, layering, and decoupling of subsystems, the role of trusted computing bases as building blocks, and the extent to which good software-engineering practice should pervasively affect the development effort. Design issues in the small relate to specific subsystems, components, and modules, and include the use of abstraction and encapsulation within components, and types of protocols and mechanisms for intercommunication and synchronization. Use of the object-oriented paradigm in the system design itself may be beneficial (particularly with respect to system integrity)—for example, creating a layered system in which each layer can be looked on as an object manager.

The **object-oriented** paradigm combines four principles of good software engineering—abstraction, encapsulation, polymorphism, and inheritance. **Abstraction** takes many forms; in the present context, it implies the removal of unnecessary details from the representation of a particular system component. **Encapsulation** with respect to a particular interface involves the protection of internal mechanisms from tampering and the protection of internal data structures from disclosure. **Polymorphism** is the notion that a computational resource can accept arguments of different types at different times and still remain type safe; it enhances programming generality and software reuse. **Inheritance** is the notion that related classes of objects behave similarly, and that subclasses should inherit the proper behavior of their ancestors; it allows reusability of code across related classes. Choice of a design methodology can have a considerable influence on the ensuing development. Arguments over which methodology is best are often second-order; use of any methodology can be beneficial if that methodology is reasonably well defined, is well understood, and has been used previously with success. In any particular development, some methods may be more effective than others, depending on the requirements, the nature of the application, and the composition of the development team. Careful design specification is beneficial throughout the development process, and should be considered as an integral part of the design rather than as an afterthought.

Overt design flaws are a significant source of problems in the design process; they can be combatted somewhat by consistent use of the good design principles emphasized here. Examples of situations cited here that might have been avoided through such practice include the 1980 ARPAnet collapse (Section 2.1), the first shuttle backup-computer clock synchronization problem (Section 2.2.1), the Aegis and Patriot-missile problems (Section 2.3), the Therac-25 (Section 2.9.1), and the design of nonsecure computer operating systems (Chapters 3 and 5), to name a few.

Consistency. Evaluation of the consistency of a design with respect to its design criteria and requirements should be done with considerable care prior to any implementation, determining the extent to which the design specifications are consistent with the properties defined by the requirements. It should also be possible at this stage to do a preliminary assessment of the system design with respect to the intended evaluation criteria. Such an evaluation was clearly lacking in many of the cases discussed here. Much greater emphasis could be placed on analytic processes and tools that could aid in early system evaluations.

Implementation. Some developers view system implementation as an anticlimax following the seemingly successful completion of the previous stages: Given a design, you simply write the code. Unfortunately, the intricacies of the implementation process are often given short shrift, and the pitfalls are ignored:

- The choice of **programming language** (or languages) is fundamental. Security-critical subsystems may sometimes necessitate the use of a different language from that used in applications when greater discipline is required, or possibly more stringently enforced conventions in the use of the same language. Of particular importance in the choice of programming language are issues concerning modularization, encapsulation, use of types and strong type checking, program definable extensions, initialization and finalization, synchronization, aliasing, control of argument passing, handling of exceptions, and run-time libraries. In weaker programming languages, each of these facilities can lead to serious security compromises. Furthermore, use of lower-level programming languages is typically more error-prone than is use of higher-level programming languages of comparable sophistication.

- **Good programming discipline** is essential. Choice of an untyped freewheeling language (such as C) may be effective with disciplined programmers, but disastrous otherwise. Choice of a discipline-demanding language (such as C++, Modula-2+, or Modula-3) may potentially produce a sounder system, but requires disciplined programmers; besides, each of those languages has some severe limitations. C++ is a low-level language, although it does contain certain modern features. Modula-3 has considerable potential, but is in its infancy in terms of widespread availability of practical compilers. Ada, despite its strong advocates, presents difficulties. All of these languages are deficient when it comes to real-time and asynchronous programming (including Ada's inherently synchronous attempt at asynchrony—that is, its rendezvous mechanism). Estelle and Real-Time Euclid are candidates for developing real-time systems, but are also deficient. Besides, even the best programming language can be misused. Object-oriented programming may fit naturally, particularly if the system design follows the object-oriented paradigm. Object-oriented programming languages include C++, Modula-3, Eiffel, Simula, and Smalltalk. Note that the object-oriented paradigm has also been studied relative to multilevel secure systems and databases [43, 114, 65, 85, 172].

The synchronization problem in the first shuttle was partly a design error and partly a programming flaw. The Patriot clock-drift problem was largely attributable to a programming error, using two different and nonequal representations for the same number. A lack of type checking was certainly evident in the Mercury Fortran program statement with DO 1.10 instead of DO 1,10. The lack of bounds checking on the length of the typed password was partly to blame for the master-password flaw noted in Section 3.1.

Correctness of the implementation. Evaluation of the implementation with respect to its design must be done to determine whether the source code and ultimately the object code are consistent with the system specification. Concepts carefully enforced by a design may be undermined by the implementation. For example, a design that carefully adheres to modular separation and encapsulation may be compromised by overzealous optimization or inadequate hardware protection. Also, a poor choice of the underlying hardware can completely undermine the security requirements. Formal or semiformal techniques may be desirable in ensuring consistency. Formal analysis of code-spec consistency can be greatly simplified through the use of a discipline-requiring programming language, if the semantics of that language have been suitably axiomatized. Although testing is never completely satisfactory, its absence is a serious deficiency, as in the case of the untested code patch in Signaling System 7 that led to the telephone system outages of June 27, 1991, noted in Section 2.1. Simulations successfully detected several problems in the shuttle program and in airplane controls—as in the F-16 that would have flipped over each time it crossed the equator, noted in Section 2.3. Analytical processes and tools can be beneficial—for example, with respect to system security, reliability, and safety.

Evaluation. Careful evaluation of the overall system is necessary throughout the development process rather than just at the end. Note that each stage of development has a corresponding assessment of conceptual soundness, requirement appropriateness, criteria compatibility, verification, validation, and so on, at various layers of abstraction. In case of verification, formal reasoning may be appropriate for demonstrating consistency of specifications with requirements and consistency of code with specifications. In any case, overall system testing is essential. (Lack of end-to-end testing was clearly unfortunate in the Hubble Space Telescope.)

Management of development. Managing the development of a system is generally a complex task. Increasingly, managers of system development efforts need to understand the technology and its limitations. Constructive use of management tools and computer-aided software-engineering (CASE) tools can be beneficial, but can also be misleading. If programmers and managers optimize the development only to satisfy the tools, they may be in for major surprises later on—for example, if it is discovered that the code solves the wrong problems, or is hopelessly inefficient, or does not easily integrate with anything else, or that the tools are checking for the wrong properties. Many problems noted here had as contributing factors poor management throughout system development.

Management of the system build. Given an implemented system, there is a remaining step to configure the system for a particular installation. This step is itself a potential source of serious vulnerabilities, including the introduction of security flaws and Trojan horses, mishandling of privileged exceptions in the trusted computing base, and erroneous tailoring of the system to the given application. One view of controlling certain aspects of this phase of the development cycle is given in [2]; it is referred to as **trust engineering**, which attempts to ensure that the potential for system security is not compromised by the installation. Configuration control is vital, but widely ignored, especially in personal computer systems—where viruses are a problem primarily because there are often no such controls.

System operations. Anticipation of operational needs is also an important part of system design, requiring vision as to the intended uses of the system, experience with human interfaces, and understanding of human limitations. The implications must be addressed throughout the design rather than being merely tacked on at the end. With respect to security, the system operator functions should respect the principles noted in Section 7.6.2, particularly separation of concerns and separation of duties, least privilege, and least common mechanism. With respect to reliability, the Patriot comes to mind again.

System maintenance. The needs of short-term system maintenance and long-term system evolution must be anticipated throughout system development, beginning with the initial system conception. Very few system developments are ever completely finished; instead, they tend to continue indefinitely, to adapt to changing requirements and to remove detected flaws. Yogi Berra's dictum is particularly appropriate here: "It ain't over 'til it's over." The moral of the development story is that difficult problems must be wrestled with early; otherwise, they will continue to plague you. Another Berra saying is also relevant: "It gets late early." Too often, difficult problems are deferred until later, in which case maintenance and evolution become not only burdensome but also extremely difficult. Unless evolvability and ease of maintenance are design goals from the beginning of system development, the task tends to become even harder as the development progresses. System redevelopment should permit incremental closure of the entire analytic process, following any changes to code, specifications, design, or even requirements—each necessitating iteration. The loss of the *Phobos 1* mission (Section 2.2.2) is a poignant example of the criticality of maintenance.

From a security viewpoint, it is important that the mechanisms for maintenance and evolution adhere to the basic system security and integrity controls, insofar as possible. Clearly, part of the process of system bootloading and physical reconfiguration may be beyond the control of the system control mechanisms. However, to the extent possible, the directories used for the system source- and object-code files should be completely subjected to the system-control mechanisms. The same is true for the hardware and software responsible for bootloading. The problem of overly powerful processes in maintenance is similar to the superuser problem noted in Section 3.1. It is startling to realize how many systems (telephone systems, control systems, and computer systems generally) can be brought to their knees through misuse of the maintenance interface.

Overview. Good system- and software-engineering practices can influence the entire system-development effort, offering many contributions toward the satisfaction of stringent requirements, such as security, reliability, and performance. These good practices are reflected inadequately in the existing criteria sets. In addition, good management practice is essential throughout system development, as is the incisive vision to anticipate and avoid development problems that otherwise might have a serious negative effect on the development. For an interesting historical perspective of system development, see F.J. Corbató's 1991 Turing Address lecture [28].

Implications of the software-development practice are discussed next.

7.8.2   **Benefits of Software Engineering**

Satisfaction of each relevant property requires assiduous adherence to various software-engineering principles. Such principles include abstraction, hierarchical layering of abstractions, formal specification [123], encapsulation, information hiding (for example, Parnas [122]), abstract data types and strong typing, trusted computing bases, strict isolation as in virtual machine monitors that share no resources, separation of concerns in design such as distinguishing among different layers of trustworthiness or different layers of protection, along with allocation of least privilege, separation of duties (for example, Clark and Wilson [25]), client–server architectures, least common mechanism, and avoidance of aliases. Although usually lacking in software-engineering efforts, good documentation is fundamental. It can also be a basis for formal analysis, as in the recent work of Parnas.

Trusted computing bases (TCBs) are a manifestation of information hiding and encapsulation, with several desiderata: all accesses to the objects of the abstract type must be mediated by the TCB; the TCB must be tamperproof; and the TCB must be small enough to permit rigorous analysis. These requirements by themselves are not sufficient to imply noncompromisibility from above. As defined here, a TCB may enforce any set of properties P, not just a security property such as multilevel security. The basic MLS property is that information shall never be visible to security levels that are not at least as trusted.

One of the most fundamental concepts is that of abstraction — for example, defining a particular entity in its own terms rather than in terms of its implementation. An abstract representation of a directory might be in terms of operations on sets of symbolically named entries rather than (say) on list-linked collections of secondary-storage addresses and other preferably hidden information. There are various forms of abstraction, principally procedure abstraction with encapsulation and data abstraction with information hiding (invisibility), both of which are addressed by the object-oriented paradigm noted in Section 7.8.1. These include virtualized resources, such as virtualized data location and virtual memory, with the hiding of physical memory addresses; virtualized flow of control, with reentrant or recursive code and remote procedure calls (RPCs); virtualized caching, masking the mere existence of performance-oriented cache memories; virtualized networking, as in network file servers and hiding the remoteness of data; virtualized remote execution; virtualized transaction management, in which logically atomic actions are indeed implemented indivisibly; virtualized concurrency management, particularly in distributed systems and networks; virtualized replication, hiding the existence of multiple versions; virtualized recovery; and other general forms of fault tolerance, in which faults are either masked or recovered from. Note that there are arguments for and against virtualization with respect to any resource, depending on the context (for example, [168, 54]), sometimes both valid simultaneously.

Of particular interest here are the problems of addressing the different requirements, observing the most useful principles, and developing robust systems that can dependably and simultaneously satisfy all of the requirements, including when operating under recovery and other emergency conditions. Distributed systems and networks are of special concern, because many of the problems are less controllable, and enforcement of proper hierarchical ordering is more difficult [109]. For example, workstations that do not implement adequate reliability, security, and system integrity greatly complicate the attainment of an overall dependable system; in particular, a Byzantine system design that assumes that workstations are completely untrustworthy (for example, with respect to confidentiality, integrity, and availability) is inherently complex. Furthermore, many existing designs are based on unreasonable assumptions, such as that certain weak-link components have to be perfectly reliable, or that certain subordinate transactions are always atomic, or that faults may occur only one at a time within a given time interval during which fault recovery occurs. In such systems, the invalidation of any such assumption could have disastrous effects, particularly if the system design has not considered the resulting consequences. Furthermore, in the extreme, optimization of an implementation can often negatively affect the design goals if the design is flawed or poorly implemented: The problem of untrustworthy optimization is noted in the earlier paragraph on implementation correctness; it results from the possibility of blurring or eliminating distinctions carefully made in the design. Thus, the challenges are to develop a framework that respects the real world,

TABLE 7.3 Summary of Clark–Wilson
integrity properties

CW rule	Clark–Wilson Integrity Properties for Enforcement (E) and Certification (C)
CW-E1	Encapsulation of abstract data types
CW-E2	User authorization
CW-E3	User authentication
CW-E4	Nondiscretionary controls
CW-C1	External data consistency
CW-C2	Transformation (internal) consistency
CW-C3	Separation of privilege and least privilege
CW-C4	Complete nontamperable auditing
CW-C5	Atomic input validation

and to make rigorous the assumptions of dependence on components of unknown or limited trustworthiness.

7.8.3   Integrity

One illustration of a set of application-layer properties that need
to be enforced by the application software is provided by the integrity model of Clark and Wilson [25]. Their model establishes a
set of application-layer integrity properties generally based on good
business accounting practice, but which are subliminally merely
good software-engineering practice in disguise. These properties
are summarized in Table 7.3, couched not in terms of their original Clark–Wilson formulation but rather in terms of their familiar
software-engineering equivalents, relating to abstract data types
and their proper encapsulation, atomic transactions, and various
forms of consistency. It thus becomes clear that good software-
engineering practice can contribute directly to the enforcement of
the Clark–Wilson properties and to other generalized forms of system integrity.

Unless a Clark–Wilson type of application is implemented directly on hardware with no underlying operating system, the
sound enforcement of the Clark–Wilson properties will typically
depend on lower-layer integrity properties. Sound implementation
is considered by Karger [63] using a secure capability architecture
(SCAP [64]) and by Lee [78] and Shockley [156] employing an un-

derlying MLS/MLI trusted computing base that uses the notion of "partially trusted subjects." Multilevel integrity is a dual of multi-level security. The basic MLI property is that no entity shall depend on another entity (for example, process, program, or data) whose integrity level is not at least as trusted for integrity.

A useful report analyzing Clark–Wilson integrity is found in [1].

7.8.4 Summary of Software-Development Principles

Table 7.4 summarizes the ways in which software engineering can potentially contribute to the prevention and detection of the misuse techniques of Table 3.1, and to the avoidance of or recovery from unreliability modes (through reliability and fault tolerance mechanisms). In the table, a plus sign indicates a positive contribution, whereas a minus sign indicates a negative effect; square brackets indicate that the contribution (positive or negative) is a second-order effect or a potential effect.

The table illustrates in overview that good software engineering can contribute significantly to system security and integrity, as well as to system reliability and human safety, with respect to the underlying systems and to the applications. However, the mere presence of a technique is not sufficient. All of these techniques are frequently touted as magical answers, which they certainly are not. Each can be badly misused.

Software engineers may find it an interesting challenge to explore the implications of individual table entries.

7.9 Techniques for Increasing Security

Security in computer systems and networks requires enormous attention throughout the requirements, design, and implementation stages of development, and throughout potentially every aspect of system operation and use. Because it is a weak-link phenomenon, considerable effort must be invested in avoiding the vulnerabilities discussed in Chapter 3. Easy answers are almost never available in the large, although occasionally an isolated problem may have a simple solution in the small.

Appropriate techniques for increasing security include the structuring approaches noted in Section 7.6.2, especially those that apply the principle of separation of concerns (duties, privileges, etc.).

TABLE 7.4 Software-engineering principles and their potential effects

Principles	Properties to Be Ensured					
	Secure data	System integrity	System reliability, availability	Identity, authentication	Auditing	Application properties
Modular decomposition	+	+	+	[+]	+	+
Modular composition	[+]	[+]	[+]	+		+
Strict isolation	+	+	+	+	+	[+]
Abstraction, encapsulation, information hiding	+	+	+	+	+	+
Hierarchical layering	+	+	+	+	+	+
Type safety	+	+	+	+	[+]	+
Object orientation	+	+	+	+	+	+
Parameterization	[+]	+	[+]	[+]	[+]	[+]
Inheritance	+	+	+	+	+	+
Separation of duties	+	+	[+]	+	+	+
Least privilege	+	+	+	+	+	+
Virtualized location	+	+	+	+	[+]	+
Virtualized networking	+	+	+	+−	[+−]	+
Virtualized concurrency	+	+	+			+
Virtualized replication	+	+	+			+
Virtualized recovery	+	+	+		[+]	+
Fault tolerance	[+−]	+	+		[+]	+

Legend:
"Secure data" includes data confidentiality and data integrity
+   a primary contribution
−   a potential negative implication
[]   a second-order or potential effect

They also include essentially all of the techniques of system and software engineering, as suggested by Table 7.4. But perhaps most important is an awareness throughout of the types of vulnerabilities that must be avoided, of which this book provides copious examples.

The following subsection addresses a portion of the general problem of increasing security by considering a particular application: computer-based voting. Although that application is not completely representative, it serves to provide specific focus. After that, the section concludes with general considerations and a discussion on authentication.

7.9.1 **An Example: Computer-Based Voting Systems**

We begin by reconsidering the problems of attaining reliability, security, and integrity in computer-based voting, summarized in Section 5.8.[27] These problems are, in many respects, illustrative of the more general security and reliability problems illustrated in this book. Thus, we can derive considerable insight from taking a specific application such as voting and attempting to characterize approaches to avoiding or minimizing the problems.

Criteria for Computer-Based Voting

At present, there is no generally accepted standard set of criteria that voting systems are required to satisfy. Previous attempts to define criteria specifically for voting systems, such as [143, 152], the Federal Election Commission voluntary guidelines, and the New York City requirements,[28] are inadequate, because they fail to encompass many of the possible risks that must ultimately be addressed. Indeed, existing security criteria such as the U.S. TCSEC (the Orange Book, TNI, TDI, etc.), the European ITSEC, the Canadian CTCPEC, and the draft U.S. Federal Criteria are also inadequate, for the same reason. Furthermore, essentially all existing voting systems would fail to satisfy even the simplest of the existing criteria. The risks lie not only in the inherent incompleteness of those criteria but also in the intrinsic unrealizability of such criteria. Nevertheless, such criteria are important.

Generic criteria for voting systems are suggested here as follows.

- **System integrity.** The computer systems (in hardware and system software) must be tamperproof. Ideally, system changes must be prohibited throughout the active stages of the election process; once certified, the code, initial parameters, and configuration information must remain static. No run-time self-modifying software can be permitted. End-to-end configuration control is essential. System bootload must be protected from subversion that could otherwise be used to implant Trojan horses. (Any ability to install a Trojan horse in the system must be considered as a potential for subverting an election.) Above all, vote counting must produce reproducibly correct results.

- **Data integrity and reliability.** All data involved in entering and tabulating votes must be tamperproof. Votes must be recorded correctly.

- **Voter authenticity.** In the context of today's voting systems, questions of voter authenticity are typically handled procedurally, initially by presentation of a birth certificate or other means of supposed identification, and later by means of a written verifying signature. In future systems in which remote voting will be possible, some sort of electronic or biometric authentication may be required.

- **Voter anonymity and data confidentiality.** The voting counts must be protected from external reading during the voting process. The association between recorded votes and the identity of the voter must be completely unknown within the voting systems.

- **Operator authentication.** All people authorized to administer an election must gain access with nontrivial authentication mechanisms. Fixed passwords are generally not adequate. There must be no trapdoors — for example, for maintenance and setup — that could be used for operational subversions.

- **System accountability.** All internal operations must be monitored, without violating voter confidentiality. Monitoring must include votes recorded and votes tabulated and all system programming and administrative operations such as pre- and post-election testing. All attempted and successful changes to configuration status (especially those in violation of the static system integrity requirement) must be noted. This capability is similar to that of an aircraft flight recorder, from which it is possible to recover all important information. Furthermore, monitoring must be nonbypassable — it must be impossible to turn off or circumvent. Monitoring and analysis of audit trails must themselves be nontamperable. All operator authentication operations must be logged. (Greenhalgh [55] analyzes accountability further in this context.)

- **System disclosability.** The system software, hardware, microcode, and any custom circuitry must be open for random inspections (including examination of the documentation) by appropriate evaluators, despite cries for secrecy from the system vendors.

- **System availability.** The system must be protected against both accidental and malicious denials of service, and must be available for use whenever it is expected to be operational.

- **System reliability.** System development (design, implementation, maintenance, etc.) should attempt to minimize the likelihood of accidental system bugs and malicious code.

- **Interface usability.** Systems must be amenable to easy use by local election officials, and must not be so complicated that they encourage the use of external personnel (such as vendor-supplied operators). The interface to the system should be inherently fail-safe, foolproof, and overly cautious in defending against accidental and intentional misuse.

- **Documentation and assurance.** The design, implementation, development practice, operational procedures, and testing procedures must all be unambiguously and consistently documented. Documentation must also describe what assurance measures have been applied to each of those system aspects.

- **Other lower-level criteria.** Further criteria elements are also meaningful, such as the TCSEC trusted paths to the system, trusted facility management, trusted recovery, and trusted system distribution. All of these criteria require technological measures and some administrative controls for fulfillment.

- **Personnel integrity.** People involved in developing, operating, and administering electronic voting systems must be of unquestioned integrity. For example, convicted felons and gambling entrepreneurs may be considered inherently suspect.[29] Satisfaction of this requirement involves primarily nontechnological factors.

- **Other factors.** This skeletal criteria set is by no means complete. There are many other important attributes that election computing systems need to satisfy operationally. For example, Roy Saltman [143] notes that voting systems must conform with whatever election laws may be applicable, the systems must not be shared with other applications running concurrently, ballot images must be retained in case of challenges, pre- and postelection testing must take place, warning messages must occur during elections whenever appropriate to reflect unusual circumstances, would-be voters must be properly authorized, handicapped voters must have equal access, it must be possible to conduct recounts manually, and adequate training procedures must exist.

Realizability of Criteria

No set of criteria can completely encompass all the possible risks. However, even if we ignore the incompleteness and imprecision of the suggested criteria, numerous intrinsic difficulties make such criteria unrealizable with any meaningful assurance.

System Trustworthiness

System trustworthiness depends on design, implementation, and operation.

Security vulnerabilities are ubiquitous in existing computer systems, and also inevitable in all voting systems — including both dedicated and operating-system-based applications. Vulnerabilities are particularly likely in voting systems developed inexpensively enough to find widespread use. Evidently, no small kernel can be identified that mediates security concerns, and thus potentially the entire system must be trustworthy.

System operation is a serious source of vulnerabilities, with respect to integrity, availability, and, in some cases, confidentiality — even if a system as delivered appears to be in an untampered form. A system can have its integrity compromised through malicious system operations — for example, by the insertion of Trojan horses or trapdoors. The presence of a superuser mechanism presents many opportunities for subversion. Furthermore, Trojan horses and trapdoors are not necessarily static; they may appear for only brief instants of time, and remain totally invisible at other times. In addition, systems based on personal computers are subject to spoofing of the system bootload, which can result in the seemingly legitimate installation of bogus software. Even in the presence of cryptographic checksums, a gifted developer or subverter can install a flaw in the system implementation or in the system generation. Ken Thompson's Turing Lecture stealthy Trojan horse technique [167] illustrates that such perpetrations can be done without any modifications to source code.

System integrity can be enhanced by the use of locally non-modifiable read-only and once-writable memories, particularly for system programs and preset configuration data, respectively.

Data confidentiality, integrity, and reliability can be subverted as a result of compromises of system integrity. Nonalterable (for example, once-writable) media may provide assistance in ensuring integrity, but not if the system itself is subvertible.

Voter anonymity can be achieved by masking the identity of each voter so that no reverse association can be made. However, such an approach makes accountability much more difficult. One-way hashing functions or even public-key encryption may be useful for providing later verification that a particular vote was actually recorded as cast, but no completely satisfactory scheme exists for guaranteeing voter anonymity, consistency of the votes tabulated with respect to those cast, and correct results. Any attempt to maintain a bidirectional on-line association between voter and votes cast is suspect because of the inability to protect such information in this environment.

Operator authentication that relies on sharable fixed passwords is too easily compromised, in a wide variety of ways such as those noted in Section 3.3.2. Some other type of authentication scheme is desirable, such as a biometric or token approach, although even those schemes themselves have recognized vulnerabilities.

System accountability can be subverted by embedded system code that operates below the accounting layers or by other low-layer trapdoors. Techniques for permitting accountability despite voter anonymity must be developed, although they must be considered inherently suspect. Read-only media can help to ensure nontamperability of the audit trail, but nonbypassability requires a trusted system for data collection. Accountability can be subverted by tampering with the underlying system, below the layer at which auditing takes place. (See also [55].)

System disclosability is important because proprietary voting systems are inherently suspect. However, system inspection is by itself inadequate to prevent stealthy Trojan horses, run-time system alterations, self-modifying code, data interpreted as code, other code or data subversions, and intentional or accidental discrepancies between documentation and code.

System Robustness

System robustness depends on many factors.

System availability can be enhanced by various techniques for increasing hardware-fault tolerance and system security. However, none of these techniques is guaranteed.

System reliability is aided by properly used modern software-engineering techniques, which can result in fewer bugs and greater assurance. Analysis techniques such as thorough testing and high-assurance methods can contribute. Nevertheless, some bugs are likely to remain.

Use of redundancy can in principle improve both reliability and security. It is tempting to believe that checks and balances can help to satisfy some of the criteria. However, we rapidly discover that the redundancy management itself introduces further complexity and further potential vulnerabilities. For example, triple-modular redundancy could be contemplated, providing three different systems and accepting the results if two out of three agree. However, a single program flaw or a Trojan horse can compromise all three systems. Similarly, if three separately programmed systems are used, it is still possible for common-fault-mode mistakes to be made (there is substantial evidence for the likelihood of that occurring) or for collusion to compromise two of the three versions. Furthermore, the systems may agree with one another in the presence of bogus data that compromises all of them. Thus, both reliability and security techniques must provide end-to-end protection, and must check on each other.

In general, Byzantine algorithms can be constructed that work adequately even in the presence of arbitrary component failures (for example, due to malice, accidental misuse, or hardware failure). However, such algorithms are expensive to design, implement, and administer, and introduce substantial new complexities. Even in the presence of algorithms that are tolerant of n failed components, collusion among $n+1$ components can subvert the system. However, those algorithms may be implemented using systems that have single points of vulnerability, which could permit compromises of the Byzantine algorithm to occur without n failures having occurred; indeed, *one* may be enough. Thus, complex systems designed to tolerate certain arbitrary threats may still be subvertible through exploitation of other vulnerabilities.

Interface usability is a secondary consideration in many fielded systems. Complicated operator interfaces are inherently risky, because they induce accidents and can mask hidden functionality. However, systems that are particularly user friendly could be even more amenable to subversion than those that are not.

Correctness is a mythical beast. In reliable systems, a probability of failure of 10^{-4} or 10^{-9} per hour may be required. However, such measures are too weak for voting systems. For example, a 1-bit error in memory might result in the loss or gain of 2^k votes (for example, 1024 or 65,536). Ideally, numerical errors attributable to hardware and software must not be tolerated, although a few errors in reading cards may have to be acceptable within narrow ranges — for example, because of hanging chaff. Efforts must be made to detect errors attributable to the hardware through fault-tolerance techniques or software consistency checks. Any detected but uncorrectable errors must be monitored, forcing a controlled rerun. However, a policy that permits any detected inconsistencies to invalidate election results would be dangerous, because it might encourage denial-of-service attacks by the expected losers. Note also that any software-implemented fault-tolerance technique is itself a possible source of subversion.

System Assurance

High-assurance systems demand discipline and professional maturity not previously found in commercial voting systems (and, indeed, not found in most commercial operating systems and application software). High-assurance systems typically cost considerably more than conventional systems in the short term, but have the potential for payoff in the long term. Unless the development team is exceedingly gifted, high-assurance efforts may be disappointing. As a consequence, there are almost no incentives for any assurance greater than the minimal assurance provided by lowest-common-denominator systems. Furthermore, even high-assurance systems can be compromised, via insertion of trapdoors and Trojan horses and operational misuse.

Conclusions on Realizability

The primary conclusion from this discussion of realizability is that certain criteria elements are inherently unsatisfiable because assurance cannot be attained at an acceptable cost. Systems could be designed that will be operationally less amenable to subversion. However, some of those will still have modes of compromise without any collusion. Indeed, the actions of a single person may be sufficient to subvert the process, particularly if preinstalled Trojan horses or operational subversion can be used. Thus, whereas it is possible to build better systems, it is also possible that those better systems can also be subverted. Consequently, there will always be questions about the use of computer systems in elections. In certain cases, sufficient collusion will be plausible, even if conspiracy theories do not always hold.

There is a serious danger that the mere existence of generally accepted criteria coupled with claims that a system adheres to those criteria might give the naïve observer the illusion that an election is nonsubvertible. Doubts will always remain that some of the criteria have not been satisfied with any realistic measure of assurance and that the criteria are incomplete:

- Commercial systems tend to have lowest common denominators, with potentially serious security flaws and operational deficiencies. Custom-designed voting systems may be even more risky, especially if their code is proprietary.
- Trojan horses, trapdoors, interpreted data, and other subversions can be hidden, even in systems that have received extensive scrutiny. The integrity of the entire computer-aided election process may be compromisible internally.
- Operational misuses can subvert system security even in the presence

of high-assurance checks and balances, highly observant poll watchers, and honest system programmers. Registration of bogus voters, insertion of fraudulent absentee ballots, and tampering with punched cards seem to be ever-popular low-tech techniques. In electronic voting systems, dirty tricks may be indistinguishable from accidental errors. The integrity of the entire computer-aided election process may be compromisible externally.

- The requirement for voter confidentiality and the requirement for non-subvertible and sufficiently complete end-to-end monitoring are conceptually contradictory. It is essentially impossible to achieve both at the same time without resorting to complicated mechanisms, which themselves may introduce new potential vulnerabilities and opportunities for more sophisticated subversions. Monitoring is always potentially subvertible through low-layer Trojan horses. Furthermore, any technique that permitted identification and authentication of a voter if an election were challenged would undoubtedly lead to increased challenges and further losses of voter privacy.

- The absence of a physical record of each vote is a serious vulnerability in direct-recording election systems; the presence of an easily tamperable physical record in paper-ballot and card-based systems is also a serious vulnerability.

- Problems exist with both centralized control and distributed control. Highly distributed systems have more components that may be subverted, and are more prone to accidental errors; they require much greater care in design. Highly centralized approaches in any one of the stages of the election process violate the principle of separation of duties, and may provide single points of vulnerability that can undermine separation enforced elsewhere in the implementation.

Finally, a fundamental dilemma must be addressed. On one hand, computer systems can be designed and implemented with extensive checks and balances intended to make accidental mishaps and fraud less likely. As an example pursuing that principle, New York City is embarking on a modernization program that will attempt to separate the processes of voting, vote collection, and vote tallying from one another, with redundant checks on each. The New York City Election Project hopes to ensure that extensive collusion would be required to subvert an election, and that the risks of detection would be high. However, that effort permits centralized vote tallying, which has the potential for compromising the integrity of the earlier stages.

On the other hand, constraints on system development efforts and expectations of honesty and altruism on the part of system developers seem to be generally unrealistic; the expectations on the operational practice and human awareness required to administer such systems also may be unrealistic.

We must avoid the lowest-common-denominator systems and instead try to approach the difficult goal of realistic, cost-effective, reasonable-assurance, fail-safe, and nontamperable election systems.

Vendor-embedded Trojan horses and accidental vulnerabilities will remain as potential problems, for both distributed and centralized systems. The principle of separation is useful, but must be used consistently and wisely. The use of good software engineering practice and extensive regulation of system development and operation are essential. In the best of worlds, even if voting systems were produced with high assurance by persons of the highest integrity, the operational practice could still be compromisible, with or without collusion. Vigilance throughout the election process is simply not enough to counter accidental and malicious efforts that can subvert the process. Residual risks are inevitable.

Although this section considers election systems, many of the concepts presented here are applicable to secure computer systems in general.

7.9.2   Criteria for Authentication

The example of electronic voting machines is not entirely representative of the fully general security problem in several respects. For example, the "end-users" (the voters) normally do not have direct access to the underlying systems, and the system operators are generally completely trusted. Nevertheless, the example demonstrates the need for overcoming many of the vulnerabilities noted in Chapter 3.

One type of vulnerability at present specifically not within the purview of computer systems in the voting application is the general problem of authenticating users and systems. In this section, we consider techniques for user authentication in the broad context of distributed and networked open systems, such as all of those systems connected to the Internet or otherwise available by dialup connections.

Section 3.3.2 considers risks inherent in reusable passwords. We consider here alternatives that considerably reduce those risks.

We also characterize the overall system requirements for authentication, including the mechanisms and their embedding into systems and networks.

Various approaches and commercially available devices exist for nonsubvertible one-time passwords, including smart-cards, randomized tokens, and challenge-response schemes. For example, a hand-held smart-card can generate a token that can be recognized by a computer system or authentication site, where the token is derived from a cryptographic function of the clock time and some initialization information, and where a personal identification number (PIN) is required to complete the authentication process. Some devices generate a visually displayed token that can be entered as a one-time password, while others provide direct electronic input. These devices typically use one-key symmetric cryptographic algorithms such as the Digital Encryption Standard (DES) or two-key asymmetric algorithms such as the RSA public-key algorithm (noted at the end of Section 3.5), with public and private keys. Less high-tech approaches merely request a specified item in a preprinted codebook of passwords.

Following is a basic set of idealized requirements relating to secure authentication.

- **User authenticity and nonrepudiation.** Authentication compromises such as those noted in Section 3.3.2 must be prevented. For example, guessing and enumeration must be practically hopeless. Capturing and (p)replaying either a token or a PIN must not be successful. Nonrepudiation is also necessary, preventing the authenticatee from later proving that the authentication had been subverted by a masquerader. (Public-key systems have an advantage over one-key systems, because shared-key compromise can lead to repudiation.)

- **Ease of use.** Authentication must be easy for the authenticatee, with system operation as invisible as possible. The human interfaces to computer systems and token-generating devices should be inherently fail-safe, fool-proof, overly cautious in defending against accidental and intentional misuse, and unobtrusive.

- **Device integrity and availability.** Ideally, the security of the system should not depend on the secrecy of its cryptographic algorithms. The design of a token-generating device should make it difficult for anyone to determine the internal parameters and nonpublic encryption keys. The device should be nontamperable. Reinitialization following battery or circuit failure must not permit any security bypasses.

- **System integrity and reliability.** Systems that provide authentication must be resistant to tampering, with no bypasses and no Trojan horses that can subvert the authentication or simulate its acceptance of a password. System development (design, implementation, maintenance, etc.) should minimize the likelihood of accidental system bugs and installed malicious code.

- **Network integrity.** Networks generally do not need to be trusted for confidentiality if the encryption used in generating the token is strong enough, which can hinder replay attacks. However, denials of service can result from encrypted tokens corrupted in transit.
- **System accountability.** All security-relevant operations and configuration changes must be nonbypassably and nontamperably monitored.
- **Emergency overrides.** Many systems provide intentional trapdoors in case of failures of the authentication mechanism or loss of ability to authenticate. Such trapdoors should be avoided, and if unavoidable must be audited nonbypassably. Unusual operator actions must also be audited. All persons authorized to perform system-administration functions must be nontrivially authenticated (not to mention that they must be well trained and experienced!), with no exceptions.

These requirements must be satisfied by systems involved in authentication. They are applicable to one-time passwords. They are also generally applicable to biometric authentication techniques, such as matching of fingerprints, handwriting, voiceprints, retina patterns, and DNA. However, even if these requirements are completely satisfied, some risks can still remain; weak links in the computer systems or in personal behavior can undermine even the most elaborate authentication methods. In any event, we need much more stringent authentication than that provided by reusable passwords.[30]

7.10 Risks in Risk Analysis

The application of risk analysis and management to software development is gaining increasing interest and attention in the software community. The numbers of articles, books, and conferences on the subject are increasing rapidly. The benefits of applying risk analysis and management are obvious, but their hazards are often hidden. The Gulf War and the erroneous conclusions drawn in many of the

Section 7.10 originally appeared as an *Inside Risks* column, *CACM, 34,* 6, 106, June 1991, and was written by **Robert N. Charette** of ITABHI Corp., Springfield, Virginia.

risk assessments—such as those concerning enemy strength, potential battle casualties, possible chemical attack, and Arab and other Moslem countries' reactions to the American presence, serve to highlight this often-interlocked issue and make it appropriate to discuss a few of the risks inherent in risk analysis.

As the Gulf War aptly demonstrated, the premier risk in doing any risk analysis is that the recommendations for the management of the risks are inaccurate. Minor inaccuracy is usually tolerable, but significant inaccuracy can hurt in many ways.

On one hand, if the analysis *overestimates* the risk, it can cause an excessive amount of mitigation effort to be expended in overcoming the perceived risk, compared to the effort that was truly required. This overreaction can cause substantial side effects, such as the withholding of assets from other key problem areas that could have made the endeavor a (greater) success, or missing the chance to exploit a new opportunity.

On the other hand, if the analysis *underestimates* the risk, it can result in surprise that the problem has indeed occurred. More often than not, a secondary consequence is management panic about what to do next, because the problem was not planned for, the analysis having led to a false sense of security (itself another risk of risk analysis). Instead of being proactive, management then finds itself reacting to events.

In either case, the *next* time an analysis is required or performed, there is an increased skepticism at either the need for an analysis or the validity of the recommendations, regardless of circumstance.

Perversely, the second major risk with risk analysis occurs if the analysis is *too accurate.* In this case, we often cannot later show the true value of the analysis, because by the recommendation of the analysis, the risk was avoided. Since nothing went awry, the analysis is seen as not contributing anything beneficial, and is viewed as an unjustifiable cost. Thus, the next time an analysis is required, it may not be performed. It is like terrorism prevention. If terrorism does not occur, it is hard to prove that terrorism was stopped by the preventive actions rather than by other, unrelated, events.

Another type of risk is that risk analysis frequently can be used as a form of **organizational snag hunting**, meant to keep the status quo, to stifle innovation or change. Another form of this risk occurs when risk analysis becomes **blame analysis**, and thus becomes a means of intimidation instead of a means to improve the situation for the better.

A fourth major risk is that risk analysis often overrelies on producing numbers and relies insufficiently on human analysis and common sense to interpret the results. Similarly, if competing analyses exist, arguments over the analysis techniques usually ensue, rather than arguments over what the results may be indicating.

A fifth risk is performing the risk analysis itself may impede project success. One reason is that performing a risk analysis is not cost free, and will take up resources that might better be applied to the endeavor at hand. The other reason is psychological. If risk is viewed as "bad" within an endeavor, especially by management, then the fact of conducting a risk analysis may stigmatize the endeavor as one that is in trouble and should be avoided. This attitude can lead to a self-fulfilling prophecy.

The final risk with risk analysis is that there is no quality control on risk analyses themselves. Risks are only that—that is, potential events. They are not certainties. Only afterward can the value of the analysis be ascertained.

When dealing with risk analyses, we should always remember the physician's motto: "First, do no harm." However, by understanding the risks in risk analysis, you can ultimately increase the value of the analysis.[31]

7.11 **Risks Considered Global(ly)**

[E]very change, any change, has myriad side effects that can't always be allowed for. If the change is too great and the side effects too many, then it becomes certain that the outcome will be far removed from anything you've planned and that it would be entirely unpredictable.
  DORS VENABILI[32]

In this section, we examine problems in *assessing* risks, continuing the thread begun in Section 7.1, which considers the importance of an overall system perspective in *avoiding* risks, and continued in Section 7.10, which deals with risks inherent in risk analysis itself.

As noted throughout this book, it is essential to understand the vulnerabilities and the threats before we can undertake a meaningful analysis of the risks. It is clear that risk analysis is important; it is also clear that it can be highly speculative.

Whether quantitative or qualitative, risk assessment is much like statistics; it can demonstrate almost any conclusion, depending on the assumptions and the frame of reference. In the small, it may emphasize the likelihood and consequences of death, loss of funds, or system failure. In the large, it may factor in global considerations such as environmental hazards and world economic implications. It may also be used for devious purposes, with parameters or interpretations influenced by politics, ideologies, greed, or special-interest constituencies. Occasionally, controverting evidence (sometimes in the form of a disaster) may expose invalid assumptions on which earlier risk analyses were based. In a few cases, *retrospective* attempts at corrective risk analyses have been hindered by uncertainty as to what really went wrong, as in the case of a damaged aircraft flight recorder or a subverted audit trail.

Several risky situations in recent years spring to mind, in defense systems, Chernobyl, and the savings and loan fiascoes.

- In the defense systems considered in Section 2.3, numerous cases are recorded of systems for which the risks were high or where disasters occurred.

- Ideally, nuclear power seems attractive, economical, and clean. In a global, practical sense (including waste-disposal problems, worldwide health issues, and infrastructure and decommissioning costs, for example), it is potentially much more expensive and risky when all of its implications are considered.

- Financial planning and management lead to wildly differing strategies, depending on whether you are optimizing your own gain or the stability of a bank, a state, a nation, or indeed the world economy. The selfish individual and the global altruist often have diametrically opposed views. (In the savings and loan cases, various accounting firms were also implicated.)

There are enormous potential benefits from using advanced software-development practices and sound system infrastructure. However, the extent to which a development effort or an operational application is willing to invest in such approaches tends to vary dramatically, depending on how extensively long-term considerations are factored into realistic analyses of costs, benefits, and risks. For example, security, reliability, and real-time performance requirements must be thoroughly anticipated if they are to be realized effectively in any complex system. Furthermore, operational requirements must all be carefully established from the outset and adhered to throughout, including day-to-day system maintainability, long-term system evolvability in response to changing needs, system portability and subsystem reusability, the need for robust distributed-system implementations, flexible networkability, and facile interoperability. Such requirements tend not to be satisfied by themselves, with benign neglect, and are generally difficult to retrofit unless planned in advance.

In all of these factors on which risks may depend, it is essential to consider a priori the risks that would result if the requirements were not satisfied or—worse yet—if the requirements were not even stated. However, in most situations, short-term considerations tend to drive the decision-making process away from long-term benefits (for example, by overemphasizing immediate cost effects). The resulting long-term deficiencies often subsequently come back to haunt us; furthermore, those deficiencies are usually difficult to overcome a posteriori. Therefore, we must use risk analysis with great care, and must be sure that it is as realistic, as global, and as far-sighted as possible. Failure to do so can easily result in major disasters. The numerous examples in this book provide ample illustrations of the importance of global thinking.

7.12 Summary of the Chapter

An overall system perspective is essential with respect to subsystems, systems, networks, networks of networks, and applications. Risk analysis is important, but difficult to do wisely. There are many pitfalls throughout system development and use; the avoidance of those pitfalls requires the broadest possible system sense as well as meticulous attention to detail.[33]

Challenges

C7.1   Identify events described in this book that arose primarily because of an inadequate system perspective. Explore what could have been done differently—for example, with respect to system conceptualization, requirement definition, design, implementation, operation, use, and evolution.

C7.2   From your experience as a system user or developer, identify and describe at least one case in which the user interface was poorly conceived and was itself a source of risks.

C7.3   Consider the computer-based voting problems of Section 5.8. How relevant do you think are the techniques noted in this chapter for increasing the reliability and security of voting systems? Can you identify and isolate the functionality that must be trusted and the people who must be trusted?

C7.4   Can you describe a voting system that would meet all of the criteria given in Section 7.9.1 and still be subvertible? Explain your answer.

C7.5   Consider direct-recording equipment, in which votes are entered directly into a computer system without any physical evidence. How might the absence of physical evidence affect the assurance that election results are correct and untampered? In what ways does it make the security and reliability problems either easier or more difficult?

C7.6   Carry out the conceptual design of a voting system that is intended to satisfy criteria in Section 7.9.1. What residual vulnerabilities remain?

C7.7   (Project) For any application area that is of particular interest to you (other than electronic voting machines in Challenges C7.3 through C7.6), contemplate a set of requirements that includes both reliability and security. For those requirements, outline applicable criteria. Then sketch the design of a system that would meet those requirements subject to those criteria. Then choose at least three types of problems in this book that are relevant to your application and that would not have been avoided by your design. Can you refine your requirements to cover these cases? Can you improve your design to accommodate these problems, or are these problems intrinsic?

CHAPTER 8

A Human-Oriented Perspective

To err is human.
SENECA

8.1 The Human Element

Experience is what you get when you were expecting something else.

In the earlier chapters, we discuss various system-related disasters and their causes, both accidental and intentional. In almost all cases, it is possible to allocate to people—directly or indirectly—those difficulties allegedly attributed to "computer problems." But too much effort seems directed at placing blame and identifying scapegoats, and not enough on learning from experiences and avoiding such problems. Besides, the real causes may implicitly or explicitly involve a multiplicity of developers, customers, users, operators, administrators, others involved with computer and communication systems, and sometimes even unsuspecting bystanders. In a few cases, the physical environment also contributes—for example, power outages, floods, extreme weather, lightning, earthquakes, and animals. Even in those cases, there may have been system people who failed to anticipate the possible effects. In principle, at least, we can design redundantly distributed systems that are able to withstand certain hardware faults, component unavailabilities, extreme delays, human errors, malicious misuse, and even "acts of God"—at least within limits. Nevertheless, in surprisingly many systems (including systems designed to provide continuous availability), an entire system can be brought to a screeching halt by a simple event just as easily as by a complex one.

261

Many system-related problems are attributed—at least in part, whether justifiably or not, and albeit differently by different analyses—to errors or misjudgments by people in various capacities or to just being in the wrong place at the wrong time. Examples include the following:

- **Requirements definition:** The *Stark*'s missile defense system, the *Sheffield* communication system
- **System design:** The 1980 self-propagating ARPAnet contamination
- **Human-interface design:** Therac-25, *Mariner 1*, and the Aegis shootdown of the Iranian Airbus
- **Implementation:** The first launch of the Shuttle *Columbia*, the DIVAD ("Sergeant York"), the Patriot missile system
- **Modeling and simulation:** Northwest Flight 255 (in which the aircraft and the MD-80 flight-training simulator behaved differently from one another), the Hartford Civic Center roof cave-in (in which an erroneous computer model was used)
- **Testing:** The Hubble space telescope and the untested code patches that resulted in serious telephone outages
- **Users, operators, and management:** For example, the Chernobyl shutdown-recovery experiments, the *Exxon Valdez* and KAL 007 running on autopilots, the Black Hawks shot down by friendly fire in the absence of proper identification, the French and Indian Airbus A320 crashes, operation at low temperature despite the known limitations of the *Challenger* O-rings, use of nonsecure systems in sensitive environments, operation under stress of battle as in the Iran Air 655 and the Patriot defense system, operation in the presence of degraded human abilities as in the *Exxon Valdez* case
- **Maintenance and system upgrades:** *Phobos 1* (lost after a botched remote patch), *Viking*
- **Innocent bystanders:** Victims of Trojan horses, of personal-computer viruses, and of privacy violations

This book describes numerous instances of each type. The human element also transcends the systems themselves. The seemingly epidemic flurry of work crews downing telephone systems and computer connections by inadvertently severing telephone cables (White Plains, New York; Chicago, Illinois; Newark, New Jersey; Annandale, Virginia; and San Francisco's East Bay) is noted in Section 2.1. The lessons of the past have taught us not to put multiple critical links in the same conduit (which was the 1986 problem in White Plains when New England was separated from the ARPAnet, all seven supposedly independent links being cut in one swell foop). Nevertheless, in June 1991 the Associated Press lost both its primary and backup links in the Annandale area, despite their being in separate (but adjacent) cables! (See Sections 2.1 and 4.1.)

Human fallibility abounds. The Aeromexico case (noted in Section 2.4) is particularly worth examining, because the blame can be distributed among the Piper pilot who crashed into the airliner in restricted airspace, the controller for not noticing him on radar, the Grumman Yankee pilot who was also in restricted airspace (which distracted the controller), the radar developers for not having been able to detect altitude, the U.S. government for not having required collision-avoidance systems earlier, perhaps even the Aeromexico pilot, and so on.

There are also Heisenbergian effects in which the mere fact that people are being observed affects their behavior. Bell Laboratories had a home-grown operating system for IBM 709x computers in the early 1960s. The system tended to crash mysteriously, but never when the system-programming wizards were in the computer room. It took months to discover an input–output timing glitch that was triggered only because the tape-handling operators were just a little sloppy in punching buttons, but only when they were not being observed.

Henry Petroski [129] has illustrated how we often learn little if anything from our successes, but that we have an opportunity to learn much from our failures. (Petroski's observation is highly relevant to us in the computer profession, even though it is based largely on experiences gained in the engineering of bridges.) Better understanding of the notable failures that have been ongoing grist for the *Risks Forum* is fundamental to our hopes for building better systems in the future. However, it appears that the risks are even greater for computer professionals than in more traditional engineering fields. It is clear that we need systems that are not only fault tolerant and secure against malicious misuse, and more predictable in their behavior, but also less sensitive to the mistakes of people involved in system development and use.[1]

8.2 **Trust in Computer-Related Systems and in People**

It is incumbent upon us to devise methodologies for designing verifiable systems that meet . . . stringent criteria, and to demand that they be

implemented where necessary. "Trust us" should not be the bottom line for computer scientists.
    REBECCA MERCURI[2]

Many of the risks of using computers in critical environments stem from people trusting computer systems *blindly* — not realizing the possibilities that the underlying models are wrong or incomplete; the software designs basically flawed; the compilers buggy; the hardware unreliable; and the programmers and operators inadequately trained, untrustworthy, negligent, or merely marginally competent.

It has long been common to find inordinate trust placed in those who develop, operate, use, administer, and regulate the technology, or in the technologies themselves. However, there are a few signs that this situation is changing. In connection with an article[3] on the 46 U.S. senators who were seeking to cut back the proposed SDI budget, Senator William Proxmire was quoted as follows:

> Challenger and Chernobyl have stripped some of the mystique away from technology.

Concern is temporarily elevated after such incidents as Chernobyl and the sequence of space failures beginning with the *Challenger*; soon afterward, that concern seems to dwindle. Indeed, there may be cases where the risks are so great that neither the people nor the computers should be trusted, or that the system should not be built at all.

Furthermore, politically motivated positions persist that are totally oblivious to the harsh technological realities of intrinsic vulnerabilities. Anthony Lewis[4] made this statement:

> Now President Reagan has shown us that he has failed to learn a fundamental lesson of Chernobyl: the folly of relying on the perfectability of dangerous high technology and the human beings who run it. In the teeth of Chernobyl and the American space rocket failures, he has renewed his insistence that we can have a shield against nuclear weapons in space. He has demanded that Congress vote all the funds for his Strategic Defense Initiative, a vision so dependent on perfectly functioning rockets and computers and software [and people!] that to believe in it any longer is close to irrational.

Recall the scene near the end of the movie *WarGames*,[5] when the computer system (WOPR) comes to a rather poignant conclusion regarding the game strategies involved with the apparent escalation of nuclear attacks and counter-attacks, in a context associated with WOPR learning to play tic-tac-toe:

A strange game. The only winning move is not to play.

There are many attributes with respect to which computer systems, networks, and applications are trusted to behave properly (explicitly or implicitly), whether or not the systems are adequately dependable:[6]

- Data confidentiality
- System integrity
- External data integrity (consistency with the real world)
- Internal data integrity (for example, consistency of various internal representations, as in file-system pointers and double-entry bookkeeping ledgers)
- Availability of resources (including systems, programs, and data)
- Protection of human safety
- Protection against loss of financial assets or other resources
- Functional correctness of applications, database-management systems, operating systems, and hardware

The desired properties interact in many subtle ways. In some cases, they are mutually antagonistic; in other cases, apparent antagonism can be reduced or even eliminated by constructive designs that address the requirements explicitly. The stringency of the requirements involving each of these properties may vary widely from one property to another, and from one system to another.

8.2.1   Misplaced Trust in Computer-Based Systems

People often tend to anthropomorphize computer systems, endowing the machines and software with humanlike traits such as intelligence, rational and intuitive powers, and (occasionally) social conscience, and even with some superhuman traits such as infallibility. Here are a few highly oversimplified types of misplaced trust, exemplified by the cited cases. The first example involved extensive wildlife deaths and long-term environmental damage; examples of each of the subsequent eight types resulted in human lives being lost.

- **Blind faith.** "Just leave it to the autopilot computer." The *Exxon Valdez* oil spill noted in Section 2.6 was alternately blamed on the captain's alcohol problem and the third mate's "severe fatigue" — according to a report of the National Commission on Sleep Disorders Research.[7] The third mate and helmsman were both unaware that their rudder controls were being ignored, because they did not realize that the ship was running on autopilot. The Coast Guard had radar tracking abilities, but it had not been using them—because there had never been a need. In addition, computer records were destroyed after the accident—in spite of a federal court order that they be preserved.

- **Trust in technology.** "With all these checks and balances, nothing can go wrong." The "friendly-fire" shootdown of the Black Hawk helicopters over northern Iraq suggests that even the most stringent preventive measures may not be enough, especially when a prevailing assumption becomes invalid.

- **Trust in foolproofedness.** "But the system did something it was *not* supposed to do." The Therac-25 software permitted the therapeutic radiation device to be configured unsafely in X-ray mode, without its protective filter in place, as discussed in Section 2.9.1.

- **False sense of safety.** "But the system did *not* do something it was supposed to do." A DC-10 crash was attributed to a stall alarm that failed to alert the pilot; the power for the alarm was expected to come from the missing engine.

- **Reliance on fragmentary data.** "The big picture was not readily available." The Aegis system's main user displays did not indicate the speed, range, and altitude of the Iranian Airbus; determination of those attributes required explicit action to bring up an auxiliary small display on which they were included among many other data items—but not including rates of change. The design of the Aegis' human interface thus had a significant role in the *Vincennes'* shootdown of the Airbus.

- **Complacency.** "We know that this [program, data item, configuration] is wrong, but it probably won't matter anyway." An Air New Zealand plane crashed into Mt. Erebus in Antarctica because erroneous instrument-flight data had been discovered by controllers but not reported to the pilots, who had never previously had to depend on the data in previous visual-only flights.

- **Overconfidence.** "The controls are too constraining. We need to turn them off while we experiment." The folks at Chernobyl did just that.

- **Impatience or annoyance.** "That alarm system is a nuisance; let's turn it off." Prior to the September 1991 New York telephone outage discussed in Section 2.1, alarms had been disabled because they had been going off frequently during construction, and thus there was no indication that the standby battery was being depleted. There were unverified reports that the pilots of the Northwest 255 flight noted in Sections 2.4 and 7.5 had disabled an alarm similar to the one that had failed on a *different* MD-80 two days before the crash.

- **Trust in emergency administrative procedures and system logic.** "The emergency procedures were never tested adequately under live circumstances." The British Midland Airways 737 shutdown of the wrong engine points to difficulties in responding to real emergencies. Deployment of the Strategic Defense Initiative's Star Wars concept would have this difficulty as well, because thorough testing under live attacks is essentially impossible.

- **Trust in recovery to overcome system failures.** "If something goes wrong, our backup procedures will save us." The $32-billion-dollar overdraft at the Bank of New York noted in Section 5.7 resulted accidentally from an unchecked program counter overflow. The effects were compounded significantly by a recovery procedure that overwrote the backup by mistake. But it's only money—one day's interest, $5 million.

- **Credulity.** "The computer will do it right. It never failed before." An F-16 whose computer system was designed to prevent the aircraft from stalling stalled—because a novice pilot managed to find a flight configuration unanticipated by the program. He bailed out, but the plane crashed.

- **Incredulity.** "The data or the program must be wrong. That's never happened before." Because the system analyzing ozone depletion had been programmed to reject far-out results, the correct data values were deemed *too anomalous,* and the first evidence showing a dramatic depletion in the Antarctic ozone layer was rejected for 8 years.

- **Confusion.** "The outputs [data values or exception conditions] don't make any sense. What do we do now?" In the Three Mile Island accident, the control indicators did not show the *actual* positions of the valves but instead the *intended* positions. The resulting ambiguity as to the actual settings caused enormous confusion.

- **Confusion in redundancy.** "The computer results are mutually inconsistent. Which of them is correct?" Dual control noncomparisons may leave ambiguity. Section 2.3 notes the case of two incorrect programs that outvoted the correct program in an 3-version fly-by-wire programming experiment.

- **Wishful thinking.** "Distributed systems are more reliable than centralized systems, and could not possibly fail totally." The 1980 ARPAnet collapse and the 1990 AT&T collapse noted in Section 2.1 both illustrated global effects that can result from local phenomena.

- **Oversimplification.** "Our computer system is completely secure." Numerous penetrations and internal frauds have shown that fundamental system flaws and sloppy practice are pervasive.

- **Chutzpah.** "We verified everything formally, and tested everything; therefore it will work correctly the first time we try it." Fortunately, this has not yet been a serious problem—although that sounds a little like the fantasy of Star Wars.

- **Loss of human control and initiative.** "The computer is down. Sorry, we can't do anything for you." This problem seems altogether too frequent. The *RISKS* archives include cases in banking, airline reservations, electric power, and supermarkets (for example).

In the case of the Midland 737 crash, one engine would have been sufficient to fly the plane—but not after the one still-working engine was shut down by mistake in an engine emergency. (The pilot may have misinterpreted smoke in the cabin and increased vibration as signs that it was the *right* engine that was failing. Normally, 70 percent of the air conditioning comes from the right engine, but apparently there was a misconception at the time that 100 percent came from that engine.) Originally, crosswiring of the alarm systems was suspected, leading to inspections of other aircraft—and to the discovery of undetected crosswiring problems in the alarm systems of at least 30 other commercial airliners. In general, it is extremely difficult to ensure that subsystems to be invoked only in true emergencies will actually work as planned when they are needed, especially if they have never before been invoked. In the Air France Airbus A-320 crash, initial reports implicated pilot error in turning off some of the automatic safety controls and flying too low. Subsequent unverified reports suggest that the fly-by-wire Airbus computer system had been suspect on previous occasions, with false altimeter readings, sudden full-throttling during landing, and sudden losses of power. The Iranian Airbus shootdown may be attributable to a combination of computer-interface problems (incompleteness of information in the Aegis system displays and inconvenience of the multiple displays—the altitude of the Airbus was not displayed directly, and its identity was mistaken for a military plane still on the runway) and human frailty—real-time pressures under fire, confusion, inexperience, and inability to question the incorrect initial assumption that was contradicted by the information that could have been displayed on the auxiliary screen. In the case of the *Exxon Valdez*, although the autopilot may have worked as intended (apart from the attempt by the third mate to override it?), all of the safety measures and contingency plans appear to have been of minimal value. Indeed, contrasting the *Exxon Valdez* situation with systems that are designed to minimize the effects of weak links, there were mostly weak links.

With respect to any of the requirements noted, trust is often misplaced. It is clear that computer systems (1) cannot ensure completely adequate system behavior, and (2) cannot enforce completely adequate human behavior. Unfortunately, these two limiting factors are usually discarded as "theoretical" and "of no practical significance"—after all, perfection is admittedly impossible. In its place, however, people are often willing to accept mediocre or incomplete systems. The desire for quick and easy answers leads to short-cut solutions that are fundamentally inadequate, but that still may persist for years—until a catastrophe illuminates shortcomings that had hitherto been systematically ignored. Ironically, such misuses of technology are generally exposed only in response to disasters (as noted by Henry Petroski). Subsequently, after some improvements are made, the previously "theoretical" arguments retrospectively become "of historical interest"—with the added emphasis, *"Of course, it couldn't happen again."*

It is difficult to raise the issue of misplaced trust in computer systems without being accused of being a Luddite—that is, a technology basher. Sound technological and social arguments are often emotionally countered by narrowly based economic arguments—such as "We can't afford to change anything" or "Why bother with defensive measures? There's never been a problem." The common strategy of expending the least possible effort for (short-term) economic reasons leaves uncomfortably narrow margins for error; experience with marginally engineered systems is not reassuring. On the other hand, consideration of longer-term goals and costs often provides more than adequate justification for better systems, better administration of them, and higher levels of awareness.

8.2.2 **Misplaced Trust in People**

Let us also examine some of the ways in which misplaced trust in computer systems interacts with misplaced trust in people, whether or not those people are adequately dependable. In some cases, computer systems become untrustworthy because of what people do—for example, errors in design, implementation, operation, and use. In other cases, people may behave undependably because of what computer systems do—for example, because the computer systems demand too much of them (especially in real-time applications). Another common problem involves placing trust in other people, who, in turn, place excessive trust in technology — oblivious to the limitations.

In essentially every computer system, there are privileged individuals who in some sense have to be more trustworthy than others — for example, system programmers, database administrators, and operators. Most system designs do not permit or encourage carefully compartmentalized privileges, and instead provoke the use of omnipotent mechanisms (for example, superusers). Such mechanisms are intrinsically dangerous, even if used with good intent — particularly if they can be subverted by someone masquerading as a privileged user — or if they are misused by privileged users.

8.2.3   "Trust" Must Be Trustworthy

Several principles of good software engineering are helpful in reducing the excessive assignment of trust — such as abstraction and information hiding. For example, the principle of separation of duties (for example, Clark and Wilson [25]) and the principle of least privilege (Section 7.8) together provide an aid to designing systems and applications so that only critical portions of the system need be trustworthy and so that privileges may indeed be partitioned. In a well-structured system that observes these principles, it is possible to reduce the extent to which successful operation must depend on the proper behavior of both ordinary users and partially privileged people. That is, the system should be capable of protecting itself against both intentional and accidental misuse. In exactly the same way that computer systems can be made fault tolerant through appropriate use of redundancy in hardware and software, there is a challenge in design and administration to make system use human-error tolerant.

In some applications, we mistakenly trust systems — as in systems that fail to operate acceptably because of bad design and implementation, or whose security controls are implemented on weak computer systems that are actually easy to subvert. In other applications, we mistakenly trust people — to develop systems whose use is much more critical than generally realized, or to use systems that can easily be compromised. In the worst case, we can trust neither the systems nor the users and therefore must go to great pains to design systems and administrative controls that constrain and monitor system use. Unfortunately, any system necessitates that certain system components and certain people be trusted —

whether or not they are trustworthy—even in the presence of fault-tolerance techniques (including Byzantine algorithms, which make few if any assumptions about what cannot happen). Intentional or accidental subversion of those system components can in many cases be devastating. In particular, both trusted people and interlopers have the ability to subvert the system and its applications. But systems that of their own accord simply fail to do what is required or expected can also be disastrous.

8.2.4   What and Whom Should We Trust?

As we see from the foregoing examples, risks come from many sources—not just from design and implementation flaws, human maliciousness, and accidents, but also from unforeseen combinations of problems and difficulties in responding to them. Any computer systems in which trust can justifiably be placed should be able to anticipate all such risks.

A few generalizations are in order.

Predictability. No system can ever be guaranteed to work acceptably all of the time. In a complex system, it is essentially impossible to predict all the sources of catastrophic failure. This caveat is true even in well-engineered systems, where the sources of failure may be subtle. Risks may come from unexpected sources. A system that has run without serious failure for years may suddenly fail. Hardware may fail. Lurking software flaws may surface. The software—and indeed the entire system—may be impossible to test fully under live conditions (as in Star Wars), especially in systems involving life-critical responses to real-time events. Software may fail because of changes external to it—for example, as a result of reconfiguration or updates to other programs on which that software depends. Classical quantitative risk assessment is superficially attractive but sorely limited in practice, especially if based on false assumptions—which often can have devastating consequences. Experience with past disasters is valuable, but only partially useful in anticipating future disasters.

System structure and complexity. It is important to understand the ways in which trust is placed in different components. It is usually a fantasy to believe that critical concerns such as security and reliability can be confined to a small portion of a computer system or replicated portion of a distributed system, particularly with conventionally designed computer systems. A realistic, generalized, trusted computing base — on which the adequacy of system operation can depend — tends to be large, especially if the totality of requirements is encompassed and the requirements and interactions with one another are explicitly recognized. This difficulty is particularly relevant for human safety. Nevertheless, hierarchical design, encapsulation, and careful distributed implementation can help to confine bad effects. Thus, a fundamental design goal is to partition a system so that different properties are maintained with high integrity by corresponding components, and that the interactions among different components can be controlled carefully.

Defensive design. Complex systems must be designed conservatively and defensively, especially when they operate under extreme circumstances. In critical applications, weak links are particularly dangerous; great care should be taken to avoid them. Assume the worst; then you can be thankful if things go well. Systems should identify different levels of trustworthiness and prevent dependence on less trustworthy subjects (for example, users) and objects (programs and data). Various notions of integrity (for example, system integrity, application integrity, and data integrity) are vital. Responses should be anticipated for the widest range of unexpected behavior. Furthermore, systems and applications should observe the many principles of good design (of which separation of duties and least privilege are cited as examples — for reliability and for security as well). Sound software-engineering practice provides no easy answers, but even riskier are the archaic techniques often found in lowest-bidder or overly simplistic efforts.

Distributed systems. The notion that distributed control solves problems not easily solved with central control is also largely a myth. Problems of updating, synchronization, concurrency, backup, and verifiability (for example) may simply appear in different guises, and some manifestations may be much harder to analyze than others.

The environment. Vagaries of the operating environment (such as power interruptions, extreme weather conditions, interference, and lightning strikes) may defeat sound design and implementation — irrespective of how well the computer systems are engineered. Thorough awareness of all risks can lead to systems with substantially fewer and less critical risks.

People. People in the loop may make the risks worse rather than better — especially if the people must operate under tight real-time constraints. Complex human interfaces are inherently risky, but the importance of sound interface design is generally underestimated. Emergency preparedness is difficult at best, and often is hampered by people taking inappropriate emergency actions. Beware of people who think they are more reliable than the computer system. But also beware of anyone in authority who has an inordinate trust—and lack of suspicion—in computers and those who employ them. Such people constitute a serious risk, especially when they give up their own responsibility to the technology.

To reduce the serious risks associated with excessive or inappropriate trust being placed in computer technology, we can take several steps:

- The many different senses in which trust is conferred must be made explicit—identifying potentially all assumptions about technology, people, and the environment.

- Systems must be designed and implemented defensively with respect to all senses of trust, and operated with continual awareness of the risks. Despite significant advances in system and software engineering, there is still too much ad-hoc-ery.

- All possible modes of human behavior must be considered, and those that are plausible must be anticipated in the system design, implementation, and operation.

- The myth of technological infallibility must be thoroughly debunked, repeatedly. This theme is revisited in Sections 9.5 and 9.8.1.

8.3 Computers, Ethics, and the Law

As high-risk uses of computer-related systems continue to increase, it is important to consider some of the critical roles that people play relative to those systems, and, in particular, the potential roles of ethics and values.

We have considered problems such as system penetrations, abuses of authority, tampering, and other system misuses, spoofed E-mail, and risks in ballot recording and tabulating. Relevant cases of misuse in the past have also included financial fraud, antisocial surveillance, and telephone phreaking.

There has been extensive discussion regarding whether access requiring no authorization violates any laws. Irrespective of the laws, Gene Spafford [158] concludes that computer breakins are

categorically unethical. But what good are computer ethics in stopping misuse if computer security techniques and computer fraud
laws are deficient? Relating back to Section 3.1, techniques to
narrow the sociotechnical gap are not particularly effective if the
technological gap and the social gap are both wide open.

In [110][8] I wrote the following:

> Some *Risks Forum* contributors have suggested that, because at-
> tacks on computer systems are immoral, unethical, and (hopefully)
> even illegal, promulgation of ethics, exertion of peer pressures, and
> enforcement of the laws should be major deterrents to compromises
> of security and integrity. But others observe that such efforts will
> not stop the determined attacker, motivated by espionage, terrorism,
> sabotage, curiosity, greed, or whatever. . . . It is a widely articulated
> opinion that, sooner or later, a serious collapse of our infrastruc-
> ture—telephone systems, nuclear power, air traffic control, finan-
> cial, and so on—will be caused intentionally.
>
> Certainly, better teaching and greater observance of ethics are
> needed to discourage computer misuse. However, we must try
> harder not to configure computer systems in critical applications
> (whether proprietary or government sensitive but unclassified, life-
> critical, financially critical, or otherwise depended on) when those
> systems have fundamental vulnerabilities. In such cases, we must
> not assume that everyone involved will be perfectly behaved, wholly
> without malevolence and errors; ethics and good practices address
> only a part of the problem—but are nevertheless important.

Superficially, it might seem that computer security would be
unnecessary in an open society. Unfortunately, even if all data and
programs were freely accessible, integrity of data, programs, and
systems would be necessary to provide defenses against tampering,
faults, and errors.

A natural question is whether the value-related issues raised by
the use of computer systems are substantively different from those
that arise in other areas. The advent of computer technology has
brought us two new ethical dilemmas.

- People seem naturally predisposed to *depersonalize* complex systems.
  Computers are not people, and therefore need not be treated humanely.
  Remote computer access intensifies this predisposition, especially if access can be attained anonymously or through masquerading. General
  ambivalence, a resulting sublimation of ethics, values, and personal
  roles, and a background of increasingly loose corporate moralities (for

example, savings and loan and other insider manipulations, and eco-
logical abuses) seem to encourage in some people a rationalization that
unethical behavior is the norm, or somehow justifiable.

- Computers have opened up radically *new opportunities*, such as
distributed and multipartner fraud, high-speed crosslinking, global
searching and matching of enormous databases, junk E-mail, undetectable surveillance, and so on. These capabilities were previously
impossible, inconceivable, or at least extremely difficult.

Most professional organizations have ethical codes. Various
nations and industries have codes of fair information practice.
Teaching and reinforcement of computer-related values are vi-
tally important, alerting system purveyors, users, and would-be
misusers to community standards, and providing guidelines for
handling abusers. But we still need sound computer systems and
sound laws.

Each community has its own suggestions for what to do about
these problems.

- System technologists typically see the need for better systems and networks—with increased security, reliability, and safety. For example,
improved operating systems, user-to-system and system-to-system authentication, network encryption, and privacy-enhanced mail (PEM)[9]
can significantly increase the security attainable. The evidence of this
book suggests that we must do better in developing and using life-
critical systems—and indeed some progress is being made in reliability
and human safety.

- Some legislators and lawyers see a need for laws that are more clearly
enforceable and in some cases more technology specific. Issues raised
include familiar topics such as liability, malpractice, intellectual property, financial crimes, and whistle-blowing. In these and other areas,
difficulties arise in applying the existing laws—which often were not
written with all of the idiosyncrasies of the computer era in mind.
Examples include remote access from another country with different
laws, and definitions of what constitutes authorization and misuse.
Law-enforcement communities typically seek more arrests, more prose-
cutions, and more jails—which might become less relevant if the technology were doing its job better. Insurers also can play a constructive
role, particularly if they encourage the development of systems that
help to reduce the risks—not just the risks to insurers but also the
risks to the insured.

- Social scientists see many needs that transcend technology and the
law. Examples include restructuring our societies, providing better
education, encouraging greater human interaction and cooperation

generally, reducing inequities between people with access to the emerging information superhighway and everyone else, and pervasively reinforcing and encouraging ethical behavior from cradle to grave.

Such a diversity of perspectives is typical when a new technology emerges. At any one time, certain interest groups may seek economic, political, ideological, or emotional leverage; each group may view its goals as predominant, and may ignore the other groups. It is dangerous to believe that one approach is more correct or has a higher priority than another. Each approach can contribute positively—whereas its absence can lead (and has led) to serious consequences. Each of the three perspectives must be respected, within a coordinated effort that unifies them. Consequently, these perspectives and others must evolve further so that the technology, the laws, and the social norms all become much more compatible with one another than they are now.[10]

8.4 **Mixed Signals on Social Responsibility**

What is the appropriate role of computer professionals in determining how their work is used? Should they consider the societal implications of their work?

Computer scientists receive mixed answers to these questions. On the one hand, there has been increasing talk about the importance of scientists and engineers playing a major role in shaping the social environment in which their work is used. Statements to this effect issue regularly from some of our most prominent universities. In the January 1991 issue of *Computing Research News*, Rick Weingarten, Executive Director of the Computing Research Association, stressed the need for computer scientists to play an active role in science and technology policy. The ACM issued a strongly worded statement calling on its members to adhere to the privacy guidelines in the ACM Code of Professional Conduct. The code advises members to consider the influence of their work on individual privacy, to express their professional opinions to employers or clients "regarding any adverse consequences to the public which might re-

Section 8.4 originally appeared as an *Inside Risks* column, CACM, 34, 8, 146, August 1991, and was written by **Ronni Rosenberg**, manager of the Documentation Department at Kendall Square Research, Waltham, MA. She is a member of the ACM Committee on Computers and Public Policy.

sult from work proposed," and to "consider the health, privacy, and general welfare of the public" as part of their work.

More generally, National Science Foundation director Walter Massey urged all scientists to devote more time to the public-policy aspects of their work: "Members of the science and engineering communities should play a more significant role in our representative democracy. Being a member of these professions does not preclude participation in the political process." In 1989, a National Academy of Sciences report said, "science and technology have become such integral parts of society that scientists can no longer abstract themselves from societal concerns. . . . [D]ealing with the public is a fundamental responsibility for the scientific community. Concern and involvement with the broader issues of scientific knowledge are essential if scientists are to retain the public's trust."

Having seen what these scientific institutions *say* about the context in which technologists should conduct their work, let's look at what the computing profession *does*.

The computing profession encourages computer scientists to be narrow technocrats. Most computer-science curricula pay little or no attention to "social impacts." This shortcoming reflects a widespread view that a computer-science degree is a (purely) technical degree. Where computers-and-society courses are available, they often are offered by departments other than computer science (for example, philosophy or sociology), and are taught by people other than computer scientists. In this way, computer-science students are taught that social effects of computing are topics for other disciplines, rather than their own, to consider.

Few senior computer scientists devote time to public service or consider the social implications related to their work. Through the example of their professional role models and the policies of their schools, computer-science students learn these lessons well: The "best" work is what extends the technical state of the art, and computer scientists should not care about how (or whether) the fruits of their work are used.

Outside of school, whether a computer scientist is employed in academia or in industry, an interest in social implications of computing must be satisfied outside of working hours, after the real work is done, if it is to be satisfied at all. Businesses may enable employees to attend technical conferences on the company's time, but such flexibility is not likely to be extended to testify before Congress. Expressing an opinion about the effects of a person's work on the public is not a recipe for professional advancement. Professional rewards in computer science—tenure, promotion, salary increase, publication opportunities—are too often proportional to the single-minded devotion to the technical aspects of one's job.

In short, the profession demonstrates, as clearly as it knows how, that the relationship between computing and society is not a valid part of computer science. Of course, not all computer science departments, businesses, and computer-scientists adhere to this view! Nonetheless, this broadly painted picture accurately captures the spirit of many participants in the field.[11]

Why should we care? Because Rick Weingarten, the ACM Code, Walter Massey, and the National Academy of Sciences are right. The context in which computer systems exist—who pays for them, who participates in their design, how they are used, and how they are viewed by policymakers—is at least as significant an indicator of the systems' impact and value as are technical factors. Computer scientists are not the only ones who should consider the context of computer-system use, but their expertise imposes a special obligation to participate actively in the discussion.

8.5 Group Dynamics

Above all, by formally recognizing the existence of fuzziness, we will realize why management isn't the way it's supposed to be—why it probably shouldn't be the way it's supposed to be. We'll learn that the problems caused by fuzziness are not to be avoided at all costs, but instead are problems to be worked on and lived with. Perhaps most important of all, we will come to find that the fuzzy side of management not only poses serious problems but opens up unusual opportunities as well—and only then may we claim to fully understand what properly unbusinesslike management is all about.
    ROGER GOLDE [51]

In this section, we review some of the influences governing collaborative and other multiperson interactions in the development and use of computers and communications, from the perspectives of the risks involved.

8.5.1 Large Programming Projects

"Too many cooks spoil the broth." This proverb certainly identifies a risk in programming projects. Large teams often cause more serious problems than they solve. However, many systems are intrinsically so complex that they cannot be concocted by a few superchefs—and so large teams are used. Controlling a multiperson development project that encompasses multiple system versions can become complicated. This book includes discussion of various systems and system developments (for example, see Section 7.4) that failed at least partly because of the unmanageability of their complexity—for which system engineering and software engineering can provide only limited help. We must increasingly question the viability of huge computer-system developments, especially if the use of those systems is life-critical or otherwise societally risky.[12]

8.5.2   **Fast, Far-Reaching Interactions**

Computer and communication technologies are radically changing the ways in which people can collaborate, both locally and worldwide. Faxes and E-mail messages are able to reach out to multitudes at arbitrary distances, economically and almost instantaneously. The enormous potential influence of such networking is evident from the 30,000 people who asked within a very short time to have themselves removed from the Lotus Marketplace Households database (Section 6.1). The influence is also evident from the electronic dissemination of news after Tienanmen Square and during the failed Soviet coup attempt against Gorbachev. These potentially unifying technologies can play a major role in the establishment and maintenance of democratic institutions and the spread of information. But they can be used repressively as well. For example, there was a report from the Northwest Information Agency via Aldis Ozols in Sydney, Australia, about high-powered electronic retaliation during the Soviet coup: "All fax machines and computers at publishing houses of democratic newspapers *Smena* and *Nevskoye* were burnt by strong electric impulses."

Easy communications and rapid interactions entail some risks. Proprietary rights can be flagrantly abused as software and text migrate on their merry ways. Trojan horses and personal-computer viruses can propagate more easily. Messages may be spoofed. The ability for people to vote instantaneously from their homes or offices in referenda on important issues would also present risks, such as emotional, simplistic, or knee-jerk responses to complex issues, sometimes with irreversible consequences.

On-line newsgroups have proliferated wildly, covering every

imaginable topic. The more carefully moderated newsgroups are providing serious international educational and cultural benefits. Other newsgroups act as sandboxes for newsgroupies. There is considerable potential for overzealous flaming and rapid spread of false information.

8.5.3   Collaborative Attacks on Security

One of the security notions aimed at defeating single weak-link security attacks is separation of duties—for example, splitting administrative and technical duties, or partitioning a superuser facility into distinct subprivileges. Another is requiring two persons to authorize a particularly sensitive action—for example, two-key systems. Perhaps it is only twice as difficult to bribe two people as it is to bribe one, unless they happen to be working together. The concept of fault tolerance could be generalized to security in the sense that an authorization system (for example) could be made n-person tolerant. However, the vagaries of human behavior suggest that Byzantine fault tolerance would be a more appropriate model but might merely encourage further collaborative attacks.

8.5.4   International Perspectives

National boundaries are rapidly fading in the electronic world. However, there are still isolationist or nationalistic self-interest movements that mitigate against increased collaborations in spite of a changing world.

- **Marketplace competition.** Computer-system vendors seeking proprietary advantages may hinder development of open systems and networks (which themselves, rather ironically, require data confidentiality and system integrity to protect against abuses of openness).

- **National security, law enforcement, and international privacy.** Encryption-based systems have raised many concerns regarding policy, standards, and export controls, as noted in Clark Weissman's *Inside Risks* column, "A National Debate on Encryption Exportability," *CACM 34*, 10, 162, October 1991. One concern is that government actions in the name of national security can have a chilling effect on international cooperation and on the domestic marketplace, as well as counterproductively stimulating competing international efforts. For example, there has been considerable discussion in the on-line *Risks Forum* regarding the proposed digital-signature standard (DSS).[13] The Escrowed Encryption Standard (EES) involving the classified SKIP-JACK encryption algorithm and its implementation in the Clipper Chip for secure telephony, and the Capstone chip for secure data communications (Section 6.2), have added further fuel to the fire. The U.S. government sees the EES as providing increased privacy while at the same time not defeating the purposes of national security and law enforcement. The privacy community sees the EES as a further threat to privacy, especially if other uses of encryption were to become illegal.

Good ideas and good software (especially if free!) tend to propagate, irrespective of attempted controls that impede the construction of new means of communication.

We are now entering an era of much greater international effort, particularly in Europe and Japan. There are various stumbling blocks — economic and governmental more than technological. However, open collaboration that constructively uses the emerging computer and communication technologies can significantly reshape our world.

8.6 Certification of Computer Professionals

The *Risks Forum* has covered numerous cases in which software developers were at least partially responsible for disasters involving computer systems. We summarize here an on-line discussion on whether software developers should undergo professional certification, as in engineering disciplines.[14]

John H. Whitehouse made various arguments in favor of certification. There are not enough qualified people. Managers are not sufficiently knowledgeable about technical issues. Many practitioners survive despite poor performance, whereas many excellent people do not receive adequate credit. "Hiring is expensive and usually done pretty much in the blind. Firing is risk-laden in our litigious society. . . . It is my contention that the vast majority of software defects are the product of people who lack understanding of what they are doing. These defects present a risk to the public, and the public is not prepared to assess the relative skill level of software professionals." Fear of failing may cause some people to oppose voluntary certification. "Furthermore, academics have not joined in the debate, because they are generally immune from the problem."

Theodore Ts'o presented an opposing view. He sees no valid way to measure software "competence." "There are many different software methodologies, all with their own adherents; trying to figure out which ones of them are 'correct' usually results in a religious war." He also expressed serious concern that, under a certification system, the software profession might become a guild, protecting mediocrity and excluding really qualified people.

Martyn Thomas noted that certification does not necessarily help. Also, creating a closed shop is inherently risky because it enhances the status and incomes of those admitted at the expense of those excluded, and can easily become a conspiracy to protect the position of the members. However, on balance, some certification is desirable, "for staff who hold key positions of responsibility on projects that have significance for society." He added that many countries already have mandatory certification for other engineers. The United Kingdom defense standards for developing safety-critical software, DEFSTAN 00-55 and 56, are noted in Section 7.8.1, and have significant implications for the competence and experience required for developers of safety-critical systems.

Gary Fostel noted the problem of scale: There are significant differences between small systems and large ones.

> Large, complex software systems have problems that are not readily visible in the small-scale applications. In my software development courses, I commonly tell students that the methods that will be required of them are not necessarily the most efficient methods for the class project required of them. For the trivial sort of work I can require of students in a semester, there is really no need for comments . . . requirements analysis . . . and formal design, and so on for most of the techniques of software engineering. On the other hand, as the size of the problem grows, and the customer becomes distinct from the development, and the development stuff becomes fluid, and the effort expands in numerous other dimensions toward bewildering complexity, the methods . . . are in fact necessary.

Paul Tomblin observed the "Ritual of the Calling of an Engineer" (the Iron Ring), created by Rudyard Kipling before there was a legal status for engineers; Kipling's "Obligation" included this statement: "For my *assured* failures and derelictions, I ask pardon beforehand of my betters and my equals in my calling . . . ." Paul added, "So we admit that everyone fails at some time, and we aren't going to crucify you if you screw up, providing you did so honestly, and not because you were lazy or unprofessional."

Russell Sorber noted the voluntary certification provided by the Institute for Certification of Computer Professionals in Park Ridge, Illinois. Nurses, physicians, pilots, civil engineers (even hair stylists) are licensed; he reiterated the thought that he would like life-critical systems to be built by licensed or certified professionals. John Whitehouse added that the ICCP takes great pains to prevent development of a guild mentality—for example, with continual review and updating of the certification process.

There was also some discussion of whether certification would stifle creativity, originality, and excellence; in summary, it might, but not necessarily.

This debate is an old one. In this exchange of views, the sentiments generally favored certification, with various caveats. There is need for a balanced position in which there is some certification of both individuals and institutions involved in the development of high-risk computer systems, but in which the certification process itself is carefully circumscribed. Certification of the systems produced is also important. Teaching and systematic use of modern development techniques are also important pieces of the puzzle, as is the reinforcement of ethical behavior. Martyn Thomas noted that certification is only a mechanism for control; it has to be exercised in the right direction if there is to be an improvement.

8.7 **Summary of the Chapter**

Most of the problems exhibited in this chapter are ultimately human problems. Difficulties in system use and operation have strong human components. Problems in conception, requirement specification, design, and implementation are also people intensive. The technological factors and the human factors must be considered together. People involved in system development and operation must be more aware of the critical roles that they play. Significantly better education and training in computer-related activities are needed at all levels, with greater emphasis on system-oriented thinking.[15]

Challenges

C8.1   Put yourself in the shoes and mindset of the individuals who were involved in a few of the disasters described in the earlier chapters. Try to choose disasters that were induced or directly caused by human behavior. What would you have done differently at the time? What would you do differently now, having read this book up to this point? (After contemplating those questions, you are ready to read my conclusions in Chapter 9.)

C8.2   Choose two particularly disastrous cases from this book. See how widely or narrowly you can spread the blame. What portion of it falls on nonhuman shoulders? Under what circumstances do you think it is reasonable to try to allocate blame? If possible, dig beyond the details presented in the book. (In numerous cases, the identification of the real causes remains either unresolved or closely guarded.)

C8.3   Consider the types of misplaced trust itemized in Section 8.2.1. In particular, address the last type (loss of human control and initiative), and analyze it in detail. Enumerate cases in which this problem has affected you personally. Choose three other types, and find examples among the cases in this book other than those explicitly noted in Section 8.2.1.

C8.4   Can you conceive of a set of standards for certification of professionals that, on one hand, would be attainable by enough system designers and programmers to satisfy the demand for their skills, and that, on the other hand, would be stringent enough that satisfying it would necessarily imply a suitable level of competence for the development of life-critical systems? Explain your answer.

C8.5   Try to obtain a set of professional ethics (with no clues given here as to how to go about it) for some organization of interest to you, such as the ACM, the Institute of Electrical and Electronics Engineers (IEEE), the IEEE Computer Society, the American Bar Assocation, the American Medical Association, or the Federal Bureau of Investigation. How difficult was it to acquire? What does the level of difficulty suggest? Consider three dissimilar cases of malicious system misuse, such as those in Sections 5.1, 5.4, and 5.6, related to the field of your choice. How might your chosen ethical code have made a difference? What else might have been helpful?

C8.6   Do you believe that computer-related systems raise value-related issues that are substantively different from those in other kinds of technologically based systems? Explain your answer.

C8.7   Under what circumstances might you accept employment in a company whose primary objective ran counter to your own principles? Would you then strive to change that company's policies? What would you do if you discovered what you considered to be a serious breach — legal, ethical, moral, or otherwise? Discuss your answer. Discuss the implications of your being a whistle-blower — a role that by itself represents some high risks relating to technology.

CHAPTER 9

Implications and Conclusions

*Data without generalization
is just gossip.*

PHAEDRUS, IN *LILA,
AN INQUIRY INTO MORALS,*
ROBERT M. PIRSIG [133]

THUS FAR, WE HAVE RECOUNTED a large number of strange cases relating to computer-communication systems, including many that involve people who have either misused those systems or been victimized by them. Interspersed throughout are various analyses of the underlying causes and the nature of the effects, along with some philosophical and technological views on what might be done to lessen the risks. In this chapter, we draw some general conclusions about the underlying problems, and assess our chances for the future.

9.1 Where to Place the Blame

*To err is human.
To blame it on a computer is even more.*[1]

Increasingly, we hear of blame being allocated rather simplistically and conveniently to one particular cause, such as the operator, the computer, or some external factor. In most cases, however, there are multiple factors that contribute. We have discussed attempts to place blame, such as in various air accidents (Section 2.4) and in the *Exxon Valdez* oil spill (Section 8.2). We have also considered many cases with identifiable multiple causes (Section 4.1).

Often, people are blamed—perhaps to perpetuate the myth of infallibility of the technology. For example, the blame for Chernobyl was attributed in Soviet reports to a few errant people; the

285

long-term health effects were suppressed completely, reflecting an attempt to downplay the real risks. In the *Vincennes'* shootdown of Iran Air 655, blame was directed at a single crew member (and on the Iranians for flying over the ship), irrespective of whether the Aegis computer system was appropriate for the job at hand. In the Patriot case, the clock-drift problem was seemingly critical; had the program fix not taken so long to arrive (by plane), the Dhahran disaster might have been averted. On the other hand, the analysis of Ted Postol noted in Section 2.3 suggests that the system was fundamentally flawed and would have been deficient even if it had been rebooted every 14 hours.

We noted in Section 8.1 that most system problems are ultimately and legitimately attributable to people. However, human failings are often blamed on "the computer"—perhaps to protect the individuals. This attribution of blame seems to be common in computers affecting consumers, where human shortcomings are frequently attributed to "a computer glitch." Computer system malfunctions are often due to underlying causes attributable to people; if the technology is faulty, the faults frequently lie with people who create it and use it.

Systems must be designed to withstand reasonable combinations of multiple hardware faults, system failures, and human mistakes. An obvious problem with this conclusion is that, no matter how defensive a design is, there will be combinations of events that have not been anticipated. In general, it is easy to ignore the possibility of a devastating event. Furthermore, Murphy's Law suggests that even seemingly ridiculous combinations of improbable events will ultimately occur. Not surprisingly, many of the cases cited here illustrate that suggestion.

9.2 **Expect the Unexpected!**

What we anticipate seldom occurs; what we least expected generally happens.

BENJAMIN DISRAELI[2]

One of the most difficult problems in designing, developing, and using complex hardware and software systems involves the detection of and reaction to unusual events, particularly in situations that were not understood completely by the system developers. There have been many surprises. Furthermore, many of the problems have arisen as a combination of different events whose confluence was unanticipated.

Prototypical programming problems seem to be changing. Once upon a time, a missing bounds check enabled reading off the end of an array into the password file that followed it in memory. Virtual memory, better compilers, and strict stack disciplines have more or less resolved that problem; however, similar problems continue to reappear in different guises. Better operating systems, specification languages, programming languages, compilers, object orientation, formal methods, and analysis tools have helped to reduce certain problems considerably. However, some of the difficulties are getting more subtle—especially in large systems with critical requirements. Furthermore, program developers seem to stumble onto new ways of failing to foresee all of the lurking difficulties.

Here are a few cases of particular interest from this perspective, most of which are by now familiar.

Air New Zealand. The Air New Zealand crash of November 28, 1979 (Section 2.4) might be classified as a partially anticipated event—in that a serious database error in course data had been detected and corrected locally, but had not yet been reported to the pilots.

British Midland. The crash of the British Midland 737-400 on January 8, 1989 (Section 2.4) illustrates the possibility of an event that was commonly thought to be impossible—namely, both engines being shut down at the same time during flight. The chances of simultaneous failure of both engines are commonly estimated at somewhere between one in 10 million and one in 100 million—which to many people is equivalent to "it can't happen." In this case, the pilot mistakenly shut down the only working engine.

F-18. The F-18 crash due to an unrecoverable spin (Section 2.3) was attributed to a wild program transfer.

Rail ghosts. As noted in Section 2.5, the San Francisco Muni Metro light rail system had a ghost train that appeared in the computer system (but not on the tracks), apparently blocking a switch at the Embarcadero station for 2 hours on May 23, 1983. The problem was never diagnosed. The same ghost reappeared on December 9, 1986.

BoNY. The Bank of New York (BoNY) accidental $32-billion overdraft due to an unchecked program counter overflow, with BoNY having to fork over $5 million for a day's interest, was certainly a surprise. (See Section 5.7 and *SEN 11*, 1, 3-7.)

Reinsurance loop. A three-step reinsurance cycle was reported where one firm reinsured with a second, which reinsured with a third, which unknowingly reinsured with the first, which was thus reinsuring itself and paying commissions for accepting its own risk. The computer program checked only for shorter cycles (*SEN 10*, 5, 8-9).

Age = 101. In Section 2.11, we note the Massachusetts man whose insurance rate tripled when he turned 101. He had been converted into a youthful driver (age 1 year!) by a program that mishandled ages over 100.

Monkey business. Chimpanzee Number 85 (who, for the launch, was named Enos, which is Greek for man) had some hair-raising adventures aboard the Mercury-Atlas MA-5 mission on November 29, 1962. His experimental station malfunctioned, rewarding proper behavior with electric shocks instead of banana pellets. In response, he tore up his restraint suit and its instrumentation.[3]

Another monkey made the news in mid-October 1987, aboard *Cosmos* 1887, a Soviet research satellite. Yerosha (which is Russian for *troublemaker*) created havoc by freeing its left arm from a restraining harness, tinkering with the controls, and playing with its cap fitted with sensing electrodes.

A monkey slipped out of its cage aboard a China Airlines 747 cargo plane before landing at Kennedy Airport, and was at large in the cabin. After landing, the pilot and copilot remained in the cockpit until the animal-control officer thought that he had the monkey cornered at the rear of the plane. After the pilot and copilot left, the monkey then entered the cockpit (macaquepit?) and was finally captured while sitting on the instrument panel between the pilot and copilot seats.[4]

Stock-price swing. Mark Brader reported a case of a sanity check that backfired. Following speculation on Canadian Pacific Railway stock over disputed land ownership, the stock dropped $14,100 (Canadian) per share in 1 day when the lawsuit failed. The stock was reported as "not traded" for the day because a program sanity check rejected the large drop as an error (*SEN 12*, 4, 4-5).

The ozone hole. As noted briefly in Section 8.2, the ozone hole over the South Pole would have been recognized from the computer-analyzed data years before it was actually accepted as fact, but it was explicitly ignored by the software for 8 years because the deviations from the expected normal were so great that the program rejected them (*SEN 11*, 5). Years later, when the *Discovery* shuttle was monitoring the ozone layer and other atmospheric gases, a high-rate data-channel problem was blocking transmission. Because the shuttle computer system does not have enough storage for the full mission data, much of the mission data could not be recorded.[5]

ARPAnet collapse. The ARPAnet network collapse (Section 2.1) was triggered by dropped bits in a status message. That problem had been partially anticipated in that checksums had been created to detect single-bit errors in transmission but not in memory. In this case, a single parity-check bit would have detected the first bit dropping in memory, in which case the second would not have been able to occur undetected. Indeed, newer node hardware now checks for an altered bit.

Other unexpected examples. We can also note the AT&T outage, the Therac-25, and the clock overflows, discussed in Sections 2.1, 2.9, and 2.11, respectively. Before the Internet Worm, the sendmail debug option feature was fairly widely known, although the fingerd trapdoor was not (Section 5.1). However, the massive exploitation of those system flaws was clearly unexpected.

9.2.1 Good Practice

Systematic use of good software-engineering practice, careful interface design, strong typing, and realistic sanity checks are examples of techniques that can help us to overcome many such problems. We must strive much harder to develop better systems that avoid serious consequences from unexpected events. (Section 7.8 gives further examples of systems that did not adhere to good software engineering practice.)

There are wide ranges in the degree of anticipation. In some cases, events occur that were completely unanticipated. In some cases, events were considered but ignored because they were thought to be impossible or highly unlikely. In other cases, an event might have been anticipated, and an attempt made to defend against it, but nevertheless that event was handled improperly (for example, incompletely or erroneously). In other cases, great care may have gone into anticipating every eventuality and planning appropriate actions. Even then, there are cases of unexpected events.

In some of these cases, the designers and implementers were like ostriches with their heads in the sand. In others, their eyes were open, but they mistakenly assumed the presence of another ostrich instead of a charging lion.

The distinction among different degrees of anticipation is often not clear, especially a priori, which suggests the need for extensive analytical techniques above and beyond the routine testing that is done today. As Section 7.10 makes clear, however, there are many pitfalls in risk analysis.

Although some of the occurrences of inadequately anticipated events may be noncritical, others may be devastating. There are many examples of serious unanticipated events and side effects given here—for example, the loss of the *Sheffield* in the Falklands War due to an unanticipated interference problem, cancer radiation-therapy deaths due to a programming flaw, two deaths due to microwaves interfering with pacemakers, and so on.

The paradoxical maxim, *"Expect the Unexpected!"* relates to the anticipation of unusual events with potentially critical side effects, and their avoidance or accommodation. The paradox, of course, arises in trying to know that all of the previously unanticipated events have indeed now been anticipated. Approaching fulfillment of this maxim is decidedly nontrivial. In the context of a single program, it may be attainable; involving the entire environment in which the computing systems operate, and including all of the people in the loop, it is essentially impossible.

9.2.2   **Uncertainty**

Perhaps the most frustrating of all are those cases in which uncertainty and doubts remain long after the event. Missing evidence is a contributing problem—for example, when an aircraft flight recorder goes down with the aircraft or when the appropriate audit trail is not even recorded. As with people, whose behavior may be altered as a result of being observed (as noted in Section 8.1), computer systems are also subject to the Heisenberg phenomenon. It may be difficult to conduct experiments that permit adequate diagnostics (barring system redesign), or to simulate such events before they happen in real systems. Asynchronous systems tend to compound the diagnostic problems, as we observe from Sections 2.1 and 7.3.

Much greater care and imagination are warranted in defending against computers that go bump in the night due to unexpected events. Ensuring adequate diagnostic ability *before, during,* and *after* such events is particularly desirable.

Informed speculation is a necessary part of the detective and preventive processes, particularly in the absence of discernible causes. It permits the true ghostbusters to emerge. Press reports tend toward gross oversimplifications, which are especially annoying when the facts are not adequately ascertainable. *Risks Forum* discussions remind us that blame is too often (mis)placed on "computer error" and "acts of God" (which serve as euphemisms for "human error" — particularly in system development and in use). On the other hand, "human error" by users often has as a cause "bad interface design" by developers. The blame must not be placed solely on people when the interface itself is unwieldy, confusing, or erroneous. Too much effort is spent on arguing the chicken-and-egg problem rather than on building systems better able to cope with uncertainty; see Section 9.1.

A somewhat extreme example of how we might learn to expect the unexpected happened to me in the early 1960s. I had just boarded a local two-car train in Peapack, New Jersey, to return to Bell Telephone Laboratories in Murray Hill after attending a funeral, and was standing in the center aisle of the train holding my wallet while waiting for the conductor to make change. It was a hot and sultry day. Suddenly a gust of wind swept across the aisle and blew my wallet out of my hand through the nearest window. The conductor kindly asked the engineer to back up the train until he found the wallet at track-side. I learned to realize that something seemingly ridiculous (the wallet disappearing) and something extremely unusual (an engineer backing up a train to pick up an object) could actually happen. That event significantly colored my perspective of anticipating what might happen.

Herb Caen noted another unusual occurrence of a man pitching horseshoes who missed. The spark from the horseshoe hitting a rock caused a 15-acre grass fire.[6] High-tech or low-tech, the risks abound.

9.3   **Avoidance of Weak Links**

[A]ll mechanical or electrical or quantum-mechanical or hydraulic or even wind, steam or piston-driven devices, are now required to have a certain

legend emblazoned on them somewhere. It doesn't matter how small the object is, the designers of the object have got to find a way of squeezing the legend in somewhere, because it is their attention which is being drawn to it rather than necessarily that of the user's. The legend is this:

> *The major difference between a thing that might go wrong and a thing that cannot possibly go wrong is that when a thing that cannot possibly go wrong goes wrong it usually turns out to be impossible to get at or repair.*

DOUGLAS ADAMS[7]

Attaining security, safety, high availability, and other critical requirements may be viewed as a weak-link problem, as discussed in Section 4.1; potentially, weak links may be broken or combinations of events may exceed the defensive capabilities of the system, no matter how defensively the system is designed and implemented. Systems can be designed to minimize the presence of such vulnerabilities, but there are inevitably circumstances in which the defenses can be overcome, accidentally or intentionally, and, in the latter case, with or without malice.

In general, it is desirable to cover all likely modes of faults, malicious misuses, and external circumstances, but also to ensure that the system will do something reasonable in the case of less likely events. Too often, however, unanticipated events may actually be much more likely than they seemed, with unpredictable consequences. Furthermore, the inability to anticipate unforeseen breakdown modes often results in those occurrences being difficult to diagnose and repair.

9.3.1 **Lessons**

Allegorically speaking, there are various morals to this story, with a meta(eu)phoria of (o)variety.

- *Do not put all your eggs in one basket.* Centralized solutions are inherently risky if a weak-link failure can knock out the entire system. Even if the centralized mechanism is designed to be highly robust, it can still fail. If everything depends on it, the design is a poor one.

- *Do not have too many baskets.* A risk of distributed systems (see Section 7.3) is that physical dispersion, intercommunications, distributed control, configuration control, and redundancy management may all become so complex that the new global fault modes cannot be accommodated adequately, as exemplified by the 1980 ARPAnet and 1990 AT&T collapses discussed in Section 2.1. There is also a risk of overdependence on individual baskets, as suggested by the Lamport quote at the beginning of Section 7.3.

- *Do not have too many eggs.* There are saturation effects of trying to manage too many objects all at the same time, irrespective of whether the eggs are all in one basket or are dispersed widely.

- *Do not have too few eggs.* There are problems relating to multiplexing among inadequate resources, recovering from malfunctions, and providing timely alternatives.

- *Avoid baskets and eggs of poor quality.* Poor quality may result from improper care in the production process and shabby quality control. One rotten egg can spoil the whole crate, just as entire networks have had great falls because of uncovered fault modes. Furthermore, a rotten egg in one basket rather surprisingly may be able to spoil the other baskets as well.

- *Know in advance what you are trying to do.* Look at the big picture. Are you trying to make a cake, an omelet, an operating system, or a worldwide network?

- *Be careful how you choose and organize your roosters.* Chief programmers and chief designers can be very effective, but only if they are genuinely competent. Otherwise, they can lead to more problems than they can solve.

- *Be careful how you choose and organize your hens.* Structuring your system into layers can help, or am I egging you on too much?

9.3.2 Defenses

Mechanisms for increasing system dependability (for example, security controls such as access controls and authentication; reliability measures such as fault avoidance, fault masking, and recovery, where faults may be introduced accidentally or maliciously; real-time checking; and proofs of algorithmic, design, or code correctness) may require vastly more complexity than the mechanisms they attempt to make dependable. Consequently, increased complexity may actually introduce greater risks.

The attainment of human safety typically may depend on security, availability, real-time performance, and reliability (among other requirements), and on the hardware, software, and operating environment behaving appropriately. Interactions among reliability, availability, and security are particularly intricate. Security flaws often may be exploited in combination with one another, and in combination with correlated fault modes. Exploitation of security flaws may also accidentally trigger reliability problems. In general, it is desirable to plan defensively to protect a system against both accidental and malicious correlated events.

It is risky to make oversimplified design assumptions, and even more dangerous to build systems that critically depend on the perpetual validity of those assumptions. Defensive design must be layered to accommodate failures of underlying mechanisms through higher-layer recovery, alternative strategies, or backups.

It is often self-defeating to pin the blame on a donkey — for example, on a designer, programmer, system operator, or penetrator, or worse yet, *on the computer.* Blame is often simplistically misplaced. Several factors may be involved. Especially in distributed systems, blame is typically distributable. (See Section 9.1.)

The faithful reader may by now be numbed by the continual reappearance of several of the examples. In fact, cases such as the ARPAnet and AT&T outages are multipurpose parables for our time. They serve to illustrate many different points, most notable of which is that seemingly isolated events are often related and — in combination with other events — may induce serious problems that were not adequately anticipated during system development and operation. They suggest that much greater care is needed in developing critical systems.

9.4 **Assessment of the Risks**

If I don't know I don't know, I think I know.
If I don't know I know, I think I don't know.
  R.D. LAING, *KNOTS*, VINTAGE BOOKS, RANDOM HOUSE, 1972.[8]

In the presence of computer-related risks as well as the difficulties inherent in risk analysis (see Section 7.10), risk assessment and its subsequent implications may necessitate tradeoffs among technical, social, economic, and political factors (among others). These tradeoffs are generally difficult to quantify, because each person's basis for judgment is likely to be different. Some risks are intrinsic in the use of technology; others can be surmounted with suitable effort and cost. The basic question to be addressed is this: Under what circumstances are the risks acceptable? An honest assessment of that question involves an analysis of *all* of the relevant factors, as well as an analysis of the analysis. But the decisions must be based on more than just narrowly conceived reasons such as bottom-line short-term profit.

It is exceedingly difficult to predict the future based only on our (incomplete) knowledge of the past and the present. Worse yet, in an apparently sound system, there always exists some risk of a malfunction or misuse that never previously occurred. Even afterward it may be impossible to find out with certainty what caused the problem.

In making supposedly rational arguments about why hardware and software will operate correctly or might continue to operate correctly, we make all sorts of implicit underlying assumptions that may be true most of the time, but which may indeed break down—particularly in times of stressed operation. Some of these are noted here. At a lower level of detail, some nasty problems seem to involve unanticipated conditions in timing and sequencing, in both synchronous and asynchronous systems, and particularly in distributed systems that rely on interdependencies among diverse components. We have various examples of such problems in the past—once again, for example, the 1980 ARPAnet collapse (due to what might be called an accidentally propagated data retrovirus after years of successful operation, noted in Section 2.1) and the delay in the first shuttle launch (Section 2.2.1).

In our lives as in our computer systems, we tend to make unjustified or oversimplified assumptions, often that adverse things will not happen. In life, such assumptions make it possible for us to go on living without inordinate worry (paranoia). In computer systems, however, greater concern is often warranted—especially if a system must meet critical requirements under all possible operating conditions to avoid serious repercussions. Thus, it seems essential that we try to make our assumptions about computer systems and their use both more explicit and more realistic. Basing a system design on assumptions that are almost always *but not quite always* true may seem like a close approximation, but may imply the presence of serious unanticipated risks. In systems such as those involved in the Strategic Defense Initiative, for example, many potentially critical assumptions have to be sufficiently correct. Certain erroneous assumptions could be catastrophic. Besides, we understand relatively little about long-term effects (whether they eventually manifest themselves as obvious effects or remain undetected as invisible side effects).

Many of the computer-related problems noted here involve unanticipated interactions between components that appeared to work correctly in isolation, or short-sighted assumptions that certain events could never happen. Furthermore, scapegoats are often found for someone else's problem.

These cases illustrate the dangers of relying on a set of assumptions that supposedly underlie proper system behavior. There are also lessons that we can learn from environmental risks such as toxic substances in our food, drink, and environments; some of those risks were known in advance but were ignored—for example, for commercial reasons; others came as "surprises" (thalidomide, for example), but probably represented a lack of due care and long-term testing. In some cases, the risks were thought of, but were considered minimal (Bhopal, Chernobyl, Three Mile Island). In other cases, the risks were simply never considered.

Greater humility is required. Science (especially computer science) does not have all the answers. Furthermore, the absence of any one answer (and indeed suppression of a question that should have been asked) can be damaging. But, as we see from the nature of the problems observed here, some people keep their heads in the sand—even after being once (or multiply) burned. Eternal vigilance is required of all of us. Some bureaucrats and technocrats may be fairly naïve about the technology, making statements such as "Don't worry, we can do it, and nothing can go wrong." Further, after a disaster has happened, the common response is that "We've fixed that problem, and it will never happen again."

The cases presented here may help to cast doubts. But technocrats who say "we can't do it at all" also need to be careful in their statements; in the small, anything is possible. (Both the Cassandra and the Pollyanna attitudes are unwise—although the original Cassandra ultimately turned out to be correct!)

We must remember that systems often tend to break down when operating under conditions of stress—particularly when global system integration is involved. Furthermore, it is under similar conditions that people tend to break down.

9.5 **Assessment of the Feasibility of Avoiding Risks**

What is the use of running when we are not on the right road?
OLD PROVERB

By now you may have detected a somewhat schizoid alternation between pessimism and optimism in this book—for example, concerning the issue of trust discussed in Section 8.2 or the issue of attaining reliability, safety, and security. There is optimism that we can do much better in developing and operating computer-related systems with less risk. There is pessimism as to how much we can justifiably trust computer systems and people involved in the use of those systems. People active in the forefronts of software engineering, testing, and formal methods tend to have greater optimism regarding their *own* individual abilities to avoid or at least identify flaws in systems and to provide some real assurances that a system will do exactly what is expected (no more and no less, assuming the expectations are correct), at least most of the time and under most realistic anticipated circumstances. However, serious flaws abound in systems intended to be secure or reliable or, worse yet, correct! Further, we have seen repeatedly that the operating environments are not always what had been expected, and that the expectations of human and system behavior are not always accurate either.

9.5.1 Progress

Is our ability to develop dependable computer-related systems generally improving? A retrospective perusal of this book suggests that there is a continual increase in the frequency of horror stories being reported and relatively few successes; new problems continue to arise, as well as new instances of old problems. One *Risks Forum* reader noted that the cases being reported seem to include many repetitions of earlier cases, and that the situation indeed does not seem to be improving.

Several comments are in order:

- Unqualified successes are rare.
- Failures are easier to observe than are successes, and are more eye-catching. Besides, the *Risks Forum* is explicitly designed for reporting and analyzing the difficulties.
- Henry Petroski's oft-quoted observation that we tend to learn much more from our failures than from our successes suggests that the re-porting of failures may be a more effective educational process.
- The people who desperately need to learn how to avoid repetitive recur-rences are not doing so. Robert Philhower suggested that the longevity of the *Risks Forum* itself attests to the fact that not enough people are properly assimilating its lessons.
- Experience is the best teacher, but once you have had the experience, you may not want to do it again (and again) — or even to teach others.
- We still do not appreciate sufficiently the real difficulties that lurk in

the development, administration, and use of systems with critical requirements.

- Developers badly underestimate the discipline and effort required to get systems to work properly—even when there are no critical requirements.
- Many computer systems are continuing to be built without their developers paying consistent attention to good software-engineering and system-engineering practice. However, reducing one risk may increase others, or at best leave them unaffected.
- Technological solutions are often sought for problems whose solutions require reasonable human actions and reactions more than sound technology.

For such reasons, the same kinds of mistakes tend to be made repeatedly, in system development, in operation, and in use. We desperately need more true success stories, carefully executed, carefully documented, and carefully evaluated, so that they can be more readily emulated by others with similar situations.

It is interesting to note that we have improved in certain areas, whereas there has been no discernible improvement in others. If you consider the sagas relating to shuttles, rockets, and satellites discussed in Section 2.2, and defense-related systems in Section 2.3, the incidence and severity of cases are both seemingly dwindling. In other areas—particularly those that are highly dependent on people rather than technology—the incidence and severity seem to be increasing.

9.5.2   **Feasibility**

The foregoing discussion brings us to familiar conclusions. Almost all critical computer-related systems have failure modes or security flaws or human interface problems that can lead to serious difficulties. Even systems that appear most successful from a software viewpoint have experienced serious problems. For example, the shuttle program used such extraordinarily stringent quality control that the programmer productivity was something on the order of a few lines of debugged and integrated code per day overall. Nevertheless, there have been various difficulties (noted in Section 2.2.1)—the synchronization problem with the backup computer before the first *Columbia* launch, multiple computer outages on a subsequent *Columbia* mission (STS-9), the output misreading that caused liquid oxygen to be drained off just before a scheduled *Columbia* launch (STS-24), *Discovery*'s positioning problem in a laser-beam experiment over Hawaii (STS-18), *Discovery*'s having the shutdown procedure for two computers reversed (STS-19), *Endeavour*'s difficulties in its attempted rendezvous with *Intelsat* (due to not-quite-identical values being equated), and others. The variety seems endless.

Systems with critical requirements demand inordinate care throughout their development cycle and their operation. But there are no guaranteed assurances that a given system will behave properly all of the time, or even at some particularly critical time. We must be much more skeptical of claimed successes. Nevertheless, we need to try much harder to engineer systems that have a much greater likelihood of success.

9.6 Risks in the Information Infrastructure

The future seems to be leading us to an emerging **national information infrastructure** (NII) (for example, see [174]) and its global counterpart, which we refer to here as the **worldwide information infrastructure**, or WII. The WII represents many exciting constructive opportunities. (This concept is sometimes referred to as the **information superhighway** or the **Infobahn**—although those metaphors introduce problems of their own.) The WII also encompasses a wide range of risks. In a sense, the emerging global interconnection of computers brings with it the prototypical generic *RISKS* problems; it encompasses many now familiar risks and increasingly involves human safety and health, mental well-being, peace of mind, personal privacy, information confidentiality and integrity, proprietary rights, and financial stability, particularly as internetworking continues to grow.

On September 19, 1988, the National Research Council's Computer Science and Technology Board (now the Computer Science and Telecommunications Board) held a session on computer and communication security. At that meeting, Bob Morris of the National Computer Security Center noted that "To a first approximation, every computer in the world is connected with every other computer." Bob, K. Speierman, and I each gave stern warnings—particularly that the state of the art in computer and network security was generally abysmal and was not noticeably improving, and that the risks were considerable. Ironically, about six weeks later, a single incident clearly demonstrated the vulnerability of many computer systems on the network—the Internet Worm of November 1988 (see Sections 3.3, 3.6, and 5.1.1). Since that time, numerous innovative system penetrations (including wholesale password capturing that began anew in the fall of 1993) have continued. The 1980 ARPAnet collapse and the 1990 AT&T long-distance collapse (Section 2.1) illustrate reliability problems. The security and reliability problems of the existing Internet can be expected to continue to manifest themselves in the WII even with improved systems and networking, and some of those problems could actually be more severe.[9]

In addition, many social risks can be expected. National cultural identities may become sublimated. Governments will attempt to regulate their portions of the WII, which attempts could have chilling effects. Commercial interests will attempt to gain control. Aggregation of geographically and logically diverse information enables new invasions of privacy. Huge volumes of information make it more difficult to ensure accuracy. The propagation of intentional disinformation and unintentionally false information can have many harmful effects. Rapid global communications may encourage overzealous or misguided reactions, such as instantaneous voting on poorly understood issues. Hiding behind anonymous or masqueraded identities can result in bogus, slanderous, or threatening E-mail and Trojan horseplay. Although modern system design and authentication can reduce some of these risks, there will still be cases in which a culprit is completely untraceable or where irrevocable damage is caused before the situation can be corrected.

Enormous communication bandwidths are certainly appealing, particularly with the voracious appetite of modern graphics capabilities and commercial entrepeneurs for consuming resources. However, past experience suggests that Parkinsonian saturation (of bandwidth, computational capacities, or human abilities) will be commonplace, with massive junk E-mail advertising tailored to patterns of each individual's observed behavior, hundreds of video channels of home shopping, interactive soap operas and community games, movies and old television programs on demand, live access to every sporting event in the world, and virtual aerobic exercise for armchair participants. Virtual reality may subliminally encourage some people to withdraw from reality further, providing additional substitutes for human contacts and real experiences. Personal disassociation and technological addictions are likely, along with diminished social skills. Cafés and other meeting places may qualify for the endangered species list, becoming the last refuge of antitechnologists. Risks of the technology being subverted by short-sighted commercializations are considerable. Recent studies linking on-line living with depression and obesity may also be relevant. Many of Jerry Mander's 1978 concerns [87] about the potential evils that might result from television, computers, and related technologies are still valid today (if not already demonstrated), and can be readily applied to the WII. (See also Section 9.8.1.)

The interconnective technologies may further divide people into haves and have-nots according to whether they are able to participate. There is great potential for improving the lives of those who are physically handicapped. However, the hopes for other minorities—such as the homeless, impoverished, elderly, or chronically unemployed—may be bleak in the absence of significant social change. Furthermore, even if everyone *could* participate (which is most unlikely), people who *choose* not to participate should not be penalized.

Educational uses could easily degenerate to lowest common denominators, unless educators and learners are keenly aware of the pitfalls. The WII can be much more than a public library, although it may not be free to all. It will clearly present unparalleled opportunities for the sharing of knowledge and for creative education. However, it will require educators and facilitators who truly understand the medium and its limitations, and who can resist the cookie-cutter phenomenon that tends to stamp out people with identical abilities.

The information-superhighway metaphor suggests analogies of traffic jams (congestion), crashes (system wipeouts), roadkill (bystanders), drunken drivers (with accidents waiting to happen), carjackers (malicious hackers), drag racers and joyriders, switched vehicle identifiers (bogus E-mail), speed limits (on the Infobahn as well as the Autobahn), onramps and gateways (controlling access, authentication, and authorization), toll bridges (with usage fees), designated drivers (authorized agents), drivers' licenses, system registration, and inspections. All of these analogies are evidently applicable. Although use of the superhighway metaphor may deemphasize certain risks that other metaphors might illuminate, it serves to illustrate some of the technological, social, economic, and political dangers that we must acknowledge and strive to overcome.

The risks noted here are genuine. I urge you all to increase your awareness and to take appropriate actions wherever possible.

9.7 Questions Concerning the NII

The previous section considers risks in the U.S. national information infrastructure and its international counterpart. We now pose some questions that need to be asked about both the NII and the WII. These questions are generally open-ended, and intended primarily to stimulate further discussion.

1. *What should the NII be?* Will it be primarily passive (500 movie and home-shopping channels) or active (two-way communications)? Will it support both commercial applications (consumers) and civic applications (citizens)? Should it have both government and private involvement? Who should oversee it?

2. *Guiding principles.* How can socially desirable services be provided if they are not directly profitable? Who determines standards and compliance for interconnectivity, quality, and so on?

3. *Accessibility.* Does **universal access** imply a connection, a terminal, and knowledge of how to access the NII? What is the NII goal? How can the government ensure that goal, and fund the NII adequately? Should providers be required to subsidize those who cannot afford it? Who determines what should be the minimum service? How can the NII be affordable and easily usable, especially for the underprivileged and disadvantaged? How can social risks be dealt with, including sexual harassment and character defamation? Should equal-access opportunity be facilitated and actively encouraged, independent of gender, race, religion, wealth, and other factors? Are fundamental changes in the workplace required? The French Minitel system is ubiquitous and cost-effective; it gives a free terminal to anyone who requests one. Is this approach effective, and could it work elsewhere? Should open access be guaranteed? If so, how? Will the existing notion of common carriers for communications services apply in the emerging union of telephones, computers, cable, and broadcast television?

4. *Censorship.* Should there be censorship of content? If so, who establishes the rules? Will there be protected forms of free

Section 9.7 originally appeared as an *Inside Risks* column, *CACM 37*, 7, 170, July 1994, written by **Barbara Simons**, who chairs the U.S. Public Policy Committee of the ACM (USACM).

speech? How do libel laws apply? Should offensive communications be screened? What about controls over advertising and bulk mailing?

5. *Access to public information.* Should the NII support the government mandate to improve the availability of information? If so, should NII users be charged for accessing this information?

6. *Privacy.* Should the NII protect an individual's privacy? Can it? Is additional legislation required for medical, credit, and other databases? Who owns the use rights for data? What permissions will be required? What should be the role of encryption and escrowed keys? Should/could the government determine that the use of nonauthorized encryption algorithms is illegal? Who should be able to monitor which activities, and under what conditions and authority? What recourse should individuals have after violations?

7. *International cooperation.* Are we studying and evaluating the activities of other countries, such as the French Minitel system, to emulate their successes and avoid their mistakes? What are we or should we be doing to ensure cooperation with other countries, while allowing them to maintain local control?

8. *Electronic democracy.* The NII could be a form of electronic democracy—an electronic town hall. Given that the current Internet users are far from representative of the entire population, to what extent should the NII be used to allow more people to have input into policy-making decisions? Do we have to be concerned about the development of an electronic oligarchy?

9. *Usability.* Legislation and research support have focused on advanced users and network technology, with little discussion about the design of the user interface. What is being done to study usability issues and to develop basic standards about the complexity of interfaces, the ease in authoring new materials, capacity for access in multiple languages, design for the elderly population, support for cooperation among users, and design methods to reduce learning times and error rates? What should be done, and who should provide the funding? Should we have testbeds to study what people would like and what constitutes a user-friendly interface?

10. *Libraries.* Should there be a knowledge base of electronic libraries? If so, who should be responsible? How should it be funded? How can the financial interests of writers and publishers be protected? With declining support for conventional libraries, how can electronic libraries become realistic?

11. *Public schools.* How can equitable NII access be provided for public schools when funding for public education varies greatly from wealthy areas to impoverished ones? How can these institutions be brought on-line when many classrooms don't even have telephone jacks? How will access to pornography be dealt with?

12. *Emergencies.* What should be the NII's role in dealing with natural and political emergencies?

9.8 Avoidance of Risks

I hate quotations. Tell me what you know.
RALPH WALDO EMERSON [10]

There is a widespread and growing disillusionment with technology. Fewer young people are aspiring to technology-oriented careers. Doubts are increasing as to technology's ability to provide lasting solutions for human problems. For example, heavy-industry technology has become a major polluter throughout the world. The use of chlorofluorocarbons in refrigeration, propulsion systems, and aerosols is threatening the ozone layer. Networked information that affects the activities of people is routinely sold and distributed without the knowledge or consent of those to whom it pertains, irrespective of its accuracy. [11]

9.8.1 Jerry Mander's Aphorisms

Jerry Mander has recently published a remarkable book, *In the Absence of the Sacred: The Failure of Technology & the Survival of the Indian Nations* [88]. He offers a list of aphorisms about technology, quoted below. From within our present ways of thinking, these aphorisms might appear as Luddite anti-technology. But they point the way to a new common sense that needs cultivation. Please read them in that spirit. [12]

1. Since most of what we are told about new technology comes from its proponents, be deeply skeptical of all claims.
2. Assume all technology "guilty until proven innocent."
3. Eschew the idea that technology is neutral or "value free." Every technology has *inherent and identifiable* social, political, and environmental consequences.
4. The fact that technology has a natural flash and appeal is meaningless. Negative attributes are slow to emerge.

5. Never judge a technology by the way it benefits you personally. Seek a holistic view of its impacts. The operative question is not whether it benefits you but who benefits most? And to what end?

6. Keep in mind that an individual technology is only one piece of a larger web of technologies, "metatechnology." The operative question here is how the individual technology fits the larger one.

7. Make distinctions between technologies that primarily serve the individual or the small community (for example, solar energy) and those that operate on a scale of community control (for example, nuclear energy).

8. When it is argued that the benefits of the technological lifeway are worthwhile despite harmful outcomes, recall that Lewis Mumford referred to these alleged benefits as "bribery." Cite the figures about crime, suicide, alienation, drug abuse, as well as environmental and cultural degradation.

9. Do not accept the homily that "once the genie is out of the bottle, you cannot put it back," or that rejecting a technology is impossible. Such attitudes induce passivity and confirm victimization.

10. In thinking about technology within the present climate of technological worship, emphasize the negative. This brings balance. Negativity is positive.

9.8.2   A New Common Sense

Peter Denning [34] proposes that it is time to start cultivating a new common sense about technology. By **common sense** Denning means the general, instinctive way of understanding the world that we all share. The disillusionment suggests that our current common sense is not working. Questions such as "If we can get a man to the moon, why can't we solve the urban crisis?" are overly simplistic; technology is not fundamentally relevant to the answer.

An example of an understanding in the old common sense is that we must obtain a precise description of a problem and then apply systematic methods to design a computing system that meets the specifications. In the new common sense, we must identify the concerns and the network of commitments people make in their organizations and lives, and then design computing systems that assist them in carrying out their commitments. The new common sense does not throw out precise specifications and systematic design; it simply regards these techniques as tools and does not make them the center of attention.

Many of the cases that are noted in the *RISKS* archives corroborate both Mander's aphorisms and the need for Denning's new common sense. In the new common sense, we would see organizations as networks of commitments, not hierarchical organization charts. Daily human interactions would be mini-instances of the customer–provider loop, and attention would be focused on whether the customer of every loop is satisfied with the provider's work. Technology would help people to fulfill their promises and commitments. Communication would serve for successful coordination of action rather than merely for exchanges of messages.

To begin the needed rethinking about technology, we can ask ourselves questions such as Mander asks. This introspection requires a rethinking of not merely military versus nonmilitary budgets but also the proper role of technology as a whole. Technology *by itself* is not the answer to any vital social questions. Ultimately, more fundamental human issues must be considered. Nevertheless, technology can have a constructive role to play—if it is kept in perspective.

9.9 **Assessment of the Future**

The future isn't what it used to be.
ARTHUR CLARKE, 1969, LAMENTING THAT IT WAS BECOMING MUCH MORE DIFFICULT TO WRITE GOOD SCIENCE FICTION

The past isn't what it used to be, either.
PETER NEUMANN, 1991, SPECULATING ON WHY HISTORY IS SO QUICKLY FORGOTTEN AND WHY PROGRESS BECOMES SO DIFFICULT

As stated at the outset, this book presents a tremendously varied collection of events, with diverse causes and diverse effects. Problems are evidenced throughout all aspects of system development and use. The diversity of causes and effects suggests that we must be much more vigilant whenever stringent requirements are involved. It also suggests that it is a mistake to look for easy answers; there are no easy answers overall, and generally no easy answers even with respect to any of the causative factors taken in isolation (doing which, as we note, is dangerous in itself).

There are many techniques noted in this book that could contribute to systems better able to meet their requirements for confidentiality, integrity, availability, reliability, fault tolerance, and human safety—among other requirements. However, the case must be made on each development effort and each operational system as to which of these techniques is worthwhile, commensurate with the risks. A global perspective is essential in determining which are the real risks and which techniques can have the most significant payoffs. Short-term benefits are often canceled out by long-term problems, and taking a long-term view from the outset can often avoid serious problems later on.

There are many lessons that must be learned by all of us — including system developers and supposedly innocent bystanders alike. And we must remember these lessons perpetually. However, history suggests that the lessons of the past are forgotten quickly. I sincerely hope that this book will provide a basis for learning, and that, in the future, we will be able to do much better — not only in avoiding past mistakes but also in avoiding potential new mistakes that are waiting to emerge. Nevertheless, we can expect the types of problems described in this book to continue. Some will result in serious disasters.

System-oriented (Chapter 7) and human-oriented (Chapter 8) viewpoints are both fundamental. In attempting to develop, operate, and use computer-related systems in critical environments, we do indeed essay a difficult task, as the Ovid quote suggests at the beginning of Chapter 1; the challenge confronting us is imposing. As the extent of our dependence on computer-based systems increases, the risks must not be permitted to increase accordingly.

9.10 Summary of the Chapter and the Book

Computers make excellent and efficient servants, but I have no wish to serve under them. Captain, a starship also runs on loyalty to one man. And nothing can replace it or him.
SPOCK, *THE ULTIMATE COMPUTER*, STARDATE 4729.4 (*STAR TREK*)

This chapter provides several perspectives from which to consider the problems addressed in the foregoing chapters.

Chapter 1 gives an introductory summary of potential sources of problems arising in system development (Section 1.2.1) and use (Section 1.2.2), as well as a summary of the types of adverse effects that can result (Section 1.3). Essentially all of the causes and effects outlined there are illustrated by the cases presented in this book.

Overall, this book depicts a risk-filled world in which we live, with risks arising sometimes from the technology and the surrounding environment, and frequently from the people who create and use the technology. We see repeatedly that the causes and the effects of problems with computers, communications, and related technologies are extraordinarily diverse. Simple solutions generally fall short, whereas complex ones are inherently risky. Extraordinary care is necessary throughout computer-system development, operation, and use, especially in critical applications. However, even in seemingly benign environments, serious problems can occur and—as seen here—have occurred.

Table 9.1 gives a rough indication of the types of risks according to their applications. The entries represent the number of incidents included in the *RISKS* archives through August 1993, classified according to the *Software Engineering Notes* index [113]. Many of those cases are included in this book. The numbers reflect individual incidents, and each incident is counted only once in the table. That is, a number in the column headed "Cases with deaths" is the number of cases, not the number of deaths. Where an incident resulted in death or risk to life and also caused material damage, it is counted under death or risk to life only. Other risks include all other cases except for those few beneficial ones in which the technology enabled risks to be avoided. The table was prepared by Peter Mellor[13] for the use of one of his classes. It is included here primarily for illustrative purposes.

I hope that this book will inspire many people to delve more deeply into this collection of material, and to address subsequent disasters with a scrutiny that has not generally been present up to now. The cited articles by Eric Rosen [139] and Jack Garman [47] are notable exceptions. Nancy Leveson's book [81] pursues various safety-related cases in considerable detail, and also provides techniques for increasing system safety. Ivars Peterson [127] provides some greater details on several cases discussed here. Appendix A gives further relevant references.

The potential for constructive and humanitarian uses of computer- and communication-related technologies is enormous. However, to be realistic, we must accept the negative implications regarding the abilities and inabilities of our civilization to wisely develop and apply these technologies. We must continually endeavor to find a balance that will encourage socially beneficial applications in which the risks are realistically low. Above all, we must remember that technology is ideally of the people, for the people, and by

TABLE 9.1   Number of cases of various types (as of August 1993)

Problem Area	Cases with deaths	Cases with risks to lives	Cases with resource losses	Cases of other risks	Bene-ficial cases	Totals
			Type of Case Effects			
Communication reliability	3	28	30	7	2	70
Space	1	25	23	12	1	62
Defense	6	26	13	6		51
Military aviation	3	15	5	2		25
Commercial aviation	17	49	9	5		80
Public transport	7	18	1	6		32
Automobiles	3	14	2	3		22
Environmental	0	3	0	1		4
Control systems	6	12	10	5		33
Robots/AI	6	1	3	3		13
Medical	17	13	4	3	1	38
Electric power	2	23	2	6		33
Computer-aided design	0	3	1	1		5
Financial (fraud)	0	0	56	6		62
Financial (accidental)	0	1	58	11	1	71
Stock market	0	0	20	1		21
Elections	0	1	1	30	2	34
Telephone fraud	0	0	22	3		25
Insurance fraud	0	0	2	0		2
Other security/privacy	2	10	72	78		162
Accidental service denials	2	11	28	26		67
Motor-vehicle databases	2	4	12	4		22
Law enforcement	0	14	11	15		40
Other legal	1	9	29	5	4	48
Other aggravation	3	5	45	43	1	97
Development fiascos	0	0	12	0		12
Miscellaneous	0	1	5	37		43
Totals	81	286	476	319	12	1174

the people. For the protection of the people and the global environment, constraints need to be placed on the development and use of systems whose misuse or malfunction could have serious consequences. However, in all technological efforts we must always remember that people are simultaneously the greatest strength and the greatest weakness.

Challenges

C9.1   Jim Horning notes that there is a risk in using the information superhighway metaphor (Section 9.6), because doing so tends to limit people's thinking to only highway-related risks. Describe additional risks that would be exposed by an alternative metaphor, such as the global village, the global library, the information monopoly, the net of a thousand lies (Verner Vinge), the global role-playing game (multiuser dungeon), the megachannel boob tube (these suggestions are Horning's), or another metaphor of your own choosing.

C9.2   Choose one of the questions on the information infrastructure given in Section 9.7, and discuss in detail the issues it raises.

C9.3   Based on your intuition and on what you have read here or learned elsewhere, examine the technologies related to the development of computer-based systems. Identify different aspects of the development process that correspond to artistic processes, scientific method, and engineering discipline. What conclusions can you draw about improving the development process?

C9.4   Identify and describe the most essential differences between ordinary systems and critical systems, or else explain why there are no such differences. Include in your analysis issues relevant to system development and operation.

C9.5   Choose an application with widespread implications, such as the Worldwide Information Infrastructure, domestic or worldwide air-traffic control, the Internal Revenue Service Tax Systems Modernization, or the National Crime Information Center system NCIC-2000. Without studying the application in detail, what potential risks can you identify? What would you recommend should be done to avoid or minimize those risks, individually and globally, as relevant to your application?

C9.6   Contrast the various types of application areas (for example, as in the various summary tables) with respect to shifts in causes and effects over time.[14] Is the nature of the causes changing? Is the nature of the consequences changing? Is the nature of the risks changing? Do you think that the risks are diminishing, increasing, or remaining more or less the same? In your analysis of any changes, consider such factors as (among others) the effects of the rapidly advancing technologies; the tendencies for increased interconnectivity; vulnerabilities, threats, and risks; education, training, and experiential learning; governmental and other bureaucracy; technical skill levels in your country and throughout the world, particularly with respect to the risks and how to combat them; the roles of technology in contrast with geosocioeconomic policy; and the levels of awareness necessary for ordinary mortals having to cope with technology. If you have chosen to view the problem areas that you understand best, estimate the potential significance of interactions with other aspects that you have not considered.

C9.7   Assess the relative roles of various factors noted in Challenge C9.6. Are people and organizations (including developers, operators, end-users, governments, corporations, educational organizations, and innocent bystanders) adequately aware of the real risks? How could their awareness be increased? Can social responsibility be legislated or taught? Why? Can the teaching and practice of ethical behavior have a significant effect? If so, who must do what?

C9.8   In what ways is the technology causing an increase in the separation between the *haves* and the *have-nots*? Is this gap intrinsic? If it is not, what can be done to shrink it?

C9.9   What are your expectations and hopes for our civilization in the future with respect to our uses of computer-related technologies?

C9.10   Describe changes in policies, laws, and system-development practices that would significantly improve the situation regarding risks to society at large and to individuals. Which changes would be most effective? What, in your opinion, are the limiting factors?

C9.11   Do you still agree with your responses to the challenges in earlier chapters? What, if anything, has changed about your earlier perceptions? Do you agree with my conclusions in this chapter? Explain your answers. Detail the issues on which you disagree (if any), and provide a rationale for your viewpoint.

Epilogue

As a civilization, we have become increasingly dependent on computers and communications. In this rush to technologize, however, we must not lose sight of our need to retain contact with ourselves, our fellow citizens, our environment, our planet, and our solar system.

In a 1954 story,[1] Isaac Asimov depicts a world in the year 2117 in which people use a virtual "Door" to teleport themselves from one place to another, worldwide, thereby avoiding the dangers of the natural world. When one of the Doors fails to operate, a 12-year-old, Dickie Hanshaw, is forced to use an emergency egress (a "door") to go to school. For the first time in his life, he walks through the outdoors.

After this experience, Dickie's behavior changes radically, taxing his mother and his mekkano (robot), who is instructed to destroy his clothing each time he returns. Dickie's schoolteacher recommends analysis in the form of a computer-controlled psychic probe. Instead, Dickie is brought to a psychiatrist, Dr. Hamilton Sloane, who happens to be concerned about the "rising, choking tide of machinery," as well as the risks of psychic probes and Doors failing to operate properly.

In attempting to communicate with Dickie, Dr. Sloane agrees to take a walk outdoors with the boy. After their walk, the doctor returns Dickie to his anxious mother and assures her that she doesn't need to worry. As Dr. Sloane prepares to depart through his Door, he utters the final line of the story:

You know, it's such a beautiful day that I think I'll walk.

APPENDIX A

Background Materials

A.1 *RISKS* References

In this book, the references to issues of the ACM SIGSOFT *Software Engineering Notes* are given in the form *SEN i*, j, where *i* is the volume number and j is the issue within the volume. The year and date of each issue can be obtained from the following table.

SEN regular issue numbers (Note: Vol 1 no 1 was dated May 1976.)

year	76	77	78	79	80	81	82	83	84	85	86	87	88	89	90	91	92	93	94
vol	1	2	3	4	5	6	7	8	9	10	11	12	13	14	15	16	17	18	19
Jan	1	1	1	1	1	1	1	1	1	1	1	1	1	1	1	1	1	1	1
Apr	3	2	2	2	2	2	2	2	2	2	2	2	2	2	2	2	2	2	2
Jul	<1>	4	3	3	3	3	3	3	4	3	3	3	3	5	3	3	3	3	3
Oct	2	5	4	4	4	5	4	5	5	5	5	4	4	6	5	4	4	4	4

The occasional references to the on-line *Risks Forum* generally do not include the dates of each issue. For reference purpose, the ranges of issues and dates for each volume are as follows.

Volume 1:	began Aug 1, 1985,	46 issues
Volume 2:	began Feb 1, 1986,	57 issues
Volume 3:	began Jun 4, 1986,	92 issues
Volume 4:	began Nov 2, 1986,	97 issues
Volume 5:	began Jun 18, 1987,	85 issues
Volume 6:	began Jan 2, 1988,	95 issues

Volume 7:	began Jun 1, 1988,	99 issues
Volume 8:	began Jan 4, 1989,	88 issues
Volume 9:	began Jul 6, 1989,	98 issues
Volume 10:	began Jun 1, 1990,	86 issues
Volume 11:	began Feb 4, 1991,	96 issues
Volume 12:	began Jul 1, 1991,	73 issues
Volume 13:	began Jan 6, 1992,	90 issues
Volume 14:	began Nov 4, 1992,	90 issues
Volume 15:	began Sep 2, 1993,	82 issues
Volume 16:	began May 1, 1994,	ongoing

A.2 On-Line Sources

There are no guarantees of continuity or longevity in the Internet. People come and go. Addresses change incessantly. As of the time that this book went to press, the following information was valid.

A.2.1 The *Risks Forum*

The on-line *Risks Forum (RISKS)* is a moderated, digested, E-mail forum for discussion of risks related to the use of computer systems, including many security, safety, and reliability problems; **comp.risks** is its Usenet counterpart. It is distributed in digest form, but undigestifiers are available from news wizards. Send administrative requests (for subscriptions, back issues, and so on) to risks-request@csl.sri.com and send contributions to risks@csl.sri.com for consideration. Archives dating back to August 1985 are available by anonymous file transfer (FTP) from crvax.sri.com (for which the IP address is [128.18.30.65]), typing cd risks: to get into the main archive directory. Each volume other than the most recent is located in its own subdirectory— [.1], [.2], and so on. *RISKS* is also available through the Wide Area Information Server (WAIS), which provides contextual search and retrieval; consult your local net wizard.

If you do *not* have Internet access, *RISKS* can be obtained by FAX; *call* +1 (818) 225-2800 or *fax RISKS* at +1 (818) 225-7203, courtesy of Lauren Weinstein of Vortex.

Highlights from the on-line *Risks Forum* appear in quarterly issues of the ACM SIGSOFT *Software Engineering Notes*, available from the Association for Computing Machinery, 1515 Broadway, New York, NY 10036. The monthly *Inside Risks* column appears in each issue of the *Communications of the ACM*, just inside the back cover.

A.2.2   *PRIVACY* Digests

There are currently two useful digests related to privacy.

- The *PRIVACY Forum Digest (PFD)* is run by Lauren Weinstein. He manages it as a selectively moderated digest, somewhat akin to *RISKS*; it spans the full range of both technological and nontechnological privacy-related issues (with an emphasis on the former). For information regarding the *PRIVACY Forum Digest,* please send E-mail to `privacy-request@cv.vortex.com` with `information privacy` on one and only one line of message text.
- The *Computer PRIVACY Digest (CPD)* (formerly the *Telecom Privacy Digest*) is run by Leonard P. Levine, who succeeded Dennis G. Rears. It is gatewayed to the USENET newsgroup **comp.society.privacy**. It is a relatively open (that is, not tightly moderated) forum, and was established to provide a forum for discussion on the effect of technology on privacy. Send E-mail to `comp-privacy-request@uwm.edu` for administrative requests.

A.2.3   The *VIRUS-L Digest*

The *VIRUS-L Digest* is a moderated, digested E-mail forum for discussing computer virus issues; **comp.virus** is its Usenet counterpart. Information on accessing anti-virus, documentation, and back issue archives is distributed periodically on the list. A FAQ (Frequently Asked Questions) document and all of the back issues are available by anonymous FTP on cert.org [192.88.209.5]. Administrative mail (comments, suggestions, and so forth) should be sent to Ken van Wyk at `krvw@first.org` (formerly `krvw@cert.org`). Send contributions to `virus-l@lehigh.edu` and use `virus-l@assist.ims.disa.mil` for administrative requests.

A.3   **General Bibliography Items**

You might wish to study some of the following references, which provide general background.

- Ulrich Beck, *Risk Society: Towards a New Modernity* [8].
- Nathaniel S. Borenstein, *Programming As If People Mattered: Friendly Programs, Software Engineering, and Other Noble Delusions* [15].

- Steven M. Casey, *Set Phasers on Stun, and Other True Tales of Design Technology and Human Error* [21].
- John Gall, *Systemantics: How Systems Work and Especially How They Fail* [46].
- Nancy Leveson, *Safeware: System Safety and the Computer Age* [81].
- Jerry Mander, *In the Absence of the Sacred: The Failure of Technology & the Survival of the Indian Nations* [88].
- Ralph Nader and Wesley J. Smith, *Collision Course: The Truth about Airline Safety* [99].
- Ivars Peterson, *Fatal Defect: Why Computers Fail* [127].
- Charles Perrow, *Normal Accidents* [126].
- Henry Petroski, *To Engineer Is Human: The Role of Failure in Successful Design* [129].
- Henry Petroski, *Design Paradigms: Case Histories of Error and Judgment in Engineering* [130].
- Steve Talbott, *The Future Does Not Compute* [165].
- Lauren Wiener, *Computer Woes: Why We Should Not Depend on Software* [177].
- National Research Council, *Computers at Risk: Safe Computing in the Information Age* [26].

Notes

Chapter 2

1. This reference is the first of many to the *RISKS* section of the ACM SIGSOFT *Software Engineering Notes*, cited by volume and issue number, and, in the more recent issues, page number. The month and year are omitted, and can be derived from the table in Appendix A; in this case, "*SEN 12*, 1" corresponds to January 1987.

2. *Telephony*, p. 11, January 22, 1990.

3. *The New York Times*, National Edition, October 16, 1990, page A14; *SEN 16*, 1.

4. See an Associated Press item, January 5, 1991; *SEN, 16*, 1, 14.

5. See an article by Carl Hall, *San Francisco Chronicle*, July 16, 1991.

6. See John Noble Wilford, *The New York Times*, August 26, 1985.

7. *SEN 11*, 5; *San Francisco Chronicle*, August 6, 1986.

8. Up to and including STS-27, the STS mission-planning serial number also indicates the sequence number of the launch. Beginning with STS-28, which was actually the thirtieth mission, and STS-29, which was the twenty-eighth mission, the numbers ceased to reflect the chronological order of the launch. The STS numbers are given here to provide specificity.

9. This summary of "Wrong Computer Instructions Were Given to *Discovery* Before Liftoff" by AP science writer Lee Siegel, October 10, 1990, was contributed by Fernando Pereira; *SEN 16*, 1.

10. See *Aviation Week and Space Technology*, May 25, 1992, p. 79, and June 8, 1992, p. 69; *SEN 17*, 3.

11. *SEN 18*, 3, A-14, summarizing *San Francisco Chronicle*, April 6, 1993, p. A2, and April 7, 1993, p. A3. See also a detailed subsequent report by Paul Robichaux that appeared in the on-line *RISKS, 14*, 47, April 7, 1993.

12. *San Francisco Chronicle*, October 15, 1993, p. A13.

13. From *The Compleat Computer*, which reprinted it with permission from *Fortune*, March 1967 — "Help Wanted: 50,000 Programmers" — by Gene Bylinsky, *Fortune*; contributed to *RISKS* by Ed Joyce. See *SEN 10*, 5.

14. A detailed account of this case is given by Paul Ceruzzi in *Beyond the Limits — Flight Enters the Computer Age*, Smithsonian Air and Space Museum (Appendix), 1989, quoted in *SEN 14*, 5.

15. From *San Francisco Chronicle* wire services, Aug 28, 1986; see *SEN 11*, 5.

16. See Joseph M. Fox, *Software and Its Development*, Prentice-Hall, Englewood Cliffs, New Jersey, pp. 187–189; contributed by David B. Benson; see also *SEN 9*, 1.

17. *The New York Times*, August 3, 1993.

18. See an Associated Press item, *San Francisco Chronicle*, July 20, 1993, p. 3.

19. See *Science*, September 16, 1988; *San Francisco Chronicle*, September 10, 1988, p. A11; *SEN 13*, 4; *14*, 2, and *Science* 245, p. 1045, September 8, 1989; *SEN 14*, 6 for *Phobos 1* and *2*, respectively.

20. See an article by Kathy Sawyer, "NASA Change in Flight Plan Blamed for Mars Probe Mishap," *The Washington Post*, January 19, 1994.

21. *San Francisco Chronicle*, October 9, 1993.

22. This report is based on articles by David Perlman in the *San Francisco Chronicle*, August 25–26, 1993; by John Noble Wilford of *The New York Times*, August 23; and from the *Los Angeles Times*, August 24.

23. *Newsweek*, April 24, 1994.

24. See various press reports in *The New York Times*, April 15 and 18, and July 1, 1994.

25. See *The Washington Post*, April 15, 1994.

26. See an article by Christopher Bellamy in *The Independent*, April 23, 1992, and a later item in *The Guardian*, October 24, 1992.

27. See an article by Steve Komarow in *USA Today*, October 27, 1993, p. 1A, which also noted the sinking of the USS *Thresher* in 1963, killing 129 men aboard, apparently because of a leak. Both submarines were nuclear-powered.

28. Daniel F. Ford, *The Button: The Pentagon's Strategic Command and Control System*, Simon and Schuster, New York, 1985.

29. For example, see E.C. Berkeley, *The Computer Revolution*, Doubleday, New York, pp. 175–177, 1962.

30. From a talk by Mark Groves, reported by Earl Boebert in *SEN 5*, 2.

31. *Aviation Week and Space Technology*, pp. 28–30, June 10, 1991; *SEN 16*, 3.

32. *Flight International*, October 13–19, 1993.

33. *The Washington Post*, August 21, 1987; *San Francisco Chronicle*, p. A5, May 11, 1988; *SEN 12*, 4; *13*, 1; *13*, 3; *14*, 5; *15*, 5.

34. *Flight International*, April 1, 1989; *SEN 14*, 2; *14*, 5; *15*, 3; *16*, 3.

35. There were various reports on-line and in *SEN 13*, 4; *14*, 2; *14*, 5; *15*, 3; *16*, 3. However, the analysis of this case has been marred by considerable confusion.

36. *Flight International*, October 13–19, 1993.

37. *Flight International*, September 15–21, 1993.

38. See the *New York Review*, April 25, 1985; *SEN 9*, 1; *10*, 3; *12*, 1; and an article by Murray Sayle, "Closing the File on Flight 007," *The New Yorker*, December 13, 1993, pp. 90–101.

39. *Flight International*, February 27 and March 5, 1991; *SEN 16*, 2.

40. See a letter to *Aviation Week and Space Technology*, January 30, 1989; *SEN 14*, 2.

41. *IEEE Spectrum*, August 1991, p. 58; *SEN 16*, 4; *17*, 1; *18*, 1, 24.

42. *San Francisco Chronicle*, January 15, 1987.

43. Literally, *Thus passes away the glory of the world;* alternatively, ailing transit systems can create a glorious start of the week—for the news media, perhaps, but certainly not for commuters.

44. Reported in *SEN 14*, 6 by Michael Trout, excerpting an article in *Call Board* of the Mohawk & Hudson Chapter National Railway Historical Society.

45. *San Francisco Chronicle*, February 9, 1986; *SEN 11*, 2.

46. John E. Woodruff, *Baltimore Sun*, datelined Tokyo, in *San Francisco Chronicle*, May 15, 1991, p.A7; *SEN 16*, 3.

47. "Results of Train Accident Investigations Indicate Driver's Neglect of Traffic Signals Direct Cause of Accident"—abridged from the *China Times*, November 23, 1991, by Jymmi C. Tseng in *SEN 17*, 1.

48. Debora Weber-Wulff, Technische Fachhochschule Berlin, based on information from *Tagespiegel*, April 14, 1993; *SEN 18*, 3, A-3.

49. See "British Train Accidents Signal Systemic Problems" by Fred Guterl and Erin E. Murphy, *IEEE Institute*, May 1989, p. 4; excerpted in *SEN 14*, 6, summarized by Jon Jacky.

50. Patrick Donovan, BR Signalmen '"Worked Blind'; Computer Software Problems Admitted at Key Commuter Train Centre," *The Guardian*, July 23, 1990, front page; excerpted by Pete Mellor, in *SEN 15*, 5.

51. Noted in *SEN 16*, 2 by Peter Mellor from an article by Dick Murray, (London) *Evening Standard*, January 24, 1991.

52. Roy Hodson, *Financial Times*, March 15, 1990, excerpted by Brian Randell in *SEN 15*, 3.

53. Stephen Page, summarizing an article by Dick Murray, (London) *Evening Standard*, April 12, 1990, with further comment from Gavin Oddy; see *SEN 15*, 3.

54. Tony Collins, "Autumn Leaves Fox BR's Signal System," *Computer Weekly*, November 7, 1991, noted by Graeme Tozer, with further comments from Geraint Jones, in *SEN 17*, 1.

55. *The Denver Post*, November 12, 1991, noted by Bob Devine in *SEN 17*, 1.

56. Noted by Olivier M.J. Crepin-Leblond in *SEN 17*, 1.

57. *San Francisco Chronicle*, July 8, 1987; noted in *SEN 12*, 3.

58. Harry W. Demoro and Carl Nolte, *San Francisco Chronicle*, December 10, 1986, p. 2; see *SEN 12*, 1.

59. Carl Nolte, *San Francisco Chronicle*, April 6, 1993; Phillip Matier and Andrew Ross, *San Francisco Chronicle*, April 7, 1993, summarized in *SEN 18*, 3, A-3.

60. *Computing Australia*, August 29, 1988; George Michaelson in *SEN 13*, 4.

61. "Worlds of Fun Timber Wolf Incident Blamed on Computer," *ACE News* (from *The American Coaster Enthusiasts*), Volume XII, Issue 6, May 1990, contributed by Gary Wright, in *SEN 15*, 3.

62. See an article by Chuck Ayers, *The Morning Call*, Allentown, Pennsylvania, July 28, 1993, p. B5, contributed to *SEN 18*, 4 by Steven D. Walter.

63. Deeann Glamser, *USA Today*, February 25, 1987; *SEN 12*, 2; see also subsequent items in *SEN 14*, 2 and *SEN 15*, 2.

64. This report is based on comments by John Sullivan, *The New York Times*, August 12, 1992, and subsequent *Vineyard Gazette* reports.

65. *The Independent*, June 5, 1992, from Brian Randell in *SEN 17*, 4.

66. Penelope M. Carrington, "Ship Makes List—the Hard Way," *The Seattle Times*, August 5, 1992, p. D1, from Jon Jacky in *SEN 17, 4*.

67. See *The New York Times*, August 14 and 24, 1985; *SEN 10, 5, 6*.

68. I. Nimmo, S.R. Nunns, and B.W. Eddershaw, "Lessons Learned from the Failure of a Computer System Controlling a Nylon Polymer Plant," *Safety and Reliability Society Symposium*, Altrincham, United Kingdom, November 1987.

69. These are just two of a series of incidents noted by Jon Jacky, excerpted from an article by Trevor Kletz, "Wise After the Event," *Control and Instrumentation* (UK), 20, 10, October 1988, pp. 57, 59, in *SEN 14, 2*.

70. Based on a report contributed by Meine van der Meulen, in *SEN 18, 2, 7*, which in turn was based on Piet van Beek, "FACTS, Database for Industrial Safety Acc. 11057, Extended abstract," The Netherlands Organization for Applied Scientific Research, Department of Industrial Safety, Apeldoorn, The Netherlands, July 8, 1992.

71. Associated Press, Johannesburg, South Africa, December 28, 1988, from Nicholas Gegg in *SEN 14, 2*.

72. *The Ottawa Citizen*, June 28, 1989, p. B1, and June 29, 1989, p. A1-A2, noted by Walter Roberson in *SEN 14, 5*.

73. *Montreal Gazette*, September 9, 1988, noted by Henry Cox in *SEN 13, 4*.

74. *Toronto Star*, April 20, 1989, noted by Mark Brader in *SEN 14, 5*.

75. *San Jose Mercury*, November 16, 1988, noted by Ira Greenberg in *SEN 14, 1*.

76. Dick Lilly, *Seattle Times*, January 8, 1990, p. 1, reported by Jon Jacky in *SEN 15, 2*.

77. *Asbury Park Press*, August 30, 1992, from George Sicherman in *SEN 18, 1, 8*.

78. This case was reported by a former factory employee, Joe Pistritto, in the early days of the on-line *Software Engineering Digest*.

79. *Electronic Engineering Times*, December 21, 1981, noted by Thomas Litant in *SEN 10, 3*.

80. See *SEN 10, 2* and "In the Lion's Cage," *Forbes*, October 7, 1985, contributed by Bill Keefe in *SEN 11, 1*.

81. Abstracted in *SEN 16, 1* by Brad Dolan from the Maryville/Alcoa (Tenn.) *Daily Times*, September 10, 1990, p. 1; Brad commented that "This looks like (1) poor work practice and (2) poor vehicle design."

82. Ron Cain, contributed to *SEN 11, 3* by Bill Park.

83. From a Reuters item in the June 26, 1985, issue of the *Halifax Gazette*, via *Digital Review*, September 15, 1986, in *SEN 11, 5* courtesy of Brad Dolan.

84. See a UPI item, October 10, 1992, noted by Les Earnest in *SEN 18, 1, 7*, and a subsequent *San Francisco Chronicle* article by Mary Madison, December 13, 1993, p. A19.

85. Peter Boyer, "At Networks, Cheap Is Chic, so Please Pardon the Robots," *The New York Times*, Television, May 2, 1988, contributed to *SEN 13, 3* by Donn Seeley.

86. See *Motor Trend*, November 1986, in *SEN 13, 3*, noted by Tom Slone.

87. *San Francisco Chronicle*, January 3, 1993, p. B-6.

88. *Science, 262*, October 22 1993, p. 495.

89. *San Francisco Chronicle*, August 27, 1993, p. A8.

90. Joan Temple Dennett, *Science 80*, 1980; *SEN 5, 1*.

91. For background on pacemakers, see *PACE*, vol. 7, Nov/Dec 1984, part 2.

92. See the series of three articles in *The New Yorker* by Paul Brodeur, June 12, 19, and 26, 1989; see also *SEN 11*, 3; *11*, 5; *15*, 5, including discussion of an article on VDT radiation by Paul Brodeur in *MacWorld*.

93. Reported by Edward Joyce from a United Press International item, March 19, 1983; *SEN 10*, 3.

94. *Computer Weekly*, February 20, 1992; *SEN 17*, 3.

95. From an article by Christine Spolar of *The Washington Post*, in *The Times-Picayune*, New Orleans, February 2, 1992, p. A-22; submitted by Sevilla Finley.

96. *Journal of the American Medical Association*, December 8, 1989, page 3132; *Chemical and Engineering News*, p. 168, February 26, 1989; *SEN 15*, 2.

97. See *New Scientist*, November 14, 1992; see also *SEN 17*, 3; *SEN 18*, 1, 26–28.

98. The primary early public source on the Therac-25 accidents is the series by Edward Joyce in the weekly *American Medical News*, beginning on October 3, 1986. Another early report on the Therac-25 is given by Jon Jacky in *Inside Risks, Communications of the ACM, 33*, 12, 138, December 1990. He notes several background sources. For background on the medical electronics industry and accounts of computer-related product recalls, see H. Bassen, J. Silberberg, F. Houston, W. Knight, C. Christman, and M. Greberman, "Computerized Medical Devices: Usage Trends, Problems, and Safety Technology," in *Proc. 7th Annual Conference of IEEE Engineering in Medicine and Biology Society*, September 27–30, 1985, Chicago, Illinois, pages 180-185. See also "Product Recalls," Mylene Moreno, *The Boston Globe*, April 10, 1989, p. 14, cited by B.J. Herbison. Food and Drug Administration Director Frank Young described his agency's views in *Annals of Internal Medicine 106*, 4, April 1987, 628–629.

99. These cases are taken mostly from *The Washington Post*, April 29, 1986.

100. See an extensive and well-written case study by Daniel F. Ford, *Three Mile Island: Thirty Minutes to Meltdown*, Viking Press, 1981, Penguin paperback, 1982, noted by J. Paul Holbrook in *SEN 11*, 3.

101. *The Washington Post*, May 24, 1986, in *SEN 11*, 3.

102. See *The Washington Post*, May 24, 1986.

103. David E. Kaplan (Center for Investigative Reporting in San Francisco), "It's Not Russia's First Meltdown," *San Francisco Chronicle*, May 1, 1986.

104. *San Francisco Examiner*, April 14, 1991, p. A-6; *San Francisco Chronicle*, April 14, 1991, p. A10, and April 17, 1991.

105. *The Washington Post*, May 22, 1986.

106. See *The New York Times*, August 16, 1986.

107. *The New York Times*, July 25, 1986.

108. *The New York Times*, August 18, 1986.

109. *San Francisco Chronicle*, July 24, 1991, p. A8, in *SEN 16*, 4.

110. *San Francisco Chronicle*, June 4, 1986.

111. These two paragraphs are adapted from an editorial by the author in *SEN 4*, 2.

112. Eliot Marshall, "NRC Takes a Second Look at Reactor Design," *Science*, 207, pp. 1445-48, March 28, 1980, contributed to *SEN 10*, 3 by Nancy Leveson.

113. Susan Watts, "Computer Watch on Nuclear Plant Raises Safety Fears," *The (London) Independent*, October 13, 1991, contributed by Antony Upward. Upward also submitted two long articles that appeared in the on-line forum,

RISKS 12, 49. A precursor of this item on Sizewell was included in *SEN 16, 2*, April 1991.

114. Tom Wilkie and Susan Watts, "Sellafield Safety Computer Fails," *The Independent*, November 24, 1991, noted by Peter Ilieve. See *SEN 17*, 1 and *SEN 18*, 1, 27.

115. "Group Questions Software's Reliability after Bruce Accident," *Canadian Press*, February 1, 1990, noted by Mark Bartelt; *SEN 15, 2* and *SEN 16, 2*.

116. Abstracted from *Nucleonics Week 32*, 1, January 3, 1991, and 2, January 10, 1991, McGraw-Hill, contributed to *SEN 15*, 1 by Martyn Thomas.

117. *New Scientist*, February 17, 1990, p. 18, noted in *SEN 15*, 2 by Steve Strassmann.

118. "Sabotage Fails—Virus in Power-Plant Program for the Lithuanian Atomic-Power Plant in Ignalina Vaccinated," *Berliner Zeitung* ([East] Berlin), February 3, 1992, translated and contributed to *SEN 17*, 2 by Debora Weber-Wulff, Institut für Informatik, Berlin.

119. See Keith Schneider, "Power Surge Causes Failure of Systems in New York Nuclear Plant," *The New York Times*, August 15, 1991, noted in *SEN 16*, 4.

120. Condensed from the *Albany (NY) Times Union*, April 26, 1989, p. B-17, noted by William Randolph Franklin in *SEN 14*, 5.

121. *San Francisco Chronicle*, October 4, 1984, *SEN 9*, 5.

122. *San Jose Mercury News*, January 19, 1994.

123. This item is excerpted from the *Ottawa Citizen*, August 8, 1986, noted in *SEN 11*, 5 by Dan Craigen.

124. Contributed by Bryan MacKinnon, Fermi National Accelerator Lab, in *SEN 17*, 3.

125. "Lost Squirrel Causes Troublesome Power Surge," *Providence Journal*, October 30, 1986, from Ross McKenrick in *SEN 12*, 1.

126. This event was reported by David L. Edwards in *SEN 14*, 5.

127. See *Science News*, May 11, 1989, noted by Peter Scott in *SEN 14*, 5.

128. This item was noted on the same day by David Lamb in the newsgroup comp.os.linux.announce and also appeared in *SEN 19*, 1, 4.

129. The time shift seems to have resulted in Braunschweiger Clockwurst. Perhaps in the foreshortening of time, the process controller was related to Ingot Zwergman.

130. *New Scientist*, September 8, 1988; *SEN 13*, 4.

131. Roger Fea, "Year Too Long for Money Machines," *New Zealand Herald*, January 2, 1993.

132. "Leap-Year Spikes Cashcards," NZPA, *Waikato Times*, January 2, 1993.

133. It is perhaps helpful that dates and times prior to the introduction of the Gregorian calendar are not particularly relevant to modern computing.

134. "The Subjectivity of Computers," *Communications of the ACM, 36*, 8, 15–18, August 1993, noted in *RISKS* by Dave Wortman.

Chapter 3

1. The basic notions underlying security vulnerabilities are contained in or referred to in this chapter. Landwehr, Bull, McDermott, and Choi [75] have developed a taxonomy that classifies program security flaws according to the mo-

tive (intentional or inadvertent), the time of introduction (during development, maintenance, or operation), and the place of introduction (software or hardware). Subdividing intentional flaws into malicious and nonmalicious types, and further substructuring these types, they provide examples for almost all the classifications. These distinctions are useful for understanding the modalities of misuse, but are often not constructively distinguishable from an operational point of view.

Two books relating more specifically to pest programs and security flaws are edited by Lance Hoffman [57] and by Peter Denning [35]. Each book reprints various relevant papers and contains background on personal-computer viruses—in a few cases with identical material appearing in both. However, recent activities in the personal-computer virus world suggest that someone wishing to stay abreast of the situation must diligently read the *VIRUS-L* newsgroup. (See Appendix A.)

Bill Cheswick and Steve Bellovin [24] have written an outstanding book on firewalls and Internet security, enumerating many of the major security flaws and recommending what to do about them. This book is an absolute requirement for anyone concerned about the risks of living in the Internet world.

A reader interested in the acts of computer crime, as opposed to the technological modalities, might wish to read books by Donn Parker [119, 120] and Buck BloomBecker [12].

Chapter 4

1. An insightful analysis of such interactions is given by R.I. Cook, "Reflections on a Telephone Cable Severed near Chicago," *SEN 16*, 1, 14-16.

2. See *The Washington Post*, May 24, 1986, and *SEN 11*, 3.

3. See *Science*, May 3, 1985, p. 562, and *SEN 10*, 3.

4. Butler Lampson [72] wrote an early paper recognizing that a hardware memory-protection mechanism cannot provide security unless it is reliable. That concept is readily extended to systems as a whole, in hardware and in software. A hierarchical approach to integrating security and reliability (along with requirements) is suggested in [107].

Chapter 5

1. See *SEN 12*, 4; *13*, 1; *13*, 2; *14*, 2; *14*, 6; and *15*, 2. See also *RISKS 8*, 36 to 38, including a response from "pengo" (an alias for Hans Huebner) in *RISKS 8*, 37.

2. See *SEN 16*, 3; *17*, 2; see also *RISKS 13*, 11 and 12.

3. John Markoff, *The New York Times*, April 4, 1990; *SEN 15*, 3.

4. An article from the now-defunct *Palo Alto Times Tribune*, February 7, 1988, is summarized in *SEN 13*, 2.

5. *Los Angeles Times*, March 23, 1991; *SEN 16*, 3.

6. *SEN 14*, 1; *Los Angeles Times*, December 23, 1988. See also [12].

7. *London Daily Mail*, November 2, 1984; *SEN 10*, 1.

8. *Wall Street Journal*, August 15, 1985; *SEN 10*, 5.

9. This situation was reported by a Computer Emergency Response Team (CERT) Internet Security Advisory; see *SEN 14*, 6.

10. *Los Angeles Times*, November 5, 1991; *SEN 17*, 1.

11. *The Washington Post*, May 31, 1988; *Ft. Worth Star-Telegram*, September 19, 1988; *SEN 13*, 3; *13*, 4.

12. *The Times* of London, June 9, 1992; *SEN 17*, 4.

13. Readers seriously interested in a detailed perspective on viruses should study the *VIRUS-L* archives, which include pointers to various catalogs such as that of Klaus Brunnstein. There are many books, including Ferbrache [44], Hoffman [57], and Kane [62].

14. See *The New York Times*, July 30, 1993, p. B5.

15. Ashland, Oregon, news article from August 23, 1986; *SEN 11*, 5.

16. A few other earlier computer-related perpetrations are reprinted in a special section of the *CACM 27*, 4, 343–357, April 1984.

17. This message appeared in *RISKS 6*, 52, April 1, 1988, courtesy of Cliff Stoll, and subsequently in *SEN 13*, 3, 9-10.

18. *SEN 9*, 2, 4-5, from an Associated Press report, "Cal Tech Prankster to Get Course Credit for Scoreboard Takeover," January 3, 1984.

19. *Chicago Tribune*, February 3, 1993, noted by Tony Scandora in *SEN 18*, 2, 14.

20. Jay Rolls, Stuttgart, "Computer Cheats Take Cadsoft's Bait," from *info-mac*, in *SEN 18*, 2, 14, via Gio Wiederhold.

21. We note in Section 4.2 that failures in reliability could alternatively have resulted from malicious human actions; in some other cases, the effects of malicious human actions could alternatively have been caused by hardware malfunctions or software flaws. This duality should be kept in mind here.

22. This computer-communication spy flick was based on Robert Lindsey's true story of the same name, describing the saga of Andrew Daulton Lee and Christopher John Boyce; Simon and Schuster, 1979.

23. *Los Angeles Times*, July 24, 1986.

24. See an article by Richard March, *PC Week*, p. 1, November 27, 1989, *SEN 15*, 1.

25. *SEN 19*, 2, 2; *The Boston Globe*, December 3, 1993.

26. See *Datamation*, p. 67, December 15, 1986; *SEN 12*, 1.

27. *The Boston Globe*, May 16, 1986.

28. *Aviation Week*, March 11, 1985.

29. Numerous cases of interference problems experienced in commercial aviation are listed in "The Electronic Safety Threat," *Airline Pilot*, June 1993, p. 30.

30. See the *Martha's Vineyard Times*, p. 1, August 4, 1988, summarized in *SEN 13*, 4.

31. See Fernando M. Esparza, "The Importance of EMC in the Preparation and Selling of Big Macs," *EMC Technology*, September-October 1989; *SEN 15*, 1.

32. John Darnton, "London Journal," *The New York Times*, June 30, 1993, p. A4; *SEN, 18*, 3, A-10.

33. Noted by Paul Leyland and Mark Huth in *SEN 16*, 2.

34. See the *San Francisco Chronicle*, p. A2, February 2, 1989; *SEN 14*, 2.

35. See Ari L. Goldman, *The New York Times*, June 30, 1993, p. B6; *SEN 18*, 3, A-9.

36. *The Boston Globe*, July 2, 1993, p. 19.

37. With apologies to Thomas Morley, 1557–1603.

38. See John Stebbins, "Fischer Victory Upheld," *St. Petersburg Tribune*, April 6, 1993, Florida/Metro section.

39. The Virginia, Durham, Rome, Yonkers, and Michigan cases were discussed in *SEN, 15, 1*, 10-13. The 1992 cases are documented in *SEN, 18, 1*, 15-19. For further background, see a report by Roy G. Saltman [143] and a subsequent paper [144]. Saltman also contributed an on-line piece on the role of standards, in *SEN, 18*, 1, 17. Four papers from the *Proceedings of the 16th National Computer Security Conference* are relevant, by Saltman [145], Rebecca Mercuri, [92], Peter Neumann [112], and Gary L. Greenhalgh, [55]. See also publications by two nongovernmental organizations, Computer Professionals for Social Responsibility (P.O. Box 717, Palo Alto, CA 94302, including a voluminous collection of study items) and Election Watch (a project spearheaded by Mae Churchill of the Urban Policy Research Institute, 530 Paseo Miramar, Pacific Palisades, CA 90272).

40. Article by Bill Johnson, *Los Angeles Herald Examiner*, prior to September 14 1987; noted by Bill Weisman in *SEN 12*, 4.

41. See "Fraudulent Fax Gets Forger Freed" in the *San Francisco Chronicle*, December 18, 1991, p. A3, excerpted in *SEN 17*, 1.

42. *San Francisco Chronicle*, July 6, 1987.

43. See a note from Paul Molenaar, via Patrick van Kleef, in *SEN 12*, 4.

44. See the *San Jose Mercury News*, December 14, 1984; *SEN 10*, 1.

45. From an Associated Press item in the *Montreal Gazette*, September 22, 1988, via Henry Cox, in *SEN 13*, 4.

46. *SEN 18, 2, 4*, from an article by Peter Fimrite in the *San Francisco Chronicle*, December 30, 1992, p. A14.

47. Ibid.

48. See "New Software Fails to Fix Jail's Computer System" by Judy Kuhlman, *Daily Oklahoman*, February 26, 1993, contributed to *SEN 18*, 2 by Jennifer Smith, who noted that "Having computer-controlled doors with not even a surge protector, not to mention no one in the state running the system, is unfortunately quite typical." Smith believes that this jail was the same allegedly "escape-proof" jail from which two inmates escaped within the first month of operation.

49. Some of the general issues relating to security are considered in a National Research Council report, *Computers at Risk* [26], which surveys the situation existing in 1990, and makes various recommendations. A useful book on computer security is provided by Charles Pfleeger [131]. There are few definitive treatises on how to do it right. Morrie Gasser [48] has written an excellent book on designing secure systems. Sape Mullender [97] has edited a useful book on distributed systems, although security is not the driving requirement. System authentication in distributed systems is discussed by Lampson, Wobber, and colleagues [71, 178], based on important earlier work by Needham, Schroeder, and others. An earlier view of distributed-system security is provided by Gasser and others. [49]. Bill Cheswick and Steve Bellovin [24] provide an outstanding analysis of how to attain better security in the Internet. There are many articles and books that inadvertently describe how *not* to do it, although that can be inferred only from a deeper understanding of the weaknesses of the resulting systems. In addition, system penetrators are examined by Bruce Sterling [161].

Chapter 6

1. Lawrence Ferlinghetti, March 31, 1993, in response to the city of San Francisco, which was trying to impose a $600 license fee for poetry reading.

2. ACM Code of Professional Conduct, Ethical Consideration 5.1.

3. *Records, Computers and the Rights of Citizens,* Report of the Secretary's Advisory Committee on Automated Personal Data Systems, U.S. Dept. of Health, Education & Welfare, 1973.

4. R. Rosenberg, "The Role of Computer Scientists in Privacy Policy," *Information Technology Quarterly IX,* 2, 24, Summer 1990.

5. "Proposed FBI Crime Computer System Raises Questions on Accuracy, Privacy: Report Warns of Potential Risk Data Bank Poses to Civil Liberties," *The Washington Post,* Feb. 13, 1991. The full report, J.J. Horning, P.G. Neumann, D.D. Redell, J. Goldman, and D.R. Gordon, *A Review of NCIC 2000,* report to the Subcommittee on Civil and Constitutional Rights of the Committee on the Judiciary, United States House of Representatives, February 1989, is available from Computer Professionals for Social Responsibility.

6. L. Winner, "A Victory for Computer Populism," *Technology Review,* p. 66, May/June 1991.

7. See *"National Crime Information Center: Legislation Needed to Deter Misuse of Criminal Justice Information,"* statement of Laurie E. Ekstrand, U.S. General Accounting Office, as testimony before the U.S. House of Representatives Subcommittee on Information, Justice, Agriculture, and Transportation, of the Committee on Government Operations, and the Subcommittee on Civil and Constitutional Rights, of the Committee on the Judiciary, July 28, 1993. The appendix to that testimony documents 61 additional cases of misuses of NCIC and other law-enforcement computer systems. Many of the cited cases are the result of misuse of state and local computer systems rather than the NCIC system. The GAO report recommends that (1) Congress enact legislation with strong criminal sanctions for misuse of NCIC, and (2) NCIC's security policy requirements be reevaluated.

8. Reported in *Harpers,* and noted in *SEN 17,* 3.

9. *San Francisco Examiner,* November 1, 1992; see also *SEN 18,* 1, 20.

10. Jay Sharbutt, *Los Angeles Times,* March 1, 1989; *SEN 14,* 2.

11. *The New York Times,* February 7, 1993, p. 32.

12. This item is excerpted from an article by Evan Ramstad, Associated Press, December 19, 1991; see *SEN 17,* 1.

13. See issues of the on-line *Risks Forum,* beginning with *RISKS 14,* 51. Also, see an unclassified description of the process by Dorothy Denning [32].

14. *De Volkskrant,* February 22, 1991.

15. See a Reuters item in the *Los Angeles Times,* September 19, 1993.

16. Both of these cases came from articles by Simon Hoggart in the *Observer,* contributed to *SEN 16,* 2, 13 by Pete Mellor.

17. *The Sydney Morning Herald,* July 23, 1988, from John Colville in *SEN 13,* 4.

18. In *The Illuminatus! Trilogy,* Robert J. Shea and Robert Anton Wilson ([153], p. 692).

19. See an article by David Burnham, *The New York Times,* February 12, 1985, with followup items in *SEN 11,* 1; *12,* 4; *13,* 2.

20. Mike Zehr in *SEN 19*, 3, 7, from an article in *The Boston Globe*, March 7, 1994.

21. Excerpted from an article by Catherine Bowman, "Sly Imposter Robs S.F. Man of Good Name," *San Francisco Chronicle*, March 14, 1994, p. 1, contributed by Mike Crawford.

22. *Ottawa Citizen*, November 23, 1992, from Stanley Chow in *SEN 18*, 1, 22.

23. See a front-page article by Yasmin Anwar in the *San Francisco Chronicle*, August 30, 1991, reprinted with permission in the on-line *RISKS 12*, 20.

24. Chris Hibbert (`hibbert@netcom.com`) has written an excellent discussion of SSNs, "What to Do When They Ask for Your Social-Security Number. Social-Security Number FAQ (Frequently Asked Questions)." Updated versions appear periodically in various on-line newsgroups, and can be obtained by anonymous FTP from rtfm.mit.edu in the file /pub/usenet-by-hierarchy/news/answers/ssn-privacy, or by E-mail sent to `mail-server@rtfm.mit.edu` containing the one-line text: `send usenet-by-hierarchy/news/answers/ssn-privacy`. Sending E-mail with the one-line `help` will get you general information about the mail server, which also has many other FAQs.

25. Some of these items are from alt.folklore.computers, contributed by John Miller, John Switzer, Jeff Hibbard, Jay Maynard, Joel Sumner, Jeff DelPapa, Hugh J.E. Davies, Terry Kennedy, Jake Richter, Kevin Stevens, Scott Telford, and Brad Heintz; those items were collected for *RISKS* by Mark Brader. Jay Maynard noted that having a comma before the 'III' tends to avoid the problem with his name. The Goleta case was reported by Arthur L. Shapiro.

26. See the on-line *RISKS 14*, 15-17, December 7–8, 1992, for the entire discussion; see Section 6.5 for examples.

27. References to authentication and access controls are noted in the previous chapter. Privacy-enhanced mail is discussed by Kent [66]. Some of the implications of computer-communication privacy are discussed by Rotenberg [140] and Tuerkheimer [141].

Chapter 7

1. Translation by Stephen Mitchell, Harper and Row, 1988.

2. See *SEN 15*, 2; *15*, 3; *15*, 5; see also M.M. Waldrop, *Science 249*, pp. 735–36, August 17, 1990.

3. Adapted from *Inside Risks, Communications of the ACM*, 33, 9, 202, September 1990.

4. *San Francisco Chronicle*, September 4, 1993, p. B1.

5. It appears that this statement is also true of many people, but I persevere nonetheless—perhaps encouraged by Freud's remark that the true test of maturity is a person's ability to generate and appreciate humor.

6. This section is drawn on material originally presented in [109].

7. For an excellent article on fault tolerance in distributed systems in general, see Cristian [30].

8. Translation by Stephen Mitchell, Harper and Row, 1988.

9. Contributed by Ross Anderson in *RISKS 14*, 41, March 12, 1993, from British press reports.

10. See the *Richmond Times-Dispatch*, June 8, 1987, p. B1, from Nick Condyles, *SEN 12*, 3.

11. See *SEN 12*, 4; *13*, 1; *13*, 2, contributed by Rodney Hoffman, who also contributed the subsequent five items, abstracted from *Business Week*, November 7, 1988; see *SEN 14*, 1.

12. See *The Washington Times*, February 15, 1989, from Joseph M. Beckman in *SEN 14*, 2.

13. See the *Los Angeles Daily News*, February 25, 1991, summarized in *SEN 16*, 2.

14. See Jeff Gerth, *The New York Times*, December 1, 1989, noted in *SEN 15*, 1 by Gary Chapman, who also contributed the subsequent 5 items to *SEN 15*, 1, 21–22.

15. This item was noted by James Paul in *SEN 17*, 3.

16. James H. Paul and Gregory C. Simon, "Bugs in the System: Problems in Federal Government Computer Software Development and Regulation" (from the Subcommittee on Investigations and Oversight of the House Committee on Science, Space, and Technology, U.S. Government Printing Office, Washington, D.C., September 1989).

17. This quote is included in a summary of the Paul-Simon report by M. Mitchell Waldrop in *Science*, 246, p. 753, November 10, 1989. See also *SEN 15*, 1.

18. See *Aviation Week*, May 27, 1991, and Henry Spencer in *SEN 16*, 4.

19. From the *Minneapolis Star Tribune*, p. 1 and 4D, November 28, 1987, excerpted by Scot E. Wilcoxon in *SEN 15*, 5.

20. *The New York Times*, July 4, 1983.

21. See Epstein and Smith, "Hartford Roof Failure: Can We Blame the Computer?", *Proceedings of the Seventh Conference on Electrical Computation*, 1979, noted by Richard S. D'Ippolito in *SEN 11*, 5. Peter Desnoyers later reported in *SEN 14*, 5 that there was only a single part-time weld inspector.

22. *Sail Wars* was broadcast on *NOVA* on December 9, 1986; this case was noted in *SEN 12*, 1 by Bruce Wampler.

23. This section is derived from [111].

24. See the assured-pipeline approach based on the LOgical Coprocessor Kernel, LOCK [13].

25. In the language of state machines, a TCB is basically a nontamperable-type manager for an abstract data type.

26. System-level concepts include dual redundancy as in Tandem's NonStop systems [53], triple-modular redundancy (TMR) with majority voting as in the Software Implemented Fault Tolerant (SIFT) aircraft flight-control system [18, 19, 91, 98, 175, 176], and combinations such as the dual-dual-plus-separately-programmed-backup quintuple redundancy of the space-shuttle systems. Subsystem-level concepts include techniques for server fault tolerance, such as highly available file servers (ranging from complete but slower coverage at one extreme to possibly incomplete but rapid recovery, as in the Sprite strategy for speedy recovery [7] using local contextual knowledge in a distributed state), and two-phase commits in transaction-based systems to defend against crashes and other unexpected events during updates of distributed data and during the execution of nonatomic transactions. Lower-layer examples include error-correcting and error-detecting codes in memory and communications, instruction retry to overcome transient errors in processing, reliable and efficient broadcast communication protocols (for example, [61, 160]), multiple paths in communications, and retries following failed communications or timeouts. Related techniques are also used for information integrity, such as

check sums and cryptoseals. Byzantine algorithms [70] provide an interesting subject of research, but may be impractical except in truly critical situations. (Simplifying assumptions that reduce the complexity and the time to completion have been considered by Flaviu Cristian [29], at the expense of diminished fault-tolerance coverage.) The reader seriously interested in reliability and fault tolerance will find an enormously rich literature, including the proceedings of the *Fault Tolerant Computing Conferences* and historically interesting volumes such as [3]. There are also many early works of significant historical interest, such as John von Neumann's paper on building reliable circuits out of unreliable components [173] and a corresponding article by Ed Moore and Claude Shannon [94] for switching circuits built out of what were affectionately referred to as "crummy relays." An early guide to error-correcting codes is given by Wes Peterson and Ed Weldon [128]; the literature since then has specialized into all sorts of varieties, considering binary and nonbinary codes, random and burst errors, arithmetic codes, and so on. A useful book on error-correcting coding is that by Thammavarapu (T.R.N.) Rao [135].

Additional references relating to techniques for increasing system reliability in response to hardware faults and communications failures are explored (for example) in [11, 38, 56, 69, 76, 107, 125, 134, 157]. The contributions of good software-engineering practice are considered in Section 7.8.

A fundamental survey article on software safety is given by Nancy Leveson [79], whose work on software safety, fault-tree analysis, hazard analysis [80, 82] and fault-tolerant software [68, 154] is particularly relevant for analyzing system safety.

A set of criteria for evaluating system safety is in use in the United Kingdom [169, 170].

27. This section is derived from [112].

28. Electronic Voting System, Request for Proposal, Appendix G, Security and Control Considerations, New York City Board of Elections, New York City Elections Project, September 1987.

29. This statement can also be applied to persons employed by state lotteries.

30. A client–server authentication scheme has been proposed that encrypts seemingly randomized data with a *fixed* password [52]. This scheme overcomes a potential weakness in Kerberos — namely, that a key derived from a fixed password may be compromisible by off-line guessing. The complexity of this scheme is comparable to the use of cryptographic tokens, and may have advantages over certain token implementations.

31. Robert Formaini [45] considers the risks of risk assessment in establishing public policy. See also books by Barry Boehm [14], Robert Charette [22, 23], and Capers Jones [60], as well as [151].

32. Elucidating her view of minimalism in psychohistory to Hari Seldon, in *Forward the Foundation*, by Isaac Asimov [5].

33. Various references to specific aspects of software engineering are given in Section 7.8. The reader may wish to delve into one of many comprehensive books on the subject, such as that by Stephen R. Schach [147]. An excellent book on modern operating systems by Andrew Tanenbaum [166] is also suggested. However, the references given here are only a few of those necessary to gain a grasp of the problems of system development.

Chapter 8

1. See articles by Dorothy Denning [31], Peter Denning [33], and Don Norman [117], and books by Norman [116] and Charles Perrow [126]. For some psychosocial implications relating to the development and use of computer systems, see [106], written by the author in response to Robert Pirsig's *Zen and the Art of Motorcycle Maintenance* [132].

2. From "Corrupted Polling" (*Inside Risks*), *CACM*, 35, 11, November 1992, p. 138.

3. *The Washington Post*, May 23, 1986.

4. *The New York Times*, June 2, 1986.

5. Some computer-minded critics have faulted the movie for bearing little resemblance to reality. To be sure, extremely critical and data-sensitive computer systems should generally not permit remote dialup access with easily compromised user authentication. However, the movie's computer-related effects are in fact based on events that have happened (many of which are noted in this book)—mistaken detections of what appeared to be incoming missiles, such as BMEWS failing to identify the moon properly; capture and use of a code by record-and-playback (in this case, touch-tone telephone signals); computer-based searching for modem-answering telephone numbers; the presence of a hidden and supposedly private trapdoor access path for the convenience of the system developers; the use of an easily guessed password; the presence of game programs (notably tic-tac-toe) in unexpected places and their unexpected interactions with other programs, and so on.

6. The remainder of this section is drawn on material originally presented in [108].

7. See *Science*, 259, p. 305, January 15, 1993.

8. See also Article 35 of the same book [35], which includes four separately authored pieces on ethics related to computers.

9. The PEM standard [66] has various implementations for message confidentiality and authenticity, including RSA Data Security's RIPEM.

10. A fascinating collection of ethical conflicts worthy of detailed study is provided by Donn Parker [121]. An important book on computer ethics is authored by Deborah Johnson [59]. Ethical behavior in engineering is considered by Stephen Unger [171]. See also the *Proceedings of the National Conference on Computing and Values*, August 12 through 16, 1991, New Haven, Connecticut; for information, contact Terry Bynum, Research Center on Computing and Society, Southern Connecticut State Univ., New Haven CT 06515, telephone 1-(203) 397-4423.

An *Invitational Conference on Legal, Ethical, and Technological Aspects of Computer and Network Use and Abuse* was held on December 17–19, 1993, sponsored by the joint National Conference of Lawyers and Scientists of the American Association for the Advancement of Science (AAAS) and the American Bar Association (ABA). The collection of position papers addresses the subject from a wide range of viewpoints. A second conference in this series was held on October 7–9, 1994. For information, contact Elizabeth Gehman, AAAS, 1333 H St NW, Washington DC 20005,egehman@aaas.org.

An important book on value conflicts and social choices is edited by Charles Dunlop and Rob Kling; its second edition [67] represents a substantial revision of the first edition, and includes many recent articles.

11. In the years since the precursor of this section originally appeared as the

Inside Risks column identified in the previous note, the number of universities offering courses or seminars in social implications of computers and other technologies has increased, and the number of readers of *RISKS* has expanded enormously, suggesting a marked increase in awareness. SRI has been most gracious in tolerating the *RISKS* activities. Perhaps this book will help to overcome some of the resistance that Ms. Rosenberg cites.

12. Various approaches to structuring and constraining the development team have been contemplated, such as chief-programmer teams and Harlan Mills' clean-room approach [93], plus countless development methodologies aimed at helping the managers. See also Fred Brooks' "Mythical Man Month" [17].

13. See a letter to Congress from Jim Bidzos of RSA (*RISKS 12*, 37, September 20, 1991), as well as subsequent letters to the National Institute of Standards and Technology (NIST) from Ron Rivest (*RISKS 12*, 57, October 28, 1991) and from Martin Hellman (*RISKS, 12*, 63, November 13, 1991).

14. This section is based on the *Inside Risks* column of the *Communications of the ACM, 34*, 2, 130, February 1991.

15. For a critical appraisal of today's bureaucratized computer education in our schools, and for some acerbic recommendations on what might be done in the future, see Seymour Papert, *The Children's Machine: Rethinking School in the Age of the Computer* [118]. For another view, see Steve Talbott, *The Future Does Not Compute* [165].

Chapter 9

1. Display in front of PJ Auto Sales in Revere, Massachusetts, January 1993, observed and contributed by Helen K. Neumann.

2. *Henrietta Temple*, book II,1837.

3. See Tom Wolfe, *The Right Stuff*, 1979, pp. 300–306.

4. UPI, in *San Francisco Chronicle*, July 31, 1987; *SEN 12*, 4.

5. See the *San Francisco Chronicle*, April 10, 1983, p. A5 and *SEN 18*, 3, A-14.

6. *San Francisco Chronicle*, July 28, 1993, p. C1.

7. *Mostly Harmless*, book 5 of the *Hitch Hiker's Guide to the Galaxy* trilogy, Heinemann, London, 1992, contributed by Pete Mellor, in *SEN 18*, 2, 5.

8. Thanks to R. Jagannathan.

9. The remainder of this section is based on the "Inside Risks" column in the *Communications of the ACM, 37* 6, 114, June 1994.

10. Quoted by Jerome Agel and Walter D. Glanze in *Cleopatra's Nose, The Twinkie Defense & 1500 Other Verbal Shortcuts in Popular Parlance*, Prentice Hall Press, Simon and Schuster, 1990.

11. The material in this section is taken from *Inside Risks, Communications of the ACM, 36*, 3, 130, March, 1993.

12. See the Winter 1991 issue of the *Whole Earth Review*, which includes a diverse collection of articles on technology by Jerry Mander, Howard Levine, Langdon Winner, Patricia Glass Schuman, Linda Garcia, Gary T. Marx, Ivan Illich, and Amory and Hunter Lovins. See also "a remarkable essay by the eccentric and curmudgeonly fluid dynamicist Clifford Truesdell, "The Computer: Ruin of Science and Threat to Mankind," in *An Idiot's Fugitive Guide to Science*, Springer-Verlag, 1984, pointed out to me by Michael Tobis.

13. Centre for Software Reliability, City University, Northampton Square, London EC1V 0HB, England.

14. The number of events recorded here and the volume of space occupied in the *RISKS* archives during any time interval are not necessarily indicative of the frequency or seriousness of observed problems. Over the years, I have become increasingly selective about what gets included in the on-line *RISKS* newsgroup and its ensuing published highlights, and have worked harder to make the printed descriptions more incisive. Thus, certain types of recent cases may be somewhat underrepresented in this book. For example, occurrences of cases nearly identical to those already reported would otherwise tend to overwhelm the reader — as in the case of naming problems considered in Section 6.5, personal-computer viruses, and security misuses.

Epilogue

1. Isaac Asimov, "It's Such a Beautiful Day," Copyright 1954, Ballantine Books, Inc., reprinted in Isaac Asimov, *The Complete Stories*, volume 1, A Foundation Book, Doubleday, New York, 1990.

References

[1] M.D. Abrams, E. Amoroso, L.J. LaPadula, T.F. Lunt, and J.N. Williams. Report of an integrity working group. Technical report, Mitre Corp. (Abrams), McLean, Virginia, November 1991.

[2] J.P Alstad, C.M. Brophy, T.C. Vickers Benzel, M.M. Bernstein, and R.J. Feiertag. The role of "System Build" in trusted embedded systems. In *Proceedings of the Thirteenth National Computer Security Conference*, pages 172–181, Washington, D.C., October 1–4, 1990. NIST/NCSC.

[3] T. Anderson and P.A. Lee. *Fault-Tolerance: Principles and Practice*. Prentice Hall International, Englewood Cliffs, New Jersey, 1981.

[4] I. Asimov. Runaround. *Astounding Science Fiction*, April 1941. Also anthologized in *I, Robot* and *The Complete Robot*.

[5] I. Asimov. *Forward the Foundation*. Doubleday, New York, 1993. Also Bantam paperback, 1994.

[6] M. Asseline. *Le pilote — est-il coupable? (The Pilot: Is He to Blame?)*. Edition #1 (4, rue Galleria, 75116 Paris), 1992.

[7] M. Baker and J.K. Ousterhout. Availability in the Sprite distributed file system. *ACM SIGOPS Operating System Review*, 25(2):95–98, April 1991.

[8] U. Beck. *Risk Society: Towards a New Modernity*. Sage Publications, Beverly Hills, California, 1992.

[9] K.J. Biba. Integrity considerations for secure computer systems. Technical Report MTR 3153, The Mitre Corporation, Bedford, Massachusetts, June 1975. Also available from USAF Electronic Systems Division, Bedford, Massachusetts, as ESD-TR-76-372, April 1977.

[10] M. Blaze. Protocol failure in the escrowed encryption standard. AT&T Bell Laboratories, June 3, 1994.

[11] K.P. Birman and T.A. Joseph. Reliable communication in the presence of failures. *ACM Transactions on Computer Systems*, 5(1):47–76, February 1987.

[12] B. BloomBecker. *Spectacular Computer Crimes: What They Are and How They Cost American Business Half a Billion Dollars a Year*. Dow Jones–Irwin, New York, 1990.

[13] W.E. Boebert and R.Y. Kain. A practical alternative to hierarchical integrity policies. In *Proceedings of the Eighth DoD/NBS Computer Security Initiative Conference*, Gaithersburg, Maryland, October 1–3, 1985.

[14] B. Boehm. *Tutorial: Software Risk Management*. IEEE Computer Society Press, Piscataway, New Jersey, 1989.

[15] N.S. Borenstein. *Programming As If People Mattered: Friendly Programs, Software Engineering, and Other Noble Delusions*. Princeton University Press, Princeton, New Jersey, 1991.

[16] S.S. Brilliant, J.C. Knight, and N.G. Leveson. Analysis of faults in an n-version software experiment. *IEEE Transactions on Software Engineering*, 16(2):238–247, February 1990.

[17] F.P. Brooks. *The Mythical Man-Month: Essays on Software Engineering*. Addison-Wesley, Reading, Massachusetts, 1975.

[18] J.E. Brunelle and D.E. Eckhardt, Jr. Fault-tolerant software: An experiment with the SIFT operating system. In *Proceedings of the Fifth AIAA Computers in Aerospace Conference*, pages 355–360, 1985.

[19] R.W. Butler, D.L. Palumbo, and S.C. Johnson. Application of a clock synchronization validation methodology to the SIFT computer system. In *Digest of Papers, Fault-Tolerant Computing Symposium 15*, pages 194–199, Ann Arbor, Michigan, June 1985. IEEE Computer Society.

[20] *Canadian Trusted Computer Product Evaluation Criteria*. Canadian Systems Security Centre, Communications Security Establishment, Government of Canada. Draft Version 3.0e, April 1992.

[21] S.M. Cascy. *Set Phasers on Stun, and Other True Tales of Design Technology and Human Error*. Aegean Publishing Company, Santa Barbara, California, 1993.

[22] R.N. Charette. *Software Engineering Risk Analysis and Management*. McGraw-Hill, New York, 1989.

[23] R.N. Charette. *Application Strategies for Risk Analysis*. McGraw-Hill, New York, 1990.

[24] W.R. Cheswick and S.M. Bellovin. *Firewalls and Internet Security: Repelling the Wily Hacker*. Addison-Wesley, Reading, Massachusetts, 1994.

[25] D.D. Clark and D.R. Wilson. A comparison of commercial and military computer security policies. In *Proceedings of the 1987 Symposium on Security and Privacy*, pages 184–194, Oakland, California, April 1987. IEEE Computer Society.

[26] D.D. Clark et al. *Computers at Risk: Safe Computing in the Information Age*. National Research Council, National Academy Press, 2101 Constitution Ave., Washington, D.C. 20418, December 5, 1990. Final report of the System Security Study Committee.

[27] F. Cohen. Computer viruses. In *Seventh DoD/NBS Computer Security Initiative Conference*, NBS, Gaithersburg, Maryland, pages 240–263, September 24–26, 1984. Reprinted in Rein Turn (ed.), *Advances in*

Computer System Security, Vol. 3, Artech House, Dedham, Massachusetts, 1988.

[28] F.J. Corbató. On building systems that will fail (1990 Turing Award Lecture, with a following interview by Karen Frenkel). *Communications of the ACM*, 34(9):72–90, September 1991.

[29] F. Cristian. Probabilistic clock synchronization. Technical Report RJ 6432, IBM Almaden Research Center, San Jose, California, September 1988.

[30] F. Cristian. Understanding fault-tolerant distributed systems. *Communications of the ACM*, 34(2):56–78, February 1991.

[31] D.E. Denning. Responsibility and blame in computer security. In *Proceedings of the National Conference on Computing and Values*, Southern Connecticut State University, New Haven, Connecticut, August 12–16, 1991.

[32] D.E. Denning. The Clipper encryption system. *American Scientist*, 81(4):319–323, July-August 1993.

[33] P.J. Denning. Human error and the search for blame. *Communications of the ACM*, 33(1):6–7, January 1990.

[34] P.J. Denning. Designing new principles to sustain research in our universities. *Communications of the ACM*, 36(7):98–104, July 1993.

[35] P.J. Denning (ed.). *Computers Under Attack: Intruders, Worms, and Viruses*. ACM Press, New York, and Addison Wesley, Reading, Massachusetts), 1990. ACM order number 706900.

[36] J. DeTreville. A cautionary tale. *ACM Software Engineering Notes*, 16(2):19–22, April 1991.

[37] E.W. Dijkstra. The structure of the THE multiprogramming system. *Communications of the ACM*, 11(5): 341–346, May 1968.

[38] J.E. Dobson and B. Randell. Building reliable secure computing systems out of unreliable unsecure components. In *Proceedings of the 1986 Symposium on Security and Privacy*, pages 187–193, Oakland, California, April 1986. IEEE Computer Society.

[39] R. Dugger. Annals of democracy (voting by computer). *New Yorker*, November 7, 1988.

[40] T. ElGamal. A public key cryptosystem and a signature scheme based on discrete logarithms. In *Advances in Cryptology: Proceedings of CRYPTO 84* (G.R. Blakley and David Chaum, editors), pages 10–18, Springer-Verlag, New York, 1985.

[41] T. ElGamal. A public key cryptosystem and a signature scheme based on discrete logarithms. *IEEE Transactions on Information Theory*, 31:469–472, 1985.

[42] European Communities Commission. *Information Technology Security Evaluation Criteria (ITSEC), Provisional Harmonised Criteria (of France, Germany, the Netherlands, and the United Kingdom)*, June 1991. Version 1.2. Available from the Office for Official Publications of the

European Communities, L-2985 Luxembourg, item CD-71-91-502-EN-C. Also available from UK CLEF, CESG Room 2/0805, Fiddlers Green Lane, Cheltenham UK GLOS GL52 5AJ, or GSA/GISA, Am Nippenkreuz 19, D 5300 Bonn 2, Germany.

[43] R.J. Feiertag and P.G. Neumann. The foundations of a provably secure operating system (PSOS). In *Proceedings of the National Computer Conference*, pages 329–334. AFIPS Press, 1979.

[44] D. Ferbrache. *A Pathology of Computer Viruses*. Springer-Verlag, Berlin, 1992.

[45] R. Formaini. *The Myth of Scientific Public Policy*. Transaction Publishers (Social Philosophy & Policy Center), New Brunswick, New Jersey, 1990.

[46] J. Gall. *Systemantics: How Systems Work and Especially How They Fail*. Quadrangle/New York Times Book Co., New York, 1977. Also, Pocket Books, New York, 1975.

[47] J. Garman. The bug heard 'round the world. *ACM SIGSOFT Software Engineering Notes*, 6(5):3–10, October 1981.

[48] M. Gasser. *Building a Secure Computer System*. Van Nostrand Reinhold Company, New York, 1988.

[49] M. Gasser, A. Goldstein, C. Kaufman, and B. Lampson. The Digital distributed system security architecture. In *Proceedings of the Twelfth National Computer Security Conference*, pages 305–319, Baltimore, Maryland, October 10–13, 1989. NIST/NCSC.

[50] A. Goldberg. Reliability of computer systems and risks to the public. *Communications of the ACM*, 28(2):131–133, February 1985.

[51] R.A. Golde. *Muddling Through: The Art of Properly Unbusinesslike Management*. AMACOM (a division of the American Management Associations), New York, 1976.

[52] L. Gong, T.M.A. Lomas, R.M. Needham, and J.H. Saltzer. Protecting poorly chosen secrets from guessing attacks. *IEEE Journal of Selected Areas in Communications*, 11(5):648–656, June 1993.

[53] J. Gray. Why do computers stop, and what can be done about it? Technical report, TR85.7, Tandem Computers, Inc., Cupertino, California, 1985.

[54] J. Gray. Transparency in its place. Technical report, TR89.1, Tandem Computers, Cupertino, California, 1989.

[55] G.L. Greenhalgh. Security and auditability of electronic vote tabulation systems: One vendor's perspective. In *Proceedings of the Sixteenth National Computer Security Conference*, pages 483–489, Baltimore, Maryland, September 20–23, 1993. NIST/NCSC.

[56] R.W. Hamming. Error detecting and error correcting codes. *Bell System Technical Journal*, 29:147–60, 1950.

[57] L.J. Hoffman (ed.). *Rogue Programs: Viruses, Worms, and Trojan Horses*. Van Nostrand Reinhold, New York, 1990.

[58] M. Jaffe, as reported by P.G. Neumann. Aegis, Vincennes, and the

Iranian Airbus. *ACM SIGSOFT Software Engineering Notes*, 14(5):20–21, July 1989.

[59] D. Johnson. *Computer Ethics (2nd ed.)*. Prentice Hall, Englewood Cliffs, New Jersey, 1994.

[60] C. Jones. *Assessment and Control of Software Risks*. Yourdon Press, 1994.

[61] M.F. Kaashoek and A.S. Tanenbaum. Fault tolerance using group communication. *ACM SIGOPS Operating System Review*, 25(2):71–74, April 1991.

[62] P. Kane. *V.I.R.U.S., Protection of Vital Information Resources Under Siege*. Bantam Software Library, New York, 1989.

[63] P.A. Karger. Implementing commercial data integrity with secure capabilities. In *Proceedings of the 1988 Symposium on Security and Privacy*, pages 130–139, Oakland, California, April 1988. IEEE Computer Society.

[64] P.A. Karger. *Improving Security and Performance for Capability Systems*. PhD thesis, Computer Laboratory, University of Cambridge, Cambridge, England, October 1988. Technical Report No. 149.

[65] T.F. Keefe, W.T. Tsai, and M.B. Thuraisingham. A multilevel security model for object-oriented systems. In *Proceedings of the Eleventh National Computer Security Conference*, October 1988.

[66] S.T. Kent. Internet privacy enhanced mail. *Communications of the ACM*, 36(8):48–60, August 1993.

[67] R. Kling (ed.). *Computerization and Controversy: Value Conflicts and Social Choices*. Academic Press, New York, 1995.

[68] J.C. Knight and N.G. Leveson. An experimental evaluation of the assumption of independence in multi-version programming. *IEEE Transactions on Software Engineering*, SE-12(1):96–109, January 1986.

[69] L. Lamport. The implementation of reliable distributed multiprocess systems. *Computer Networks*, 2:95–114, 1978.

[70] L. Lamport and P.M. Melliar-Smith. Synchronizing clocks in the presence of faults. *Journal of the ACM*, 32(1):52–78, January 1985.

[71] B. Lampson, M. Abadi, M. Burrows, and E. Wobber. Authentication in distributed systems: Theory and practice. *ACM Transactions on Computer Systems*, 10(4):265–310, November 1992.

[72] B.W. Lampson. Redundancy and robustness in memory protection. In *Information Processing 74 (Proceedings of the IFIP Congress 1974)*, Hardware II: pages 128–132. North-Holland, Amsterdam, 1974.

[73] S. Landau, S. Kent, C. Brooks, S. Charney, D. Denning, W. Diffie, A. Lauck, D. Miller, P. Neumann, and D. Sobel. *Codes, Keys, and Conflicts: Issues in U.S. Crypto Policy*. ACM report, June 1994.

[74] S. Landau, S. Kent, C. Brooks, S. Charney, D. Denning, W. Diffie, A. Lauck, D. Miller, P. Neumann, and D. Sobel. Crypto policy perspectives. *Communications of the ACM*, 37(8):115–121, August 1994.

[75] C.E. Landwehr, A.R. Bull, J.P. McDermott, and W.S. Choi. A taxonomy of computer program security flaws, with examples. Technical report, Center for Secure Information Technology, Information Technology Division, Naval Research Laboratory, Washington, D.C., November 1993.

[76] J.C. Laprie. Dependable computing and fault tolerance: Concepts and terminology. In *Digest of Papers, FTCS 15*, pages 2–11, Ann Arbor, Michigan, June 1985. IEEE Computer Society.

[77] M. Lee, E. Lee, and J. Johnstone. *Ride the Tiger to the Mountain*. Addison-Wesley, Reading, Massachusetts, 1989.

[78] T.M.P. Lee. Using mandatory integrity. In *Proceedings of the 1988 Symposium on Security and Privacy*, pages 140–146, Oakland, California, April 1988. IEEE Computer Society.

[79] N.G. Leveson. Software safety: Why, what, and how. *ACM Computing Surveys*, 18(2):125–163, June 1986.

[80] N.G. Leveson. Software safety in embedded computer systems. *Communications of the ACM*, 34(2), February 1991.

[81] N.G. Leveson. *Safeware: System Safety and the Computer Age*. Addison-Wesley, Reading, Massachusetts, 1995.

[82] N.G. Leveson, S.S. Cha, and T.J. Shimeall. Safety verification of Ada programs using software fault trees. *IEEE Software*, 8(7), July 1991.

[83] N.G. Leveson and C. Turner. An investigation of the Therac-25 accidents. *IEEE Computer*, pages 18–41, July 1993.

[84] T.F. Lunt. Aggregation and inference: Facts and fallacies. In *Proceedings of the 1989 IEEE Symposium on Research in Security and Privacy*, May 1989.

[85] T.F. Lunt. Multilevel security for object-oriented database systems. In *Proceedings of the Third IFIP Database Security Workshop*, September 1989.

[86] T.F. Lunt, R.R. Schell, W.R. Shockley, M. Heckman, and D. Warren. A near-term design for the SeaView multilevel database system. In *Proceedings of the 1988 Symposium on Security and Privacy*, pages 234–244, Oakland, California, April 1988. IEEE Computer Society.

[87] J. Mander. *Four Arguments for the Elimination of Television*. William Morrow/Quill, New York, 1978.

[88] J. Mander. *In the Absence of the Sacred: The Failure of Technology & the Survival of the Indian Nations*. Sierra Club Books, San Francisco, California, 1991, paperback 1992.

[89] M.D. McIlroy. Green light for bad software. *Communications of the ACM*, 33(5):479, May 1990.

[90] G.H. Mealy. A method for synthesizing sequential circuits. *Bell System Technical Journal*, 34:1045–79, September 1955.

[91] P.M. Melliar-Smith and R.L. Schwartz. Formal specification and verification of SIFT: A fault-tolerant flight control system. *IEEE Transactions on Computers*, C-31(7):616–630, July 1982.

[92] R. Mercuri. Threats to suffrage security. In *Proceedings of the Sixteenth National Computer Security Conference*, pages 474–477, Baltimore, Maryland, September 20–23, 1993. NIST/NCSC.

[93] H.D. Mills. *Principles of Information Systems Analysis and Design.* Academic Press, New York, 1986.

[94] E.F. Moore and C.E. Shannon. Reliable circuits using less reliable relays. *Journal of the Franklin Institute*, 262:191–208, 281–297, September, October 1956.

[95] M. Moriconi and T.C. Winkler. Approximate reasoning about the semantic effects of program changes. *IEEE Transactions on Software Engineering*, 16(9):990–1004, September 1990.

[96] R. Morris and K. Thompson. Password security: A case history. *Communications of the ACM*, 22(11):594–597, November 1979.

[97] S.J. Mullender (ed.). *Distributed Systems.* ACM Press, New York, and Addison-Wesley, Reading, Massachusetts, 1989.

[98] *Peer Review of a Formal Verification/Design Proof Methodology.* NASA Conference Publication 2377, July 1983.

[99] R. Nader and W. J. Smith. *Collision Course: The Truth about Airline Safety.* TAB Books, McGraw-Hill, Blue Ridge Summit, Pennsylvania, 1994.

[100] NCSC. *Trusted Network Interpretation (TNI).* National Computer Security Center, August 1, 1990. NCSC-TG-011 Version-1, Red Book.

[101] NCSC. *Department of Defense Trusted Computer System Evaluation Criteria (TCSEC).* National Computer Security Center, December 1985. DOD-5200.28-STD, Orange Book.

[102] NCSC. *Guidance for Applying the Trusted Computer System Evaluation Criteria in Specific Environments.* National Computer Security Center, June 1985. CSC-STD-003-85.

[103] P.G. Neumann. Beauty and the beast of software complexity – elegance versus elephants. In *Beauty Is Our Business, A Birthday Salute to Edsger W. Dijkstra* (W.H.J. Feijen, A.J.M. van Gasteren, D. Gries, and J. Misra, editors), pages 346–351 (Chapter 39). Springer-Verlag, Berlin, New York, May 11, 1990.

[104] P.G. Neumann. The role of motherhood in the pop art of system programming. In *Proceedings of the ACM Second Symposium on Operating Systems Principles, Princeton, New Jersey*, pages 13–18. ACM, October 1969.

[105] P.G. Neumann. Computer security evaluation. In *AFIPS Conference Proceedings, NCC*, pages 1087–1095. AFIPS Press, January 1978. Reprinted in Rein Turn (ed.), *Advances in Computer Security*, Artech House, Dedham, Massachusetts, 1981.

[106] P.G. Neumann. Psychosocial implications of computer software development and use: Zen and the art of computing. In *Theory and Practice of Software Technology*, pages 221–232. North-Holland, 1983. D. Ferrari, M. Bolognani, and J. Goguen (eds.).

[107] P.G. Neumann. On hierarchical design of computer systems for critical applications. *IEEE Transactions on Software Engineering*, SE-12(9), September 1986. Reprinted in Rein Turn (ed.), *Advances in Computer System Security*, Vol. 3, Artech House, Dedham, Massachusetts, 1988.

[108] P.G. Neumann. The computer-related risk of the year: Misplaced trust in computer systems. In *Proceedings of the Fourth Annual Conference on Computer Assurance, COMPASS '89*, pages 9–13. IEEE, June 1989.

[109] P.G. Neumann. The computer-related risk of the year: Distributed control. In *Proceedings of the Fifth Annual Conference on Computer Assurance, COMPASS '90*, pages 173–177. IEEE, June 1990.

[110] P.G. Neumann. A perspective from the Risks Forum. In *Computers Under Attack: Intruders, Worms, and Viruses*, Article 39, pages 535–543, ACM Press, New York, 1990.

[111] P.G. Neumann. Managing complexity in critical systems. In *Managing Complexity and Modeling Reality: Strategic Issues and an Action Agenda*, pages 2-36–2-42, ACM, New York, 1991. In a report edited by D. Frailey, based on an ACM Conference on Critical Issues, Arlington, Virginia, November 6–7, 1990. This paper includes a discussion of papers by David Parnas, Edward S. Cheevers and R. Leddy in the conference track on Managing Complexity.

[112] P.G. Neumann. Security criteria for electronic voting. In *Proceedings of the Sixteenth National Computer Security Conference*, pages 478–482, Baltimore, Maryland, September 20–23, 1993.

[113] P.G. Neumann. Illustrative risks to the public in the use of computer systems and related technology, index to *RISKS* cases as of October 7, 1993. *ACM Software Engineering Notes*, 19(1):16–29, January 1994. (At-least quarterly cumulative updates to this index are available on request.).

[114] P.G. Neumann, R.S. Boyer, R.J. Feiertag, K.N. Levitt, and L. Robinson. A provably secure operating system: The system, its applications, and proofs. (2nd ed.) Technical report, SRI International Computer Science Lab, Menlo Park, California, May 1980. Report CSL-116.

[115] P.G. Neumann and D.B. Parker. A summary of computer misuse techniques. In *Proceedings of the Twelfth National Computer Security Conference*, pages 396–407, Baltimore, Maryland, October 10–13, 1989. NIST/NCSC.

[116] D.A. Norman. *The Psychology of Everyday Things*. Basic Books, New York, 1988.

[117] D.A. Norman. Human error and the design of computer systems. *Communications of the ACM*, 33(1):4–5,7, January 1990.

[118] S. Papert. *The Children's Machine: Rethinking School in the Age of the Computer*. Basic Books, New York, 1993.

[119] D.B. Parker. *Crime by Computer*. Scribner, New York, 1976.

[120] D.B. Parker. *Fighting Computer Crime*. Scribner, New York, 1983.

[121] D.B. Parker. *Ethical Conflicts in Information and Computer Science,*

Technology, and Business. QED Information Sciences, Wellesley, Massachusetts, 1990.

[122] D.L. Parnas. On the criteria to be used in decomposing systems into modules. *Communications of the ACM*, 15(12), December 1972.

[123] D.L. Parnas. A technique for software module specification with examples. *Communications of the ACM*, 15(5), May 1972.

[124] D.L. Parnas. On a "buzzword": Hierarchical structure. In *Information Processing 74 (Proceedings of the IFIP Congress 1974)*, Software, pages 336–339. North-Holland, Amsterdam, 1974.

[125] M. Pease, R. Shostak, and L. Lamport. Reaching agreement in the presence of faults. *Journal of the ACM*, 27(2):228–234, April 1980.

[126] C. Perrow. *Normal Accidents.* Basic Books, New York, 1984.

[127] I. Peterson. *Fatal Defect: Why Computers Fail.* Random House, New York, 1995.

[128] W.W. Peterson and E.J. Weldon, Jr. *Error-Correcting Codes* (2nd ed.). MIT Press, Cambridge, Massachusetts, 1972.

[129] H. Petroski. *To Engineer is Human: The Role of Failure in Successful Design.* St. Martin's Press, New York, 1985.

[130] H. Petroski. *Design Paradigms: Case Histories of Error and Judgment in Engineering.* Cambridge University Press, Cambridge, England, 1994.

[131] C.P. Pfleeger. *Security in Computing.* Prentice Hall, Englewood Cliffs, New Jersey, 1989.

[132] R.M. Pirsig. *Zen and the Art of Motorcycle Maintenance.* William Morrow, Bantam Books, New York, 1974.

[133] R.M. Pirsig. *Lila, An Inquiry into Morals.* Bantam Books, New York, 1991.

[134] B. Randell. System design and structuring. *Computer Journal*, 29(4):300–306, 1986.

[135] T.R.N. Rao. *Error-Control Coding for Computer Systems.* Prentice Hall, Englewood Cliffs, New Jersey, 1989.

[136] R. Rivest. The MD4 message digest algorithm. Technical report, MIT Laboratory for Computer Science, October 1990. TM 434.

[137] R. Rivest, A. Shamir, and L. Adleman. A method for obtaining digital signatures and public-key cryptosystems. *Communications of the ACM*, 21(2):120–126, February 1978.

[138] J.A. Rochlis and M.W. Eichin. With microscope and tweezers: The Worm from MIT's perspective. *Communications of the ACM*, 32(6):689–698, June 1989.

[139] E. Rosen. Vulnerabilities of network control protocols. *ACM SIGSOFT Software Engineering Notes*, 6(1):6–8, January 1981.

[140] M. Rotenberg. Communications privacy: Implications for network design. *Communications of the ACM*, 36(8):61–68, August 1993.

[141] M. Rotenberg. The underpinnings of privacy protection. *Communications of the ACM*, 36(8):69–73, August 1993.

[142] J.M. Rushby and F. von Henke. Formal verification of algorithms for critical systems. *ACM Software Engineering Notes*, 16(5):1–15, December 1991.

[143] R.G. Saltman. Accuracy, integrity, and security in computerized vote-tallying. Technical report, National Bureau of Standards (now NIST) special publication, Gaithersburg, Maryland, 1988.

[144] R.G. Saltman. Assuring accuracy, integrity and security in national elections: The role of the U.S. Congress. In *Computers, Freedom and Privacy '93*, pages 3.8–3.17, March 1993.

[145] R.G. Saltman. An integrity model is needed for computerized voting and similar systems. In *Proceedings of the Sixteenth National Computer Security Conference*, pages 471–473, Baltimore, Maryland, September 20–23, 1993.

[146] P.H. Salus. *A Quarter Century of UNIX*. Addison-Wesley, Reading, Massachusetts, 1994.

[147] S.R. Schach. *Software Engineering* (2nd ed.). Aksen Associates, Homewood, Illinois, 1993.

[148] C.P. Schnorr. Efficient identification and signatures for smart cards. In *Advances in Cryptology: Proceedings of CRYPTO 89* (G. Brassard, editor), pages 239–251, Springer-Verlag, New York, 1990.

[149] M.D. Schroeder, A.D. Birrell, and R.M. Needham. Experience with Grapevine: The growth of a distributed system. *TOCS*, 2(1):3–23, February 1984.

[150] D. Seeley. Password cracking: A game of wits. *Communications of the ACM*, 32(6):700–703, June 1989.

[151] *SEI/NSIA Conference on Risks in the Acquisition and Development of Large-Scale Software Intensive (LSSI) Systems*, Pittsburgh, Pennsylvania, October 8–10, 1991. SEI/NSIA.

[152] M. Shamos. Electronic voting: Evaluating the threat. In *Computers, Freedom and Privacy '93*, pages 3.18–3.25, March 1993.

[153] R.J. Shea and R.A. Wilson. *The Illuminatus! Trilogy*. Dell, New York, 1975.

[154] T.J. Shimeall and N.G. Leveson. An empirical comparison of software fault tolerance and fault elimination. *IEEE Transactions on Software Engineering*, SE-17(2):173–183, February 1991.

[155] J.F. Shoch and J.A. Hupp. The "Worm" programs — early experience with a distributed computation. *Communications of the ACM*, 25(3):172–180, March 1982. Reprinted in Denning (ed.), *Computers Under Attack*.

[156] W.R. Shockley. Implementing the Clark/Wilson integrity policy using current technology. Technical report, Gemini Computers, P.O. Box 222417, Carmel California, 1988. GCI-88-6-01.

[157] S.K. Shrivastava and F. Panzieri. The design of a reliable remote procedure call mechanism. *IEEE Transactions on Computers*, C - 31(7):692–687, July 1982.

[158] E. Spafford. Are computer hacker break-ins ethical? *Journal of Systems and Software*, January 1992. Purdue Technical Report CSD-TR-994, March 91.

[159] E.H. Spafford. The Internet Worm: Crisis and aftermath. *Communications of the ACM*, 32(6):678–687, June 1989.

[160] P. Stephenson and K. Birman. Fast causal multicast. *ACM SIGOPS Operating System Review*, 25(2):75–79, April 1991.

[161] B. Sterling. *The Hacker Crackdown: Law and Disorder on the Electronic Frontier*. Bantam, New York, 1992 (paperback 1993).

[162] C. Stoll. Stalking the Wily Hacker. *Communications of the ACM*, 31(5):484–497, May 1988.

[163] C. Stoll. *The Cuckoo's Egg: Tracking a Spy Through the Maze of Computer Espionage*. Doubleday, New York, 1989.

[164] A. Swasy. *Soap Opera: The Inside Story of Proctor & Gamble*. Times Books, New York, 1993.

[165] S. Talbott. *The Future Does Not Compute*. O'Reilly & Associates, Sebastopol, CA 95472, 1994.

[166] A.S. Tanenbaum. *Modern Operating Systems*. Prentice Hall, Englewood Cliffs, New Jersey, 1992.

[167] K. Thompson. Reflections on trusting trust (1983 Turing Award Lecture). *Communications of the ACM*, 27(8):761–763, August 1984.

[168] I.L. Traiger, J. Gray, C.A. Galtieri, and B.G. Lindsay. Transactions and consistency in distributed database systems. *ACM TODS*, 7(3):323–342, September 1982.

[169] UK–Ministry of Defence. *Interim Defence Standard 00-55, The Procurement of Safety-Critical Software in Defence Equipment*. U.K. Ministry of Defence, April 5, 1991. DefStan 00-55; Part 1, Issue 1: Requirements; Part 2, Issue 1: Guidance.

[170] UK–Ministry of Defence. *Interim Defence Standard 00-56, Hazard Analysis and Safety Classification of the Computer and Programmable Electronic System Elements of Defence Equipment*. U.K. Ministry of Defence, April 5, 1991. DefStan 00-56.

[171] S.H. Unger. *Controlling Technology : Ethics and the Responsible Engineer* (2nd ed.). John Wiley and Sons, New York, 1994.

[172] V. Varadharajan and S. Black. Multilevel security in a distributed object-oriented system. *Computers and Security*, 10(1):51–68, 1991.

[173] J. von Neumann. Probabilistic logics and the synthesis of reliable organisms from unreliable components. In *Automata Studies*, pages 43–98, Princeton Univeristy, Princeton, New Jersey, 1956.

[174] F.W. Weingarten. Public interest and the NII. *Communications of the ACM*, 37(3):17–19, March 1994.

[175] J.H. Wensley et al. SIFT design and analysis of a fault-tolerant computer for aircraft control. *Proceedings of the IEEE*, 66(10):1240–1255, October 1978.

[176] J.H. Wensley et al. Design study of software-implemented fault-tolerance (SIFT) computer. NASA contractor report 3011, Computer Science Laboratory, SRI International, Menlo Park, California, June 1982.

[177] L. Wiener. *Digital Woes: Why We Should Not Depend on Software*. Addison–Wesley, Reading, Massachusetts, 1993.

[178] E. Wobber, M. Abadi, M. Burrows, and B. Lampson. Authentication in the Taos operating system. *ACM Operating Systems Review*, 27(5):256–269, December 1993. Proceedings of the Fourteenth ACM Symposium on Operating Systems Principles.

[179] W.D. Young and J. McHugh. Coding for a believable specification to implementation mapping. In *Proceedings of the 1987 Symposium on Security and Privacy*, pages 140–148, Oakland, California, April 1987. IEEE Computer Society.

Glossary

ARPAnet A research network developed by the Advanced Research Projects Agency (ARPA) of the U.S. Department of Defense (DoD). It initially linked a few research organizations in the United States. The **Milnet** is a spinoff of the ARPAnet, for DoD use. The ARPAnet is the precursor of the Internet.

Compromise An accidentally or intentionally caused situation that prevents a system from fulfilling its intended requirements. Of particular concern are compromises resulting from malicious human actions such as system penetrations, subversions, and other intentional misuses. The term is also used more generally; a compromise may also result from a system malfunction, spontaneous external event, or other causes.

COMPUSEC Computer security.

COMSEC Communications security.

CTCPEC The Canadian Trusted Computer Product Evaluation Criteria [20].

Criteria Definitions of properties and constraints to be met by system functionality and assurance. See **TCSEC**, **ITSEC**, and **CTCPEC**.

Criticality A characteristic of a requirement whose nonsatisfaction can result in serious consequences, such as damage to national or global security or loss of life. A system is critical if any of its requirements is critical.

Dependability Defined with respect to some set of properties, a measure of how or whether a system can satisfy those properties.

Dependence A subject is said to depend on an object if the subject may not work properly unless the object (possibly another subject) behaves properly. One system may depend on another system.

DES Data Encryption Standard.

Digital signature A string of characters that can be generated only by an agent that knows some secret, and hence provides evidence that such an agent must have generated it.

Digital Signature Standard (DSS) A standard for digital signatures based on a variant of an ElGamal algorithm [40, 41] due to C.P. Schnorr [148].

DOS Disk Operating System (as in MS-DOS for personal computers).

DSS *See* **Digital Signature Standard.**

Feature **1**. An advantage attributed to a system. **2**. A euphemism for a fundamental flaw that cannot or will not be fixed.

Formal Having a punctilious respect for form—that is, having a rigorous mathematical or logical basis.

Gateway A system connected to different computer networks that mediates transfer of information between them.

Guard A component that mediates the flow of information and/or control between different systems or networks.

Human safety A property that a system must satisfy to preserve personal and collective safety.

Identification The association of a name or other identifier with a user, subject, object, or other entity. Note that no authentication is implied in identification by itself.

Implementation A mechanism (in software or hardware, or both) that attempts to correctly realize a specified design.

INFOSEC Information security. Includes both **COMPUSEC** and **COMSEC**.

Internet A worldwide network of networks linking computer systems.

ITSEC The Information Technology Security Evaluation Criteria, the Harmonized criteria of France, Germany, the Netherlands, and the United Kingdom [42].

Letter bomb A logic bomb contained in electronic mail, which will trigger when the mail is read.

Logic bomb A Trojan horse set to trigger on the occurrence of a particular logical event.

Mediation The action of an arbiter interposition (literally, being in the middle) that decides whether to permit a subject to perform a given operation on a specified object.

Message digest A checksum, hash-code, compression code, or other generally nonreversible transformation of a message into a generally much shorter form. Message digests can be used in authentication and certification. (MD4 [136] is an example of a message digest algorithm.)

Milnet The U.S. Department of Defense spinoff of the ARPAnet.

MLI *See* **Multilevel integrity**.

MLS *See* **Multilevel security**.

Model An expression of a policy or a system design in a form that can be used for analysis or other reasoning about the policy or the system.

Monitoring Recording of relevant information about each operation by a subject on an object, maintained in an audit trail for subsequent analysis.

Multics An operating system developed beginning in 1965 by MIT, with participation of Bell Laboratories from 1965 to 1969, and with hardware and software support initially from General Electric and then Honeywell. Multics (Multiplexed Information and Computing Service) was an early pioneer in virtual memory, directory hierarchies, several innovative approaches to security, multiprocessing, abstraction, symbolic naming, and the use of a higher-level programming language for system development.

Multilevel integrity (MLI) An integrity policy based on the relative ordering of multilevel integrity labels.

Multilevel security (MLS) A confidentiality policy based on the relative ordering of multilevel security labels (really multilevel confidentiality).

NCSC The National Computer Security Center.

Noncompromisibility The ability of a system to withstand compromise.

Nonrepudiation An authentication that, with high assurance, can not be refuted subsequently.

Nontamperability The ability of a system to withstand tampering.

Operating system A collection of programs intended to control directly the hardware of a computer, and on which all the other programs running on the computer generally depend.

OPSEC Operations security. Encompasses security concepts that transcend system and network technology per se—that is, COMPUSEC and COMSEC, respectively). Includes such techniques as TEMPEST, communication channel randomization, and covert channel masking.

Orange Book The familiar name for the basic document defining the TCSEC [101], derived from the color of its cover. The Orange Book provides criteria for the evaluation of different classes of trusted systems, and has many documents relating to its extension and interpretation. *See* **Red Book, Yellow Book**.

Pest program A collective term for programs with deleterious and generally unanticipated side effects—for example, Trojan horses, logic bombs, viruses, and malicious worms.

Policy An informal, generally natural-language description of intended system behavior. Policies may be defined for particular requirements, such as confidentiality, integrity, availability, and safety.

Private key **1.** In a public-key (asymmetric) cryptosystem, the private-key counterpart of a public key—namely, the key that is private to the owner and does not need to be shared at all. In contrast, see **Public key**. **2.** In a shared-key (symmetric) cryptosystem, the key that must be shared by the encrypter and decrypter, but (hopefully) by no one else. See **Shared key** (also referred to as a secret key). (We avoid the confusion between these two definitions by referring to the key in the latter case as a shared key rather than as a private key.) **3.** In a symmetric cryptosystem, a key that is not shared, but rather is held by only one entity—used, for example, for storage encryption. See **Secret-key cryptosystem**, definition 2.

Process Generally, a sequential locus of control, as in the execution of a virtual processor. It may take place on different processors or on a single processor, but with only a single execution point at any one time.

Public key In a public-key (asymmetric) cryptosystem, the public-key counterpart of a private key—namely, the key that is public and does need not to be protected. In contrast, see **Private key**.

Public-key cryptosystem An encryption algorithm or its implementation, using a public key and a corresponding private key. Also known as an asymmetric cryptosystem. See **RSA** as an example of a public-key encryption algorithm.

Red Book Familiar name for the Trusted Network Interpretation of the TCSEC [100].

Reference monitor A system component that mediates usage of all objects by all subjects, enforcing the intended access controls. It might typically include a kernel plus some trusted functionality.

Requirement A statement of the system behavior needed to enforce a given policy. Requirements are used to derive the technical specification of a system.

Risk Intuitively, the adverse effects that can result if a vulnerability is exploited or if a threat is actualized. In some contexts, risk is a measure of the likelihood of adverse effects or the product of the likelihood and the quantified consequences. There is no standard definition.

RSA Acronym for the Rivest–Shamir–Adelman public-key encryption algorithm [137].

Secret key A key that is (supposedly) kept secret. See **Shared key**; see also **Private key**, definition 2. It is sometimes actually a key known only to one entity; see **Secret-key cryptosystem**, definition 2.

Secret-key cryptosystem **1**. In common usage, equivalent to shared-key (symmetric) cryptosystem. **2**. One-key (symmetric) encryption and decryption (perhaps of a file) in which the single key is known only to one entity (such as a person or computer system).

Security **1**. Protection against unwanted behavior. In present usage, computer security includes properties such as confidentiality, integrity, availability, prevention of denial of service, and prevention of generalized misuse. **2**. The property that a particular security policy is enforced, with some degree of assurance. **3**. *Security* is sometimes used in the restricted sense of confidentiality, particularly in the case of multilevel security (that is, multilevel confidentiality).

Separation of duties A principle of design that separates functions of differing security or integrity into separate protection domains. Separation of duties is sometimes implemented as an authorization rule in which two or more subjects are required to authorize an operation.

Shared key In a shared-key (symmetric) cryptosystem, the key that must be shared by encrypter and decrypter, and (hopefully) by no one else. *See* **Secret key**.

Shared-key cryptosystem A symmetric system for encryption and decryption, using a single key that is shared presumably only by the sender and the recipient. *See* **DES** as an example of a shared-key algorithm.

Signature *See* **Digital signature**.

Smart card A small computer with the approximate dimensions of a credit card. It is typically used to identify and authenticate its bearer, although it may have other computational functions.

Specification A technical description of the intended behavior of a system. A specification may be used to develop the implementation and provides a basis for testing the resulting system.

Spoofing Taking on the characteristics of another system or user for purposes of deception. In the present contexts, spoofing is generally prankish rather than overtly malicious, although it is often used elsewhere in a malicious context.

State An abstraction of the total history of a system, usually in terms of state variables. The representation could be explicit or implicit.

State machine In the classical model of a state machine (attributable to George Mealy [90]), the outputs and the next state of the machine are functionally dependent on the inputs and the present state. This model is the basis for all computer systems.

Subversion A compromise that undermines integrity.

System **1**. A state machine with an associated state, which, when provided with inputs, yields a set of outputs and results in a new machine state. (*See* **State machine**.) **2**. An interdependent collection of components that can be considered as a unified whole — such as a networked collection of computer systems, a distributed system, a compiler, an editor, or a memory unit.

Tampering An intentionally caused event that results in modification of the system and of its intended behavior.

TCB *See* **Trusted computing base**.

TCSEC The Department of Defense Trusted Computer System Evaluation Criteria. *See* **Orange Book** [101], **Red Book** [100], and **Yellow Book** [102].

TENEX An operating system developed by Bolt, Beranek and Newman for Digital Equipment Corporation mainframe computers.

Threat A potential danger that a vulnerability may be exploited intentionally, triggered accidentally, or otherwise exercised.

Time bomb A Trojan horse set to trigger at a particular time.

Token authenticator A pocket-sized computer that can participate in a challenge–response authentication scheme. The authentication sequences are called tokens.

Trapdoor A hidden flaw in a system mechanism that can be triggered to circumvent the system's security. A trapdoor is often placed intentionally, but can be created accidentally.

Trojan horse A computer entity that contains a malicious component whose use by an unsuspecting user can result in side effects desired by the creator of the Trojan horse and generally unanticipated by the user. A Trojan horse typically operates with all of the privileges of the unsuspecting user. It may give the appearance of providing normal functionality.

Trust Belief that a system (or person) meets its specifications or otherwise lives up to its expectations.

Trusted computing base (TCB) The portion of a system that enforces a particular policy. The TCB must be nontamperable and noncircumventable. Under the TCSEC, it must also be small enough to be systematically analyzable.

Trusted guard A computer system that acts as a guard and that is trusted to enforce a particular guard policy, such as ensuring the flow of only unclassified data from a classified system or ensuring no reverse flow of pest programs from an untrusted system to a trusted system.

Trusted system A system believed to enforce a given set of attributes to a stated degree of assurance (confidence).

Trustworthiness Assurance that a system or person deserves to be trusted.

Unix A family of extremely popular multiprogramming operating systems, originally developed by Ken Thompson and Dennis Ritchie at Bell Laboratories, beginning in 1969. See [146].

Vaccine A program that attempts to detect and disable viruses.

Virus A program that attaches itself to other programs and has the ability to replicate. In personal computers, viruses are generally Trojan horse programs that are replicated by inadvertent human action. In general computer usage, viruses are self-replicating Trojan horses.

Vulnerability A weakness in a system that can be exploited to violate the system's intended behavior. There may be security, integrity, availability, and other types of vulnerabilities. The act of exploiting a vulnerability represents a **threat,** which has an associated **risk** of exploitation.

Worm A program that distributes itself in multiple copies within a system or across a distributed system. A worm may be beneficial or harmful.

Worm attack The harmful exploitation of a **worm** that may act beyond normally expected behavior, perhaps exploiting security vulnerabilities or causing denials of service.

Yellow Book Familiar name for a document providing guidance for applying the TCSEC to specific environments [102].

Index

Boldfaced page numbers indicate a primary description. Italic page numbers indicate a glossary item.

Parnas, David L. *(cont.)*
  hierarchies, 240
  specification, 240
Passwords
  attacks, 103, 127
  bypassed by trapdoors, 109
  capture, 109, 211
  compromise by compiler Trojan
    horse, 115
  derivation, 109
  encrypted in Unix, 109, 127, 133
  file unprotected against writing,
    110
  flaws in mechanisms, 108
  guessable, 108
  nonatomic checking, 110
  unencrypted, 109
  universal, 109
  vulnerabilities, 108, 127
Patriot, 124, 234
  clock drift, 34, 237
Paul, James H., 328
Penetration of telephone network
    controls, 129
Pentagon DP system upgrade, 217
People, failures due to, 262
Pereira, Fernando, 317
Performance, very high, 213
Perrow, Charles, 5, 330
  Normal Accidents, 316
Personal identification numbers, 165
Pest programs, **103–105**, *347*
Peterson, Ivars, 316
Petroski, Henry, 263, 269, 297, 316
Pfleeger, Charles, 325
Phaedrus, 285
Philhower, Robert, 297
Phobos 1, 29, 121, 156, 239
Phobos 2, 29, 156
Pig-farm spoof, 146
Piggybacking, 113
  in TENEX, 107
  of up-links, 128
Pinkerton scammed, 167
PINs, *see* Personal identification
    numbers
Pirate TV, 153
Pirsig, Robert M., 285
Pistritto, Joe, 320
Playbacks, 113
Playboy channel interruptus, 154
Policy, *347*
Pollyanna attitude, 296
Polymorphism, 235

Popp, Joseph, 141
Postol, Ted, 34, 286
Power problems, **74–85**
  Chicago flood, 84
  earthquake side-effects, 83
  Northeast U.S. blackout, 83
  Ottawa blackout, 83
  raccoon, Utah, 85
  squirrel, RI, 84
  squirrel, SRI, 84
  summary, 86
  West coast blackout, 83
Principles
  of design, 240
  object-oriented, 235
  for software engineering, 244
Prison problems, **174–176**
Privacy
  enforcement, **188–189**
  needs for, **181–183**
  problems, **181–202**
  summary of problems, 201
  violations, **183–188**
Privacy digests, 315
Private keys, *347*
Privileges
  exceptions to, in requirements, 234
  minimum, 225, 238
  mishandling of exceptions, 238
  separation of, 225
Process, *348*
  daemon, 212
Proctor & Gamble, 187
Programming languages
  choice, 236
  discipline in use, 236
Promiscuous mode in Ethernet, 211
Propagation of access rights, 99
Protocols
  communication, 235
  synchronization, 235
Proxmire, Senator William, 264
Public keys, *348*
Public-key encryption
  for authentication, 111
  for key distribution, 212
Puget Sound ferry system, 58

Quayle, Dan, 186
Queen Elizabeth II hits shoal, 58

Race conditions
  critical, 108
  noncritical, 108

This book is published as part of ACM Press Books—a collaboration between the Association for Computing Machinery and Addison-Wesley Publishing Company. ACM is the oldest and largest educational and scientific society in the information technology field. Through its high-quality publications and services, ACM is a major force in advancing the skills and knowledge of IT professionals throughout the world. For further information about ACM, contact:

ACM Member Services
1515 Broadway, 17th floor
New York, NY 10036-5701
Phone: 1-212-626-0500
Fax: 1-212-944-1318
E-mail: ACMHELP@ACM.org

ACM European Service Center
Avenue Marcel Thiry 204
1200 Brussels, Belgium
Phone: 32-2-774-9602
Fax: 32-2-774-9690
E-mail: ACM_Europe@ACM.org